IN HIS
Presence

Other Classics Compiled and Edited by Lance Wubbels

30-DAY DEVOTIONAL TREASURIES

Charles Finney on Spiritual Power
George Müller on Faith
Andrew Murray on Holiness
Hudson Taylor on Spiritual Secrets
Charles Spurgeon on Prayer
R. A. Torrey on the Holy Spirit

CHARLES SPURGEON: BELIEVER'S LIFE SERIES

Grace Abounding in a Believer's Life
A Passion for Holiness in a Believer's Life
The Power of Prayer in a Believer's Life
Spiritual Warfare in a Believer's Life
The Triumph of Faith in a Believer's Life
What the Holy Spirit Does in a Believer's Life

CHARLES SPURGEON: LIFE OF CHRIST SERIES

The Power of Christ's Miracles
The Power of Christ's Prayer Life
The Power of Christ's Second Coming
The Power of Christ's Tears
The Power of Christ the Warrior
The Power of the Cross of Christ

F. B. MEYER: BIBLE CHARACTER SERIES

The Life of Abraham: The Obedience of Faith
The Life of David: Shepherd, Psalmist, King
The Life of Joseph: Beloved, Hated, Exalted
The Life of Moses: The Servant of God
The Life of Paul: A Servant of Jesus Christ
The Life of Peter: Fisherman, Disciple, Apostle

IN HIS

Presence

DAILY DEVOTIONALS

COMPILED & EDITED BY
LANCE WUBBELS

Emerald Books
P.O. Box 635
Lynnwood, Washington 98046

In His Presence

Published by Emerald Books
P.O. Box 635
Lynnwood, WA 98046

Library of Congress Cataloging-in-Publication Data

In His presence : daily devotionals through the Gospel of Matthew /
    compiled and edited by Lance Wubbels.
            p. cm.
    ISBN 1-883002-49-4
    1. Bible. N.T. Matthew--Devotional literature. 2. Devotional
calendars. I. Wubbels. Lance. 1952-   .
BS2575.4.I5 1998
242'.2--dc21   98-40528
                                                                    CIP

Printed in Korea.

Introduction

Over fifteen years ago I had the privilege of compiling Bethany House Publishers' *Parallel Commentary of the New Testament* and *Parallel Commentary of the Old Testament*. As I searched for supplementary commentary to the three primary contributors to those volumes, I was delighted to discover a wealth of rich expositions by several pre–twentieth–century British biblical scholars and pastors. However, that material was not easily accessible to the lay person, hidden away in out–of–print books or in large, expensive pastoral volumes. It has remained my passion for all these years to return to these writings and provide readers with the wisdom that lies buried in the old volumes.

During the second half of the nineteenth century, Great Britain was home to some of the greatest expository preachers, biblical scholars, and Christian leaders and writers in all of church history. Legendary names like Charles Spurgeon, Alexander Maclaren, Joseph Parker, George Müller, Hudson Taylor, Henry Liddon, George MacDonald, Alexander Whyte, and others stand out as giants of the church. Their British predecessors, like John Wesley and Matthew Henry, left them a rich tradition of biblical and evangelical excellence to follow, and follow it they did.

From the classic writings of these revered British saints, I have compiled and edited "the very best of the best" of their inspirational insights on the *Gospel of Matthew*. Verse by verse, following the biblical text consecutively through the entire life of Jesus Christ, here are 366 devotional reading that are packed with profound biblical commentary, brilliant wisdom, and practical application to a Christian's daily walk with God that will enrich readers for years to come.

In His Presence Daily Devotionals brings a wonderfully unique approach. Readers will concentrate their readings on the *Gospel of Matthew* for an entire year, gaining an unforgettable understanding into the life, words, and ministry of Christ. And these readings, which have never been gathered together in a devotional format, come from the timeless pens of some of the church's finest expositors. It promises a year's worth of readings that will be used for a lifetime.

It is my hope and prayer that these readings will help bring the Word of God alive to you. May it be a source of biblical inspiration that leads to thoughtful meditation and worship.

LANCE WUBBELS

Contributors

CHARLES HADDON SPURGEON (1834–1892) was the remarkable British "Boy Preacher of the Fens" who became one of the truly greatest preachers of all time. Coming from a flourishing country pastorate in 1854, he accepted a call to pastor London's New Park Street Chapel. This building soon proved too small and so work on Spurgeon's Metropolitan Tabernacle was begun in 1859. Meanwhile his weekly sermons were being printed and having a remarkable sale—25,000 copies every week in 1865 and translated into more than twenty languages.

Spurgeon built the Metropolitan Tabernacle into a congregation of over 6,000 and added well over 14,000 members during his thirty-eight-year London ministry. The combination of his clear voice, his mastery of the language, his sure grasp of Scripture, and a deep love for Christ produced some of the noblest preaching of any age. An astounding 3,561 sermons have been preserved in sixty-three volumes, *The New Park Street Pulpit* and *The Metropolitan Tabernacle Pulpit,* from which the readings of this book have been selected and edited.

During his lifetime, Spurgeon is estimated to have preached to 10,000,000 people. He remains history's most widely read preacher. There is more available material written by Spurgeon than by any other Christian author, living or dead. His sixty-three volumes of sermons stand as the largest set of books by a single author in the history of Christianity, comprising the equivalent to the twenty-seven volumes of the ninth edition of the *Encyclopedia Britannica.*

ALEXANDER MACLAREN (1826–1910) was a Scottish Baptist minister who pastored successfully at Portland Chapel, Southampton (1846–1858) and Union Chapel, Manchester (1858–1903), where he acquired the reputation of "the prince of expository preachers." Next to Charles Spurgeon, Maclaren's sermons perhaps have been the most widely read sermons of their time. His preaching drew vast congregations and his sermon methods of subdivision and analogies drawn from nature and life have been widely imitated ever since. He was twice president of the Baptist Union and chairman of its Twentieth Century fund and the first president of the Baptists World Alliance (1905).

The eleven volumes of Maclaren's *Expositions of Holy Scripture*, from which the devotional readings in this book are derived, are still available today. Of those expositions, W. Robertson Nicoll, the noted New Testament Greek scholar, said, "Will there ever be such a combination of spiritual insight, of scholarship, of passion, of style, of keen intellectual power? He was clearly a man of genius. So long as preachers care to teach from the Scriptures, they will find him their best guide and help."

JOSEPH PARKER (1830–1902) was an English Congregational preacher who was ordained in 1853 to the ministry in Banbury Congregational Church, though his formal education had ceased when he was sixteen. In 1869 he moved to Poultry Chapel in London, which congregation built the City Temple, opening in 1874. There Parker ministered until his death, preaching twice each Sunday and every Thursday morning, and earning a reputation as one of the city's greatest pulpit masters, alongside Spurgeon and Liddon. His theology was the whole system of evangelical truth enshrined in the Apostle's Creed. With an impressive appearance, regal personality, commanding voice, impeccable diction, and histri-onic manner, he preached authoritatively and appealingly. Only Spurgeon at the Metropolitan Tabernacle exceeded him in attracting crowds. During 1885–1892 he preached through the Bible. Those sermons were published in the twenty–five volumes of *The People's Bible*, from which these devotional readings were selected and edited.

ALEXANDER WHYTE (1836–1921) was a Scottish minister who was often described as the "last of the Puritans." Educated at King's College, Aberdeen, and at the Free Church of Scotland's New College, Edinburgh, he was called to Edinburgh as colleague and successor to R. S. Candlish at Free St. George's. During nearly forty years there he established a reputation as a graphic and compelling preacher to an extent probably unparalleled even in a nation of preachers. In 1909 Whyte became principal of New College and taught New Testament literature there. He was moderator of the Free Church general assembly in 1898 and the author of a number of devotional books.

GEORGE MACDONALD (1824–1905), Scottish novelist, poet, and pastor, was one of the most original and influential writers of Victorian Britain. He studied at King's College, Aberdeen and Highbury Theological College and became minister of a Congregational church at Arundel, Sussex, in 1850. His more than fifty books—including fantasy, fairy tales, short stories, sermons, essays, poems, and some thirty novels—sold in the millions and made him one of the most popular authors of the day on both sides of the Atlantic.

Always one who was in pursuit of honest, practical, sensible faith, MacDonald's writing profoundly influenced the lives of many well-known Christians such as Oswald Chambers, C. S. Lewis, G. K. Chesterton, and Madeleine L'Engle. His *Unspoken Sermons*, from which the devotionals in this book originated, are available through Sunrise Books, Eureka, California 95501. Michael Phillips has provided a wonderful sampler of MacDonald's sermons in the books, *Discovering the Character of God* and *Knowing the Heart of God*, published by Bethany House Publishers.

JOHN WESLEY (1703–1791) was the founder of Methodism. Educated at Charterhouse and Christ Church, Oxford, he was elected in 1726 to a fellowship at Lincoln College in the same university. Along with his brother Charles and George Whitefield, he joined the "Holy Club" at Oxford, meeting for prayer, the study of the Greek Testament, and self-examination. After an unsuccessful missionary venture to the Indians and colonists of Georgia, John returned to London where he was "clearly convinced of unbelief, of the want of that faith whereby alone we are saved." On May 23, 1738, his heart was "strangely warmed" as he listened to a reading from Luther's preface to Romans. This experience kindled a fire in him for evangelism that was never extinguished.

Wesley embarked upon his lifework with a clear object. He set out "to reform the nation, particularly the church, and to spread scriptural holiness over the land." He declared that he had only "one point of view—to promote so far as I am able vital, practical religion; and by the grace of God to beget, preserve, and increase the life of God in the souls of men." He and Whitefield took to open-air preaching with remarkable results in conversions through their straightforward evangelical doctrine. To conserve the gains of evangelism, he formed societies that became the organization of Methodism.

MATTHEW HENRY (1662–1714), born in a Welsh farmhouse at Iscoid, Flintshire, was the son of an evangelical Church of England minister who had been ejected from the Anglican Church along with two thousand Presbyterian, Independent, and Baptist ministers. They had resisted universal adoption of the Elizabethan Prayer Book. Matthew studied at a Nonconformist academy in London, and then read law at Gray's Inn. He considered becoming an Episcopalian minister, but decided to be a Nonconformist and was privately ordained a Presbyterian. His first pastorate was in Chester (1687–1712), followed by Hackney (1712–1714).

Greatly influenced by the Puritans, he made the exposition of Scripture the central concern of his ministry. Beginning work at four or five o'clock each day, he aimed to use time to the full. In 1704 he began the seven-volume *Commentary on the Bible* for which he is remembered. It set a style in detailed, often spiritualized, exposition of Scripture that has shaped evangelical ministry ever since. Charles Spurgeon is reported to have said that "every minister ought to read Matthew Henry entirely and carefully through once at least."

Editor

LANCE WUBBELS is presently the Managing Editor of Bethany House Publishers, where he has worked for over the past seventeen years. For many of those years he also taught biblical studies courses at the Bethany College of Missions. He has also been the compiler and editor of the Charles Spurgeon and F.B. Meyer Christian Living Classic books published by Emerald Books.

Combining the skills of teacher, researcher, and editor, Wubbels has discovered a wealth of classic writings, sermons, and biblical expositions from legendary Christians that remain nearly inaccessible to most believers. It has been his desire to present these extraordinary writings in a way that will appeal to a wide audience of readers and allow their ageless messages to be as relevant today as the day they were penned. It is his belief that the readings selected for this volume, *In His Presence*, represent some of the most profound expositions ever given regarding the life of Christ.

Wubbels is also the author of six fiction books with Bethany House Publishers. THE GENTLE HILLS series contains four books that capture the heart-rending challenges of World War II and the love of family and home. *One Small Miracle* is a heartwarming novel about the profound impact of a teacher's gift of love on the life of one of her struggling students. His most recent story, *The Bridge Over Flatwillow Creek*, is a timeless country love story that begins on a quiet summer day in 1901 in southeastern Minnesota. A naturally gifted storyteller, he captivates readers with a warm, homey style filled with wit and insight that appeals to a wide readership.

He and his family make their home in Bloomington, Minnesota.

January 1

The Old Testament begins with the book of the generation of the world, and it is its glory that it does so, but the glory of the New Testament excels in that it begins with the book of the genealogy of Him who made the world. As God, His "origins are from of old, from ancient times" (Mic. 5:2), but as man, He was sent forth "when the time had fully come,...born of a woman" (Gal. 4:4), and it is that record that is here declared.

The purpose of the record is to prove a title and make out a claim; the design is to prove that our Lord Jesus is the son of both David and Abraham and therefore of that nation and family out of which the Messiah was to arise. Abraham and David were the great trustees of the promise relating to the Messiah. It was promised to Abraham and his family that Christ should descend from him (Gen. 12:3; 22:18), and to David that Christ should descend from him (2 Sam. 7:12; Ps. 89:3–4; 132:11). Therefore, unless it can be proved that Jesus is a son of David and of Abraham, we cannot admit Him to be the Messiah. This exacting record was proof from the authentic records of the heralds' offices.

In calling Christ the son of David and of Abraham, Matthew shows that God is faithful to His promise and will make good every word that He has spoken, no matter how long the fulfillment may take. When God promised Abraham a son who would be the great blessing of the world, perhaps Abraham expected it would be his immediate son, but it proved to be one at the distance of forty–two generations and about 2,000 years. Note that delays of promised mercies, though they exercise our patience, do not weaken God's promise. Also note that the Messiah came when the descendants of Abraham were a despised people and the house of David was buried in obscurity. God's timing for the performance of His promises is often when it labors under the greatest improbabilities.

MATTHEW HENRY

A record of the genealogy of Jesus Christ the son of David, the son of Abraham.

MATTHEW 1:1

January 2

Abraham was the

father of Isaac...and

Jacob the father of

Joseph, the husband of

Mary, of whom was

born Jesus.

MATTHEW 1:2–16

Some of the names in the genealogy were in the direct line of the royal succession, and some come into it indirectly, causing commentators to pause and wonder how they came into the lineage at all. We are soon puzzled by divine providences—things seldom fall into easy, straight lines; life is a complication, a problem, a difficulty. Occasionally we catch a clue and think we can unwind the whole, but then we come to a hard knot. You do not know what your relations are to the great lines of history. You may be startled someday to find how much you have been and how much you have done. Do not say that you are not upon the great lines of history, that you are not tributaries to the great river that seems to carve for itself an infinite channel through the earth and pours its noble waters into a great sea. All creeks trickle into the rivers. There is royalty of mind as well as royalty of descent. The question to consider is whether we are living up to the potential of our endowment and responsibility, and having answered that question in the affirmative, all the rest will be settled by the Supreme Power.

Note from these genealogical records that the most illustrious lines often dip into strange places and seem to become lost in great moral swamps, so much so that it appears to be impossible they can ever be found again and reunited. There are many bad men and women in this list who have broken all the commandments of God. And yet the grand purpose moves on. It is not in the power of men's hands to break the thread of the divine purpose and scheme. The Savior comes, notwithstanding at times that the whole history seems to be depraved and utterly lost. Sometimes we find ourselves where it seems to be impossible that God can ever find us. Yet the life is redeemed with great cost to God, for He pays blood for blood, but His redeemed ones are not given over to the power of the destroyer.

JOSEPH PARKER

January 3

ary, the mother of our Lord, was pledged to Joseph; a purpose of marriage had been solemnly declared in words that regarded the future, and a promise of it made if God permits. It seems that the marriage was deferred so long after the contract that she appeared to be with child before the time came for the solemnizing of the marriage, though she was pledged before she conceived. It was probably after her return from her cousin Elizabeth, with whom she stayed three months (Luke 1:56), that she was perceived by Joseph to be with child and did not deny it.

Now we may well imagine how difficult and perplexing this situation was to the blessed virgin. She herself knew the divine origin of this conception, but how could she prove it? She would be dealt with as a harlot. Never was a daughter of Eve so dignified as the Virgin Mary was and yet in danger of falling under the charge of one of the worst of crimes. One of the ancients said, "It was better it should be asked, 'Is not this the son of a carpenter?' than, 'Is not this the son of a harlot?'" Even so, we do not find that she tormented herself about it; but being conscious of her own innocence, she kept her mind calm and committed her predicament to Him who judges righteously.

From Mary, let us learn what she learned. Although she was highly favored by God with the most awesome responsibility of giving birth to the Messiah, the reproach she would bear and its potential consequences were daunting. After great and high spiritual experiences, we too must expect something or other to humble us—some reproach, some thorn in the flesh, to keep us from becoming proud or puffed up with ourselves. If that happens, we may rest in a good conscience and cheerfully trust God with the keeping of our good names, having every reason to hope that He will clear up not only our integrity but also our honor, as the sun at noonday.

MATTHEW HENRY

This is how the birth of Jesus Christ came about: His mother Mary was pledged to be married to Joseph, but before they came together, she was found to be with child through the Holy Spirit.

MATTHEW 1:18

January 4

His mother Mary was pledged to be married to Joseph, but before they came together, she was found to be with child through the Holy Spirit. Because Joseph her husband was a righteous man and did not want to expose her to public disgrace, he had in mind to divorce her quietly.

MATTHEW 1:18–19

Try to imagine the shock to Joseph of the sudden discovery, crashing in on him after he was pledged to Mary, and in what would have been the sweet interval of love and longing that is delicately and unconsciously brought out in the words "before they came together." "She was found"—how the remembrance of the sudden disclosure, blinding and startling as a lightning flash, lives in that word! And how the agony of perplexity as to the right thing to do in such a cruel dilemma is hinted at in the two clauses that pull in opposite directions! Being a just man, Joseph owed it to righteousness and to himself not to ignore Mary's condition, but as her lover and husband, how could he put her, who was still so dear to him, to public shame, some of which would cloud his own name? To divorce her was the only course possible, though it racked his soul, and to do it quietly was the last gift that his wounded love could give her. No wonder that these things kept him brooding sadly on them, nor that his day's troubled thinkings colored his sleeping hours!

The divine guidance, which is ever given to waiting minds, was given to him by the way of a dream, which is one of the Old Testament media of divine communications and occurs with striking frequency in this and the following chapter, there being three recorded as sent to Joseph and one to the Magi. We need not wonder that divine communications were abundant at such an hour, nor shall we be startled, if we believe in the great miracle of the Word's becoming flesh, that a flight of subsidiary miracles, like a bevy of attendant angels, clustered around it.

The most stupendous fact in history, the great mystery that lies at the foundation of Christianity, is announced by the angel in the fewest and simplest words.

ALEXANDER MACLAREN

*J*oseph was the man who looked on these matters with great wonder. All the ages have since crowded around him and, so to speak, have thronged him into an infinite multitude, all looking on with the same amazement, all distracted by the same perplexity. Joseph had no idea that an angel was coming to him along the crooked lines of his mental anguish.

Like Joseph, we seem to constantly misunderstand everything that is at all great and noble. We cannot understand ourselves; we can give but foolish answers to all the great questions that relate to our own being and our own destiny. No one has ever satisfied his friend fully and left him in the position in which he could ask no question or suggest no doubt regarding any movement in life that was really tragic, involving suffering when that suffering might have been escaped.

Perhaps you are looking at your life as a great perplexity, full of knots and twists. You cannot see how this knot can be untied, and yet you feel that it would be improper to attempt to cut it. Refuse to be in a hurry. I have had a thousand knots like that in my life. When I touched them, my fingers were too soft to get hold of the strings that bound them together. When I have called for a knife, I have been guilty of a coward's trick, and the angel has said, "Do not cut it. Let it alone. The answer of all things is not yet, but in due time that knot shall prove to be part of the strange yet ever beneficent ministry of the divine and Holy Father."

JOSEPH PARKER

Because Joseph her husband was a righteous man and did not want to expose her to public disgrace, he had in mind to divorce her quietly. But after he had considered this, an angel of the Lord appeared to him in a dream and said, "Joseph son of David, do not be afraid to take Mary home as your wife, because what is conceived in her is from the Holy Spirit."

MATTHEW 1:19–20

January 6

"She will give birth to a son, and you are to give him the name Jesus, because he will save his people from their sins."

MATTHEW 1:21

Bernard has delightfully said that the name of Jesus is honey in the mouth, melody in the ear, and joy in the heart—so inexpressibly fragrant that it imparts a delicious perfume to everything that it contacts. Notice its first use, when the child who was yet to be born was named Jesus. Here we find everything suggestive of comfort. The person to whom that name was first revealed was Joseph—a carpenter, a humble working man, unknown and undistinguished except for the justice of his character. It is not, therefore, a title to be monopolized by princes, sages, priests, or men of wealth. It is to be a household name among common people. He is the people's Christ.

We should also note that the angel spoke to Joseph in a dream. That name is so soft and sweet that it breaks no man's rest but rather, yields a peace unrivaled, the peace of God. With such a dream, Joseph's sleep was more blessed than his waking. The name has evermore this power, for it unveils a glory brighter than dreams have ever imagined. Under its power young men see visions and old men dream dreams, and these do not mock them but are prophecies faithful and true.

The name of Jesus was sweet at the first because of the words with which it was accompanied, for they were meant to remove perplexity from Joseph's mind, and some of them ran thus: "Do not be afraid." Truly, no name can banish fear like the name of Jesus. It is the beginning of hope and the end of despair. Hearing that name, the sinner forgets to die, he hopes to live; he rises out of the deadly lethargy of his hopelessness, and looking upward, he sees a reconciled God and fears no longer. This name is full of rare delights when we meditate upon the infinite preciousness of the person to whom it is assigned.

CHARLES SPURGEON

January 7

The cause of every man's discomfort is evil, moral evil—first of all, evil in himself, his own sin, his own wrongness, his own unrightness, and then evil in those he loves, which he cannot deal with except as he rids himself of his own sin.

No man shall be condemned for any or all of his sins that are past. He needs not dread remaining unforgiven even for the worst of them. The sin he dwells in, the sin he will not come out of—that is the sole ruin of a man. His present, his live sins—those pervading his thoughts and ruling his conduct, the sins he keeps doing and will not give up, the sins he is called to abandon and clings to—these condemn him even at this moment. "Light has come into the world, but men loved darkness instead of light because their deeds were evil" (John 3:19).

It is this indwelling badness ready to produce bad actions that we need to be delivered from. Against this sin, if a man will not strive, he is left to commit evil and reap the consequences. Jesus came to deliver us, not rescue us from needful consequences. It is the sin in our being, the miserable fact that we as a very child of God do not care for our Father and will not obey Him, causing us to desire wrong and act wrongly—this is what He came to deliver us from, not the things we have done, but the possibility of doing such things anymore.

Come, then, at the call of the Giver of repentance and light, the Friend of sinners, all you on whom lies the weight of sin or the gathered heap of a thousand crimes. He came to call such as you that He might make you clean. He cannot bear that you should live in such misery, such blackness of darkness. He wants to give you your life again, the bliss of your being. Heartily He loves you; heartily He hates the evil in you. If you know yourself to be a sinner, come to Him that He may work in you His perfect work, for He came to call sinners—us, you and me—to repentance.

GEORGE MACDONALD

"You are to give him the name Jesus, because he will save his people from their sins."

MATTHEW 1:21

January 8

All this took place to fulfill what the Lord had said through the prophet.

MATTHEW 1:22

All that we read of Jesus' birth was done in fulfillment of prophecy. God does not work extemporaneously; the suddenness of His movements is only apparent. Every word He says comes up from eternity around the birthplace of Jesus Christ. There assembled the prophets and the minstrels of ancient time, saying, "All this took place to fulfill what the Lord had said through the prophet."

The prophets were misunderstood men; they seemed to sing a song that found entrance in no heart. Their forecasts were met with derisive laughter, their predictions were considered but the protest of a disordered and unbalanced mind, and many a time, wrapping their mantles around them, travel-stained, they lay down, asking, "Why did I ever let the prophetic inspiration move me to speak?"

Prophets always suffer. It is a crucifixion to be born before your time. The man who projects himself by divine energy through centuries ahead dies a thousand deaths. The prophets suffered for us: Isaiah, Ezekiel, and Daniel, and the mighty tribe of men who never spoke to their own day but shot their thunder voices across the ages died for us. They have their reward. I cannot think of them as dead dust, scattered upon the winds and going to make up some other man's grave, and there an end of them. I must, following the instinct of justice and nobleness of compensation, think of them as seeing the triumphs they predicted and turning into songs all the tears and woes that afflicted them during their misunderstood ministry.

JOSEPH PARKER

January 9

*L*et it remain as a matter of faith that Jesus Christ, even He who lay in Bethlehem's manger and was carried in a woman's arms and lived a suffering life and died on a criminal's cross, was nevertheless "God over all, forever praised" (Rom. 9:5). He was not an angel or a subordinate deity or a being elevated to the Godhead. He was as surely God as God can be, one with the Father and the ever-blessed Spirit. All that *God* means, the Deity, the infinite Jehovah with us, this, this was worthy of the burst of the midnight song when angels startled the shepherds with their carols, singing "Glory to God in the highest, and on earth peace to men on whom his favor rests" (Luke 2:14).

This was worthy of the foresight of seers and prophets, worthy of a new star in the heavens, worthy of the care that inspiration has manifested to preserve the sacred record. This, too, was worthy of the martyr deaths of apostles and confessors who refused to count their lives dear to them for the sake of the incarnate God. And this is worthy of your most earnest endeavors to spread the glad tidings, worthy of a holy life to illustrate its blessed influences, and worthy of a joyful death to prove its consoling power.

God—therein is the glory; *God with us*—therein is the grace. Let us admire this truth. Let us stand at a reverent distance from it as Moses when he saw God in the bush and put off his shoes, feeling that the place where he stood was holy ground. This is a wonderful fact: God the Infinite dwelt in the frail body of a lowly man. "God was in Christ."

CHARLES SPURGEON

"The virgin will be with child and will give birth to a son, and they will call him Immanuel"—which means, "God with us."

MATTHEW 1:23

January 10

When Joseph woke up, he did what the angel of the Lord had commanded him and took Mary home as his wife. But he had no union with her until she gave birth to a son. And he gave him the name Jesus.

MATTHEW 1:24–25

Joseph was put to sleep by God and talked to through the medium of a dream. It is God's old plan: He puts us into a deep sleep, and behold when we awake, there is the great answer to a small difficulty that had turned our life into a sharp pain, or there is the way out of an entanglement that seemed as difficult as a labyrinth, puzzling as a thicket, devised by all the cunning cruelty of our worst enemies. Many times I have done as you have, falling off into sleep, quite unable to do the work that was pressing me. A refreshing slumber has blessed the brain, has wound it up in every energy and force, and the awakening has been as a resurrection. We have gone to the work that defied us, and lo, in the hands recovered by sleep there has been cunning enough to lift the burden or to dispel the difficulty, and we who had fainted in weariness rejoiced in a renewed and apparently inexhaustible strength.

Thank God for sleep, thank God for dreams, thank God for every ministry that gets you out of your littleness. If any minister of God in any church can charm you away from your daily experiences and make you feel even for one moment that the universe is larger than you had supposed it to be, go and hear that man: He is your soul's true friend. If by tone of voice, if by passion of appeal, if by tenderness of prayer, he can turn you to an upward look, he is God's minister to your soul.

I read the books that make me stretch. I follow the authors who tell me of bigger things than I have yet seen. I love the souls who lure me into sleep that is enriched with dreaming, that extends the horizon and doubles the stars and heightens the sky in which they shine.

JOSEPH PARKER

January 11

These men were watchers of the stars; therefore a star was used to call them. Certain other men soon after were fishermen, and by means of an amazing catch of fish, the Lord Jesus called them to be fishers of men. For a stargazer a star, for a fisherman a fish. The Master-Fisher has a bait for each one of His elect, and often He selects a point in their daily life to be the barb of the hook. Were you busy yesterday at your sales work? Did you hear no voice saying, "Buy the truth and do not sell it"? Do you make bread, and have you never asked yourself, "Has my soul tasted of the bread of heaven?" Are you a farmer who works the soil? Has God never spoken to you by those plowed fields and made you wish that your heart might be tilled and sown?

Listen! God is speaking! Hear, for there are voices everywhere calling you to heaven. You need not traverse a desert to find the link to everlasting mercy. God and human souls are near each other. How I wish that your common vocation would be viewed by you as concealing within itself the door to your high calling. Oh, that the Holy Spirit would turn your favorite pursuits into opportunities for His gracious work upon you! If not among the stars, yet among the flowers or the cattle or the waves of the sea may He find a net in which to enclose you for Christ.

It did seem that a star was an unlikely guide to head a procession of Eastern sages, and yet it was a sufficient guide. And so it may seem that your vocation is an unlikely thing to bring you to Jesus, and yet the Lord may so use it. There may be a voice for wisdom from the mouth of an ass, a call to a holy life may startle you from a bush, a warning may flash upon your wall, or a vision may impress you in the silence of night. Only be ready to hear, and God will find a way of speaking to you.

CHARLES SPURGEON

After Jesus was born in Bethlehem in Judea, during the time of King Herod, Magi from the east came to Jerusalem and asked, "Where is the one who has been born king of the Jews? We saw his star in the east and have come to worship him."

MATTHEW 2:1–2

January 12

The contrast of the Gentile Magi's joyful eagerness to worship the King of Israel with the alarm of His own people at the whisper of His name is a prelude of the tragedy of His rejection and the passing over of the kingdom to the Gentiles. Notice the scornful doubled emphasis of that *"King* Herod" in immediate connection with the mention of the true King. Herod was a usurper, caricaturing the true Monarch. Like most kings who have had "Great" tacked to their names, his greatness consisted mainly in supreme wickedness. Fierce, lustful, cunning, he had ruled without mercy, and now he was passing through the last stages of old age, ringed about by the fears born of his misdeeds. He trembles for his throne, as well he may, when he hears of these strangers. He recognizes the familiar tones of the Messianic hope, which he knew was ever lying like glowing embers in the breast of the nation, ready to be blown into flame. An evil conscience is full of fears and shrinks from the good news that the King of all is at hand. His coming should be joy, like the bursting spring or the rosy dawn, but our sin makes the day of the Lord darkness and sends us cowering into our corners to escape these searching eyes.

No less tragic is the trouble that "all Jerusalem" shared with Herod. The Magi had naturally made straight for the capital, expecting to find the newborn King there and His city jubilant at His birth. They must have felt like men who see, gleaming from afar on some hillside, a brightness that has all vanished when they reach the spot. Nobody in Jerusalem knew anything about their King. That was strange enough. But nobody wanted him! The Magi, who represented the eagerness of the Gentile hearts grasping the new hope in Israel's Messiah, saw His own people alarmed that the promise that had shone as a great light through dreary centuries was at last on the eve of fulfillment.

ALEXANDER MACLAREN

January 13

Herod's alarm over the birth of the true King of Israel is followed by the council of the theologians, with its solemn illustration of the difference between orthodoxy and life, and of the utter hollowness of mere knowledge, however accurate, of the letter of Scripture. While the ecclesiastical rulers were fully aware of the place of the Messiah's birth, notice the different conduct of Herod, the Magi, and the scribes. The first is entangled in ludicrous contradiction. Herod believes that the Messiah is to be born in Bethlehem, and yet he sets himself to oppose what he must, in some sense, believe to be God's purpose. Such a policy represents madness, and yet this is perhaps not more insane than our own actions when we set ourselves against what we know to be God's will and consciously seek to thwart it. A child trying to physically stop a train has as much chance of success.

The scribes are quite sure where the Messiah is to be born, but they do not care to go and see whether He is born. The Magi, to whom the hope of Israel is new, may rush away in their enthusiasm to Bethlehem, but they, to whom it had lost all appeal and become a commonplace, would take no such trouble. Does not familiarity with the gospel produce much the same effect on us? Might not the joy and the devotion, however ignorant if compared with our better knowledge of the letter, that marks converts from heathenism, shame the tepid zeal and unruffled composure of us who have heard all about Christ till it has become wearisome. Here on the very threshold of the gospel story is the first instance of the lesson on the worthlessness of head knowledge and the constant temptation of substituting it for that submission of the will and that trust of the heart that alone makes faith. The most impenetrable armor against the gospel is the familiar and lifelong knowledge of the gospel.

ALEXANDER MACLAREN

When he had called together all the people's chief priests and teachers of the law, he asked them where the Christ was to be born. "In Bethlehem in Judea," they replied, "for this is what the prophet has written."

MATTHEW 2:4–5

January 14

After they had heard the king, they went on their way, and the star they had seen in the east went ahead of them until it stopped over the place where the child was. When they saw the star, they were overjoyed.

MATTHEW 2:9–10

*O*bserve how graciously God directed the Magi. By the first appearance of the star they were given to understand where they might inquire for this king, and then it disappeared, and they were left to take the ordinary methods for such a search. Extraordinary helps are not to be expected where ordinary means are available. Now they had traced the matter as far as they could, to Bethlehem, but how would they find the child in such a populous town? Here they were at a loss but not at their faith's end; they believed that God, who had led them this far, would not leave them there. And He did not, for the star again led the way. If we go on as far as we can in the way of our duty, God will direct and enable us to do that which we cannot do on our own.

The star had left them a great while yet now returns. They who follow God in the dark shall find that light is still reserved for them. God would rather create a new thing than leave those at a loss who diligently and faithfully seek Him. The star is the token of God's presence with them, for He is light and goes before His people as their Guide. If we look to God in all our ways, He says, "I will instruct you and teach you in the way you should go; I will counsel you and watch over you" (Ps. 32:8). There is always a morning star that arises in the hearts of those who seek Christ (2 Pet. 1:19).

Note that when the Magi saw the star, they were overjoyed. Now they were sure that God was with them, and this token of His presence cannot but fill with joy unspeakable the souls of those who know how to value them. This is light out of darkness. Now they had reason to hope for a sight of the Lord's Christ soon. We should be glad for everything that shows us the way to Christ. The star would conduct them into the very presence–chamber of the King. "Let the hearts of those who seek the Lord rejoice" (Ps. 105:3).

MATTHEW HENRY

*O*ne should note that the Magi did not fall down and worship Mary—they hardly saw the mother. Who can see anything but Christ when He is there? To see anything in God's house but God is to waste the opportunity. The wise men worshiped the young child, they knelt before Him, they became oblivious of themselves in His presence. Not a word might they say, for worship when deepest is often silent. Words are often a hindrance in the way of spiritual progress, and they are to blame for the thousand controversies that afflict and distress the church. How much we need to become like the wise men. Whatever the word *worship* may mean here, it is evident that the Magi offered homage to the young child. The right attitude of wisdom is to bend before Christ, to be silent in His presence, to wait for Him to lead the conversation. If wisdom venture to utter its voice first, it should be in inquiry or in praise. Wisdom is always reticent of speech. It is the fool who chatters; the wise man thinks.

If we come into the house where Jesus Christ is, our business is to imitate the Magi—to bow the knee, to put our hand over our eyes, lest we be blinded by the great light, to be silent, to wait. It would be good in a church service if in our brief time of worship we could set aside a few minutes for absolute silence. No minister to speak, no organ to utter its voice, no hymn to trouble the air. If we could, with closed eyes and bent head, spend five minutes in absolute speechlessness, that would be prayer, that would be worship. The fool would misunderstand it and think nothing was being done, but the last expression of eloquence is silence, and sometimes the highest liturgy is to be dumb. Unfortunately, we have banished the angel of silence. The angel of quietude is a nuisance to our fussy civilization. We have set noise in the front, and silence has been exiled from the church. It is time we restore the worship of the wise men.

JOSEPH PARKER

On coming to the house, they saw the child with his mother Mary, and they bowed down and worshiped him.

MATTHEW 2:11

January 16

When they had gone, an angel of the Lord appeared to Joseph in a dream. "Get up," he said, "take the child and his mother and escape to Egypt. Stay there until I tell you, for Herod is going to search for the child to kill him."

MATTHEW 2:13–14

God is well aware of all the cruel purposes of the enemies of His church. How early was the blessed Jesus involved in trouble! His life and suffering began together. Pharaoh's cruelty fastens upon the Hebrew children, and a great dragon stands ready to devour the child the moment it is born (Rev. 12:4).

Joseph is directed to take the young child and mother and flee to Egypt. But why into Egypt? Egypt was infamous for idolatry, tyranny, and enmity to the people of God. It had been a house of bondage to Israel and particularly cruel to the infants of Israel, and yet it was appointed to be a place of refuge to the holy child Jesus. God, when He pleases, can make the worst of places serve the best of purposes, for the earth is the Lord's, and He makes use of it as He pleases.

Mary and Joseph might be tempted to ask, "If this child is the Son of God, has He no other way to protect Himself than this inglorious retreat? Is He unable to summon legions of angels to guard His life, or a cherubim with flaming swords? Can He not strike Herod dead or wither the hand that is stretched out against Him?" But we find no such objections. Their faith, being tried, is found firm, and they believe the child is the Son of God, though they see no miracle wrought for His preservation, and they must carry out the command on their own. Joseph had a great honor put upon him in being the husband of the blessed virgin, but that honor has trouble attending it, as all honors have in this world. He must carry the child to safety in Egypt, yet the gold that the Magi brought would help to bear their charges. God foresees His people's distresses and provides against them beforehand. And in the command to remain there until the angel returns to them, God intimates the continuance of His care and guidance. Thus God will keep His people in dependence upon Him.

MATTHEW HENRY

January 17

Herod's fierce rage, enflamed by the dim suspicion that these wily Magi have gone away laughing in their sleeves at having tricked him and by the dread that they may be stirring up armed defenders of the infant King, is in full accord with all that we know of him. A splash or two of the blood of poor innocents, more or less, found on the tyrant's bloody skirts could be of little consequence in the eyes of those who knew what a long debauchery of horrors his reign had been. And the number of infants under two years old in such a tiny place as Bethlehem would be small, so that their feeble wail might fail to reach the ears even of contemporaries. But there is no reason to question the simple truth of the story so like the frantic cruelty and sleepless suspicion of the gray-headed tyrant, who was stirred to more ferocity as the shades of death gathered about him and power slipped from his rotting hands. Of all the tragic pictures that Scripture gives of a godless old age, burning with unquenchable hatred to goodness and condemned to failure in all its antagonism, none is touched with more lurid hues than this. What a contrast between the infant King and the aged Herod going down to his loathsome death, which all longed for! Herod may well stand as a symbol of the futility of all opposition to Christ the King.

The fate of these few infants is a strange one. In their brief lives they have won immortal fame. They died as martyrs for the Christ whom they never knew. These lambs were slain for the sake of the Lamb who lived while they died, that by His death they might live forever. Even in His infancy, Christ came to bring not peace but a sword, and the shadow of suffering for Him already attended the brightness of His rising. But even in His infancy, His coming abolished death and made all who partook of His suffering, even by anticipation, sharers in His glory.

ALEXANDER MACLAREN

When Herod realized that he had been outwitted by the Magi, he was furious, and he gave orders to kill all the boys in Bethlehem and its vicinity who were two years and under.

MATTHEW 2:16

January 18

After Herod died, an angel of the Lord appeared in a dream to Joseph in Egypt and said, "Get up, take the child and his mother and go to the land of Israel, for those who were trying to take the child's life are dead."

MATTHEW 2:19–20

Those who patiently wait for guidance are never disappointed or left undirected. Joseph is a pattern of self-abnegating submission and an example of its rewards. The angel ever comes again to those who have once obeyed him and continue to wait. This third appearance describes his coming as the appearance of a familiar presence. His command begins by a verbal repetition of the former summons, "Get up, take the child and his mother and go," and then passes to the command to Moses that was the first step toward the former calling of God's son—the nation—out of Egypt. "For all the men who wanted to kill you are dead" (Exod. 4:19) was the encouragement to Moses. "Those who were trying to take the child's life are dead" is the encouragement to Joseph. It sums up in one sentence the failure of the first attempt and is like an epitaph cut on a tombstone for a man yet living—a prophecy of the end of all succeeding efforts to crush Christ and thwart His work. Christ lives and grows: Herod rots and dies.

Apparently Joseph's intention was to return to Bethlehem. He may have thought that Nazareth would hardly satisfy the angel's injunction to go to the "land of Israel" or that David's city was the right home for David's heir. At all events, his perplexity appeals to heaven for direction, and, for the fourth time, his course is marked for him by a dream (Matt. 2:22–23). Archelaus, Herod's son, who had received Judea on the partition at his father's death, was as cruel but less able. There was more security in the obscurity of Nazareth under the less sanguinary sway of Antipas, whose share of his father's vices was his lust rather than his ferocity. So, after so many wanderings and with such strange new experiences and providences, the silent, steadfast Joseph and the meek mother bring back their mysterious charge and secret to the humble old home.

ALEXANDER MACLAREN

January 19

The voice of prophecy in Israel had fallen silent for four hundred years. Now, when it is once more heard, it sounds in exactly the same key as when it ceased in Malachi. Its last word had been the prediction of the day of the Lord and of the coming of Elijah once more. John was Elijah over again—the same garb, the isolation, the fearlessness, the grim, gaunt strength, the fiery energy of rebuke that defied kings in the fury of their self-will. Elijah, Ahab, and Jezebel have their double in John, Herod, and Herodias. John's portrait is flung on the canvas with the same startling abruptness that Elijah was. Matthew leaps his readers into the arena of a full-grown and fully armed John, whose work is described by one word—*preaching,* meaning proclaiming as a king's herald.

In those days John the Baptist came, preaching in the Desert of Judea and saying, "Repent, for the kingdom of heaven is near."

MATTHEW 3:1–2

John's message is summed up in two blasts of the trumpet: the call to repentance and the rousing proclamation that the kingdom of heaven is at hand. In the former, he but reproduces the tone of earlier prophecy when he insists on a thorough change of mind and a true sorrow for sin. But in the latter, he advances far beyond his precursors, who had seen the vision of the kingdom and of the King, but not nigh. John must peal into the drowsy ears of a generation that had almost forgotten the ancient hope that it was at the very threshold. Like some solitary stern crag that catches the light of the sun yet unrisen but hastening upward, long before the shadowed valleys, John flamed above his generation all aglow with the light as the witness that in another moment it would spring above the eastern horizon. But he knows that his contemporaries thought the kingdom of heaven meant exclusive privileges and their rule over the heathen. They had all but lost the thought that it meant first God's rule over their wills and their harmony with the glad obedience of heaven. They had to be shaken out of their self-complacency and be told that the King's standard was purity, and the preparation of His coming, penitence.

ALEXANDER MACLAREN

January 20

John's clothes were made of camel's hair, and he had a leather belt around his waist. His food was locusts and wild honey. People went out to him from Jerusalem and all Judea and the whole region of the Jordan.

MATTHEW 3:4–5

Matthew gives a vivid picture of the asceticism of John which was one secret of his hold on the people. The more luxuriously self-indulgent men are, the more they are fascinated by religious self-denial. A man "clothed in soft raiment" would have drawn no crowds. A religious teacher must be clearly free from sensual appetites and love of ease if he is to stir the multitude. John's rough garb and coarse food were not assumed by him to create an impression. He was no mere imitator of the old prophets. His asceticism was the expression of his severe, solitary spirit, detached from the delights of sense and even from the softer play of loves, because the coming kingdom flamed ever before him, and the age seemed to him to be rotting and ready for the fire. The thoughts that burned in him drove him into the wilderness and might well have seemed to have tyrannized over him.

John's work produced a nearly universal excitement. He did not come out of the desert with his message. If men would hear it, they must go to him. And they went. All the southern portion of the country seemed to empty itself into the wilderness. Sleeping national hopes revived, the awe of the coming judgment seized all classes. It had been so long since a fiery soul had scattered flaming words, and religious teachers had for so many centuries been mumbling the old well-worn formulas and splitting hairs, that it was an apocalypse to hear once more the accent of conviction from a man who really believed every word he said and who himself thrilled with the solemn truths that he thundered. Wherever a religious teacher shows that he has John's qualities—his unalterable resolution, a vision of the unseen, and a message from God—the crowds will go out to see him. And even if the enthusiasm is shallow, some spasm of conviction will pass across many a conscience, and some will be pointed by him to the King.

ALEXANDER MACLAREN

January 21

*J*ohn's baptism was the sensation of the day. Everybody seemed to have more or less interest in it. Not to have heard it was to be misinformed or lacking in information, and not to have partaken of it was to have missed a great opportunity. After five hundred years without a prophet in Israel, curiosity was touched, wonder was on the alert, and national pride was excited.

But when John saw many of the great and leading religious men of the day, pure in their own estimation, not needing any such ministry as he came to conduct, except in an official and ceremonial manner, it changed his tone severely. He recognized the possibility of people coming to religious ordinances from wrong motives. They appeared willing to embrace it superficially in order to gain a great end. John startled them with tidings that struck at the root of their religious motives.

When we come to spiritual matters, we need to be warned of the meaning of the action that they are intended to accomplish. It is the business of the ministers of the truth to give this warning, to keep back those who have not the right credentials. This is a kingdom that can be entered only by one right—the right of sin, affirmed, confessed, deplored. Blind man, your blindness is your certificate; you have no other. Broken-hearted, wounded man, your contrition is your credentials; seek for none beside. Weary, tired soul, altogether overborne and distressed by the burdens and difficulties of life, your weariness is your claim. Do not try to get up your strength. When you lie flat in your weakness, your attitude is most acceptable to heaven. To try to appear with some decorousness in His presence is to enhance your sin. To come panting, heaving, out of breath, gasping, dying—that is a guarantee of good hearing in the presence of God. He resents our fullness, not our poverty: It is when we are great that He has nothing to say to us, not when we are small in our own esteem.

But when he saw many of the Pharisees and Sadducees coming to where he was baptizing, he said to them: "You brood of vipers! Who warned you to flee from the coming wrath?"

MATTHEW 3:7

JOSEPH PARKER

January 22

"Produce fruit in keeping with repentance."

Matthew 3:8

The Pharisees were self-righteous pedants who had turned religion into a jumble of petty precepts. The Sadducees were very superior persons who keenly appreciated the good things of this world and were too enlightened to have much belief in anything. These highest and coldest classes of the nation had the very same red-hot words flung at them as the general public—all fared alike. So they should and always will if a real prophet has to talk to them. Honeyed words were not in John's line. John had not lived in the desert for all these years and held converse with God without having learned that his business was to smite on the conscience with a strong hand and tear away the masks that men hid behind. His brusque, almost fierce address was true of all the old prophets. Charging the religious elite with moral corruption and creeping earthliness went far beyond a scolding.

The summary of John's preaching is like a succession of lightning flashes. In his hands the great hope of Israel became a message of terror set forth as "the wrath to come" by the imagery of the axe lying at the root of the trees, the fan winnowing the wheat from the chaff, the destroying fire. That wrath was inseparable from the coming of the King, for His righteous reign necessarily meant punishment of sin. We need today a clearer discernment of the truth that flamed before John's eyes, that the full proclamation of God's kingdom includes the wrath to come.

Then follows the urgent demand for reformation of life as the sign of real repentance. John's exhortation does not touch the deepest ground for repentance that is laid in the heart-softening love of God, but it is based wholly on the certainty of judgment. So far, it is incomplete, but the demand for righteous living as the only test of religious emotion is fully Christian and needed in this generation as it never was. Repentance must get beyond an emotional response to the solid fruits that alone guarantee the worth of the emotion.

ALEXANDER MACLAREN

January 23

There is an amazing number of excuses that carnal hearts put up to prevent the convincing, commanding power of the Word of God from entering in—vain thoughts that lodge within those who are called to "wash the evil" from their hearts and be saved (Jer. 4:14). The word of caution is clear—"Do not pretend, do not presume, do not rock yourselves to sleep with this, nor flatter yourselves into a fool's paradise." God takes notice of what we say *within* ourselves which we dare not speak out loud, and He is acquainted with all the false rests of the soul and the fallacies with which it deludes itself but which it will not discover lest it should be undeceived. Many hide the lie that ruins them and roll it under their tongue because they are ashamed to own it. They keep in the devil's interest by keeping the devil's counsel.

The false pretense disclosed by John was the Jewish claim to Abraham as their father. "We are Jews, a holy nation, a peculiar people. The covenant with Abraham makes us holy. Why should we repent like Gentile sinners?" John warns that it is a vanity to trust in the fact that we descended from godly ancestors, have been blessed with a religious education, live within the circle of a family where the fear of God is uppermost, and have good friends to advise and pray for us. What will all this avail us if we do not repent and live a life in keeping with repentance? It will not keep us from judgment.

When John spoke these words, he was baptizing in the Jordan River at Bethany (John 1:28), where the children of Israel had passed over as they entered the promised land and where they had placed twelve stones, one for each tribe, which Joshua set up for a memorial (Josh. 4:20). It is possible that John pointed to those stones, which God could raise to be, more than in representation, the twelve tribes of Israel. God prefers a stone over a hard, dry, barren sinner who refuses to bow before Him.

MATTHEW HENRY

"And do not think you can say to yourselves, 'We have Abraham as our father.' I tell you that out of these stones God can raise up children for Abraham."

MATTHEW 3:9

January 24

John knew that his baptism was, like the water in which he immersed, cold and incapable of giving life. It symbolized but did not effect cleansing, any more than his preaching righteousness could produce righteousness. But the King would come, bringing the gift of a mighty Spirit whose life–giving energy, transforming dead matter into its own likeness, burning out the foul stains from character, and melting cold hearts into radiant warmth, should do all that John's poor, cold, outward baptism only shadowed. Form and substance of this great promise gather up many Old Testament utterances. From of old, fire had been the emblem of the divine nature, not only, nor chiefly, as destructive, but rather as life–giving, cleansing, gladdening, transforming. It speaks of the might of His transforming power, the melting and vitalizing influence of His communicated grace, the warmth of His conquering love. From of old, the promise of the divine Spirit poured out on all flesh had been connected with the kingdom of Messiah, and John but reiterates the uniform voice of prophecy, even as he anticipates the crowning gift of the gospel, in this saying.

So where is the Spirit that was poured out on Pentecost? Where is the flame that Christ died to light up? Has it burned down to gray ashes? Has it gone out after a little ineffectual crackling without ever reaching the solid mass of obstinate coal? Where? The question is not difficult to answer. His promise remains faithful. But our sin, our negligence, our eager absorption with worldly cares, and our withdrawal of mind and heart from the patient contemplation of His truth have quenched the Spirit. Is it not so? We sit frostbitten and almost dead among the snows, and all the while the gracious sunshine is pouring down that is able to melt the white death that covers us and to free us from the bonds that hold us prisoned in their numbing clasp. Are our souls on fire with the love of God, aglow with the ardor caught from Christ's love? "He will baptize you with the Holy Spirit."

ALEXANDER MACLAREN

January 25

Fire purifies. The Holy Spirit, who is fire, produces holiness in heart and character by torching the flame of love to God that burns our souls clear with its white fervors. This is the Christian method of making men good—first, know God's love, then believe it, then love Him back again, and then let that genial heat permeate all your life, and it will bring forth everywhere blossoms of beauty and fruits of holiness that shall clothe the pastures of the wilderness with gladness. Did you ever see a blast furnace? How long would it take a man with a hammer and chisel to get the bits of ore out from the stony matrix? But fling it into the fiery great cylinder, and by evening you can run off a golden stream of pure and fluid metal, from which all the dross and rubbish are parted and which has been charmed out of all its sullen hardness and will take the shape of any mold into which you like to run it.

So with us when the love of God is shed abroad in our hearts by the Holy Spirit. His love will purify us and sever us from our sins. Nothing else will. Moralities and the externals of religion will wash away the foulness that lies on the surface, but stains that have sunk deep into the very substance of the soul and have dyed every thread in warp and woof to its center are not be gotten rid of so. God be thanked, there is a mightier detergent than all these—even the divine Spirit that Christ gives and that divine forgiveness that Christ brings. There, and there alone, we can lose all the guilt of our faultful past and receive a new and better life that will mold our future into growing likeness to His great purity. Do not resist that merciful searching fire that is ready to penetrate our very bones and marrow and burn up the seeds of death that lurk in the inmost intents of the heart! Let Him plunge you into that gracious baptism as we put some poor piece of foul clay into the fire, and like it, as you glow, you will whiten, and all the spots will melt away before the conquering tongues of the cleansing flames.

ALEXANDER MACLAREN

"He will baptize you with the Holy Spirit and with fire."

MATTHEW 3:11

January 26

Then Jesus was led by the Spirit into the desert to be tempted by the devil.

MATTHEW 4:1

From our Lord's temptation, let it always be remembered that there is no sin in being tempted. Even when our first parents were in their perfect state, they were liable to temptation. Their fault was in yielding, not in being tempted. Our Lord was tempted to what would have been the worst of sins, yet He did not yield.

Remember also that temptation does not necessitate sinning. Jesus "has been tempted in every way, just as we are—yet was without sin" (Heb. 4:15). Joseph was sorely tempted but remained pure. A man may walk in the midst of the furnace of temptation, yet not even the smell of fire shall be upon him. Amid the worst temptations, he is one "who through faith [is] shielded by God's power until the coming of salvation" (1 Peter 1:5).

Indeed, temptation may be necessary for you. It evidently was so in the case of our Lord. He was led by the Holy Spirit to face the devil. Temptation may be necessary for us for the purpose of testing and trying us. There are no champions in God's army who are fair-weather soldiers. They must all endure hardness; their valor must be tried and proven. God sends none of his ships to sea without having first tested them, and when their seaworthiness is proven, then they may go on their long voyages. Like Abraham, we may be severely put to the test yet come to hear the Angel of the Covenant's marvelous commendation: "Now I know that you fear God" (Gen. 22:1, 12).

Where would our patience be if there were no suffering to test it? Where would be the grace of forgiveness if we never had to suffer injury from others? It is for our growth in grace that the storms of temptation are let loose upon us, that, like a stalwart oak, we may be firmly rooted. By this stern experience, Christians grow "strong in the Lord and in his mighty power" (Eph. 6:10). They break the power of the world, and they take a firmer grip on the invisible things of God as they are tried and tempted.

CHARLES SPURGEON

January 27

Never question the validity of your baptism into spiritual life because it is followed by a fierce temptation. Read the life of your Lord and find from that life that you are just as much a son of God when the dove descends from heaven as when you are tormented and vexed by all the forces of hell in the wilderness. God is not variable; His elections are not so many opportunities of recalling His decrees.

We sometimes speak of temptation as if it were an accident of life: We forget the words "led by." These words indicate that temptation is part of a plan, a step in a succession to a better life. Sometimes we delude ourselves with the foolish imagination that if we step very softly, we shall get past the serpent's nest without the serpent hearing us, safely eluding the devil. Take no such a view. Life itself is a temptation. To *be* is to be nearly lost. To be here at all is to be in the devil's domain.

Understand that you have to be tempted. The wilderness is not a sphere lying thousands of miles from your course. Your eye is fixed on heaven, and right across, from sea to sea, lies the wilderness, and you cannot escape it. There is no way to sneak into heaven. I must be assailed, tried, vexed, thrown down, battered, and if I have not passed through experiences of this kind, the whole priesthood of Christ has been lost upon me, and if there are not experiences of this kind to pass through, then the cross of Christ is an exaggeration of remedial measures, and there was no need for the heart of the Son of God to burst in pity or in sacrifice. Count it no strange thing, then, when temptations come; to be finite is to be tempted.

Such are the violent alternations of human experience, baptized and tempted, approved of God and assailed by the devil, standing with a grand inaugural sign upon our heads on the river's bank, and then driven to fight life's determining battle.

JOSEPH PARKER

Then Jesus was led by the Spirit into the desert to be tempted by the devil.

MATTHEW 4:1

January 28

After fasting forty days and forty nights, he was hungry. The tempter came to him and said, "If you are the Son of God, tell these stones to become bread."

MATTHEW 4:2–3

The devil is the tempter, and therefore he is Satan, the adversary, for our worst enemies are those that entice us to sin and are Satan's agents carrying out his work and designs. He is called emphatically the tempter because he was so to our first parents and still is so, and all other tempters are set to work by him.

Observe the subtlety of the tempter to take advantage of Christ's hunger, in that to make his point of attack. Satan is an adversary no less watchful than spiteful, and the more ingenious he is to take advantage against us, the more industrious we must be to give him none. Christ's hunger in the wilderness, where there was nothing to be eaten, made the notion of turning stones into bread seem very proper. Satan states that if Jesus really is the Son of God, the Father would never allow Him to be in such a difficulty. Either God is not His Father, or He is a very unkind one.

The primary thing Satan aims at in tempting good people is to overthrow their relationship to God as a father and so to cut off their dependence on Him and their communion with Him. Outward afflictions, needs, and burdens are the great arguments Satan uses to make the people of God question their sonship, as if afflictions and difficulties were not consistent with God's fatherly love. The devil aims to shake our faith in the Word of God and bring us to question the truth of that. He implants within people hard thoughts of God, as if He were unkind or unfaithful and had forsaken or forgotten those who have ventured their all with Him. He used the tree of knowledge in this manner with our first parents, and here he insinuates to our Savior that His Father has cast Him off and left Him to fend for Himself.

Let us answer temptations of this sort with the words of holy Job: "Though he slay me, yet will I hope in him" (Job 13:15). Though I starve to death, I will trust and love God as a Friend. It is better to starve to death than live and thrive by sin.

MATTHEW HENRY

Always have "It is written" ready by your side. Some believers, when a spiritual conflict begins, are ready to give up all hope. Do not act so cowardly; seek grace to be a soldier. You must fight if you are to enter heaven. Look to your weapon; it cannot bend or grow blunt; wield it boldly and plunge it into the heart of your enemy. "It is written" will cut through soul and spirit and wound the old dragon himself.

I commend to you the hiding of God's Word in your heart, the pondering of it in your minds. Be rooted and grounded in its teaching and saturated in its spirit. To me it is an intense joy to search diligently in my Father's book of grace that grows upon me daily. The Bible was written by inspiration in old times, but I have found that not only *was* it inspired when written but also is so still. It is not a mere historic document. It is a letter fresh from the pen of God to me. It is not a flower dried and put in a vase, with its beauty clouded and its perfume evaporated. It is a fresh blooming flower in God's garden, as fragrant and as fair as when God planted it.

I look not upon the Scriptures as a harp that once was played by skillful fingers and is now hung up as a memorial upon the wall. No, they are an instrument of ten strings still in the minstrel's hand, still filling the temple of the Lord with divine music, which those who have ears to hear delight to listen to. Holy Scripture is an Aeolian harp through which the blessed wind of the Spirit is always sweeping and creating mystic music such as no man's ears shall hear elsewhere, nor hear even there indeed, unless they have been opened by the healing touch of the Great Physician. The Holy Spirit is in the Word, and the Word is therefore living truth. Be assured of this, and because of it, take the Word as your chosen weapon of war.

CHARLES SPURGEON

Jesus answered [the devil], "It is written."

MATTHEW 4:4

January 30

Then the devil took [Jesus] to the holy city and had him stand on the highest point of the temple. "If you are the Son of God," he said, "throw yourself down."

MATTHEW 4:5–6

What do you think were the temptations that came upon the Savior on account of His position on the high and holy place? We frequently forget that the Savior was most truly man. He was divine without mitigation of royalty and splendor of Deity. But He was man, altogether as we are. Did He not tremble with fear of falling? It is natural that a shivering emotion of dread should creep over anyone standing in so lofty and unprotected a position. The temptation, though, lies in doing something desperate to escape from the position that is so full of peril. It is right for me to be afraid of falling into sin; it is not right for me either to mistrust God's grace that will sustain me or to run to foolish means to escape from the particular peril in which I happen to be involved. Jesus did not doubt His Father's care, but He did tremble because of the danger in which He was placed.

Notice the point of attack: It was our Lord's sonship. Satan knows that if he can make any of us doubt the Father's love, doubt our regeneration and adoption, he will have us very much in his power. How can I pray "Our Father in heaven" if I do not know Him to be my Father? If the dark suspicion crosses my mind that I am no child of His, I cannot say with the prodigal, "I will arise and go to my father." Having a Father, I feel sure that He will pity my weaknesses, feel for my needs, forgive my wrongs, protect me in the hour of danger, and save me in the moment of peril. But if I have no Father in heaven, then, miserable orphan! what shall I do, where shall I flee? Standing on the pinnacle as God's child, I shall stand there erect though every wind should seek to whirl me from my foothold.

"If you are the Son of God." Beware of unbelief; those who justify unbelief hold a candle to the devil. God is faithful: Why should we doubt Him? God is true: How can we suppose that He will be false?

CHARLES SPURGEON

January 31

_T_his third temptation may be regarded as the contest of the seen and the unseen, of the outer and inner, of the likely and the true, of the show and the reality. The evil clearly lay in that it was a temptation to do good instead of doing the will of His Father.

We forget that Jesus was a man and prone to the same ambitions that lure men's hearts. It must have been a sore temptation to think that Jesus might, if He would, lay a righteous grasp upon the reins of government, leap into the chariot of power, and ride forth conquering and to conquer. Glad visions no doubt arose before Him of the prisoner breaking jubilant from the cell of injustice, of the widow lifting up her bowed head, of weeping children bursting into shouts, of oppression and wrong shrinking and withering before the wheels of the chariot. What glowing visions of holy vengeance, what rosy dreams of human blessedness would crowd such a brain as His!

But how would He, thus conquering, be a servant of Satan? In a word, would it not have been a serving of Satan to desert the mission of God, who knew that men could not be set free in that way and so sent Jesus to be a man, a true man, among them, that His life might become their life, so they might be as free in prison or on the cross as upon a hillside or on a throne. Nothing but the obedience of the Son, the obedience unto the death, the absolute doing of the will of God because it was the truth, could redeem the prisoner, the widow, the orphan. And it would redeem them by redeeming the conquest–ridden conqueror, too, the stripe–giving jailer, the unjust judge, the devouring Pharisee himself with the insatiable moth–eaten heart.

The earth should be free because Love was stronger than Death! Man would be free—not merely man as he thinks of himself but man as God thinks of him. The great and beautiful and perfect will of God would be done.

GEORGE MACDONALD

Again, the devil took him to a very high mountain and showed him all the kingdoms of the world and their splendor. "All this I will give you," he said, "if you will bow down and worship me."

MATTHEW 4:8–9

February 1

"Worship the Lord your God, and serve him only."

MATTHEW 4:10

Jesus says that not only should we not tempt the Lord our God, but we should worship Him, give Him our heart's adoration, the spirit's whole fire of love, without one spark falling elsewhere. Your spiritual life should be a concentrated offering, intense as flame. That is what keeps a man right, spiritually and theologically. We are not propped up by little clevernesses, ecclesiastical and theological; we are not shored up by some religious mechanism of man's design; we are only right in proportion as our worship is right. If we live in our ideas and logic, if we secure ourselves behind the defense of our own way of stating theological propositions, the very first thunderstorm that comes will carry us away. I am right only when I rightly pray; I am secure only while I truly worship; I am delivered from fear of death and hell only in proportion as my fellowship with the Father is intimate and sweet. We are in great danger if we trust a formulated faith of theological words, but worship, deep as the life, silent as the springs of being, mighty as the urgency of love, is the only thing that keeps a man right amid all this swirl and hurry, tumult and danger, of a probationary life.

Religion is not a contemplation only; religion is a service. Religion is not a folding of the hands and an upturning of the eyes to measurable heavens, and a silent expectation of something that shall fall upon our indolence. Religion is activity, service, sacrifice, devotion, wholehearted consecration of every power of the life to one object. If we have not attained that height, let us strive after it with sweet modesty and with burning energy in our heart. Do we love God, wait for Him, trust in Him, believe every syllable He has spoken, and do we know Him, not by some trained act of the intellect but by an inexplicable and ineffable operation of that sympathetic power of the soul that makes us men? The only supreme religion is the sacrifice of the broken heart in complete and affectionate trust in the living God.

JOSEPH PARKER

February 2

*J*esus was tempted in every way as we are. How otherwise could He be our Priest and Savior in every sense of those immeasurable terms? He had to pass under the universal experience: He should know the devil, He should have met him face to face, He should have felt the keenness of his subtlest approaches and the blow of his heaviest assault. Jesus Christ was thus prepared to preach the gospel to the world and to accomplish mankind's redemption.

No man can be prepared for any deep and vital work in the world who has not gone through the school of the devil. You cannot be taught to preach by reading books, however good and eloquent. You overshoot my life; I must hear something in your tone and accents that tell me that you too have been in the pit, have been dragged through the lake of fire, and have understood what it is to be almost—gone. He has wonderful influence over me who can pity me in the distresses of my temptation. He who can only make my intellect wonder, touch my imagination with new and flashing lights, has but momentary fascination for me, and I must say good-bye. But he who knows the devil in and out, all the temptations in me, and who has come away from the life-battle feeling that the enemy is no small one, and who says to me, "The battle is very heavy, do not underrate it. Your strength will be tried to its very limit, but God will help you"—this man becomes a teacher, wise and true, a sympathetic friend, with whose soul mine has fellowship and blessing.

Have you been prepared for your work? If so, why are you not doing it? We have been trained in music, yet we do little but mumble in the vocal worship of Almighty God. We have read many books, yet are silent as the grave. We have passed through many temptations, but the word of sympathy never falls from our lips. We have proved the vanity of the world, yet we never tell the young that the world is a gigantic lie and life but an empty wind apart from God and the infinite Savior. Our Lord, having been qualified for His work, went to it. Arise, let us do the same.

JOSEPH PARKER

Then the devil left him, and angels came and attended him.

MATTHEW 4:11

February 3

"The people living in darkness have seen a great light; on those living in the land of the shadow of death a light has dawned."

MATTHEW 4:16

When Christ came to live in Capernaum, which was a great city of Galilee, the gospel came to all those places surrounding it, such diffusive influences did the Sun of righteousness cast. We observe that before He came, the inhabitants were living in darkness. Those who are without Christ are in the dark, living in the land of the shadow of death, which denotes not only great darkness, as the grave is a land of darkness, but also great danger. A man who is desperately sick and not likely to recover is in the valley of the shadow of death, though not quite dead; so these people were on the borders of damnation, though not yet damned—dead in law. What is worst of all, they were sitting in this condition. Sitting is a continuing posture; where we sit, we mean to stay. They were in the dark, despairing to find the way out. And it is a contented posture. They were in the dark, and they loved darkness; they chose it rather than light; they were willing ignorant. What a privilege they enjoyed when Christ and His gospel came among them! It was as great a reviving as ever light was to a traveler lost in the darkness of night. When the gospel comes, light comes; when it comes to any place, when it comes to any soul, it makes day there (John 3:19; Luke 1:78–79). Light is discovering, it is directing; so is the gospel.

It was a great light, denoting the clearness and evidence of gospel revelations. It was not like the light of a candle but like the light of the sun when he goes forth in his strength. Great is Christ in comparison with the light of the law, the shadows of which were now done away. It was a great light, for it discovers great things and things of great consequence; it will last long and spread far. And it was a growing light, implied by the word *dawned*. The light had its dawn, which afterward shone more and more. Such is the gospel kingdom as morning light in our souls—small in its beginnings, gradual in its growth, but great in its perfection.

MATTHEW HENRY

February 4

*R*epentance, however unpopular a theme, is an *indispensable condition* of entering the kingdom of God. I believe God has made human salvation as easy as the Almighty, Infinite mind could make it! And there is a necessity that my mind and feelings be changed and brought to repentance toward God.

Repentance is not merely a conviction of sin. Thousands of people are convinced of sin, but they go no further. They live this week as they did last. Neither is repentance a mere sorrow for sin. I have seen people weep bitterly and writhe and struggle but yet hug their idols, and in vain you try to shake them from them. Yes, some weep but will not yield to the Holy Spirit. You may be ever so sorry and all the way down to death be hugging some forbidden possession, as the young ruler hugged his wealth.

Repentance is simply renouncing sin, turning from darkness to light, from the power of Satan to God. This is giving up sin in your heart, in purpose, in intention, in desire, resolving that you will give up every evil thing and do it now. Of course, this involves sorrow, for he regrets the course he has taken. It implies, also, a hatred of sin. Like the prodigal, Jesus Christ's own beautiful illustration of true penitence, he hates the course he formerly took and turns from it. He cuts off the particular thing that the Holy Spirit reveals to him.

Never say that you do not have the power to repent. You have that power, or God would not command it. You can repent. You can this moment lift up your eyes to heaven and say with the prodigal, "Father, I have sinned, and I renounce my sin." You may not be able to weep—God nowhere requires it—but you are able to renounce sin in purpose, in resolution, and in intention. Surrender it. The more you struggle, the more you sink. Jesus will come to you. His glorious, blessed presence will lift you out of the mire and put your feet on the rock of salvation.

CATHERINE BOOTH

From that time on Jesus began to preach, "Repent, for the kingdom of heaven is near."

MATTHEW 4:17

February 5

"Come, follow me,"
Jesus said, "and I will
make you fishers of
men."

MATTHEW 4:19

When Christ calls us by His grace, we should not only remember what we are but also think of what He can make us. We should repent of what we have been but rejoice in what we may be. It did not seem a likely thing that lowly fishermen would develop into apostles, that men so handy with the net would be quite as much at home in preaching sermons and leading the church. One would have said, "How can this be? You cannot make founders of churches out of peasants of Galilee." But that is exactly what Christ did.

We cannot tell what God may make of us in the new creation, since it would have been quite impossible to have foretold what He made of chaos in the old creation. Who would have imagined all the beautiful things that came forth from darkness and disorder by that one flat, "Let there be light"? And who can tell what lovely displays of everything that is divinely fair may yet appear in a man's formerly dark life when God's grace has said to him, "Let there be light"?

We are not made all that we shall be, nor all that we will desire to be, when we are ourselves fished for and caught. This is what the grace of God does for us at first, but it is not all. The good Lord comes, and with the gospel net He takes us and delivers us from the life and love of sin. But He also works a higher miracle to make us who were fish to become fishers, making the saved ones saviors, the convert into converter, the receiver of the gospel into an imparter. Christ's word is: Follow me, not merely to be saved, nor even sanctified, but that I may use you to fish for men. Each of us must take to the business of a man catcher. If Christ has caught us, we must catch others. Let us ask Him to give us grace to go fishing and so to cast our nets that we may take a great multitude of fish. Oh, that the Holy Spirit may raise up from among us some master-fishers who shall sail their boats in many seas and surround great shoals of fish!

CHARLES SPURGEON

February 6

From John 1, we know that the response of Simon and Andrew, James and John, to Jesus' call was no sudden impulse but was the deliberate surrender of men who knew well what they were doing though they had not fathomed the whole truth as to His kingdom and their place in it. They had already attached themselves to Him as disciples, although it had not interfered with their trade. Now they were led on, little by little, to posts and tasks they never dreamed at the beginning. The same is true for us. Duty opens before the heart bit by bit. Obedience is rewarded by the summons to more complete surrender.

"Come, follow me,"

Jesus said.

MATTHEW 4:19

Christ's call is authoritative in its brevity. All duty lies in "Come, follow me." Jesus does not need to use arguments. From the very first, this meek and lowly man assumed a tone that on other lips we call arrogant. His style is royal. His mouth is autocratic. He knows that He has the right to command. And strangely enough, the world admits the right and finds nothing unworthy in this unconditional claim of absolute submission to His orders. That same peremptory summons reaches beyond these four fishermen to us all. The very same voice speaks to us, and we are as truly summoned by the King to be His servants and soldiers.

Their prompt self-surrendering response is the witness of the power over their hearts that Jesus had won. One pair of brothers left their nets floating in the water; the other left their father. It was not much wealth to leave. But he surrenders much who surrenders all, however little that all may be; and he surrenders nothing who keeps back anything. One sweet portion of their earthly happiness He left them to enjoy, heightened by discipleship, for each had his brother by his side, and natural affection was ennobled by common faith and service. So both the surrender that outwardly gives up possession or friends and that which keeps them, sanctified by being held and used as for and from Him, were exemplified in their obedience to the King's call.

ALEXANDER MACLAREN

February 7

Jesus went throughout
Galilee, teaching in
their synagogues,
preaching the good
news of the kingdom,
and healing every
disease and sickness
among the people.

MATTHEW 4:23

*M*atthew presents the broad features of the early Galilean ministry and the triumphal progress of the King, painting it as a time of joyful activity, of universal recognition, of swift and far-spreading fame. As Jesus makes His way through His dominions, note that all who were sick and diseased were healed and that His fame spread across the border into heathendom. From His first preaching, the kingdom is diffusive.

Note, too, the contrast between John's ministry and Christ's. While John stayed in one spot and the crowds had to go out to him, the very genius of Christ's mission expressed itself in that this shepherd king actively sought out the sad and sick.

Observe, too, that Jesus teaches and preaches the good news of the kingdom before He heals. John's proclamation of the kingdom had been so charged with threatenings and mingled with fire that it could hardly be called a "gospel." But here that joyous word, used for the first time, is in place. As the tidings came from Christ's lips, they were good tidings, and to proclaim them was His first task. The miracles of healing came second. They were not "the bell before the sermon" but the benediction after it. They flowed from Christ in rich abundance and were not only attestations of His claim to be the King but also illustrations of the nature of His kingdom. They were tokens of His inexhaustible fountain of power and of the swift and equally inexhaustible treasures of sympathy that dwelt in Him. The eager receptiveness of the people, ignorant as it was, was greater then than ever afterward, and the flow of miraculous power was less impeded.

Thus, the King appeared encompassed with enthusiasm and aspirations of greatness. But no illusions deceived His calm prescience. From the beginning He knew that the transient loyalty of His followers was leading toward the cross, but the sight did not make Him falter.

ALEXANDER MACLAREN

February 8

What a world Jesus came into! And He knew it before He entered it. If the world had been less damned, He need not have come. In this verse you have a picture of the real state of humanity as Jesus Christ found it. I want to go where the people are well. Tell me of lepers and various diseases, and I flee. What are terrors to me were attractions to the infinite heart of Jesus.

This is the real condition of the world in every age—it is a world full of sickness and disease and torment, a world in which men are possessed with demons and every sort of disorder. Do we want men of culture to go into such a world and faint at the sight of blood and shudder if they see a paralytic in the streets? If we send those who are infinitely gifted in the art of saying nothing in many words, they will soon return with a sigh for a better class of people. The world is a sick world, a dying world, a mad world, and clever sentences will never touch it. The world wants blood: No other price will redeem it. O church of the living God, called by a thousand tender names, what are you doing but running away to pick flowers when you should be laboring with your coat off, with both hands earnestly at the deliverance and healing of souls.

If you do not buy the world with the blood of Jesus Christ, you will never buy it. Redemption is always by blood, and he who has paid less than blood for any redemption has bought it at the wrong counter and paid for it with counterfeit coin. When we go near the city we must weep over it, and when we go into the city we must die for it. We must never stand back in fear. What is the complaint of any heart? Jesus can heal it. Mark the infinite ease of the expression "He healed them." The blood of Jesus cleanses from all sin, and the healing fountain has been opened for all to receive deliverance.

JOSEPH PARKER

News about him spread all over Syria, and people brought to him all who were ill with various diseases, those suffering severe pain, the demon-possessed, those having seizures, and the paralyzed, and he healed them.

MATTHEW 4:24

February 9

He went up onto a mountain, into a pulpit not made with hands. He did not go in conventional methods. We wait until the church is built. He said the church was not made with hands. Wherever there is a sky, there is a roof; wherever there is a floor, there is a platform; wherever there is a person, there is a congregation; wherever there is a human heart, there is an opportunity for preaching the kingdom of God.

Then He sat while he talked, as the Jewish rabbis did but on a larger and grander scale. He begins royally: There is a subtle claim of dominion in this very attitude of His. He does not beg to be heard, but He sits, and the mountain gives Him hospitality. He fills the mountain, and it seems like a king's throne. Close your eyes and open the vision of your hearts and look at Him. When He sits, He sits as one who has a right to the mountain, and when He speaks, it is as one whose gentle voice fills the spaces like a healing breeze.

"He began to teach them." The ages had been waiting for the opening of those lips. When some great men open their lips in high places, they seem to have the power of making history. When this man opened His mouth, He uttered words that would fill creation and that would be a gospel set in every language spoken by mankind. The words of Jesus Christ go everywhere and fall into languages with infinite ease—light, love, life, truth, and peace.

When we listened to Jesus Christ before, He was preaching; now He is teaching. The preacher was a herald: "Repent," said He. The air was startled by the cry. Now He changes the tone: He sits down and teaches, explains, simplifies, draws the listeners into confidence and sympathy with Himself, and makes them co-partners of the infinite secret of the divine truth and love. "Blessed," He now says. Repentance first, then inspiration. This is His way always.

JOSEPH PARKER

February 10

One enjoys a sermon all the better for knowing something of the preacher. It is natural that, like John on Patmos, we should turn to see the voice that speaks to us. Turn then, and learn that the Christ of God is the Preacher of the Sermon on the Mount. He who delivered the Beatitudes not only was the Prince of preachers but also was beyond all others qualified to inform us who are indeed the blessed of the Father.

Seven of the Beatitudes Jesus presented relate to character, and the eighth is a benediction upon the persons described when their excellence has provoked the hostility of the wicked. The whole seven describe a perfect character and make up a perfect benediction. Each blessing is precious separately, more precious than much fine gold. But we do well to regard them as a whole, for as a whole they were spoken, and from that point of view they are a wonderfully perfect chain of seven priceless links. No such instruction in the art of blessedness can be found anywhere else. Our Lord has, in a few sentences, told us all about happiness without using a solitary redundant word or allowing the slightest omission. The seven gold sentences are perfect as a whole, and each one occupies its appropriate place. Together they are a ladder of light, and each one is a step of purest sunshine.

Observe carefully that each step in the ladder rises above those that precede it. It would have been a grievous discouragement to struggling faith if the first blessing had been given to the pure in heart. Our divine Instructor begins at the beginning with those who know too well their own poverty of spirit and so enables us as babes in grace to learn of Him. Come, then, for there is not one link in the wonderful chain of grace in which there is a withdrawal of the divine smile or an absence of real happiness. Blessed is the first moment of the Christian life on earth, and blessed is the last.

CHARLES SPURGEON

Now when he saw the crowds, he went up on a mountainside and sat down. His disciples came to him, and he began to teach them.

MATTHEW 5:1–2

February 11

"Blessed are the poor in spirit, for theirs is the kingdom of heaven."

MATTHEW 5:3

The utmost the law can accomplish for our fallen humanity is to lay bare our spiritual poverty and convince us of it. Its greatest service is to tear away a man's fancied wealth of self-righteousness, show him his overwhelming indebtedness to God, and bow him to the earth in self-despair. To this point in our lives, Jesus descends.

Poverty of spirit is the porch of God's temple of blessedness. As a wise man never builds the walls of his house till he has first dug the foundation, so no person skillful in divine things will hope to see any of the higher virtues where poverty of spirit is absent. Till we are emptied of self, we cannot be filled with God; stripping must come first before we can be clothed with the righteousness from heaven. Christ is never precious till we are poor in spirit; we must see our own needs before we can perceive His wealth. Pride blinds the eyes, and sincere humility must open them, or the beauties of Jesus will be forever hidden from us.

God's first blessing is given to the absence rather than to the presence of praiseworthy qualities. It is a blessing upon the man whose chief characteristic is that he confesses his own sad deficiencies. God wants nothing of us except our needs, and these furnish Him with room to display His bounty when He supplies them freely. When the poor in spirit come to Him with their utter destitution and distress, He not only accepts them at once but also bows the heavens to bless them and opens His storehouses to satisfy them. Let everyone come and drink comfort from this well.

The Lord's eye of favor rests only upon hearts broken and spirits humbled before Him. Poverty of spirit in the publican was better than fullness of external excellence in the Pharisee. The highest grade of outward religiousness is unblessed, but the very lowest form of spiritual grace is endowed with the kingdom of heaven. Are you spiritual enough to be poor in spirit?

CHARLES SPURGEON

February 12

Each beatitude springs from the preceding and must be understood within that context. Jesus speaks of the sorrow that arises from the contemplation of the same facts concerning self as lead to poverty of spirit. He who takes the true measure of himself cannot but sorrow over the frightful gulf between what he should and might be and what he is. The grim reality of sin has to be reckoned in. Personal responsibility and guilt are facts.

"Blessed are those who mourn, for they will be comforted."

MATTHEW 5:4

The soul that has once seen its own past as it is and looked steadily down into the depths of its own being cannot choose but "mourn." Brought into the light of God's face, we realize what sin against God is, what must necessarily come from it, what aggravations His gentleness, His graciousness, His constant love cause, how we choose to do the evil thing and then still can say, "I have done no harm." In the divine light, we discover the depths of our self-life.

This is Christ's account of discipleship. We must creep through a narrow gate that is passed only on our knees, leaving all our treasures outside. But once through, we are in a great temple with far-reaching aisles and lofty roof. Such sorrow is sure of comfort. The comfort it needs is the assurance of forgiveness and cleansing, and that assurance has never been sought from the King in vain. Blessed is the sorrow that leads to the experience of the tender touch of the hand that wipes away tears from the face and plucks evil from the heart! Blessed the mourning that prepares for the festal garland and the oil of gladness and the robe of praise!

You will never know the deep and ineffably precious comforts of Christ unless you have learned to despair of self and have come helpless, hopeless, and yet confident to that great Lord. Empty your heart, and He will fill it; recognize your desperate condition, and He will lift you up. The deeper you descend, the surer the rebound and the higher the soaring to the zenith. Only those who go this way find the sweet, sacred, secret recess of Christ's heart, and there find all-sufficient consolation.

ALEXANDER MACLAREN

February 13

"Blessed are the meek, for they will inherit the earth."

MATTHEW 5:5

The truly meek are submissive to God's will. Whatever God wills, they will. They are perfectly satisfied that where God has placed them is the best place. They do not talk of having been placed in circumstances unfavorable for their development. They do not quarrel with what God forms for them—whether Solomon's throne or Job's dunghill. They desire to be equally happy wherever the Lord places them or however He deals with them.

The meek are flexible to God's Word. They do not come to the Bible for texts to prove what they think should be there. But they love their God so much that they desire to obey even the least command that He gives simply out of love for Him. As the Word of God comes to them, they desire to have its image imprinted upon their hearts, becoming living epistles of the living God.

The meek man is humble. He knows that he is only a man and that the best of men are but men at the best, and he does not even claim to be one of the best of men. He knows himself in some respects to be the very chief of sinners. He is content if he may pass among his fellowmen as a notable example of the power of God's grace, as one who is a great debtor to God's mercy.

The meek man is gentle. He does not speak harshly, and his spirit is not domineering. He seeks to be a true brother among his brethren, thinking himself most honored when he can be the doorkeeper in the house of the Lord.

The meek are patient. If others grieve them, they put up with it. When their anger rises, they have the grace given to them to keep their temper in subjection. They turn their anger wholly upon the evil done and away from the person who did the wrong and are ready to extend him kindness.

The meek are content with God's providence. He knows God as the God of the hills and also the valleys. If he can have God's face shining upon him, he cares little of where he is made to walk. That his times are in God's hands is enough.

CHARLES SPURGEON

February 14

ecause man had perfect righteousness before the fall, he enjoyed perfect blessedness. If we, by divine grace, attain to blessedness hereafter, it will be because God has restored us to righteousness. As it was in the first paradise, so it must be in the second. We cannot be truly happy and live in sin. Holiness is the natural element of blessedness, and it can no more live out of that element than a fish could live in the fire. The happiness of man must come through his righteousness: his being right with God, with man, with himself. Though we have not yet attained the righteousness we desire, yet we are told by Jesus that even the longing for it makes for blessedness. The tremendous blessedness of the past and the priceless blessedness of the eternal future are joined together by a band of present blessedness. The band is not so massive as those two things that it unifies, but it is of the same metal, has been fashioned by the same hand, and is as indestructible as the treasures that it binds together.

To hunger and to thirst are the language of keen desire. He who has ever felt either of these two knows how sharp are the pangs they bring; and if the two are combined in one craving, they make up a restless, terrible, unconquerable passion. Blessed is the man who is always desiring righteousness with an insatiable longing that nothing can turn aside. He carries the desire for righteousness to his work, to his house, to his bed, wherever he goes, for it rules him with its imperative demands. He hungers and thirsts to be what God wants him to be—honesty, purity, integrity, and holiness. He cannot be content till he is himself like Jesus, who is the image of the invisible God, the mirror of righteousness and peace. He would live for righteousness and die for righteousness; the zeal for it consumes him. Oh, to be holy and pure in heart! This is the blessed hunger and thirst.

CHARLES SPURGEON

"Blessed are those who hunger and thirst for righteousness, for they will be filled."

MATTHEW 5:6

February 15

"Blessed are the merciful, for they will be shown mercy."

MATTHEW 5:7

Mercy is more than meekness. It is really love in exercise to the needy, especially the bad and the blameworthy. It embraces pity, loving forbearance, and beneficence and is revealed in acts, in words, in tears. It is a hand of helpfulness stretched out and a gush of pity and mercy in the heart if we are to do what our Master has done for us all and what our Master requires us to do for one another. It is blessed in itself. A life of selfishness is hell. A life of mercy is sweet with some fragrance of heaven; it is the consequence of mercy received from God. If I know how dark my own nature is, how prone to commit sin, how little virtue I have in my own self, and the judgment that was my due, the stern judgment and censure I am tempted to apply to others will falter on my tongue and stick in my throat. And if I have been made rich by divine forgiveness, comforted by His hand, and filled with righteousness, shall I not be impelled to communicate what I have already received? Our mercifulness, then, is a reflection of His. His mercifulness is to be the measure and pattern of ours in depth, scope, extent of self-sacrifice, and freeness of its gifts.

Our exercise of mercy is the condition of our receiving it. Merciful men get mercy from God—not that we deserve mercy by being merciful. That is a contradiction in terms; for mercy is precisely that which we do not deserve. The place of mercy in this series of beatitudes shows that Jesus regarded it as the consequence, not the cause, of our experience of God's mercy. But He teaches over and over that a hard, unmerciful heart forfeits the divine mercy. It does so because such a disposition tends to obscure the very state of mind to which alone God's mercy can be given. Such a man must have forgotten his poverty and sorrow, his longings and their rich reward, and so must have, for the time, passed from the place where he can take in God's gift. A life inconsistent with Christian motives will rob a Christian of Christian privileges.

ALEXANDER MACLAREN

February 16

The teaching of our Lord was continually aimed at the hearts of men. Other teachers had been content with outward moral reformation, but He sought the source of all the evil, that He might cleanse the spring from which all sinful thoughts, words, and actions come. He insisted that until the heart was pure, the life would never be clean. Unless the inner nature is divinely renewed, you cannot enter or even see the kingdom of God.

"Blessed are the pure in heart, for they will see God."

MATTHEW 5:8

When a man's heart is purified by the Holy Spirit, he will see God in nature. He will hear God's footfall everywhere in the garden of the earth in the cool of the day. He will hear God's voice in the tempest and behold the Lord walking on the mighty water. To an impure heart, God cannot be seen anywhere; but to a pure heart, God is seen everywhere—in the deepest caverns, in the lonely desert, in every star that gems the brow of midnight.

The pure in heart see God in the Scriptures. Impure minds cannot see any trace of God in them, but the pure in heart see God on every page of this blessed book.

The pure in heart see God in His Church. The impure in heart see nothing but a conglomeration of divided sects full of faults, failures, and imperfections. But the pure in heart see God in His Church and rejoice to meet Him there.

The pure in heart begin to discern something of God's true character. To perceive that God is eternally just and yet infinitely tender and that He is sternly severe and yet immeasurably gracious, and to see the various attributes of the Deity all blending into one another as the colors of the rainbow make one harmonious and beautiful whole—this is reserved for the man whose eyes have been first washed in the blood of Jesus and then anointed with the heavenly eye salve of the Holy Spirit. What a wonderful sight!

Yet the day shall come when those who have seen God on earth shall see Him face-to-face in heaven. What a splendor!

CHARLES SPURGEON

February 17

"Blessed are the peacemakers, for they will be called sons of God."

MATTHEW 5:9

*N*o man can bring to others what he does not possess. Vainly will he whose heart is torn by contending passions, full of animosities and unreconciled causes of alienation between him and God, between him and duty, between him and himself, ever seek to shed any deep or real peace among men. The Christian peacemaker is created by having passed through all the previous beatitudes—emptied of self, broken, hungering for and filled with righteousness—and therefore is, in heart as well as in regard to men, meek and merciful. He has been led through all these, often painful, experiences into a purity of heart that has been blessed by some measure of vision of God; and having thus been equipped and prepared, he is fit to go out into the tempestuous world and say, "Peace, be still." Something of the miracle–working energy of his Master will grace his heart.

Note that the climax of Christian character in the Beatitudes is found in our relations to men, not in our relation to God. Worship of heart and spirit, devout emotions of the sweetest sort, are absolutely indispensable. But equally if not more important is it for us to remember that the purest communion with God is meant to be the base of active service to others. If this service to others is lacking in our lives, there is good reason to question our relationship with God. The service of man is the outcome of the love of God. He who begins with poverty of spirit is perfected when, forgetting himself and coming down from the mountaintop, where the Shekinah cloud of the Glory and the audible voice are, he plunges into the struggles of the multitude below and frees the devil–ridden boy from the demon that possesses him. Begin by all means with poverty of spirit, or you will never get to this.

Men may revile God's peacemaker, but it matters little what men call us. It matters everything what God calls us. If He calls us "sons of God," what higher calling can there be?

ALEXANDER MACLAREN

February 18

The last beatitude crowns all the paradoxes of the series with what sounds like a stark contradiction. The persecuted are blessed. The previous seven sayings have perfected the portrait of what a child of the kingdom is to be. This appends a calm prophecy, which must have shattered many a rosy dream among the listeners, of what his reception by the world will certainly turn out. Jesus is summoning men not to dominion, honor, and victory but to scorn and suffering. Their relation to the world is that of peacemakers; the world's relation to them is that of hostility. Jesus' own crown, He knew, was first to be twisted of thorns, and copies of it were to wound His followers' brows.

I take these words to be as universal and permanent in their application as any that have preceded them. It is not an arbitrary promise, but it stands as integral to Christian character. Darkness hates light, and the true believer should be a standing rebuke to the world. To practice a righteous life never leads to popularity. While persecution may not come via an assassin's dagger, be assured that it will come via an assassin's tongue.

The great reason why professing Christians now know so little about persecution is because there is so little real antagonism. While the Church has leavened the world, the world has also leavened the Church, and it seems that there is to be no fanatical godliness of the New Testament pattern. Of course, then, there will be no persecution where religion goes in silver slippers, and you find Christians running neck and neck with others, and no man can tell which is which.

But to suffer persecution for righteousness is blessed, for it is to suffer for Jesus and brings elevation of spirit, a solemn joy, secret supplies of strength, and sweet intimacies of communion otherwise unknown. Theirs is the kingdom of heaven as a natural result of the development of their character.

ALEXANDER MACLAREN

"Blessed are those who are persecuted because of righteousness, for theirs is the kingdom of heaven."

MATTHEW 5:10

February 19

"If the salt loses its saltiness..."

MATTHEW 5:13

There is no need for asking the question whether in the natural realm it is possible for any forms of matter that have salt to lose it by any cause. That does not at all concern us. The point is that it is possible for us who call ourselves Christians to lose our penetrating pungency, which stops corruption, to lose all that distinguishes us from the men whom we are to influence.

Looking upon the present condition of professing Christendom, we must confess that this saying comes perilously near being true of us. It occurs when Christian men and women embrace and practice the maxims of the world in their lives as to what is pleasant and desirable and as to the application of morality to business. Too often, there is not a hair of difference in that respect between believers' lives and the lives of the ungodly. Religion has next to no influence on their general conduct and does not even keep them from the world's corruption, to say nothing of making them sources of purifying influence.

I can assure you that if you are not heating your world, the world is freezing you. Every man influences all men around him and receives influences from them, and if there is not more influences and mightier influences raying out from him than are coming into him, he is at the mercy of circumstances. Remember that if you do not salt the world, the world will rot you.

Is there any difference between your ideals of happiness and pleasure and those of the ungodly one? Is there any difference in your application of the rules of morality to daily life? Yes, or no? Might it be that we are even cooling the fervor of other believers? If the salt has diminished, you cannot expect the glories of character and the pure unworldliness of conduct that you would have where the salt is. Fellowship with Jesus is not a vague exercise of the mind but is kept vibrant by meditation on the Word of God and private prayer. If you have let these go, no power in heaven or earth can prevent you from losing the savor that makes you salt.

ALEXANDER MACLAREN

February 20

*O*ne last word warns us what is the certain end of the saltless salt. All it is fit for is to be pitched out into the road and to be trodden down between the stones by men's heels. If it has failed in doing the only thing it was created for, it has failed altogether.

Yes, where are the churches of Asia Minor, Antioch, Constantinople, or Augustine's North Africa? Over the archway of a mosque in Damascus is the half-obliterated inscription—"Thy Kingdom, O Christ, is an everlasting Kingdom," and above it, "There is no God but God, and Mohammed is His prophet"! The salt has lost its savor and been cast out.

And does anyone believe that the churches of Christendom are eternal in their present shape? I see everywhere the signs of disintegration in the existing organizations that set forth Christian life. And I am sure of this, that in the days that are coming, the storm in which we are already caught, all dead branches will be whirled out of the tree! And a great deal that calls itself Christian will have to go down because there is not vitality enough in it to stand. Where there is spiritual feebleness and inconsistency, backsliders and heretics will take root.

Unless you go back close to your Lord, you will go farther away from Him. The deadness will deepen, the coldness will become icier and icier; you will lose more and more of the life and show less and less of the likeness and purity of Jesus Christ until you hear this solemn word: "You have a reputation of being alive, but you are dead" (Rev. 3:1). Let us return to the Lord our God and keep nearer Him than we ever have done and bring our hearts more under the influence of His grace and cultivate the habit of communion with Him. Pray and trust, and leave ourselves in His hands, that His power may come into us and that we in the beauty of our characters and the purity of our lives may witness to all men that we have been with Christ.

ALEXANDER MACLAREN

"It is no longer good for anything, except to be thrown out and trampled by men."

MATTHEW 5:13

February 21

"A city on a hill cannot be hidden. Neither do people light a lamp and put it under a bowl. Instead they put it on its stand, and it gives light to everyone in the house."

Matthew 5:14–15

The nature and property of light is to radiate. Light cannot choose but shine, and the little village perched upon a hill, glittering and twinkling in the sunlight, cannot choose but be seen. So, says Christ, "If you have Christian character in you, if you have Me in you, it will manifest itself." All true Christian conviction will demand expression, and all deep experience of the purifying power of Christ upon character will show itself in conduct.

All sincere conviction will demand expression. Everything that a man believes has a tendency to convert its believer into its apostle. That is not so in regard to common everyday truths, nor in regard even to truths of science, but it is so in regard to all moral truth. When moral truth masters a man, he must speak it out. How much more so Christian truth? Do you never feel this in your heart: "His word is in my heart like a fire, a fire shut up in my bones" (Jer. 20:9)? Believer, do you know anything of the longing to speak your deepest convictions, the feeling that the fire within you is burning through all envelopings? What shall we say of the man who has it not? God forbid I should ever say there is no fire, but if you never feel that you must tell someone that you have found Jesus, you have not found Him in any very deep sense, and that if the light that is in you can be buried under a bushel, it is not much of a light after all.

On the other hand, all deep experience of the purifying power of Christ upon character will show itself in conduct. If you have received the forgiveness of sin and the inner sanctification of God's Spirit, let us see it, and see it in the commonest affairs of daily life. The communication between the innermost experience and the outermost conduct is such that if there is any real revolution deep down, it will manifest itself in the daily life. I make allowance for our imperfections clouding over our lives, but Jesus said that if we are light we shall shine.

ALEXANDER MACLAREN

February 22

The purpose of God is that we may shine and illuminate the world. The lighthouse keeper takes great pains that the ships tossing away out at sea may behold the beam that shines from his light. And that is all that you and I have to do—tend the light and do not, like cowards, cover it up. Modestly, but yet bravely, carry out your Christianity, and men will see it. Do not be as a dark lantern, burning with the shades down and illuminating nothing and nobody. Live your Christianity, and it will be beheld.

"In the same way, let your light shine before men, that they may see your good deeds and praise your Father in heaven."

MATTHEW 5:16

Candles are lit that something else may be seen by them. Men may see God through your words and conduct who never would have beheld Him otherwise because His beams are too bright for their dim eyes. It is a staggering thought that the world always—*always*—takes its conception of Christianity from the Church and not from the Bible or from Christ. What is that they see? Inconsistent believers who claim forgiveness but continue in their old sins? Unpraying, worldly people who have no elevation of character and no self-restraint of life and no purity of conduct above others? Such lives hinder the coming of Christ's kingdom, standing as disgraces to the Church. Jesus calls out that you no longer mar the clearness of your testimony and disturb with envious streaks of darkness the light that shines from His followers.

How effectual such a witness may be none who have not seen its power can suppose. Example does tell. A holy life curbs evil, ashamed to show itself in that pure presence. A good man or woman reveals the ugliness of evil by showing the beauty of holiness. More converts would be made by a Christlike Church than by many sermons. Never be content until your heart is fully illumined by Christ, having no part dark, that at your bright presence darkness would flee, ignorance would grow wise, impurity would be abashed, and sorrow would be comforted.

ALEXANDER MACLAREN

February 23

"Do not think that I have come to abolish the Law or the Prophets; I have not come to abolish them but to fulfill them."

MATTHEW 5:17

The ceremonial law, delivered by Moses to the children of Israel, containing all the injunctions and ordinances that related to the old sacrifices and service of the temple, our Lord indeed did come to destroy and utterly abolish. To this all the apostles bear witness, and it was most clearly established in Acts 15. This handwriting of ordinances our Lord did blot out, take away, and nail to His cross.

But the moral law, contained in the Ten Commandments and enforced by the prophets, He did not take away. This is a law that never can be broken. It stands on a different foundation from the ceremonial law, which was designed only for a temporary restraint upon a disobedient and stiff-necked people, whereas the moral law was from the beginning written on the hearts of all the children of men. And, however the letters once written by the finger of God are now defaced by sin, yet can they not wholly be blotted out while we have any consciousness of good and evil. Every part of this law remains in force upon all mankind and in all ages and is dependent not upon time or place or any other circumstances liable to change but on the nature of God and the nature of man and their unchangeable relation to each other.

While it cannot be doubted that Jesus fulfilled every part of the law, this does not appear to be what He means here. His meaning is, "I have come to establish it in its fullness. I have come to place in full and clear view whatsoever was dark and obscure therein. I have come to declare the true and full import of every part of it, to show the length and breadth, the entire extent, of every commandment contained therein and the height and depth, the inconceivable purity and spirituality of it in all its branches." It was never so fully explained nor so thoroughly understood till the great Author of it gave mankind this authentic comment on all the essential branches of it, at the same time declaring it should never be changed but should remain in force to the end of the world.

JOHN WESLEY

February 24

This was a strange and stunning doctrine to those who looked upon the teachers of the law and Pharisees as having arrived at the highest level of religion. The scribes were the most noted teachers of the law, and the Pharisees the most celebrated professors of it, and they both sat in Moses' seat (Matt. 23:2) and had such a reputation among the people that they were looked upon as the super elite of the law. Ordinary people would never consider themselves obliged to be as good as the Pharisees. It was therefore a great surprise to hear that they must be better than the Pharisees, or they would not go to heaven. "For I tell you" adds Christ's declaration of solemnity that this is indeed so.

The teachers of the law and the Pharisees were enemies of Christ and were great oppressors, yet there was something commendable in them. They often fasted and prayed and gave alms; they were punctual in observing the ceremonial regulations and in teaching them to others; they had such an interest in the people that they thought if but two men went to heaven, one would be a Pharisee. And yet our Lord Jesus tells His disciples that the religion He came to establish did not only exclude the badness but also excel the goodness of the teachers of the law and the Pharisees. We must do more than they, and better than they, or we shall fall short of heaven. They were partial in the law, laying most stress upon the ritual parts, but we must be universal and not think it enough to give the priest his tithe but must give God our hearts. They minded only the outside, but we must make conscience of inside godliness. They aimed at the praise and applause of men, but we must aim at the acceptance with God. They were proud of what they did in religion and trusted in it as righteousness, but we trust only in the righteousness of Christ. Thus, by our faith we may go beyond the teachers of the law and the Pharisees.

MATTHEW HENRY

"For I tell you that unless your righteousness surpasses that of the Pharisees and the teachers of the law, you will certainly not enter the kingdom of heaven."

MATTHEW 5:20

February 25

"But I tell you that anyone who is angry with his brother will be subject to judgment."

MATTHEW 5:22

As keen as the sting of fire, Jesus puts the question to us: "What about your inner life, your heart? You do not kill, but you think evil of your neighbor. You do not slay a man with the sword, but you whisper unkind words about your friend. You do not violate the open laws of decency, but yours is an unloving judgment. You have not passed a counterfeit bill, but you would take away a reputation and wound a heart. You would never lie, but if two constructions can be put upon a person's action, you pick the worse of the two." Terrible is this talk of Christ's as a great burning judgment, and it keeps us at bay like a fire. What wonder if our hearts are so dejected at times as to think that no progress is being made with our Christianity. Love thinks no evil, suffers long and is kind, believes and hopes and endures all things, never fails; without love no man can be a follower of Christ.

Jesus is very urgent about these human relations of ours. "Therefore, if you are offering your gift at the altar and there remember that your brother has something against you, leave your gift there in front of the altar. First go and be reconciled to your brother; then come and offer your gift" (Matt. 5:23–24). Our memory needs no help in recalling where others have wronged us, but we soon forget our own delinquencies. Where did my last word of fire drop? What heart did I wound in my last speech? On what right did I trample in my last transaction? Whom did I strike down in order to accomplish my last plan? Let me examine myself in this light, and I shall be a long time in getting to the altar. At the altar, whited, painted hypocrite? The very holiness of Jesus' words creates a torment in the heart that is not set upon obedience, and He is looking for genuine followers. First go away and apologize to the hearts you have broken. Then come and lay your offering on the altar purer than snow.

JOSEPH PARKER

February 26

*J*esus has been showing that righteousness is but fairness—from God to man, from man to God and to man. It is giving everyone his due. In this case, the man had better make up his mind to be righteous, to be fair, to do what he can to pay what he owes in any and all the relations of life—all the matters wherein one man may demand of another or complain that he has not received fair play. Settle your matters with those who have anything against you while you are yet together and things have not gone too far to be settled. You will have to do it one day, and then it could be under less easy circumstances than now. Putting it off is of no use. The thing must be done; there are ways to compel you.

The issue here is not whether you are right or wrong; it is a question of condition, of spiritual relation and action toward your neighbor. If in yourself you were all right toward him, you could do him no wrong. And it need not concern you whether he does you wrong. Even if he should take advantage of you, that is only so much the worse for him but does you no harm. It is a very small matter to you whether another man does you right; it is life or death to you whether you do him right. Whether he pay you what you count his debt or not, you will be compelled to pay him all you owe him. If you owe him a dollar and he owes you a million, you must pay him the dollar whether he pays you the million or not. There is no business parallel here. If, owing you love, he gives you hate, you, owing him love, have yet to pay it. A love unpaid, a justice undone you, a praise withheld you, a judgment passed on you, will not absolve you of the debt of loving, giving justice, praising, and judging fairly. You must pay him the very last penny, whether he pay you or not. We are given ample time to pay, but a crisis will come—always sooner than those who are not ready for it expect—when the demand unyielded will be forced. All must be yielded to the will of God.

GEORGE MACDONALD

"Settle matters quickly with your adversary who is taking you to court.... I tell you the truth, you will not get out until you have paid the last penny."

MATTHEW 5:25–26

February 27

"You have heard that it was said, 'Do not commit adultery.' But I tell you that anyone who looks at a woman lustfully has already committed adultery with her in his heart."

MATTHEW 5:27–28

The Pharisees, in their expositions of this command, made it to extend no further than the act of adultery, suggesting that if the iniquity was only regarded in the heart and went no further, God could not hear it, would not regard it, and therefore thought it enough to say that they were not adulterers (Luke 18:11). Jesus teaches that there is such a thing as heart–adultery, adulterous thoughts and attitudes that never proceed to the act of adultery or fornication, and that this is included in the meaning of the seventh commandment. All lusting after the forbidden object is the beginning of the sin (James 1:15). It is a bad step toward the sin; and where the lust is dwelt upon and approved, it is the commission of the sin, as far as the heart can do it. There lacks nothing but a convenient opportunity for the sin itself.

All approaches toward this sin are wrong—feeding the eye with the sight of the forbidden fruit, not only looking for that end, that I may lust, but looking till I do lust or looking to gratify the lust. The eye is both the inlet and the outlet of a great deal of wickedness of this kind, as is seen in Joseph's temptress (Gen. 39:7), Samson (Judg. 16:1), and David (2 Sam. 11:2). We read of "eyes full of adultery, they never stop sinning" (2 Pet. 2:14).

We have need to follow the example of holy Job, to make "a covenant with my eyes," to make this bargain with them, that they should have the pleasure of beholding the light of the sun and the works of God, provided they would never fasten or dwell upon anything that might occasion impure imaginations or desires (Job 31:1). We have a tremendous need to guard our eyes, to restrain corrupt glances, and to keep out their defiling impressions. This also forbids the using of any other of our senses to stir up lust. To dress or behave in a designed way to be looked at and lusted after is no less a sin. To tempt to sin is the work of devils and provides the fuel and bellows of this hellish fire.

MATTHEW HENRY

February 28

A man may have begun to love his neighbor with the hope of someday loving him as himself and yet be shocked by our Lord's next word. This seems to be another law yet harder than the first! In truth, it is not another at all, for without obedience to it, even the command to love his neighbor cannot be attained. How can we love someone who persecutes us? who is filled with bitter contempt? who is mean, unlovely, self–righteous, complaining, self–seeking, critical, sneering, and self–admiring? These actions or characteristics cannot be loved. The best man hates them most, and even the worst man cannot love them.

But do these make up the man? Does a woman, because she does these things, bear their very form? Does there not lie within the person something lovely and lovable, a pure essential humanity, slowly fading though it may be—dying under the fierce heat of vile passions or the yet more fearful cold of sepulchral selfishness—but still there? It is the very presence of this fading humanity that makes it possible for us to hate. If it were only an animal, we would not hate; we would kill. But instead of telling ourselves that there is our enchained brother, that there lies our bound, disfigured, scarcely recognizable sister, captive of the devil, we recoil into the hate that would doom them to stay there. And the dearly lovable reality of them we sacrifice to the outer falsehood of Satan's incantations, thus leaving them to perish. Rather than murder them to get rid of them, we *hate* them.

Yet within the worst person—deep, unseen, hidden, dormant— lies that which, could it but show itself as it is, would compel and draw from our hearts a devotion of love. We are told to love the real person. Begin to love him now. Refuse to listen to the many reasons not to love him. The person needs your life and mind to help him deliver himself, to help him fight within himself against that wrong, and thus to emerge into the true person he is.

GEORGE MACDONALD

"You have heard that it was said, 'Love your neighbor and hate your enemy.' But I tell you: Love your enemies..."

MATTHEW 5:43–44

February 29

> *"If you love those who love you, what reward will you get? Are not even the tax collectors doing that? And if you greet only your brothers, what are you doing more than others? Do not even pagans do that?"*
>
> MATTHEW 5:46–47

To do good to those who do good to us is a common piece of humanity, which even those whom the Jews hated and despised could give as good proofs equal to the best of them. Nature inclines them to it; interest directs them to it. The tax collectors were men of no good fame, yet they were grateful to those who had helped them to their places and courteous to those they had a dependence upon. Shall we be no better than they? In doing this much, we serve ourselves and consult our own advantage. What reward can we expect for that, unless a regard to God and a sense of duty carry us further than our natural inclination and worldly interest?

We must therefore love our enemies, that we may exceed the general love of humanity. We must go beyond the teachers of the law and the Pharisees, much more beyond the tax collectors and pagans. Christianity is something more than humanity. It is a serious question that we should frequently ask ourselves: "What do we do more than others? What excelling thing do we do? We know more than others; we profess and have promised more than others; God has done more for us and therefore justly expects more from us than from others; but what do we do more than others? How do we live above the level of the children of this world?" In this especially we must do more than others, that while everyone will render good for good, we must render good for evil; and this will speak a nobler principle and is conformant to a higher rule than the most of men act by. Others greet their brethren; they embrace those who are friends and of like mind to themselves. But we must not so confine our respect but must love our enemies; otherwise what reward do we have? We cannot expect the reward of Christians if we rise no higher than the virtue of pagans.

MATTHEW HENRY

March 1

A heart perfect toward God! What does it mean?

A *heart perfect in its loyalty to God,* thoroughly given over to God's side, irrespective of consequences. This is the heart God desires. This was the difference between David and Saul. Outwardly, their lives were similar, but David was loyal to God, and God calls him a man after His own heart. The interests of God's kingdom lay at David's heart—not his own honor, ease, fame, riches, or even building himself a house while the house of God remained unbuilt. Saul knew nothing of this heart.

A *heart perfect in its obedience.* The person with this heart ceases to pick and choose among God's commandments that he shall obey. Though he may sometimes struggle with his own will and the way that God may call him to take, when he is sure that it is God's way, the true child will not hesitate. Some look ahead and see that to obey the light will involve loss of some kind—perhaps reputation, wealth, family associations, ease, or loss of friends, comforts, or good business. And so they slip back and turn their heads away, yet hoping a partial heart toward God will do. They are willing to go a little way with God, but not all the way. Such a heart is all too common today.

A *heart perfect in its trust.* This is the root of all. How beautiful Abraham's heart was in the eyes of God, and that perfect heart expressed it in trust almost to the blood of Isaac. I dare say Abraham was compassed with weaknesses and erroneous views, but his trust was perfect toward God. Do you think God would have failed in His promise to Abraham? God showed Himself strong in Abraham's behalf and delivered him, making him the father of the faithful.

God is looking for a person sincere and thorough in his love—that goes to the ends of his fingers and his toes, through his eyes, and through his tongue, to his loved ones, to his workplace, and to his circle in the world. That is what I mean by holiness.

CATHERINE BOOTH

"Be perfect, therefore, as your heavenly Father is perfect."

MATTHEW 5:48

March 2

We are to be the salt of the earth and the light of the world, not to break one of the least of God's commandments, not to yield to anger, not to tolerate impure thoughts, not to give rash promises, never to speak evil of others. The spirit of retaliation is not to be indulged in; a yieldedness of spirit is to characterize the child of the kingdom of God; and those who hate and despitefully use us are to be pitied and loved and prayed for.

In the little frictions of daily life, as well as in the more serious trials and persecutions to which he is exposed, the Christian is manifestly to be an imitator of his heavenly Father. Now, God's perfection is an absolute perfection, while ours, at best, is only relative. A needle may be a perfect needle, in every way adapted for its work. It is not a microscopic object, and under the magnifying power it becomes a rough, honeycombed poker. So we are not called to be perfect angels or in any respect divine, but we are to be perfect Christians, performing the privileged duties that are given to us.

Now our Father makes *according to His perfection* the least little things that He makes. The tiniest fly, the smallest animal-cule, the dust of a butterfly's wing, however highly you may magnify them, are seen to be absolutely perfect. Should not the little things of daily life be as relatively perfect in the case of the believer as lesser creations of God are perfect as His work? Ought we not to glorify God in everything we do as Christians, and should it not be more than unconverted people can be expected to do? Ought we not be more thorough in our service, not simply doing well that which will be seen and noticed but, as our Father makes many a flower to bloom unseen in the lonely desert, so to do all that we can do as under His eye, though no other eye ever take note of it?

HUDSON TAYLOR

March 3

The hypocrites did indeed give to the needy, but not from any principle of obedience to God or compassion for the poor, but in pride and vain glory, that they might be extolled as good men and gain an interest in the esteem of the people. Thus they chose to give their alms in public places where there was the greatest concourse of people to observe them and who applauded their liberality but were ignorant to discern their abominable pride. The sounding of the trumpet, under pretense of calling the poor together to be served, was really to proclaim their charity and to have that taken notice of and made the subject of discussion. Jesus warns His disciples to take heed to such a subtle sin, for if it reigns in you, it will ruin you.

Now the doom that Christ passes upon this hypocrisy is very clear: "they have received their reward in full," but it is not the reward that God promises to them who do good but the reward that they promise themselves. They did good to be seen by men, and they were seen by men. Their reward is a present reward; they already have it. They chose their own delusions with which they cheated themselves, and they shall have what they chose. But they shall have no reward from God, nothing eternal to show for it, and they should expect nothing more than that. There is nothing reserved for them in the future state. They now have all that they are likely to have from God. What rewards the godly have in this life are but in part of payment; there is more to come, much more. But hypocrites have their all in this world, so shall their doom be. They have decided that for themselves. The world is but for provision to the saints; it is their spending money, but it is pay to hypocrites; it is their only portion.

MATTHEW HENRY

"Be careful not to do your 'acts of righteousness' before men, to be seen by them. If you do, you will have no reward from your Father in heaven. So when you give to the needy, do not announce it with trumpets, as the hypocrites do in the synagogues and on the streets, to be honored by men. I tell you the truth, they have received their reward in full."

MATTHEW 6:1–2

March 4

"But when you give to the needy, do not let your left hand know what your right hand is doing, so that your giving may be in secret. Then your Father, who sees what is done in secret, will reward you."

MATTHEW 6:3–4

*O*ur great Master teaches us that our Father is always watching. Does that eye never close to slumber? Is there not one moment when it tires of looking? The Holy One of Israel never slumbers nor sleeps: The darkness and the light are both alike to Him. That which is whispered in the ear he hears in thunder in heaven. This gives me a very solemn and grand view of life.

Sometimes men meet and challenge one another to do good. "I will give so much if you do." It is one thing if this is only a matter of taste, but if it relates to the consecration and offering of the heart to God, do not mention what you are going to do, ask not what other people are giving. Stand before God, calculate the whole case in His presence and hearing, have but one auditor, and that your Father who sees in secret, and then do what is right according to your sanctified conviction, and God will do the rest.

Compulsion is not to enter into giving, except self-compulsion. If you compel me to give a gift, I will undo it if I can when you are not looking, but if I am compelled by ministries within to give, I do it with my love. I could not withdraw it; it is given to God in holy sacrifice and grateful prayer. In this matter there should be no compulsion at all except the compulsion of love. That love needs continual warming. It is amazing how soon our affections become cooled by the chilling winds of the earth. I must make my way into the inner spirit of the divine Word, I must climb the sacred eminence on which stands the one cross of Jesus, and so much I renew the fire of my love.

When we give to the needy, our motive must be that we give it to Christ: "whatever you did for one of the least of these brothers of mine, you did for me" (Matt. 25:40). That is Jesus' own interpretation of my actions. Whenever I give to alleviate another's distress, Jesus feels the tingling of it in His own pierced palm and writes it down, to be spoken of another day.

JOSEPH PARKER

March 5

The way of the hypocrites was to use prayer to bring honor to themselves. When they seemed to soar upward in prayer, yet even then their eye was downward upon this as their prey. They did not love prayer for its own sake, but they loved it when it gave them an opportunity to be admired and applauded by others. Situations may be such that our good deeds be done openly and be commended by others, but the sin and the danger are when we love it and are pleased because it feeds our pride.

The result is that they have all the reward they should ever expect from God for their service. What will it avail us to have the good word of our neighbor if our Master does not say, "Well done"? We must rather avoid everything that tends to make our personal devotion to God remarkable. It is not to men that we pray nor from them that we expect answers.

Humility and sincerity are the two lessons that Christ teaches us. Secret prayer is to be performed in private, that we may be unobserved and so may avoid ostentation, undisturbed and so may avoid distraction, unheard and so may use the greater freedom. Pray to your Father, who is in secret and is ready to graciously hear and answer. His eye is upon you to accept you when the eye of no man is upon you to applaud you. There is not a secret, sudden seeking after God but that He observes it and will reward you. Sometimes prayers are rewarded in this world by clear answers to them, and in that we rejoice. However, at the great last day there will be an open reward, when all praying people shall appear in glory with the great Intercessor. Christians shall have their reward before all the world, angels and men, and it shall be a weight of glory.

MATTHEW HENRY

"And when you pray, do not be like the hypocrites, for they love to pray standing in the synagogues and on the street corners to be seen by men. I tell you the truth, they have received their reward in full. But when you pray, go into your room, close the door and pray to your Father, who is unseen. Then your Father, who sees what is done in secret, will reward you."

MATTHEW 6:5–6

March 6

"But when you pray,

go into your room,

close the door and

pray to your Father,

who is unseen."

MATTHEW 6:6

We shut our door when we wish to be alone. We shut our door when we have some special work to do that must be done today. Jesus means that just as you do every day in your household and business life, so do exactly in your spiritual life. Set aside times for prayer. He does not say how often or how long. He leaves all that to each man to find out for himself. He says, "When you have real business on hand with heaven, when the concerns of another life and another world are pressing you hard, then set about the things of God in a serious and resolved manner."

It is not that God is more present behind our closed door than in the synagogue or on the street. God is wherever we are. The difference lies in us. We all feel it the instant we shut the door and go to our knees. In that instant we are already new creatures. We feel that this is our proper and true and best place. We say, "This is the house of God: This is the gate of heaven." And if you keep the door shut and give things time to work, very soon your Father and you will be the whole world to each other.

If you pursue that, if you lay out your life to be a man of prayer, you will make continual discoveries of practices and expedients of secret devotion such as will carry you up to heights of heavenly-mindedness that at one time would have been unbelievable by you. You will find your heart being impressed with the being, the grandeur, the grace, the condescension, the nearness, and then the inwardness of God. Your imagination, when you are on your secret knees, will sweep through heaven and earth, not so much seeking God as seeing Him and finding Him in all His works. You will see Jesus and speak with Him with an intimacy and confidence not second to that of the first disciples. You will positively people your place of prayer with Jesus and His Father, and out of your place of prayer you will people your whole life, public and private, with the light of God's countenance.

ALEXANDER WHYTE

March 7

What is that spirit of a child—that sweet spirit that makes him recognize and love his father? I cannot tell you unless you are a child yourself, and then you will know. And what is "the Spirit of adoption, whereby we cry, Abba, Father" (Rom. 8:15, KJV)? I cannot tell you, but if you felt it, you would know it. It is a sweet compound of faith that knows God to be my Father, love that knows Him as my Father, joy that rejoices in Him as my Father, fear that trembles to disobey Him because He is my Father, and a confident affection and trustfulness that relies upon Him, and casts itself wholly upon Him because it knows by the infallible witness of the Holy Spirit that Jehovah, the God of earth and heaven, is the Father of my heart.

"Our Father in heaven."

Matthew 6:9

Have you ever felt the spirit of adoption? There is nothing like it beneath the sky. Other than heaven itself there is nothing more blissful than to enjoy that spirit of adoption. When the wind of trouble is blowing and waves of adversity are rising and the ship is reeling to the rock, how sweet to say "my Father" and to believe that His strong hand is on the helm! There is music, there is eloquence, there is the very essence of heaven's own bliss in that phrase "my Father" when said by us with an unfaltering tongue through the inspiration of the Spirit of God.

And so we come to Him. When I talk to my Father, I am not afraid He will misunderstand me; if I put my words a little out of place, He understands my meaning. When we are little children, we babble at times; still our father understands. Our prayers may be little broken things; we cannot put them together, but our Father hears us. What a beginning is "Our Father" to a prayer full of faults, and a foolish prayer, perhaps, a prayer in which we are going to ask what we should not ask for! The Lord reads the meaning and the desires of our heart. Let us draw near to His throne as children coming to a father, and let us declare our needs and our sorrows in the language that the Holy Spirit teaches us.

CHARLES SPURGEON

*G*od knows what will best minister to His gracious designs. He ordains all things according to the counsel of His will, and that counsel never errs. Let us adoringly consent that it shall be so, desiring no alterations. That *will* may cost us dear, yet let it never cross our wills. Let our minds be wholly submissive to the mind of God. That *will* may bring us bereavement, sickness, and loss; but let us learn to say, "He is the Lord; let him do what is good in his eyes" (1 Sam. 3:18). We should not only yield to the divine will but also acquiesce in it so as to rejoice in the tribulations that it ordains. This is a high attainment, but we set ourselves to reach it. He who taught us this prayer used it Himself in the most unrestricted sense. When the bloody sweat stood on His face and all fear and trembling of man in anguish were upon Him, He did not dispute the decree of the Father but bowed His head and cried, "Not my will, but yours be done."

If the prayer had not been dictated by our Lord Jesus, we might think it too bold. Can it ever be that this earth, a mere drop of a bucket, should touch the great sea of life and light above and not be lost in it? Can it remain earth and yet be made like heaven? The earth that is subjected to vanity, defiled with sin, furrowed with sorrow, can holiness dwell in it as in heaven? Our divine Instructor would not teach us to pray for impossibilities. He puts such petitions into our mouths as can be heard and answered. Yet it is a great prayer; it has the hue of the infinite about it. Can earth be tuned to the harmonies of heaven? It can be, and it must be, for He who taught us this prayer did not mock us with vain words. It is a brave prayer that only a heaven-born faith can utter.

Up yonder there is no playing with sacred things: They do His commandments, hearkening to the voice of His word. Would that God's will were not alone preached and sung below but actually done as it is in heaven.

CHARLES SPURGEON

March 9

Never boast of your own strength. Never say, "Oh, I shall never fall into that sin. They may try me, but they will find more than a match in me." Never indulge one thought of congratulation as to self-strength. You have no power of your own; you are as weak as water. The devil has only to touch you in the right place and you will run according to his will. Only let a loose stone or two be moved and you will soon see that feeble building of your own natural virtue come down at a tumble. Never court temptation by boasting your own capacity.

"And lead us not into temptation."

MATTHEW 6:13

The next thing is, never go into temptation. What a hypocrite a man must be who utters this prayer and then goes straight off to sin. How false is he who offers this prayer and then stands drinking in the bar and talking with depraved men and women. You need not ask the Lord to not lead you there; He has nothing to do with you. The devil and you will go far enough without mocking God with your hypocritical prayers. The man who goes into sin willfully with his eyes open and then bends his knee and says half a dozen times over in his church on Sunday morning, "Lead us not into temptation," is a hypocrite without a mask upon him.

The last word is, if you pray God not to lead you into temptation, do not lead others there. Some seem to forget the effect of their example, for they will do evil things in the presence of their children and those who look up to them. Now I pray you consider that by your shameful example you destroy others as well as yourself. Do nothing, dear friend, of which you have need to be ashamed or which you would not wish others to copy. Do the right thing at all times, and do not let Satan use you to destroy the souls of others. Put your foot down. Be steadfast about it.

The man who has felt the fowler's net about him, who has been seized by the adversary and almost destroyed, prays with amazing eagerness, "Lead us not into temptation."

CHARLES SPURGEON

"For if you forgive
men when they sin
against you, your
heavenly Father will
also forgive you."

MATTHEW 6:14

God's forgiveness creates our forgiveness and therefore can do so much more. It can take up all our wrongs, small and great, with their righteous attendance of griefs and sorrows and carry them away from between our God and us.

Christ is God's forgiveness.

God is forgiving us every day—sending from between Him and us our sins and their fogs and darkness. Witness the shining of His sun and the falling of His rain, the filling of their hearts with food and gladness, that He loves them who love Him not. When some sin that we have committed has clouded all our horizon and hidden Him from our eyes, He sweeps away a path for His forgiveness to reach our hearts, that it may, by causing our repentance, destroy the wrong and make us able even to forgive ourselves. For some are too proud to forgive themselves until the forgiveness of God has had its way with them, has drowned their pride in the tears of repentance, and has made their heart come again like the heart of a little child.

Looking at forgiveness, then, as the perfecting of a work ever going on, as the contact of God's heart and ours, we may say that God's love is ever in front of His forgiveness. God's love is the prime mover, ever seeking to perfect His forgiveness. The love is perfect, working out the forgiveness. God loves where He cannot yet forgive—where forgiveness is yet simply impossible because no contact of hearts is possible, because that which lies between has not even begun to yield to the broom of His holy destruction.

The Spirit of God lies all about the spirit of man like a mighty sea, ready to rush in at the smallest chink in the walls that shut Him out from His own—walls that even the tone of a violin afloat on the wind of that Spirit is sometimes enough to rend from battlement to base, as the blast of the rams' horns rent the walls of Jericho. He only awaits the turning of our face toward Him.

GEORGE MACDONALD

Jesus' concern is that what is *with* the treasure must fare the same as the treasure. The heart that haunts the treasure house where the moth and rust corrupt will be exposed to the same ravages as the treasure, will itself be rusted and moth-eaten. The treasures are nothing; it is the condition of the heart that is everything! Many a man, many a woman, fair and flourishing to see, is going about with a rusty, moth-eaten heart within!

Is it not the heart that is your true self that suffers? The heart that is the innermost chamber wherein springs the divine fountain of your being? Infected and interpenetrated with all the diseases of self, the decay of the heart becomes moral vileness in the soul. Then it descends with the heart into a burrow in the earth, where its wings wither away from its shoulders instead of haunting the open plains and the high-uplifted tablelands.

If God sees that heart corroded with the rust of cares, riddled into caverns by the worms of ambition and greed, then your heart is as God sees it, for God sees things as they are. And one day you will be compelled to see, no, to feel your heart as God sees it and to know that the cankered thing that you have within you is indeed the center of your being, your very heart.

This lesson applies equally to those who in any way worship the transitory, who seek the praise of men more than the praise of God, who would make a show in the world by wealth or taste or intellect or power or art or genius of any kind, and so would gather golden opinions to be treasured on earth. To all who derive their pleasure and satisfaction and joy from the transitory in all its forms, these words bear terrible warning, for the hurt lies not in the fact that these pleasures are false or that they pass away and leave a fierce disappointment behind. The hurt lies in this—that the immortal, the infinite, created in the image of the everlasting God, is housed with the fading and corrupting.

GEORGE MACDONALD

"Do not store up for yourselves treasures on earth, where moth and rust destroy, and where thieves break in and steal. For where your treasure is, there your heart will be also."

MATTHEW 6:19, 21

March 12

"For where your treasure is, there your heart will be also."

MATTHEW 6:21

Jesus Christ says, "Riches can be stolen, riches can perish, riches can fly away; therefore, look for treasures that are not subject to these contingencies." What you have in your hands may be taken out of them; therefore, have something in your heart that no man can get at and steal. He who has nothing but what he can grasp in his hands is not stronger in his possessions than his fingers. Where is your Bible? If it is only in your hands as a book, though you are pressing it to your heart, it can be taken from you. But if it is in your heart, though the book be burned with fire, the revelation is untouched.

Jesus says, "Have an inward life; have a soul." You are no richer than your heart; though you may have enough books to make a library, you are only as rich as you are in your thought, feeling, aspiration, desire after God and all things godly. Our inner nature should be so much in excess of our outer nature as to give the impression that we have no outer nature at all. We are to be so much larger in the soul than we are in the hands as to throw the hand into infinite insignificance, though in itself it have a giant's fist and can deliver a Herculean blow. Let every man therefore ask himself what he has in the bank of his heart.

If my heart is right, our Lord says that the whole outgoing of my life will be right. Provided that is the case, the Lord does not care whether my possessions are heaven-high or whether I can rise above them and stand upon them and use them with mighty strength. He is most anxious that they should not be bigger than I am; His supreme anxiety is that they should not lure my confidence and make up the sum total of my hope and expectation. But I must never treasure them or cling to them. They are to ever be used for the good of others. Jesus is not against laying up property; His concern is that our heart be free to be good stewards.

JOSEPH PARKER

March 13

The heart is the eye of the life: Always keep the heart pure and right, sincere and true, and you cannot stumble along. Let your motive be right, and you will be brought along the right road, even though you may have stumbled into the wrong path for a moment. If your heart is right, I care not how thick the bramble, you shall yet rejoin the main path that lies right up toward the light and the heaven that is at the end of it.

What is the motive of your heart? What is your purpose? Dare you throw back the screen and show the motive to heaven's light? If so, you cannot be weak. But let your motives become mixed, let them double themselves back into reservations and ambiguities and uncertainties, let the inner life become a hesitation and a compromise and a trick in expediency, and you are blinded in your very center and fount of light. And if the light that is in you is darkness, how utter is the degradation? If you have gone down in your motive, you have gone altogether. So let a man examine himself as to his motives and purposes, and keeping these right, so as to bear the very test of fire and to stand the examination of light, he may maintain his life in the quietness of spiritual confidence. If you have gone wrong in your motives, stop. Do not be lured away by inventiveness in making excuses and justifying. To your knees, and become strong by first becoming weak. No coverings up, no clever whitewashing, no assumptions of appearance, but complete, unreserved, emphatic, contrite confession, and then begin again. Remember that your eye is the center of light, and if the eye is injured, no other part of you can receive that great gift. The eye once blinded, your fingertips cannot be flamed up into illumination; your whole body is darkness. With the eye, the light is gone forever, and wisdom at one entrance quite shut out.

JOSEPH PARKER

"The eye is the lamp of the body. If your eyes are good, your whole body will be full of light. But if your eyes are bad, your whole body will be full of darkness. If then the light within you is darkness, how great is that darkness!"

MATTHEW 6:22–23

March 14

"No one can serve two masters. Either he will hate the one and love the other, or he will be devoted to the one and despise the other. You cannot serve both God and Money."

MATTHEW 6:24

There is a common notion that a man may try to serve God and Money. Jesus Christ does not ask you for one moment to believe so flagrant an absurdity. The experiment does not allow such a trial. You must get into the profound meaning of this word *cannot*. This is not a warning against hypocrisy and double-handedness. Jesus is not lifting up His voice against the ambidexters who are trying to do the same thing with both hands—He lays down a universal and everlasting law: You cannot serve two masters. The meaning is, if a man's supreme purpose in life is to seek God and to glorify Him, whatever his business upon earth may be, he elevates that business up to the level of his supreme purpose.

Where, then, is the value of your criticism upon the rich Christian man? You have said, "The man must serve God and Money to accumulate such wealth." Such reasoning is childish. Where a man's heart burns with the love of God, if he is the owner of the Bank of England, he lifts up all his property to the high level of the purpose that inspires him. It is not a matter of serving God with one hand and Money with the other. Jesus says to me, "I lay it down as a law that the supreme purpose of a man's life gives character to all he does."

Conversely, if your supreme purpose in life is selfish, narrow, little, worldly—if your one object is to accumulate money, power, property, renown, you cannot serve God, though you may sing hymns all day long, though you may attend church whenever the doors are open, though you may give your body to be burned and your goods to feed the poor.

It is impossible to go east and west at the same time. It cannot be done. And so if I want to be heavenly and worldly, it is impossible. If I am heavenly, I sanctify the world. If I am worldly, I debase the heaven. You are therefore one of two things, and there is not mixture in your character.

JOSEPH PARKER

March 15

*U*ndue anxiety is very common among believers. Some are nervous, timid, doubtful, and prone to fear. There are plenty of pessimists about, although they will hardly recognize themselves by that title. To them evil is always impending: We are about to take a leap in the dark. All their birds are owls or ravens. All their swans are black. If it rains today, it will rain tomorrow, and the next, and the next, and in all probability there will be a deluge. Or if it is a fine day today, it will be dry tomorrow, and so on for months, until the earth and all the meadows perish with drought. I suppose they cannot help it, but Christians must help it. For the Lord's word is plain and binding: "Do not worry about your life."

Fretful anxiety is forbidden for the believer, and it is needless. If you have a Father in heaven to care for you, are you not put to shame by every little bird that sits upon the bough and sings, though it has not two grains of barley in all the world? God takes charge of the birds of the air, and thus they live exempt from care; why don't we?

Our Lord also taught that such anxiety is useless, for with all our care, we cannot add a single hour to our life. Can we do anything else by fretful care? What if the farmer deplores that there is no rain? Do his fears unstop the bottles of heaven? It is infinitely wiser to do our best and then cast our care upon our God. Prudence is wisdom, for it adapts means to ends, but anxiety is folly, for it groans and worries and accomplishes nothing.

Besides, "the pagans run after all these things." Let the heir of heaven act a nobler part than the mere man of the world. Our distrust of our God is childish and dishonoring. If we could not trust Him, could we manage better ourselves?

CHARLES SPURGEON

"Therefore I tell you, do not worry about your life, what you will eat or drink; or about your body, what you will wear. Is not life more important than food, and the body more important than clothes? Look at the birds of the air..."

MATTHEW 6:25–26

March 16

> *"But seek first his kingdom and his righteousness, and all these things will be given to you as well."*
>
> MATTHEW 6:33

It is the position of our China Inland mission to invite the cooperation of fellow believers, irrespective of denomination, who fully believed in the inspiration of God's Word and were willing to prove their faith by going into Inland China with only the guarantees they carried within the covers of their pocket Bibles. God had said, "But seek first his kingdom and his righteousness, and all these things [food and clothing] will be given to you as well." If anyone did not believe that God spoke the truth, it would be better for him not to go to China to propagate the faith. If he did not believe it, surely the promise sufficed.

Again: "No good thing does he withhold from those whose walk is blameless" (Ps. 84:11). If anyone did not mean to walk uprightly, he had better stay at home; if he did mean to walk uprightly, he had all he needed in the shape of a guarantee fund. God owns all the gold and silver in the world and the cattle on a thousands hills.

Money wrongly placed and money given from wrong motives are both to be greatly dreaded. We can afford to have as little as the Lord chooses to give, but we cannot afford to have unconsecrated money or to have money placed in the wrong position. Far better to have no money at all, even to buy food with, for there are ravens in China that the Lord could send again with bread and fish. The Lord is always faithful; He tries the faith of His people, or rather their faithfulness. People say, "Lord, increase our faith." Did not the Lord rebuke His disciples for that prayer? He said, "You do not want a great faith, but faith in a great God. If your faith were as small as a grain of mustard seed, it would be enough to remove this mountain." We need a faith that rests on a great God and that expects Him to keep His word and to do just what He has promised.

HUDSON TAYLOR

Jesus had already said that we were not to worry how to lay up treasures on earth, how to increase in worldly substance; not to worry how to procure more food than we can eat or more clothing than we can put on or more money than is required from day to day for the plain, reasonable purposes of life. Now he adds that we are not to trouble ourselves with thinking what we shall do at a season that is yet far off. Perhaps that season will never come, or it will be no concern of ours; before then we will have passed through all the waves and be landed in eternity. All those distant views do not belong to us, who are but creatures of a day. Nay, what have we to do with tomorrow, more strictly speaking? Why should we perplex ourselves without need? God provides for us today what is needful to sustain the life that He has given us. It is enough; we must give ourselves up into His hands. If we live another day, He will provide for that also.

"Therefore do not worry about tomorrow, for tomorrow will worry about itself."

MATTHEW 6:34

Above all, do not make the care of future things a pretense for neglecting present duty. This is a most fatal way of worrying about tomorrow. And how common it is among men! Many, if we exhort them to keep a conscience void of offense, reply that they must continue in known, willful sin in order to provide for themselves and their families. They say, and perhaps think, they would serve God now were it not that they should lose their income. They would prepare for eternity, but they are afraid of lacking the necessities of life. So they serve the devil for a morsel of bread; they rush into hell for fear of lack; they throw away their poor souls, lest they should fall short of earthly needs.

Jesus tells us to live for today. Be it your sincere desire to improve the present hour. This is your own, and it is your all. The past is as nothing, as though it had never been. The future is nothing to you; it is not yours; perhaps it never will be. Now give Him your heart; now do His will; now be holy as He is holy!

JOHN WESLEY

March 18

> "Do not judge, or you too will be judged. For in the same way you judge others, you will be judged, and with the measure you use, it will be measured to you."
>
> MATTHEW 7:1–2

*O*ur Savior's expressions seem intended as a reproof to the teachers of the law and the Pharisees, who were rigid and severe, very magisterial and scornful in condemning all about them, as those commonly are who are proud and conceited in justifying themselves. The prohibition is that we must not judge our brother, not magisterially assume such an authority over others. We must not sit in the judgment seat to make our word a law to everybody. We must not slander our brother (James 4:11) or despise or look down upon him (Rom. 14:10). We must not make the worst of people nor infer such offensive things from their words and actions as they will not bear. We must not judge uncharitably, unmercifully, or with a spirit of revenge and a desire to harm. We must not judge another man's state by a single act nor of what he is in himself by what he is to us, because in our own cause we are apt to be partial. We must not judge the hearts of others nor their intentions, for it is God's prerogative to try the heart, and we must never step into His throne. We may counsel and help the person, but we are not to judge him.

If we presume to judge others, we may expect to be judged ourselves. He who usurps the divine throne shall be called to the throne. Both parties must appear before God (Rom. 14:10), who will surely resist the haughty scorner and punish the judging. If we decline from judging others, we shall not be judged by the Lord, for the merciful shall find mercy. "What will I do when God confronts me? What will I answer when called to account?" (Job 31:14). What would become of us if God should be as exact and severe in judging us as we are in judging our brethren, if He should weigh us in the same balance? We may justly expect this judgment if we are extreme to mark what our brethren do wrong. Let us deter ourselves from all severity in dealing with our brother.

MATTHEW HENRY

*B*eware of thinking that any person deserves this appella-
tion till there is full and incontestable proof that he is unholy and
wicked, not only a stranger but also an enemy of God, righteousness, and true holiness. Then beware of that zeal that is not
according to knowledge. When we ourselves first partake of the
heavenly gift, we wonder that all mankind does not see the
things that we see so plainly, and we have no doubt but we shall
open the eyes of all we have any conversation with. Hence, we
aggressively evangelize all we meet and pressure them to see,
whether they will or not; and by the failure of this intemperate
zeal, we often suffer in our own souls. To prevent this spending
our strength in vain, our Lord adds this needful caution: We are
not under any obligation to force these glorious truths on those
who contradict and blaspheme, who have a rooted enmity
against them. No, we ought not so to do but rather to lead them
as they are able to bear.

To those who glory in their shame, making no pretense to
purity either of heart or life, cast not your pearls before them.
Talk not to them of the mysteries of the kingdom of God—
without spiritual senses, it cannot enter their hearts to conceive.
Just as much knowledge as swine have of pearls and as much
relish as they have for them, so much relish have they for the
things of God and His gospel who are immersed in the mire of
this world. They will utterly despise what they cannot understand and speak evil of the things that they know not. Indeed, it
is probable that to press those who are unwilling to receive the
gospel will lead to them returning you evil for good, cursing for
blessing, and hatred for your goodwill. Such is the enmity of the
carnal mind against God and all the things of God.

Yet you need not despair even for these who are hard-hearted.
If all your arguments and persuasives fail, there is yet another
remedy left, and one that avails much; this is prayer.

JOHN WESLEY

"Do not give dogs what is sacred; do not throw your pearls to pigs. If you do, they may trample them under their feet, and then turn and tear you to pieces."

MATTHEW 7:6

March 20

Let us abound in prayer, for nothing under heaven pays like prevailing prayer. He who has power in prayer has all things at his call.

Ask for everything you need, whatever it may be. If it is a good and right thing, it is promised to the sincere seeker. Seek for what Adam lost you by the Fall and for what you have lost yourself by neglect, backsliding, or lack of prayer. Seek till you find the grace you need. Then knock. If you seem shut out from comfort, from knowledge, from hope, from God, then knock, for the Lord will open it to you. Here you need the Lord's own intervention: You can ask and receive, you can seek and find, but you cannot knock and open—the Lord must open the door, or you are shut out forever. There is no cherub with fiery sword to guard this gate; on the contrary, the Lord Jesus opens, and no man shuts.

Do you fear that sin has barred the gate of grace? Your desponding feelings lock the door in your judgment. Yet, it is not so. The gate is not barred. Though it may be spoken of as closed in a certain sense, yet in another sense it is never shut. In any case, it opens very freely; its hinges are not rusted; no bolts secure it. The Lord is glad to open the gate to every knocking soul. It is closed far more in your apprehension than as a matter of fact. Have faith and enter through holy courage.

And if we plead with God for a while without realized success, it makes us more earnest. David pictured himself as sinking in the miry clay, lower and lower, till he cried out of the depths, and then at last he was taken up out of the horrible pit, and his feet were set on a rock. So, our hearts need enlarging. The spade of agony is digging trenches to hold the water of life. If the ships of prayer do not come home speedily, it is because they are more heavily freighted with blessing. If you knock with a heavy heart, you shall yet sing with joy of spirit. Never be discouraged!

CHARLES SPURGEON

This is an inseparable quality of the way to heaven. So narrow is the way that leads to life everlasting that nothing unclean, nothing unholy, can enter. No sinner can pass through the gate until he is saved from all his sins. Not only saved from outward sins that are so common among men but also inwardly changed, thoroughly renewed in the spirit of his mind. Otherwise he cannot pass through the gate of life; he cannot enter into glory.

"But small is the gate and narrow the road that leads to life, and only a few find it."

MATTHEW 7:14

Narrow is the way of universal holiness. Narrow indeed is the way of poverty of spirit, the way of holy mourning, the way of meekness, and that of hungering and thirsting after righteousness. Narrow is the way of mercifulness, of love unfeigned, the way of purity of heart, of doing good to all men, and of gladly suffering evil for righteousness' sake.

Alas, how few of mankind are innocent even of outward transgressions! And how much smaller the proportion have their hearts right before God—clean and holy in His sight! Where are they, whom His all-searching eye discerns to be truly humble; to abhor themselves in dust and ashes in the presence of God; to be steadily serious, walking in the fear of God truly meek and gentle, never overcome of evil but overcoming evil with good; thoroughly athirst for God and continually panting after a renewal in His likeness? How thinly are they scattered over the earth whose souls are enlarged in love to all mankind and who love God with all their strength, who have given Him their hearts and desire nothing else in earth and heaven! How few are ready to suffer all things, even death, to save one soul from eternal death!

Here is a short, a plain, an infallible rule: If you take one step toward God, you are not as other men are. But regard not this. It is far better to stand alone than to fall into the pit. Run, then, with patience the race that is set before you, although your companions are but few. Remember your destination!

JOHN WESLEY

"Watch out for false prophets. They come to you in sheep's clothing, but inwardly they are ferocious wolves."

MATTHEW 7:15

Beware of the false in everything: If you encourage the spirit of truth, you will have no need to be instructed as to particulars. Have ever dwelling in the temple of your heart the spirit of truth; then you will know the false man the moment you look at him. The detection of falsehood will not be an act of skill or cleverness, but you will shudder when the false man is within a mile of you, as the wind in some parts of the sea has a sudden chill in it because of the far-off icebergs. Beware of the false in everything—false promises, false directions, false appearances. Then add the word *prophets.* A man is not a good man simply because he is a prophet: Do not trust the goodness of the office for its vindication.

The truth is that our life cannot be good if our teaching is bad. Doctrine lies at the basis of life. Some may turn doctrine into useless definitions; but doctrine, teaching, correct idea, lies at the root and core of our life. You are what you believe. You may profess to believe things that you do not make real in your life, but what you truly believe is the very substance and inspiration of your character. How needful, therefore, that we should be rooted and grounded in it and saved from perversion and folly, holding the truth of God with a grip that nothing false can tear us from.

How are we to know the false from the true? Jesus said by the fruit it bears. Judge all preaching by its results; judge all doctrine by its effects. The teaching may sound brilliant, but how does it come down into life? Is it an inspiration that expresses itself in love, patience, and sympathy? How does it come downstairs out of its dreamer's intellect and behave in the kitchen? Does it hush itself into gentleness and quietness, and what does it say to the pained heart? I ask you not how your doctrine titillates your intellect, inflames and pleases your fancy. How does it stand by a man when all hell seems to be against him in huge and terrible assault on his integrity and his peace?

JOSEPH PARKER

March 23

*I*f false prophets appeared as wolves, they could not destroy. You would take the alarm and flee for your life. Therefore, they take an appearance of harmlessness, coming in the most mild, inoffensive manner. And they come with an appearance of usefulness. As prophets, they are particularly commissioned to watch over your soul and to train you up to eternal life. You have been accustomed to look upon them in this light as messengers of God. Therefore, they come with an appearance of religion, saying all they do is for conscience' sake. They assure you it is out of mere zeal for God, when they are in fact making God a liar. They come with an appearance of love. They take all these pains only for your good, troubling themselves about you because of their kindness for you.

Our blessed Lord saw how needful it was for all men to know false prophets, however disguised. He saw, likewise, how unable most men were to deduce a truth through a long train of consequences. He therefore gives us a short and plain rule, easy to be understood by men of all mental capacity and easy to be applied on all occasions: Observe their fruit.

To know whether any who speak in the name of God are false or true prophets, what are the fruits of their doctrine as to their lives? Are they holy and unblamable in all things? Do they carry about in them the mind of Christ Jesus? Are they meek, lowly, patient, lovers of God and man, and zealous of good works? And what of their converts? Do they walk as Jesus walked? Do they love and serve God as their manifest proof?

Jesus states that a true prophet does not bring forth good fruit only sometimes but *always,* not accidentally but of necessity. A false prophet does not bring forth evil fruit accidentally or sometimes only, but *always* and of necessity. True prophets bring the proud, passionate, unmerciful lovers of the world to be lowly, gentle lovers of God and man.

JOHN WESLEY

"They come to you in sheep's clothing, but inwardly they are ferocious wolves."

MATTHEW 7:15

"By their fruit you will recognize them. Do people pick grapes from thornbushes, or figs from thistles? Likewise every good tree bears good fruit, but a bad tree bears bad fruit."

MATTHEW 7:16–17

We must "test everything" (1 Thess. 5:21), "test the spirits to see whether they are from God" (1 John 4:1), and the touchstone is the fruit being the discovery of the tree. You cannot always distinguish trees by their bark and leaves or by the spreading of their boughs, but the fruit tells the story. The fruit is always according to the tree. Men may make all sorts of declarations and professions, but the stream and bent of their practices will agree with what is true of their lives. Christ says that if you know what the tree is, you may know what fruit to expect. A bunch of grapes may hang upon a thornbush; so may a good truth, a good word or action, be found in a bad man, but you may be sure it never grew there. This good fruit is never to be expected from bad men, any more than getting a clean thing out of an unclean container. Unsanctified hearts are like thorns and thistles, which came in with sin and are worthless, vexing, and for the fire at last.

We know a man by his words and actions, by the course of his life when he is least observed. If you would know whether he is right or not, observe how he lives. Let his works testify for or against him. The teachers of the law and the Pharisees sat in Moses' chair, but they were proud, covetous, false, and oppressive, and therefore Christ warned His disciples of them (Matt. 23:2–3). What affections and practices will they lead others into? If they are of God, their words and actions will tend to promote humility, love, holiness, serious godliness. If what they preach has a manifest tendency to make people proud, worldly, and contentious, to make them loose and careless in their conversation, to allow them to indulge in carnal liberty, and to excuse their sin, this persuasion is not from God (Gal. 5:8). Faith and a good conscience are held together (1 Tim. 1:19). Always try doctrines of doubtful disputation by graces and duties of confessed certainty.

MATTHEW HENRY

March 25

This warning concerns the case of him who builds his house upon the sand, thinking of going to heaven by any other way than what Jesus describes. It implies all good words, all verbal religion. It includes whatever creeds we may rehearse, whatever professions of faith we make, whatever number of prayers we may repeat, whatever thanksgivings we read or say to God. We may be talking of all His mighty acts and telling of His salvation from day to day. We may explain the mysteries of His kingdom, which have been hidden from the beginning of the world. We may speak with the tongue of angels rather than men concerning the deep things of God. We may proclaim repentance with such a measure of the power of God and such demonstration of His Spirit as to save many souls from death. And yet it is very possible all this may be no more than saying, "Lord, Lord."

Second, it may imply the doing of no harm. We may abstain from every presumptuous sin and all wickedness. We may be able to say with Saul that concerning the law, we are blameless. We may be clear of all uncleanness and ungodliness as to the outward act and not hereby be justified.

Third, it may imply many of what are usually styled good works. A man may attend to the Lord's Supper, hear an abundance of excellent sermons, and omit no opportunity of partaking all the other ordinances of God. I may do good to my neighbor, give to the poor, even give all I have away for them. And I may do all this with a desire to please God and a real belief that I do please Him thereby, and still I may have no part in the glory that shall be revealed.

How short is all this of that righteousness and true holiness that Jesus has described in this great sermon! How widely distant from that inward kingdom of heaven that is opened in the believing soul!

JOHN WESLEY

"Not everyone who says to me, 'Lord, Lord,' will enter the kingdom of heaven, but only he who does the will of my Father who is in heaven."

MATTHEW 7:21

"Therefore everyone who hears these words of mine and puts them into practice is like a wise man who built his house on the rock."

MATTHEW 7:24

Jesus Christ is the foundation of our lives if we have any true life at all. He should be the foundation of all our thinking. His word should be the absolute truth, His life the final all-satisfying, perfect revelation of God to our hearts. The facts of His incarnation, earthly life, death, resurrection, ascension, and present sovereignty—these facts, with the truths that are deduced from them and the great glimpses that they afford into the heart of God and the depths of things, are the foundations of all true thinking on moral and social and religious questions. Christ in His revelation gives us the ultimate truth on which we have to build.

Jesus is also the foundation of all our hope, the foundation of all our security, the foundation of all our effort and aspiration. His cross goes before the nations and leads them. His cross stands by the individual and relieves the sense of guilt and breaks the bondage and captivity of sin and stirs to all lofty emotion and holy living and moves ever in the van, like the pillar of cloud and fire, the pattern of our lives and the guide of our pilgrimage. It is Christ Himself who is the foundation, and His death and sacrifice that are the sure basis of our hope, safety, and blessedness. And it is only because He Himself is the foundation, and what He has done for us is the basis of hope and blessedness, that He has the right to come to us and say, "Take my commandments as the foundation on which you build your lives."

We must draw near to Him in humble penitence and lowly faith, and then there comes into our heart a power that makes it possible and delightful to keep even the loftiest sayings of Jesus. The obedience of which this text speaks is second, and the building of ourselves on Jesus Christ Himself, by faith in Him, is first. Only when we build on Him as our Savior shall we build our lives upon Him in obedience to His commands.

ALEXANDER MACLAREN

March 27

*J*esus Christ is the Rock on which we build if we are Christians; the other man built his house upon the sand. That is to say, shifting inclinations, short-lived desires, fleeting aims, varying judgments of men, the trends of the day in morality, the changing judgments of our own consciences—these are the things on which men build if they are not building upon Jesus Christ. Like a vessel that has a new hand at the helm, you sometimes head one way, and then the puff of wind that fills your sails dies down, or the sails that were flat as a board belly out a little, or you are caught in some current, and round goes the bowsprit on another tack altogether.

How many of us are pursuing the objects that we pursued twenty-five years ago, if we have numbered that many years? What has become of aims that were everything to us then? We have won some of them, and they have turned out not half as good as we thought they would be. (The rabbit is never as big when it is in the bag as when it is hurrying across the fields.) We have missed some of them, and we hardly remember that we once wanted them. We have outlived a great many, and they lie away behind us, hull down on the horizon, and we are making for some other point that, in like manner, if we reach it, will be left behind and be lost. There is nothing that lasts but God and Christ and the people who build their lives upon them.

I press upon your heart this one simple thought—what an absurdity it is to choose for our life's object anything that is shorter-lived than ourselves! They tell us that sand makes a very good foundation under certain circumstances. I believe it does, but what if the water gets in? With all these temporary aims and short-lived purposes on which some build their lives, there is a certainty that the water will come in someday. So dig deeper, even to the Eternal Rock. That is the only foundation on which an immortal man or woman like you is wise to build your life.

ALEXANDER MACLAREN

"But everyone who hears these words of mine and does not put them into practice is like a foolish man who built his house on sand."

MATTHEW 7:26

When he came down

from the mountainside,

large crowds followed

him.

The great sermon had been made, the grand propagation of new ideas had begun, a wondrous intellectual apocalypse had been opened, charming and dazzling the inner vision with all its mystery of separate yet blended colors, and now the great action is to be commenced. Herein you have the hemispheres of Christianity: It is a great speech, and it is also a great healing; it is an eloquent word, and it is an eloquent practice. It requires the mountain from which to project its great deliverances of an intellectual and spiritual kind. It does not exhaust itself by that exercise; it has not only strength enough left to come down the mountain but also, having descended from the mountain and entered into the city, strength, sympathy, patience, tenderness, and every other requisite for the healing and the redemption of man.

Wonderful is that word in Isaiah 61:1, wherein Christ, forecasting the ages, says, "The Spirit of the Sovereign Lord is on me, because the Lord has anointed me to preach good news to the poor. He has sent me to bind up the brokenhearted, to proclaim freedom for the captives and release from darkness for the prisoners." Jesus Christ did not come to the scribes and the Pharisees; the Son of God did not come to our intellectual capacity and self-contented sufficiency; He came to the meek and lowly, and unless we are in this condition, He will speak to us an unknown tongue. We shall not recognize one syllable in all His gospel; it will shoot over our heads as a light not meant for our darkness. But if we are in the condition described in Isaiah, then every word He speaks will be a word to us, the very word we need, the only word as it would seem that the heart could possibly understand. We determine by our moral condition what the gospel is to be to us. Given a right state of heart, and every hymn will lift you to heaven, but given the wrong state of heart, and God's own Word would be to you an idle tale, ill-pronounced and pointless.

JOSEPH PARKER

It is marvelous how even a great multitude can shrink when a leper comes near. You thought there was no room before; let a leper come, and the space on which the multitude stands will soon lessen. Every one of us is a leper if the truth of our real character is known. Every man must feel his own leprosy and go with his own prayer and pierce the multitude and get through it to have his own interview with the Son of God. We are not saved in great swelling crowds. We must go one by one, and each state his own case in his own words to the only healer of human life. I need not teach you a prayer: Lepers are mighty in prayer. Leprosy sharpens a man's tongue into a keen accent; leprosy teaches brief speech, but ringing and telling, without one wasted word, ear-piercing and making God Himself hear. Leprosy batters upon heaven's door with a violence that God never neglects.

A sweet prayer, a full, tender prayer is the leper's: "Lord, if you are willing." Go and stand beside the tax collector, that other leper, and hear his prayer: "God, have mercy on me, a sinner" (Luke 18:13). Go beside the cross where the better thief dies and hear his prayer: "Jesus, remember me when you come into your kingdom" (Luke 23:42). A prayer in a sentence you have in each case, not a long argument, and yet you could sooner add a beam to the sun than you could add one touch of beauty to this prayer.

The leper was not skilled in phrase cutting and in word setting; he was not cunning in giving facets to words that might catch the light and throw it back again most beautifully—his only teacher was his heart. When will men listen to that great teacher, the hot heart, wild in misery, sad with despair, almost in hell because of self-reproach? Let your prayers be as real as your heart. Whatever leaves the heart untouched is barren, vexatious, and worse than useless.

JOSEPH PARKER

A man with leprosy came and knelt before him and said, "Lord, if you are willing, you can make me clean."

MATTHEW 8:2

March 30

A man with leprosy came and knelt before him and said, "Lord, if you are willing, you can make me clean." Jesus reached out his hand and touched the man. "I am willing," he said. "Be clean!" Immediately he was cured of his leprosy.

MATTHEW 8:2–3

Leprosy was a living death and misery, a center of defilement. The leper was dreaded in his every approach by others. He was considered dead while he lived and his case beyond hope. No one but our Savior would have touched this man. The touch and the "I will" of Christ drive death and hell before Him, conquer diseases, remove despair, and flood the world with mercy. His touch said, "I do not loathe you. I will not keep away from you. I will come very near and bring a heavenly, healing power to you."

As a reward to the leper's faith, our Lord gave an immediate cure. How so great a change could be wrought we cannot tell. To dissect a miracle is absurd. Every part of the body had been long out of order, and it is very likely that body parts were missing, his skin was foul, and his joints were rotting. But one command from Jesus immediately restored the leper's ruined frame. He who created can restore. God can turn a sinner into a saint in a moment. Niagara comes crashing down from the precipice of rock; could omnipotence reverse these waters and make them leap upward? God can do all things. In the moral world, He is as mighty as in the outer universe.

The heart is hard as a millstone; can He make it soft? Yes, in a moment He can make it tender as flesh. Do you believe this? If so, submit to the divine touch and ask that this be done to you. Only believe that Jesus is the incarnate God and that He has all power over human nature to pardon and cleanse and there is absolutely no spiritual need that He cannot meet for you.

Our Lord is mighty both in word and in deed. His kingdom comes not only with truth but also with power. Jesus is never known in the full authority of His Word until the Holy Spirit makes us feel the glory of His work within our hearts. Blessed be the divine power that confirms what Christ is saying to you!

CHARLES SPURGEON

March 31

I need add nothing to what has been written of the grievous complaint of this leper. Men shrink more from skin diseases than from any other. Jesus could have cured him with a word. There was no need He should touch the man. No *need* did I say? There was every need. It was a poor thing for the Lord to cure his body; He must comfort and cure the leper's sore heart. Out went the loving hand to the ugly skin that no man would touch, and there was His brother as he should be—with the flesh of a child. I thank God that the touch went before the word. It was more than the healing. It was to the leper what the word *daughter* was to the woman in the crowd (Matt. 9:22), what the *neither do I condemn you* was to the woman in the temple (John 8:11)—the sign of the perfect presence. Outer and inner are one with Him: The outermost sign is the revelation of the innermost heart.

That the Lord should send him to the priest requires no explanation. Jesus constantly recognized the sacred customs of His country, and He wished the man to fulfill the command of Moses as a testimony to him. The leper's healing was in harmony with all the forms of the ancient law, for it came from the same source.

The only other thing Jesus required of the man—silence—the man did not render, and it resulted in impeding the labors of Jesus (Mark 1:45). The Lord required silence of him, that he might think and give the seed time to root itself well before it shot its leaves out into the world. Are there not some in our own day who, having had a glimpse of truth across the darkness of moral leprosy, instantly blaze abroad the matter instead of retiring into the wilderness, for a time at least, to commune with their own hearts and be still? But he meant well, and his tongue could not be still. He would befriend his healer against His will. Yet the Lord found His popularity a great obstacle that He could have done without. Obedience is the only service.

GEORGE MACDONALD

Then Jesus said to him, "See that you don't tell anyone. But go, show yourself to the priest and offer the gift Moses commanded, as a testimony to them."

MATTHEW 8:4

April 1

When Jesus had entered Capernaum, a centurion came to him, asking for help. "Lord," he said, "my servant lies at home paralyzed and in terrible suffering."

MATTHEW 8:5–6

*O*n the surface, this is not a prayer—there is no request in this form of words; it sounds merely like a stated fact. What we don't see is the character of the man in the form of his approach. Is there no prayer in the eye, is there no agony in the look, is there no supplication in the tone? What can the printers do but catch the bare words and put them into cold blank ink? This is how it is that the written page is not the spoken discourse; it lacks the fire that glowed in the face, the inquiry that sharpened the vision of the eye, the music and the eloquence that made the tone pierce the hearer's heart like a prayer. Why you, man of few words, gifted with rare silence, often complaining that you have no language, could pray like this!

Prayer is the lifting of an eye, the falling of a tear, the outdarting of an arm as if it would snatch a blessing from on high. You do not need long sentences, intricate expressions, elaborate and innumerable phrases; a look may be a battle half won. "It will be done just as you believed it would" (vs. 13). You may pray now or in the crowded street or in the busiest scene—you can always have a word with God—you can always wing a whisper to the skies. Pray without ceasing. Live in the spirit of prayer. Let your life be one grand desire, Godward and heavenward. Then use as many words or as few as you please. Your heart is itself a prayer, and your look a holy expectation.

It is beautiful to see the pagan centurion come into worship. He does not know what to do; he wishes to be respectful and yet does not know what is proper. There is something moving in such ignorance and something instructive in such inquiry. To see one unversed in religion come to state his servant's case and to simply leave it with the Master with a beseeching look and tone is to receive a powerful lesson from uncircumcised lips.

JOSEPH PARKER

April 2

*N*otice the happy blending of this beautiful humbleness with an extraordinary degree of faith. It is a wretched error that a lowly esteem of ourselves must be connected with a lack of trust in Christ. The fact is that low thoughts of self go with high thoughts of Christ, for they are both products of the Spirit of God, and they help each other. Our unworthiness is a contrast that sets off the brightness of our Lord's infinite grace. We sink in humility but soar high in assurance. As we decrease, Christ increases.

This lowly estimate of himself brought the centurion away from dictating to Jesus how the blessing should come. Many people are always mapping out courses for the Holy Spirit. They will believe if they see signs and wonders, but not unless. Their peace must come in the way they have selected; their mind is made up as to how it should be. The centurion might have said, "Come under my roof, and then I will believe. Your presence will assure my faith." But he did not ask for a sign or a wonder or a comfort. Many wait till they have some singular feeling or see some strange vision or undergo a special experience, refusing to believe Christ's bare word. They hear of the experiences of other Christians, and they say, "If I only felt that or saw that, I would believe." Thus it seems that the Lord must bow to their will. But the sovereign Spirit will never listen to this dictation.

Be content with the centurion's "just say the word." Be content to believe God's bare word. If you walk in darkness and see no light, trust in the Lord. He who cannot believe God's Word without wonders really fixes his belief in the wonders and not in God. If every power and passion of your nature seem to be contrary to the fact of our salvation, believe in Christ. Set side by side with a deep sense of unworthiness a high appreciation of the power of Christ to cleanse you and make you holy, even as God is holy. Down with self; up with Christ.

CHARLES SPURGEON

The centurion replied, "Lord, I do not deserve to have you come under my roof. But just say the word, and my servant will be healed."

MATTHEW 8:8

April 3

When Jesus heard this, he was astonished and said to those following him, "I tell you the truth, I have not found anyone in Israel with such great faith."

MATTHEW 8:10

*J*esus now gets His chance to respond to the centurion. Oh, that we could have seen that marred and sorrow–riven face when he lifted it up and marveled! Jesus Himself had seen a miracle. His own miracles, viewed as mere expressions of power, fell into insignificance before the miracle performed by the centurion, the miracle of all–trust: living, loving, simple, unquestioning, undisputing trust. Surely a great wave of emotion swelled in Jesus' heart; forecasting the ages, He saw the crown already rounding into shape that was to sit upon His own head, and though the cross lay between Him and that crown, He endured the cross and despised the shame.

We have it in our power to gladden the heart of Jesus. How pleased He always was with faith. If a man looked trustfully at Him, He said he was a son of Abraham. How pleased He was, let me say again, with faith. A woman touched the hem of His garment in faith, and He called her daughter. He had never seen the woman before, yet He called her by endearing names and sent her home with His peace. Her house was never so rich as it was in that sunset. He does not ask our intellect, our pomp, our power, our grandeur; what can be these to Him who thickly inlaid the floor of heaven with the brightest gold? What can our gilt be to Him who spoke the sun into being and rolled the stars along? But when we look to Him and say, "Lord, I believe," it fills His very soul with joy. He keeps back nothing from faith. He says if we had faith as a grain of mustard seed, the mountains would be at our bidding and the earth would be our slave.

What can we say now but, "Lord, increase our faith"? We are keen at suggesting difficulties and clever in the creation and piling of obstacles of doubt. I would to God I could say always right in the devil's very face when he is grinding at my weakness most, "Lord, I believe."

JOSEPH PARKER

April 4

When Jesus came into Peter's house, he found a shadow there. There is a shadow in every house, a fever in every family. If we could find a house in which there was no fever, no death, no pain, no sorrow, no poverty, we should all want to live in it.

But Peter was the senior disciple, an original apostle; great honors were in store for his name in the ages, and yet the shadow was in his house. You would think that God would send all the shadows upon the atheist, yet it is not so in the divine government. "'The Lord disciplines those he loves, and he punishes everyone he accepts as a son.' Endure hardship as discipline; God is treating you as sons" (Heb. 12:6–7).

Who would not have spared the senior disciple? The thief that lived next door had less fever in his house than Peter had. Sometimes the bad man's ground brings forth plentifully; sometimes the pampered and overfed reprobate has wealth upon wealth while the praying soul is outside with the dogs for his companions and crumbs as his portion. All this cannot be reconciled within the narrow limits of time. We need more space: The line that appears to be straight is only apparently straight because of the limited points within which it is drawn. Extend the line, and it partakes of the shape of the world upon whose surface it is drawn. So within these narrow points of time, from the cradle to the tomb, there is not scope enough to reconcile all the divine purposes and actions and mysteries; we need more space, an ampler horizon. We shall get it by and by, and then we shall know how God has been dealing with us in forcing rivers of tears from our eyes and in making our heads a burning pain. O child of God, much praying one, wearied almost with crying at heaven's gate, proceed, persevere; the sigh of your weakness shall be mightier far than the thunder of your strength. Do not despair, do not yet give up, hold on.

JOSEPH PARKER

When Jesus came into Peter's house, he saw Peter's mother-in-law lying in bed with a fever.

Matthew 8:14

April 5

He touched her hand and the fever left her.

MATTHEW 8:15

The woman before us had a "high fever" (Luke 4:38), tossing from side to side in vain attempts to ease a nameless misery. Her head ached, and dreary forms, even in their terror, kept rising before her in aimless dreams. Through it all was the nameless unrest, not an aching or burning but a bodily grief, dark, dreary, and nameless. She repeated the words in the long night, "Oh, for the morning," to find but little comfort in the gray dawn.

No man can love pain. It is unlovely, an ugly, abhorrent thing. The more true and delicate the bodily and mental construction, the more it must recoil from pain. No one, I think, could dislike pain so much as the Savior must have disliked it. God dislikes it. He knows it is grievous to bear, a thing He would cast out of His blessed universe, save for reasons He alone knows.

Then a sudden coolness glides through the woman's burning skin, a sense of all-pervading well-being, of strength conquering weakness, of light displacing darkness, of urging life at the heart! Behold, the young man Jesus, of whom she has heard, is beside her. He has judged the evil thing, and it is gone. From Him, she knows, has the healing flowed. He has given of His life to her. The sun is still shining, and she rises and ministers.

But one will say, "How can this help me when the agony racks me and the weariness rests on me like a gravestone?" Is it nothing, I answer, to be reminded that suffering is in its nature transitory, that it is against the first and final will of God, that it is a means only, not an end? Is it nothing to be told that it will pass away? God made man for lordly skies, great sunshine, vibrant colors, free winds, and delicate odors. However the fogs may be needful for the soul, gladly does He send them away and cause the dayspring from on high to revisit His children. While they suffer, He is brooding over them an eternal day, suffering with them but rejoicing in their future. He is the God of the individual man, or He could be no God of the race.

GEORGE MACDONALD

April 6

We would have thought it would have been an excellent reason for staying where He was. What more could Jesus need than great multitudes? He came to teach, to preach, to heal, and to save, and behold here are great multitudes, and yet He gives their presence as a reason for leaving them.

Why did this Son of Man leave the great thronging, sweltering multitudes? Because the true spirit had left them. They were a mob, a great congregation of curious gazers, of people who wanted to be satisfied with mighty works and wondrous signs. They were swollen with their own wonder, moved by the bad inspiration of their own love of amazement. To such people, Jesus Christ never has anything to say. To the miracle–loving Herods He answers never a word; to the merely curious inquirers regarding doctrine or history He preserves a stony silence. It is not the crowd as a crowd Jesus wants or seeks; it is the needy heart, the conscious poverty, the piercing, pleading pain.

Do not suppose that we can attract Jesus by anything of a merely multitudinous or formal or ceremonial character. It is not the crowned one, whose shoulders are gowned, whose feet are plunged in soft velvet and down, to whom the Lord looks. It is to the man who is of a broken and contrite heart and who trembles at the word of the Lord. Fill your church with multitudes and with eloquence and with incense and with color till the eye is weighted by its oppressiveness, but if the waiting, panting, broken heart is not there, Christ is miles away, yes, on the other side of the horizon, with His back to us. The Son of Man came to seek and save that which is lost. He comes to our poverty, weakness, and self–renunciation, not to our wealth and strength and self–assertion.

JOSEPH PARKER

When Jesus saw the crowd around him, he gave orders to cross to the other side of the lake.

MATTHEW 8:18

April 7

Then a teacher of the law came to him and said, "Teacher, I will follow you wherever you go." Jesus replied, "Foxes have holes and birds of the air have nests, but the Son of Man has no place to lay his head."

MATTHEW 8:19–20

There is a certain almost showy air of pretension about the man and his promise. What he promised was no more than what Christ requires from each of us, no more than what Christ was infinitely glad to have laid at His feet. And the scribe promised it with absolute sincerity, meaning every word and believing he could fulfill it all. What was the fault? There were three: being caught up in emotions, making a vow with insufficient knowledge of what it meant, and foolishly relying on his own strength.

Vows that rest on no firmer foundation than these are sure to sink and topple over into ruin. Discipleship that is the result of mere emotion may be short-lived, for all emotion is so. Discipleship that enlists in Christ's army in ignorance of the hard marching and fighting that have to be gone through will very soon be skulking in the rear or deserting the flag altogether. Discipleship that offers faithful following because it relies on its own fervor and force of will, sooner or later, feel its unthinkingly undertaken obligations too heavy and be glad to shake off the yoke that it was so eager to put on. These three are the explanation for much of the stagnant Christianity that chokes our churches today.

Christ does not reject the offered devotion, but He would not have anyone coming after Him on a misunderstanding of where he is going or what he will have to do. He does not need to hide from His recruits the black side of the war for which He enlists them. To follow Jesus meant being willing to tramp after Him through the length and breadth of the land homeless. It meant to be a stranger and sojourner on the earth. "Are you really willing for that?" No resolution to follow Christ can be too enthusiastic, nor any renunciation for His sake too absolute, to correspond to His supreme authority. But there may very easily be brave words much too great for the real determination that is in them.

ALEXANDER MACLAREN

April 8

*G*od speaks in an unmistakable voice, speaking in the most direct and clearest possible way to the human heart: "Follow me."

He wants you. He wants your gifts, your influence, your money, all you have. But He wants most of all *you*! Yes, you! I do not know to what He calls you, but the question to settle is, *Will you obey?* Will you rise and follow? Will you face whatever it is He calls you to face? Shut your eyes; never mind me. Look inside. Listen to the voice within. Face God and say, "Yes!" or "No!" Face Him. Oh, this everlasting swinging to and fro like the door on its hinges! Oh, this coming to the brink and then going back again into the wilderness! Oh, this listening and thinking and saying, "I would like to—I wish I could—I will someday." It has been the damnation of thousands and the robbing of the kingdom of God.

Have you obeyed the call? I know the reason why many do not. They have too much baggage. There is something God calls you to give up, to lay down, to cut off, and you halt and shrink. You have been sitting or standing there on the bank, sometimes for years. Face the fact that you will never become what He wants you to be until you sacrifice that thing—till you put your foot on that idol, till you embrace that cross, till you say in your inmost soul, "Yes, Lord," and then arise and follow Him.

Do not suppose that God does not keep demanding fresh sacrifices and laying upon us fresh crosses. The devil takes care that we shall not get all smooth sea when we have once started. But I can tell you that whatever the sacrifice, however dear the idol may be to your bleeding heart, however much it may cost you to trample it in the dust, the gain will be ten times as much. To know Christ makes it as nothing. But the devil spreads his great black wing over all that God has in store for you. He hides it from your view and shows you only what you will miss. Now then, look over his wing. Look at the Christ whom you will gain!

CATHERINE BOOTH

But Jesus told him, "Follow me, and let the dead bury their own dead."

Matthew 8:22

April 9

Without warning, a furious storm came up on the lake, so that the waves swept over the boat. But Jesus was sleeping.

MATTHEW 8:24

Mountain-surrounded lakes are exposed to sudden storms from the wind sweeping down the glens. Such a one comes roaring down as the little boat is laboring across the six or seven miles to the eastern side. Matthew describes the desperate plight as waves are sweeping over the boat. It must have been a serious gale that frightened a crew who had spent all their lives on the lake.

Note Christ's sleep in the storm. His rest is contrasted with the hurly-burly of the tempest and the alarm of the crew. It was the sleep of physical exhaustion after a hard day's work. Jesus was too tired to keep awake or to be disturbed by the tumult. His fatigue is a sign of His true manhood, of His toil up to the very edge of His strength, a characteristic of His life of service.

Such is true for us. Though Christ is present, the storm comes, and He sleeps through it. Lazarus dies, and He makes no sign of sympathy. Peter lies in prison, and not till the hammers of the carpenters putting up the gallows for tomorrow are heard does deliverance come. He delays His help, that He may try our faith and quicken our prayers. The boat may be covered with waves, and He sleeps on, but He will wake before it sinks. He sleeps, but He never oversleeps, and there are no too-lates with Him.

He desires from us the awaking cry of fear. The broken abruptness of the disciples' appeal reveals the urgency of the case in their experienced eyes. Their summon is a curious mixture of fear and faith. "Save us" is the language of faith; "We're going to drown" is that of fear. That strange blending of opposites is often repeated by us. The office of faith is to repress fear. But the origin of faith is often in fear, and we are driven to trust just because we are so much afraid. A faith that does not wholly suppress fear may still be real; and the highest faith has ever the consciousness that unless Christ help, and quickly, we perish.

ALEXANDER MACLAREN

April 10

The quiet soul always brings quietness. Note in the worst of crises how certain persons quiet everything; their composure is so serene, their self-possession is so complete, that they bring with them half a deliverance from the distress that was overwhelming you. The Son of Peace brings peace—He creates peace.

He replied, "You of little faith, why are you so afraid?"

MATTHEW 8:26

There is only one storm to be feared, and that is the storm of unbelief. Why are you so afraid, you of little faith? There is only one loss to be deprecated, the loss of faith. "Simon, Simon, Satan has asked to sift you as wheat. But I have prayed for you, Simon, that your faith may not fail" (Luke 22:31–32). I may lose health, money, friends, power, but if I have not lost my faith, I have lost nothing. I shall come up again. Destroy this body and in three days I will raise it again. Blessed are those whose faith is greater than the power of destruction that lies around them. Lord, increase our heart's faith, that deep inner trust that lays hold of you with a tenacity that cannot be shaken off.

Learn that storms may arise even while we are following the clear directions of Jesus. If these men had taken the ship on their own and for their own convenience, we can readily understand the storm as a penalty. Let us learn the brighter lesson and encourage the grander faith. Storms arise even in the fulfilling of our service. Do not create your own difficulties. Do not reason that if you are a child of God your way will be without sorrow or terrible obstacle. Do not reason that you have missed your providential way because of the storm. These things come not for the deepening of your fear but for the quickening, the enlargement, and the completion of your faith.

Never magnify the mountain or the sea outside of you. The mountain is but huge mud, the sea but infinite water, but God towers over both to astound and awe it into submission.

JOSEPH PARKER

April 11

*The men were amazed
and asked, "What kind
of man is this? Even
the winds and the
waves obey him!"*

MATTHEW 8:27

John Bunyan, when describing the experience of his pilgrim, said, "O world of wonders! I can say no less." And so it is. The man who receives grace from Jesus is a gallery of heavenly art, an exhibition of divine power, a wonderland of mercy.

When storms come upon the Galilean lake, it turns into a boiling cauldron that is rent, upheaved, and almost hurled out of its bed by down-driving winds. Yet this billowy lake instantly was turned to glass by the word of Jesus, a fact more wonderful to those disciples who were despairing of their lives at the time than to us who read about it today.

Come, indulge your wonder. Admire and marvel at the exceeding grace of God toward you in working contrary to nature and contrary to all reasonable expectations and in bringing you to be His dear child. Marvels of mercy, wonders of grace, belong to God Most High. If your religion has never produced a wonder, if there is nothing about you through divine grace that surprises your own self, I wonder whether you believe in it. Grace must produce in you what your natural temperament and your worldly surroundings could never produce. There has been fire where you looked for snow, and cool streams where you expected flames. A growth of good wheat has come where nature had produced nothing but thorns. Where sin abounded, grace has much more abounded, and your life has become the theater of miracles.

Are not God's mercies new every morning? Do you not find a continual freshness in the manifestations of God's goodness to you? Still have I beheld fresh beauties of my Master's face, fresh glories in my Master's Word, fresh power in my Master's Spirit as He has dealt graciously with my soul. He can work in a moment what we could not effect in a year. He can change our prison into a palace and our ashes into beauty. This is a great wonder. Go and marvel at what the Lord has done for you.

CHARLES SPURGEON

April 12

There is always a testing case in every ministry. There are critical hours in every life. Jesus has been involved in wondrous healings and deliverances, but here is a test case, and it makes me tremble.

Make no mistake about the terribleness of this possession. The men were exceedingly fierce. The demons had been in possession of the men for a long time, so much so that they lived in the tombs. How will Jesus Christ do now? We have used that question regarding one another in critical circumstances when great distress has come upon the life. How will He carry Himself now?

Into this darkness Christ comes in that calm, serene, majestic presence that makes hell afraid. He was working when we did not suppose He was doing anything; He was troubling the hidden devils with light that only they could see. The cry of distress from the demons comes from hell. God is to do wonders by the brightness of His face: The silent glance of Jesus is a sword before which nothing that is evil can stand. The ever-speaking but ever-silent face, gleaming with light, glowing with fire, will ultimately burn up the devil with His divine look.

Hold your little light aloft; speak mightily or gently, in thunder or whisper as you will, and do what little lies within the realm of your little power. But understand that the final disposition of the devil, and the ultimate setting up of the dominion that is divine and beneficent, is to be done by the breath and power and the glory of God. Jesus confronts the severest demoniac and remains enthroned; when the true collision with evil comes in our lives, our God must reign.

JOSEPH PARKER

When he arrived at the other side in the region of the Gadarenes, two demon-possessed men coming from the tombs met him. They were so violent that no one could pass that way. "What do you want with us, Son of God?" they shouted.

MATTHEW 8:28–29

April 13

> "What do you want
> with us, Son of God?"
> they shouted. "Have
> you come here to
> torture us before the
> appointed time?"
>
> MATTHEW 8:29

This is a remarkable instance of the power of God over demons. Despite their fury through these poor men, they could not keep the men from meeting Jesus Christ, who ordered the matter so as to meet them. It was Jesus' overpowering hand that dragged these unclean spirits into His presence, which they dreaded more than anything else: His chains could hold them when the chains that men made for them could not. But being brought before Him, they protested against His jurisdiction and broke out into a rage.

When the demon addressed Christ as the Son of God, it spoke like a saint. It was a great word that flesh and blood did not reveal to Peter (Matt. 16:17). Even the demons know and believe and confess Christ as the Son of God, and yet they are demons still, which makes their enmity to Christ so much the more wicked. It is not knowledge but love that distinguishes saints from demons. He is the firstborn of hell who knows Christ and yet hates Him and will not be subject to Him and His law.

"What do you want with us?" Christ wants no relations to the fallen spirits whatsoever. Oh, the depth of this mystery of divine love, that fallen man has so much to do with Christ when fallen spirits have nothing to do with Him! Yet they cannot deny that the Son of God stands over them as judge; to His judgment they are bound over in chains of darkness. "Have you come here to torture us before the appointed time?" To be cast out of these men is torture to the demons, but they acknowledge a judgment day (Matt. 25:41). The very sight of Christ and His word of command made them tremble at their torment.

Christ has not only power in heaven and earth and all deep places but also the keys of hell. Principalities and powers were subject to Him, and He disarmed them (Col. 2:15). Oh, the matchless grace of Christ whose divine power reigns over physical diseases, winds and waves, and devils!

MATTHEW HENRY

April 14

To understand the weight of this verse, one must read it in its context. Jesus did not return to His own town because He wanted to. In the previous chapter we discover that He was driven away, that the people begged Him to leave. Jesus never leaves the human heart of His own will.

Jesus stepped into a boat, crossed over and came to his own town.

MATTHEW 9:1

But you tell me that Jesus Christ is no longer with you. You say you sigh to think of happier days when Jesus was the only guest of your heart, and now you mourn that He is no longer present in the sanctuary of your consciousness and your love. He never left of His own accord. I cannot allow you to think so without one or two sharp and piercing inquiries. How did you treat Him? Did His presence become a shadow in the life? Was His interference burdensome? Did He call you to sacrifices that were too painful for your love? Search yourself and see. I never knew Him to leave a human heart because He was tired of it, weary because He had expended His love upon it. But I have known Him whipped out, scourged away, begged to go, banished.

How did Jesus feel as His good deeds became the occasion of a desire on the part of those who had seen them to send Him away from their coasts? This is a mystery on which there is no light. So when my heart is empty of His presence and I wonder where He has gone, I will revive my recollection, I will command my memory to be faithful and to tell me the whole truth, the candid fact; and when it speaks, it will shame me with the intolerable reminiscence that I begged Him to go. Let us be honest, or we shall never be healed. Let us face the stern, fierce facts of life, or we shall make no progress in purity or in spiritual knowledge.

Come, say, "My Lord, my God, cast the darkness out of me, make me a sanctuary, a living temple—abide with me." This is the better course.

JOSEPH PARKER

April 15

Some men brought to him a paralytic, lying on a mat. When Jesus saw their faith, he said to the paralytic, "Take heart, son; your sins are forgiven."

MATTHEW 9:2

This word of encouragement which exhorts to both cheerfulness and courage is often upon Christ's lips. If we put together the various instances in which He speaks these words, we get a striking view of the hindrances to such an attitude of bold, buoyant cheerfulness that the world presents and of the means for securing it that Christ provides. Let me note this thought: Such a disposition in the life of a believer, facing the inevitable sorrows, evils, and toilsome tasks of life with glad and courageous buoyancy, is a Christian duty and is an attitude not merely to be longed for but consciously and definitely to be striven after.

We have a great deal more in our power, in the regulation of moods and attitudes and character, than we often are willing to acknowledge to ourselves. Our "low" times—when we fret and are dull and all things seem wrapped in gloom and we are ready to sit down and lament ourselves, as Job did—are often quite as much the result of our own imperfect Christianity as the response to our feelings to external circumstances. It is by no means an unnecessary reminder for us, who have heavy tasks set before us that often seem too heavy and who are surrounded with crowding temptation to be bitter and melancholy and sad, that Christ commands us, and therefore we ought, to "take heart."

Jesus Christ never tells people to cheer up without giving them a reason to do so. In every case where He spoke these words, they are immediately followed by words or deeds of His that hold forth something on which, if the hearer's faith lay hold, darkness and gloom will fly like morning mists before the rising sun. The world comes to us and says, in the midst of our sorrows and difficulties, "Take heart; be of good cheer," and says it in vain and generally only rubs salt into the sore by saying it. As in the case of the paralytic, Jesus gives him all the reason in the world to be encouraged: "Your sins are forgiven."

ALEXANDER MACLAREN

April 16

*I*s this not just like Jesus? He always sees the *best* in us; He never takes other than the greatest view of our life and its endeavors. "When Jesus saw their faith." Shall we amend the text? "When Jesus saw their sectarianism." That would fill up a line better than *faith;* it is a longer word; it fills the mouth better—shall we put it in? "When Jesus saw their denominationalism." There is a word that would almost make a line by itself. That word ought to have something in it; polysyllables ought not to be empty. "When Jesus saw their deep love for their church." I imagine we cannot amend the text. We can take out the little word *faith* and put in the long words I have named, but these would not be amendments: They would be spoiliations, blasphemies, belittling the occasion, tainting it with a human touch. Let the word *faith* stand; it is universal; it is a cord that stretches itself around the starlit horizon; it touches those of you who are unchurched as well as those who are devoted to religious principles and conviction.

Jesus Christ always startled His hearers by seeing something greater in them than they had ever seen in themselves and always seemed to credit His patients with their own cure. He said, "Take heart, daughter...your faith has healed you" (Matt. 9:22). He made the woman feel as if she had all the time been her own healer. And the broad and everlasting meaning of that assurance is that you and I have it in us at this moment to get the healing that we need. The physician is here; His prescription is written in syllables clear as stars and in lines open as the heavens. What He waits for is faith. "Believe in the Lord Jesus, and you will be saved" (Acts 16:31). "According to your faith will it be done to you" (Matt. 9:29). "Do you believe that I am able to do this?" (Matt. 9:28). There is something then for us to do. Find it out and do it, and God will be faithful to His Word.

JOSEPH PARKER

Some men brought to him a paralytic, lying on a mat. When Jesus saw their faith...

MATTHEW 9:2

April 17

At this, some of the teachers of the law said to themselves, "This fellow is blaspheming."

MATTHEW 9:3

There was, sitting by the paralytic, with their jealous and therefore blind eyes, a whole crowd of wise men and religious formalists of the first order, collected together as a kind of ecclesiastical inquisition. They had no care for the pity that was in Christ's looks or for the incipient hope that began to swim up into the poor, dim eyes of the paralytic. But they had a keen scent for heresy, and so they fastened with true feline instinct upon the one concern that Jesus' words of forgiveness were blasphemous.

Ah! if you want to get people blind as bats to the radiant beauty of some lofty character and insensible as rocks to the needs of a sad humanity, commend me to your religious formalists, whose religion is mainly a bundle of red tape tied around men's limbs to keep them from getting at things that they would like. These are the people who are as hard as the nether millstones and utterly blind to all enthusiasm and to all goodness.

And yet these Pharisees are right, perfectly right. Forgiveness is an exclusively divine act. Of course! For sin has to do with God only; vice has to do with the laws of morality; crime has to do with the laws of the land. The same act may be vice, crime, and sin. In the one aspect, it has to do with me; in the other, with my fellows; in the last, with God. And so evil considered as sin comes under God's control only, and only He against whom it is committed can forgive.

Jesus stands before them and declares forgiveness to the paralytic and brings a definite divine assurance of pardon. If you have ever been down into the cellar of your own heart and seen the ugly things that coil there, you know that a vague trust in a vague God and a vague mercy is not enough to still the conscience that has once been stung into action. Nothing but the King's own sign manual on the pardon makes it valid and deals with the deepest needs of our hearts. All that is given in Christ Jesus.

ALEXANDER MACLAREN

April 18

Though the teachers of the law did but think Christ was a blasphemer, Christ knew their thoughts. Our Lord Jesus has the perfect knowledge of all that we say within ourselves. Thoughts are secret and sudden yet open before Christ, and He understands them from afar (Ps. 139:2). He could speak clearly to the evil in their hearts. There is a great deal of evil in sinful thoughts which is very offensive to the Lord Jesus. He being the Sovereign of the heart, sinful thoughts invade His right and disturb His rule; therefore, He takes notice of them and is very displeased by them. In them lies the root of bitterness (Gen. 6:5). The sins that begin and end in the heart are as dangerous as any other.

Christ addresses these secret thoughts by asserting His authority in the kingdom of grace. He undertakes to show unmistakably that the Son of Man, the divine Mediator, has power on earth to forgive sins. If He has the power to give eternal life (John 17:2), He must have power to forgive sins, for guilt is a bar that must be removed or we can never get to heaven. He proves it by His power in the kingdom of nature, His power to cure diseases. His miracles, especially His miraculous cures, confirm what He said of Himself, that He was the Son of God. The power that appeared in His cures proved Him to be sent by God. And the compassion that appeared in them proved Him sent of God to heal and save. The God of truth would not set His seal to a lie.

The immediate cure of the paralytic filled the multitude with awe and praise to God. All our marveling and awe should help to enlarge our hearts in praising God, who alone does marvelous things. Others' mercies should be our praises, and we should give God thanks for them, for we are members one of another. God should be glorified in all the power that is given to men to do good, for all power is originally His.

MATTHEW HENRY

Knowing their thoughts, Jesus said, "Why do you entertain evil thoughts in your hearts? Which is easier: to say, 'Your sins are forgiven,' or to say, 'Get up and walk'?" When the crowd saw this, they were filled with awe; and they praised God, who had given such authority to men.

MATTHEW 9:4–5, 8

April 19

As Jesus went on from there, he saw a man named Matthew sitting at the tax collector's booth. "Follow me," he told him, and Matthew got up and followed him.

MATTHEW 9:9

Matthew loved money. Matthew, like Judas, must have money, and the surest and shortest way to make money in the Galilee of that day was to take sides with Caesar and to become one of Caesar's tax collectors. This, to be sure, would be for Matthew to sell himself to the service of the oppressors of his people, but Matthew made up his mind and determined to do it. He set his face like a flint for a few years, and then he will retire to spend his rich old age in peace and quiet.

And so we find Matthew, a son of Abraham, in the unpatriotic and ostracized position of a tax collector in Capernaum. The tax collectors were hard-hearted, extortionate, and utterly demoralized men; thus, they are often spoken of alongside "sinners" and "harlots." Like his fellow tax collectors, Matthew could not help squeezing the last drop of blood out of helpless debtors. His business would not allow him to stop to think who was a widow or an orphan or was being cruelly treated. The debt must be paid no matter the consequence.

Jesus of Nazareth, the carpenter's son, knew Matthew the tax collector quite well. Jesus and His mother had by this time migrated from Nazareth to Capernaum. Jesus had often been to Matthew's tax booth with His mother's taxes and perhaps with other poor people's taxes. The sweat of Jesus' own brow had often gone to settle Matthew's extortionate charges. But by this time, Jesus had left His workshop and been baptized by John into a new role. And thus it is that Jesus is back again in Capernaum, no longer a hard-working carpenter, mortgaging all His week's wages and more for His poor neighbors, but He is now the Messiah Himself! And Matthew in his tax booth has a thousand thoughts about all that, till he cannot get his columns to add up. Then came the call to follow, and the chains of a lifetime of cruelty fell on the floor, till, scarcely taking time to clasp up his books and to lock up his presses, Matthew rose up and followed.

ALEXANDER WHYTE

Luke tells us that Matthew made a great feast the night that Jesus called him to follow and gathered his former friends and acquaintances that they might see with their own eyes the Master that he is henceforth to confess and to follow and to obey. What a sight to our eyes! There sit the tax collector at the head of table and the erstwhile carpenter of Capernaum in the seat of honor. And then the whole house is full of what we may quite correctly describe as social and religious outcasts—men who had made themselves rich and at the same time made themselves outcasts from all patriotic and social and family life. For Jesus and His disciples to join this company was scandalous to the Pharisees, as we see by their question in the next verse.

When Matthew rose up and followed our Lord, the only thing he took with him out of his old occupation was his pen and ink. And it is well for us that he did, for never once did our Lord sit down on a mountainside or on a seashore to teach His disciples that Matthew was not instantly at His side. Matthew came to be known not so much as Matthew the disciple or as the former tax collector of Capernaum, but rather as that silent man with the sleepless pen and ink-horn. It needed a diligent and understanding pen to take down the Sermon on the Mount and to report and arrange the parables and to seize with such correctness and insight the terrible sermons of his Master's last week of preaching. But Matthew did all that, and we have all that to this day in his Gospel. The bag would have been safe and kept well filled in Matthew's money-managing hands, but Matthew had far more important matters to attend. What a service, above all price, were Matthew's hands ordained to do as soon as his hands were washed from sin and uncleanness in the Fountain opened in that day! What a service it was to build that golden bridge by which so many of his kinsmen discovered the covenant of Christ!

ALEXANDER WHYTE

While Jesus was having dinner at Matthew's house, many tax collectors and "sinners" came and ate with him and his disciples.

MATTHEW 9:10

April 21

"It is not the healthy

who need a doctor, but

the sick."

Matthew 9:12

This was Christ's argument for mingling with sinners when the Pharisees murmured against Him. He made it clear that a physician should be found where healing is required and that the publicans and sinners sought His merciful deliverance from sin.

Be it forever understood that Jesus Christ never came into the world merely to explain what sin is. Moses had for his mission the exposition of sin through the law; Christ has for His mission the eradication of it. Jesus did not apologize for sin; Christ never died so that sin might appear less sinful, that God might be less severe toward sin. Indeed, we never see sin to be so black as when we view its evil as revealed in the sufferings of Jesus, nor is God's wrath ever more intolerable than when we behold it consuming His only begotten Son. No, Christ came to cure sin, not to cover over it, not to make men forget the disease by drugging them with presumptuous thoughts of consolation but by absolutely removing that which is the cause of their dread and to make them whole.

Christ did not come so that you might continue in sin and yet escape hell. We preach salvation *from sin;* we say that Christ is able to save a man and to make him holy, to make him a new man. No person has any right to say, "I am saved," while he continues in sin as he did before. How can you be saved from sin while you are living in it? A man who is drowning cannot say he is saved from the water while he is sinking in it. Christ did not come to save you *in* your sins but to save you *from* your sins. He did not make the disease so that it would not kill you but to let it remain in itself mortal and, nevertheless, to remove it from you, and you from it. Christ Jesus came to heal us from the plague of sin, to touch us with His hand and say, "I will, be clean." We do but trust Christ, and sin dies; we love Him, and grace lives; we wait for Him, and grace is strengthened; we see Him, as we soon shall, and grace is perfected forever.

CHARLES SPURGEON

April 22

*J*esus Christ was always pestered by little questions. It is very seldom that you hear a great inquiry propounded to Him. Why eat with sinners and unwashed hands? Why heal on the Sabbath? Why not fast more? A man is known by the questions he asks. Let our questions be profound when we open the sacred book and be assured we shall receive great answers.

The persons who asked this question were honest men, disciples of John. They represent people who have got only as far as the gospel of abstention. Many of us are at that point in the Christian life. Our Christianity consists in *not* doing things. It is a necessary point in our growth, but the purpose of Jesus Christ is to lead us away from the negative gospel and virtue of abstention into the glorious gospel of ample and lifelong liberty.

You find people whose virtue consists in abstaining from vice— a kind of minus quantity, the mere negation of wrong. They will not drink, will not pursue this pleasure, nor will they follow after that delight, much less be seen in such and such company. That is a good step, but a man ought not always to rest there. Virtue is positive; faith is emphatic; the true spirit is one of liberty. The question we should put to ourselves is, How far am I yet in the prison of the letter, and what advancement have I made into the kingdom of liberty? True virtue consists in being able to go around the whole circle of legitimate pleasures and yet to keep that circle in its proper place. He has grown up into the fullness of Christ who can sit down with tax collectors, harlots, and sinners and not be defiled, but who has attained that height? That is the grand liberty that is yet to be realized when the spiritual shall triumph over the material and soulish. And that is the line along which our Christian growth has to proceed.

JOSEPH PARKER

Then John's disciples came and asked him, "How is it that we and the Pharisees fast, but your disciples do not fast?"

MATTHEW 9:14

Jesus answered, "How can the guests of the bridegroom mourn while he is with them? The time will come when the bridegroom will be taken from them; then they will fast."

MATTHEW 9:15

*O*ur Lord's first answer is as profound as it is beautiful and veils, while it reveals, a lofty claim for Himself and a solemn foresight of His death. His speaking of Himself as the bridegroom would recall to some of His questioners, and that with a touch of shame, John the Baptist's humble acceptance of the subordinate place of the bridegroom's friend and the elevation of Jesus to that bridegroom (John 3:29). But it was not merely a rebuking quotation from John's witness but the expression of His own unclouded and continual consciousness of what He was to humanity and of what humanity could find in Him, as well as a sovereign appropriating to Himself of many prophetic strains. What depth of love, what mysterious blending of spirit, what adoring, lowly obedience, what perfection of protecting care, what rapture of possession, what rest of heart in trust, what wealth of riches are dimly shadowing in that wonderful emblem, will never be known till the glorious hour of the marriage supper of the Lamb.

But across the light there flits a shadow. It is but for a moment, and it meant little to the hearers, but it meant much to Jesus, for He could not look forward to winning His bride without seeing the grim cross, and even across the brightness of the days of companionship with His humble friends came the darkness on His soul, though not on theirs, of the violent end when He "will be taken from them." The hint fell apparently upon deaf ears, but it witnesses to the continual presence in the mind of Jesus of His sufferings and death. The certainty that He must die was not forced on Him by the failure of His efforts as His career unfolded. It was no disappointment of bright earlier hopes, as is the case with many a disillusioned reformer who thought at the outset that he had only to speak and all men would listen. It was the clearly discerned goal of Jesus from the first to give His life as a ransom.

ALEXANDER MACLAREN

April 24

*H*erein is a wonderful figure. We are guests of the bridegroom, gathered around a wedding table, and the air vibrates
and dances under the thrill of the wedding bells. Fasting is an
alien in this fair land. We are not called to gloom and mourning
here in the Father's house where the life–wine is poured out in
rivers for the soul's ample drinking. You thought the church was
a gloomy place? If there is any gloom in it, blame the human
fingers that brought it to the place. The high ideal of the Church
is joy in its keenest accent, pleasure without alloy, the very
ecstasy and rapture of gladness. "Rejoice" is her watchword.

Yet the Lord keeps us on the right lines for one swift moment,
quicker than the twinkling of an eye. In this passage He directs
attention to the highest point of joy, and then He descends to the
day "when the bridegroom will be taken from them; then they
will fast." Then the ceremonial observances of the Church shall
not be priestly tricks, for they shall come out of the heart's
wound, out of the life's bitter grief. They will not be calendared
for punctual observance, but they shall express an inner, real,
profound grief. When that black grief seizes you, you need not
look to see whether it is a fast day or not. Every heart will be
its own calendar, every life will keep its own fasts, and no man
need ask the meaning of the dejection that shall then picture
itself on the worn face.

There are mechanical Christians who ask questions about fasts.
Is the bridegroom with you? If you can say yes, then let your
soul delight itself in the abundance, whatever the religious calendar may say. Has the bridegroom gone—is His sunlike face
no more the center of the feast and the security of its delight? I
need not exhort you to grief and mourning; the heart will know
what to do. Follow the intuitions of the heart in these matters,
and then your ceremonies will be expressions of the inner life.

JOSEPH PARKER

*"How can the guests
of the bridegroom
mourn while he is
with them? The time
will come when the
bridegroom will be
taken from them; then
they will fast."*

MATTHEW 9:15

April 25

While he was saying this, a ruler came and knelt before him and said, "My daughter has just died. But come and put your hand on her, and she will live."

MATTHEW 9:18

While Jesus was answering the disciples of John about fasting, just then a great, solemn, heart–laden prayer burst upon His startled ear. Elijah taught us that other gods might be so busy that they could not hear the cry of their devotees. He spoke so in irony and mockery that the god was on a journey or sleeping and must be called for louder. Jesus Christ was never so busy that He could not answer any question and, in proportion as that question was acute, arising from the heart's burning agony, would interrupt the matter at hand. These are the things that prove His divine quality, rising above simply being a good man, kind and sensitive. Now He stands before us as God, so much like God that were a man to say to Him, "My Lord and my God," not a heart around would feel the shock of any irreligious or painful surprise.

Yet He appears to be Servant as well as Master, for He rises and follows the man, as if He had no alternative. He never has an alternative when the heart really wants Him. A heart may indeed send Him away, but when the broken heart needs Him, He always answers. To the soul who seeks Him by the lamp of intelligence or who invites Him into the cunning arranged chambers of His fancy or imagination, and to all Herods and Pilates who tempt Him by their intellectual curiosity, Jesus answers nothing. But when a man's eyes are upon the dust, whose hand is upon his heart, and who sobs rather than says his eager prayer, Jesus will come.

Jesus hears the ruler's unspoken prayer, for it had a subtle undertone that touched His heart. If the child is dead, why call her back from glory? But the living man was also dead. The house had become a ghastly tomb; the house had shaped itself in its ghost's faces—Jesus went for the living man's sake. So wondrous is His mercy that sometimes those who are in heaven have to be called back again to make up our life!

JOSEPH PARKER

April 26

*N*otice the woman's real but imperfect faith. There was unquestionable confidence in Christ's power and a very genuine desire for healing. But the woman believes that her touch of the cloak will heal without Christ's will or knowledge, much more His pitying love, having any part of it. She thinks she may win her desire furtively, may carry it away, and Jesus be none the wiser or poorer for the stolen blessing. What ignorance of His character and way of working! My feeling is that there was even gross superstition mixed in. Yet with absolute assurance of confidence, her Healer recognized her faith as true, though blended with ignorance.

Her error was very like that which many Christians entertain with less excuse. To attach importance to external means of grace, rites, ordinances, sacraments, outward connection with Christian organizations, is the very same misconception in a slightly different form. Such error is always near us and is especially pervasive where the church has long been established. It has received a strange new vigor today and is threatening to corrupt the simplicity and spirituality of Christian worship and needs to be strenuously resisted. But let us be careful to remember that, along with this clinging to the hem of the cloak instead of to the heart of its Wearer, there may be a very real trust that might shame some of us who profess to hold a less ceremonial form of faith. Many a devout soul clasping a crucifix clings to the true cross of Christ.

The woman wanted health; she did not appear to care that much about the Healer. Love comes after, born of the experience of His love, as it did for her. But faith precedes love, and the predominant motive impelling to faith at first is distinctly self-regard. How often does God turn us around into a peaceful, thankful surrender of the cured self to His love and service?

ALEXANDER MACLAREN

Just then a woman who had been subject to bleeding for twelve years came up behind him and touched the edge of his cloak. She said to herself, "If I only touch his cloak, I will be healed."

MATTHEW 9:20–21

April 27

Jesus turned and saw her. "Take heart, daughter," he said, "your faith has healed you." And the woman was healed from that moment.

MATTHEW 9:22

Jesus could not let this woman leave with half a gift. He could not let her go away with only her healing. She must know who had healed her. Her will and His must come together; and for this, her eyes and His, her voice and His ears, her ears and His voice must meet. It is the only case recorded in which He says *daughter*. He perfectly understood her pain. His heart yearns toward the woman to shield her from her own innocent shame. Her story appealed to all that was tenderest in humanity, for the secret that her modesty had hidden, her conscience had spoken aloud. Therefore, the tenderest word that the language could afford must be hers. "Daughter," He said. It was the fullest reward, the richest acknowledgment He could find of the honor in which He held her, His satisfaction with her conduct, and the perfect love He had for her.

Some will say that the word was an Eastern mode in common usage at the time. I say that whatever Jesus did or said, He did and said like other men, and He did and said as no other man did or said. If he said *daughter,* it meant what any man would mean by it; it also meant what no man could mean by it—what no man was good enough, great enough, loving enough to mean by it. In Him the Father spoke to this one the eternal truth of His relation to all His daughters, to all the women He has made, though individually it can be heard only by those who lift up the filial eyes, lay bare the filial heart.

Perhaps she thought He was offended with her because of her approach to Him. But He soothes her with gentle, restoring words: "Take heart, your faith has made you well." What wealth of tenderness! She must not be left in her ignorance to the danger of associating power with the mere garment of the divine. She must be brought face-to-face with her Healer. See how He praises her. He is never slow to commend. The first quiver of the upturning eyelid is to Him faith. He said, "Daughter."

GEORGE MACDONALD

April 28

After another remarkable healing, like a river turned from its course for a time to fill some empty reservoir, Jesus' love comes back to its original direction. How abundant the power and mercy to which such a work as that just done was but a parenthesis! The doleful music and the shrill shrieks of Eastern mourning that met them at the ruler's house disturbed the sanctity of the hour and were in strong contrast with the majestic calmness of Jesus. Not amid laments and excited cries will He do His work. He bids the noisy crowd to exit and therein rebukes all such hollow and tumultuous scenes in the presence of the stillness of death.

Then comes the great deed. Into the silence of the room Jesus comes. There is no effort, repeated and gradually successful, as when Elisha raised the dead boy (2 Kings 4:18–37); no praying, as when Peter raised Dorcas (Acts 9:37–42); only the touch of the hand in which life throbbed in fullness and, as the other gospel narratives record, two words, spoken strangely to and yet more strangely heard by the dull, cold ear of death. But Matthew passes them by, as he seems here to have desired to emphasize the power of Christ's touch. But touch or word, the real cause of the miracle was simply His will, and whether He spoke or touched or both, little mattered. He varied his methods as the circumstances of the recipients required and so that they and we might learn that He was tied to none. The miracles of Jesus raising the dead are three: The ruler's daughter has just passed away, the widow's son at Nain was being taken to his burial, Lazarus had been dead for days. A few minutes or days or four thousand years are one to His power. These three but typify the first fruits of the great prophesied coming harvest of the final resurrection. Blessed are they who, like this little maiden, are awakened, not only by His voice but also by His touch, and to find, as she did, their hand in His!

ALEXANDER MACLAREN

When Jesus entered the ruler's house and saw the flute players and the noisy crowd, he said, "Go away. The girl is not dead but asleep."

MATTHEW 9:23–24

"The girl is not dead

but asleep."

MATTHEW 9:24

What did our Lord mean by these words? Not certainly that, as we regard the difference between death and sleep, His words were to be taken literally; not that she was only in a state of coma, for the narrative clearly intends us to believe that she was dead in the manner we call death. That this was not to be dead in the manner our Lord called death is a blessed and lovely fact.

The explanation seems to me large and simple. These people professed to believe in the resurrection of the dead. They were not Sadducees, for they were friends of a synagogue ruler. Our Lord did not bring the news of the resurrection to the world. That had been believed, in varying degrees, by all peoples and nations from the first. But as with the greater number even of Christians, although it was a part of their creed and had some influence upon their moral and spiritual condition, their practical faith in the resurrection of the body was a poor affair. In the moment of loss and grief, they thought little of it. They lived then in the present almost alone; they were not saved by hope.

The reproach therefore of our Lord was simply that they did not take from their own creed the consolation they should. If the child was to be one day restored to them, then she was not dead, as their tears and laments would imply. Any one of them who believed the words of the prophets might have stood up and said, "Why make such a commotion? The child is not dead, but sleeps. You shall again clasp her to your bosom. Hope, and fear not—only believe." It was in this sense that our Lord spoke.

It is as if Jesus told us that our notion of death is all wrong, that there is no such thing as we think it, that we would be better to call death the name of sleep, for it is but a passing appearance and no right cause of such misery as we manifest in its presence. With the girl's resurrection, the Lord brings His assurance, His knowledge of what we do not know, to feed our feeble faith. "The girl is not dead but asleep."

GEORGE MACDONALD

April 30

*J*esus did not ask the blind men what kind of characters they had been in the past, because when men come to Christ, the past is forgiven. He did not ask them whether they had tried other means of getting their eyes opened. No. Curious questions and idle speculations are never suggested by the Lord Jesus. His inquiries were all resolved into a trial upon one point, and that one point, faith. Did they believe that He, the Son of David, could heal them?

Why does our Lord everywhere, not only in His ministry but also in the teaching of the apostles, always put so much emphasis upon faith? It is because of its receptive power. Faith of itself could not contribute a penny to salvation, but as the container that holds a precious Christ within itself, it holds all the treasures of divine love. If a man is thirsty, a rope and a bucket are of little use, but if there is a well nearby, they are the very thing that is required. Faith is the bucket by means of which a man may draw water out of the wells of salvation and drink to his heart's content.

Faith is the connection link between our souls and God, and the message from God flashes along it to our souls. Faith is sometimes as weak as a thread, but it is a very precious thing, for it is the beginning of great things. Through faith, your sinfulness rests on His grace, your weakness hangs on His strength, your nothingness hides itself in His all-sufficiency. Riches, education, and position count for nothing—only faith in Christ.

The blind men came crying emphatically, persevering with an insatiable desire for sight, and passionately proclaiming the Son of David. Jesus-adoring prayers have in them the swiftness and force of eagles' wings; they must ascend to God, for the elements of heavenly power are abundant in them. A mouth open in never-ceasing prayer shall bring about the eyes open in full vision of faith.

CHARLES SPURGEON

As Jesus went on from there, two blind men followed him, calling out, "Have mercy on us, Son of David!" When he had gone indoors, the blind men came to him, and he asked them, "Do you believe that I am able to do this?"

MATTHEW 9:27–28

May 1

Then he touched their

eyes and said,

"According to your

faith will it be done to

you."

MATTHEW 9:29

*W*e find the vessel; Jesus finds its heavenly contents. If we have no vessel, we cannot catch the rain; if we have no goblet of faith, we cannot catch the wine of grace. There is a human side as well as a divine side in all this great mystery of human healing and growth. I have never seen Jesus Christ put the crown upon genius, beauty, power, but I have been present on a thousand coronations, when He encircled the brows of modesty with the choicest garlands of heaven.

There is a great law here that we would do well to ponder: *Our faith is the measure of our progress in divine things.* If your faith is equal to the occasion, you shall have what you need; if your faith falls below the occasion, you will be as blind as ever. You may touch the right Christ, but if you touch Him with a cold hand, you will receive nothing in return. Not only must we go to the right altar, we must go in the right spirit.

Why is it that the Church is not succeeding today? Because the Church has intelligence but not faith. We now have theories of inspiration, theories of the atonement, theories of justification by faith. Do you mean to say that Christ's great work for the human family requires a volume of five hundred pages to make it clear? Then the salvation of the world is impossible. The atonement is a flash of the mind, a passion of the heart, one transient glimpse of an infinite tragedy, one touch of hot heart-blood. Lord, take us away from dry systematic theology and lead us into the invisible temple, the hidden sanctuary, the house in the clouds, and show us there Your grace; then send us down the steep mountain to find the blind man and give him sight. The Church will one day take her cleverness up to some Moriah, draw her glittering knife, and slay the enemy, and then the church will put on her beautiful garments and be ashamed neither of the mystery of faith nor of the obedience of love.

JOSEPH PARKER

May 2

*A*s you read this chapter, you notice the rapidity with which the cures wrought by the Savior followed each other, how much of mercy was compressed into a short space of time. He has no sooner healed the paralytic than He cures the woman who had a flow of blood, then raising to life the young maiden, next giving sight to two blind men, and now delivering this deaf and mute man who was possessed with a demon. Christ heals again, again, and yet again. What an inexhaustible fullness there is in Christ!

Then observe the wonderful readiness of the Lord to bless men. Whether in response to the faith of friends who drop a paralytic through the ceiling or the cry of a father's heart for his dead daughter, He brings healing and forgiveness of sin immediately. But here is one who could not ask, for he could not speak. I do not suppose that he even brought a personal desire, for he was demon-possessed, and the demon had mastered the poor soul. So the Savior, though He perceived no faith in the man and no prayer could come from the man's lips, noticed and honored the faith of those who brought him, and swiftly and spontaneously did His mercy flow out to the demoniac.

Come, dear heart, you have not to plead with Jesus to make Him merciful, for He loves you better than you love yourself. You do not have to persuade Him to be gracious; Christ is no miser, holding His blessings with a tight hand as though He would rather hoard than bestow them on the needy. No. As freely as the sun scatters His light, as freely as the clouds dispense His rain, so does Christ bless where He sees that there is need of blessing. Then let us put our friends in Christ's way by breathing a secret, silent prayer for them, and let us put ourselves in Christ's way, and may the great Master speedily heal us to the praise of His glory.

CHARLES SPURGEON

While they were going out, a man who was demon-possessed and could not talk was brought to Jesus. And when the demon was driven out, the man who had been mute spoke. The crowd was amazed and said, "Nothing like this has ever been seen in Israel."

MATTHEW 9:32–33

May 3

When he saw the crowds, he had compassion on them, because they were harassed and helpless, like sheep without a shepherd.

MATTHEW 9:36

Again and again as we come along the line of the sacred narrative, we have seen Jesus' tears, have heard the pity in the tone of His voice, and have been touched by the pathos of many of His deeds. The key word of this divine life is *compassion*. If you do not seize that word in its true meaning, the life of Jesus Christ will be to you little more than either a romantic surprise or a dead letter. His was a life of love, a history of compassion, an exemplification of the tenderest aspects of the infinite mercy of God. He is a high priest who can be touched with the feeling of our infirmities. He knows us through and through, He bears our iniquities, and He took our infirmities and sustained our afflictions.

When Jesus saw the multitudes, He was moved with compassion. When we see the multitudes, we are moved with wonder or admiration, but not with compassion. Who would dare pity a multitude? It could overpower you, run you down, trample you to death. Yet the multitude touched His heart and filled His eyes with tears. Every other emotion grows dumb; wonder must sometimes close its eyes; admiration falls upon itself, sates its appetite, and dies of the fullness, but compassion grows by what it feeds on and is of the very nature of God.

Jesus sees the multitudes and sees them as vexed, disturbed, and chafed—as sheep when the wolf comes into the fold. Jesus sees beyond the sheep to the wolf—the devil and his angels, who disturb and frighten mankind by ten thousand black spirits that darken the day. He sees it all with a comprehensive and penetrating vision, and His eyes darken with tears.

Jesus has the shepherdly heart, is called the Good Shepherd, and lays down His life for the sheep. He made Himself of no reputation and took up His residence with us in all its forms of endearment and service and fellowship. He is the great Christ.

JOSEPH PARKER

May 4

*J*esus saw the multitudes thronging Him whenever He stood up to preach, and He perceived that the ordained instructors of the day were either leading the people into error or shamefully neglecting their duty. I do not think that the circumstances under which our Lord spoke these words have passed away, but rather that we are living under precisely the same conditions.

Moved with compassion for the multitudes, our Lord turned to His disciples to pray for laborers. Precious souls were perishing around the world, and this our Savior lamented. He did not say, "The laborers are few, but that matters not; God can bless a few and make them accomplish as much as many." He believed in His Father's omnipotence, but He also believed that the Lord would work through laborers and that many were required. He believed in the results being proportionate to the means used. Nor did Jesus suggest that God would do the work alone. Our Master never made too much of men, but He made a very great deal about men anointed by the Holy Spirit and sent out to preach. In fact, He taught us to pray for them, and His instructions regarding the day of Pentecost were crystal-clear and emphatic. If we despise what Christ evidently prizes as His ascension gift, we may fancy we are honoring God, but we shall grieve His Spirit. He would have us give great importance to the instrumentality.

Are you praying for laborers to go into the great harvest fields of the world? From China to Japan to Africa, the world lies before us in tremendous need of laborers. Laborers who will pour their heart and soul into the work with tears and entreaties. Laborers, not loiterers. We need men on fire, and I beseech you to ask God to send them. We need men who will take off their coats and sweat at their work, for nothing in the harvest field can be done without the sweat on the face. The church must have men sent by the Holy Spirit who can do this by God's help!

CHARLES SPURGEON

Then he said to his disciples, "The harvest is plentiful but the workers are few. Ask the Lord of the harvest, therefore, to send out workers into his harvest field."

MATTHEW 9:37–38

May 5

He called his twelve disciples to him and gave them authority to drive out evil spirits and to heal every disease and sickness.

MATTHEW 10:1

*N*ote that the Lord encouraged them to pray for harvest laborers, and then when they have prayed themselves into white heat of soul, He names them as a partial answer to their own prayers. Revelations come to men in prayer; while they are praying about others, God suddenly says, "You are the men—go!" That is a solution of ten thousand church difficulties.

Also note that Jesus was always calling these men. Again and again He called them—always calling, shaping our manhood to new and noble uses, always enlarging the definition of our sphere and ennobling the destiny of our powers. The call of Christ is a daily interview; the invitation to go nearer to Him comes with every sunrise. We have never been so near to Jesus Christ that we cannot be nearer, and the nearer we get, the softer is His voice.

What does He do when they come nearer to Him? He gave them *power* against evil spirits and to heal sicknesses and diseases. It was, then, a power to do good. Jesus Christ gave His disciples power to relieve human burden and distresses, to heal all manner of sickness. He detests the presence of evil spirits and disease—these came not from the compass of His counsel; an enemy has done this to His creation. It is His will that we should be strong, grand, royal, and if we are otherwise, an enemy has done it, and he must be found and slain.

What has become of the Church's power? It is partially, almost wholly, lost. The Church is prudent, self-admiring, self-protecting, trimming her edges, locking her gates, talking much within her borders. Where is the old world-shaking power? The Church should be a hospital, a nursery, a home for the destitute and cast out. The Church should have both hands filled with bread to give to the hungry. When she ceases her more or less impotent speculations and takes upon herself this beneficent ministry, the world will soon know that the Son of God has come in power.

JOSEPH PARKER

May 6

Half of these twelve are never heard of as doing any work for Christ. Some of them are never so much as named again other than in the list at the beginning of the book of Acts. No doubt those apostles toiled honestly and did their Lord's commands, and oblivion in history has swallowed them up.

These twelve Jesus sent out.

MATTHEW 10:5

From them let us learn the lesson that the same will sooner or later come to us all. For most of us, our service goes unnoticed and unknown, and the memory of our work will live perhaps a year or two in the hearts of some who loved us but will fade wholly when they follow us into the silent land. Well, be it so; we shall sleep none the less sweetly. The world has a short memory, and as the years go on, remembrance grows dim. All that matters very little. The notoriety of our work is of no consequence. The earnestness and accuracy with which we strike our blow is all-important, but it matters nothing how far it echoes. We shall do our work best and be saved from much festering anxiety if we make up our minds to work unknown and unnoticed. Whether our position is a conspicuous or an obscure one, we shall fill it to the utmost of our power.

Christ gave all the apostles their tasks—to some to found the Gentile churches and leave all generations precious teaching, to some of them none of these things. Was Peter more highly favored than the others? Not so. To Christ, all service done from the same motive is the same, and His measure of excellence is the quantity of love and spiritual force in our deeds, not the width of the area over which they spread. The deeds that stand highest on the records in heaven are not those that we call great. Many cups of cold water will be found to be rated higher there than jeweled golden chalices brimming with rare wines. God's treasures, where He keeps His children's gifts, will be like many a mother's secret store of relics with her children, precious in His eyes for love's sake.

ALEXANDER MACLAREN

May 7

"Do not go among the Gentiles or enter any town of the Samaritans. Go rather to the lost sheep of Israel. As you go, preach this message: 'The kingdom of heaven is near.' Heal the sick, raise the dead, cleanse those who have leprosy, drive out demons. Freely you have received, freely give."

MATTHEW 10:5–8

The specific instructions to the apostles have been abrogated by Christ in the Great Commission (Matt. 28:19), but the spirit of them remains as the perpetual obligation of all Christian workers.

The restriction to limit their sphere of work to the Jew was clearly transient, but that method could not be abandoned till the Jew himself had destroyed it by rejecting Christ. Even when the commission widened, Paul went to the Jew first, till he too was taught by uniform failure that Israel was fixed in unbelief.

How tenderly our Lord designates the nation as the lost sheep of Israel. He is still influenced by that compassion that the sight of the multitudes had moved in Him (Matt. 9:36). Lost indeed, wandering with torn fleece, in ignorance of their pasture and their Shepherd, yet they are His sheep.

The work to be done is twofold—a glad truth is to be proclaimed; gracious deeds of power are to be done. How blessed must be the kingdom, the forerunners of which are miracles of healing and life giving! If the heralds can do these, what will not the King be able to do? If such colors attend the dawn, how radiant will be the noontime! Note "as you go," indicating that they were traveling evangelists and were to speak as they went and go when they had spoken. The road was to be their pulpit, and each man they met their audience. What a different world it would be if Christians carried their message with them!

We have freely received the message of the coming kingdom and the power to work miracles. The deepest springs of the heart's love are set flowing by the gift of God which contains in itself both the most tender and mighty motive in self-forgetting labor and the pattern for Christian service. May we never seek a personal profit or advantage from preaching the gospel.

ALEXANDER MACLAREN

May 8

$\mathcal{L}$et us hear what Jesus Christ has to say to His twelve disciples when He sends them forth. It is my belief that this is the way to evangelize the world. Jesus never said a single word about going through missions with guarantees and supports and home refuges in the case of foreign disappointments. Go to a foreign land with nothing—nothing but yourself and God. Do you want to be a missionary to distant people? Then go at once and tell no one about it. If you can't pay for it, work for it, or you do not mean to go. If you have the fire of God burning in you and want to go to reclaim the moral wastes of the world, you would be off! You would not need to consult with your minister and others. We would ask of you, "Where is he?" And eventually the answer would come that Christ had sent you forth.

"Do not take along any gold or silver or copper in your belts; take no bag for the journey, or extra tunic, or sandals or a staff; for the worker is worth his keep."

MATTHEW 10:9–10

The kind of sloth seen in today's church will never conquer the world. If Christ has called you very closely to Himself and has told you to go and be a missionary, then go. This is exactly how Christ Himself came. "Who, being in very nature God, did not consider equality with God something to be grasped, but made himself nothing, taking the very nature of a servant" (Phil. 2:6–7). Believe that as you go, willing to serve in any way in order to witness to the truth, you will have bread enough and to spare. You cannot show disinterestedness, the passion of enthusiasm, the inspiration of absolute consecration, and be left to starve. There are always kind hearts, open houses, thoughtful minds; God has His elect everywhere. Our care must be about the truth; God will take care about the bread. If Jesus Christ had set up a missionary scheme with most intricate and complex and expensive mechanism, it would have come to nothing, but its conditions are so simple, so heroic, so grand and perfectly exemplified in His own person that they apply at all times and in all places.

JOSEPH PARKER

May 9

> "I am sending you out like sheep among wolves. Therefore be as shrewd as snakes and as innocent as doves."
>
> MATTHEW 10:16

Jesus encouraged no illusions in His servants as to their success or what they would face. It is He who sends them among wolves; therefore He will protect them. A strange thing for a shepherd to do! A strange encouragement for the apostles on the threshold of their work! A strange theme to drape in a metaphor, but does not the very metaphor help to lighten the darkness of the picture as well as speak of His calmness. Surely the words would often come back to them when beset by the wolf pack with their white teeth gleaming and their howls filling the night. The sheep has no claws to wound with nor teeth to tear with and therefore is defenseless. The disciples are not promised that they will not be torn, but they are assured that even if they are, the Shepherd wills it and will not lose one of His flock. Whenever believers have been misguided enough to depart from Christ's law of endurance and to give blow for blow, they have lost their cause in the long run and hurt their own Christian life more than their enemies' bodies.

What is the Christian defense? Shrewdness like the serpent's but not the serpent's malice, harmlessness like the dove's but not without the other safeguard of "wisdom." The combination is a rare one, but a possible one, and the surest way to possess it is to live so close to Jesus that we shall be progressively changed into His likeness. Then our prudence will never degenerate into cunning nor our simplicity become blindness to dangers. Mark the fine sanity of that injunction, which not only permits but also enjoins prudent self-preservation, so long as it does not stoop to crooked policy and is saved from that by dovelike guilelessness. The Christian armor is meekness, unconquerable patience, and Christlikeness. To resist is to be beaten; to endure unretaliating is to be victorious. The victorious antagonist of savage enmity is patient meekness. "Do not be overcome by evil, but overcome evil with good" (Rom. 12:21).

ALEXANDER MACLAREN

May 10

*O*ur Lord had no dreams of the swift success of the gospel but realized the long, hard fight to which He was summoning His disciples. He knew the future in store for them, yet He knew that danger and death will not appall a soul that is touched into heroic self-forgetfulness by His love.

Gentile governors and kings will unite with Jewish councils and synagogues in common hatred against you. That is a grim prospect to set before a handful of Galilean peasants. But three little words from Jesus turn its terror into joy; it is "on my account," and that is enough. Jesus believed that those words would sweeten the bitterest cup and make cowards into heroes and send men and women to their deaths triumphant. History has proven that Jesus did not trust them too much. "On my account" remains for us the power that makes the crooked straight and the rough places plain, that nerves for suffering and impels to noble acts, that molds life and takes the sting out of death.

Nor is that the only encouragement given to the twelve, who might well be appalled at the coming prospect of standing before Gentile kings. Jesus seems to discern how they shrank as they listened, and with beautiful adaptation to their weakness, He interjects a great promise that for the first time presents the divine Spirit as dwelling in the disciples' spirits. The occasion of the dawning of that great Christian thought is very noteworthy, and not less so is the designation of the Spirit as "of your Father," with all the implications of paternal care and love that that name carries. Special crises bring special helps, and the martyrologies of all ages and lands, from Stephen outside the city wall to the most recent martyr, have attested the faithfulness of the Promiser.

ALEXANDER MACLAREN

"Be on your guard against men; they will hand you over to the local councils and flog you in their synagogues. On my account you will be brought before governors and kings as witnesses to them and to the Gentiles. But when they arrest you, do not worry about what to say or how to say it. At that time you will be given what to say, for it will not be you speaking, but the Spirit of your Father speaking through you."

MATTHEW 10:17–20

"Brother will betray brother to death, and a father his child; children will rebel against their parents and have them put to death. All men will hate you because of me."

MATTHEW 10:21–22

In sending men forth to their duty, Jesus Christ shows them clearly what they will certainly have to bear. He does not promise them a down pillow; He does not promise them genteel society; He does not offer them any social bribe. There is no mistaking the lot of the true Christian witness. Goodness is always hateful to evil; the beasts that gather together in the nighttime hate the light—you torment them if you turn a sudden blaze upon them, and they will display animosity and resentment. Goodness can never establish itself anywhere without a battle; it is a daily battle. You cannot take upon you a new habit without having to fight for every inch of ground you make; you cannot exert yourself to throw off slothfulness or any self-indulgence without having to fight for the end.

What is true in discipline is true in the educational and moral conquest of the world. In proportion as you are adaptive in your methods of going into any company, taking on its manners and speaking its language, will you have an easy time of it; but if you have a grand program, a rousing and elevating purpose that disrupts the established method, you will go as sheep among wolves. Do not imagine that goodness is peaceful. Goodness is controversial. It always sends a sword upon the earth and kindles a fire, dividing families. It sets the father against the belief of the child, and the child against the father, and the brother against the brother, and it kindles a great fire upon the earth. We have succeeded now in putting the fire out and have come to the age of courteous civilities and tender regard for one another's evil habits. The old goodness, the Christ-goodness, fought every day, not with a blade of steel but with that keener blade of conviction, enthusiasm, sacrifice that counted not its life dear unto itself that it might win the battle against evil and darkness and corruption.

JOSEPH PARKER

May 12

*J*esus Christ gives His disciples the infinite consolation of knowing that when they suffer for His sake, it is because they are His followers. Christian disciples are bound to the same love of Jesus as the main motive for all their actions, to the same stripping off of dignity and lowly equalizing of themselves with those below them whom they would help, and to bringing them the cleansing and the purity that Christ gives.

A Christian life all moved and energized by self-giving love, which comes among men to make them better and purer, influencing them in the direction of ridding their foul hearts of filth—how different is that from our lives? What a grim contrast much of our lives is to the Master's example and command! Did you ever strip yourself of anything to make some poor creature a little purer and more like the Savior? Did you ever drop your dignity and go down to the low levels to lift up the people who are there? Do others see anything in your life of the Master's example of pouring out His life to make poor hearts pure and like His own?

Discipleship is likeness to Jesus Christ in conduct. There is no discipleship worth naming that does not, at least, attempt that likeness. What is the use of a man's saying he is the disciple of Incarnate Love if his whole life is incarnate selfishness? Why say you follow Jesus when you come to do your own will and never do God's will at all, or rarely so, and then reluctantly and with many a murmur? A disciple is not one whose life contradicts the life of his Master and disobeys His word.

"It is enough for the student to be like his teacher." This saying is not only a law but also a promise, for it assures us that our efforts shall not fail but will progressively succeed and lead on at last to our becoming what we behold, being conformed to Jesus and like the Master to whose wisdom we profess to listen.

ALEXANDER MACLAREN

"A student is not above his teacher, nor a servant above his master. It is enough for the student to be like his teacher, and the servant like his master."

MATTHEW 10:24–25

"Do not be afraid of them.... Do not be afraid of those who kill the body but cannot kill the soul. Rather, be afraid of the One who can destroy both soul and body in hell. So don't be afraid; you are worth more than many sparrows."

MATTHEW 10:26, 28, 31

These three encouragements come as the assurance of the certain, ultimate, worldwide manifestation of hidden things. He spoke to a handful of men in an obscure corner of the world who were commissioned to sound out the kingdom of God. But the spark is going to be a blaze, and the whisper to become a shout that fills the world. Therefore we should never allow fear to make us silent.

A second reason for fearlessness is the limitation of the enemy's power to hurt, reinforced by the thought that while the penalties that man can inflict for faithfulness are only transitory and incapable of harming the true self, the consequences of unfaithfulness fling the whole man, body and soul, down to utter ruin. There is a fear that makes cowards and apostates; there is a fear that makes heroes and apostles. He who fears God, with the awe that has no torment and is akin to love, is afraid of nothing and of no man. That holy and blessed fear drives out all others, as fire draws the heat out of a burn. He who serves Christ is lord of the world; he who fears God fronts the world and is not afraid.

The last reason for fearlessness touches a tender chord and discloses a gracious thought of God as Father. Jesus looked with pity on the difficulties His followers would face and stayed Himself on the thought of the all-embracing working of God. The very dying sparrow, with broken wing, had its place in that universal care. But the immanent God is "your Father," and because of that sonship, know that His love embraces you, no matter what happens to you. God puts our tears in His bottle, and He writes our names in His book of life. Therefore, do not fear.

ALEXANDER MACLAREN

May 14

*I*f this word is true, that the hairs of our head are all num-bered, and if providence provides for God's people all things necessary for this life and godliness and arranges everything with infinite and unerring wisdom, what manner of persons ought we to be?

"Even the very hairs of your head are all numbered."

MATTHEW 10:30

We should certainly be a bold race of people. What have we to fear? We are out at sea, the waves are dashing against the ship, she reels to and fro. Other men shake because they think this is all chance. We, however, believe that the tempest is in the hand of God, and we can confide in our God in the midst of the storm. It is for us to be peaceful and calm. Why should we shake? In all convulsions in the world, in all temporal distress and danger, it is for us to stand calm and collected, looking boldly on. Our confidence should be very much the same—in comparison with the man who is not a believer in providence—as the confidence of some experienced surgeon who, when he is going through an operation, sees something very marvelous yet never shudders at it. We are to say, "I know God is here, and I am His child, and this is all working for my good. Therefore, I will not be afraid, though the earth is removed and though the mountains be carried into the midst of the sea."

There is never a reason to be frightened at every little thing, to always imagine the worst is coming, and to live in dreadful fear. If you have evils today, do not multiply them by fearing those of tomorrow. "Therefore do not worry about tomorrow, for tomorrow will worry about itself. Each day has enough trouble of its own" (Matt. 6:34).

If good things come, thank God for them, but do not set your heart upon them. If good things go, thank God that He has taken them Himself, and still bless His name. Bear all. He who feels that everything that comes to pass is according to God's will has a great mainstay to his soul. He need not be shaken to and fro by every wind that blows. This is an anchor cast into the sea.

CHARLES SPURGEON

May 15

"Whoever acknowl-

edges me before men,

I will also acknowl-

edge him before my

Father in heaven. But

whoever disowns me

before men, I will dis-

own him before my

Father in heaven."

MATTHEW 10:32–33

This marvelous promise follows the preceding thought of a watchful Father's care, extending like a great invisible hand over the true disciple. No matter what may befall his witnesses, the extremist disaster shall not rob them of their reward. The river of the confessor's life may plunge underground and be lost amid persecutions, but it will emerge again into the brighter sunshine on the other side of the mountains.

The confession of Jesus Christ as Lord will be rewarded as long as it is maintained in one's life, and the denial is seen as a cowardly attempt to save one's skin at the cost of treason to Jesus. But the temptation seldom comes to us in that severe form. It is perhaps easier to marshal up the courage to face martyrdom than to resist the more specious flattery of the world, especially when it calls itself religious. The light laugh of scorn, the silent pressure to lower the standard of Christian character, the discrimination in the business place and public life, make many a man's tongue lie silent. The sun has more power than the tempest to make the pilgrim drop his garment. But the duty remains the same for all ages. Every man is bound to make the deepest springs of his life visible and to stand to his convictions, whatever they are. If he does not, his convictions will disappear like a piece of ice hid in a hot hand. The obligation lies with infinitely increased weight on Christ's servants, and the consequences of failure are in exact proportion of the greater preciousness of their faith.

The wonder is that our confession of Christ will be endorsed by His confession of us! What a hope for all who have trem-blingly, and aware of their unworthiness, ventured to declare Jesus as their King! He will say, "Yes, this man is Mine, and I am His." That will be glory, honor, blessedness, life, heaven.

ALEXANDER MACLAREN

May 16

We greatly impoverish the meaning of these great and penetrating words if we understand by "loses his life" only the actual surrender of physical life. It is not only the martyr on whose bleeding brow the crown of life is gently placed. There is a daily dying that is continually required of all believers and is, perhaps, as hard as the brief passage of martyrdom by which some enter into rest, for the true losing of life is the slaying of self, and that has to be done day by day and not once for all. We must take the knife into our own hands and strike, and that not once, but ever, right on through our Christian life, for by natural disposition, we are all inclined to make our own selves to be our own centers, our own aims, the objects of our trust, our own law.

We are meant to live in the absolute submission to the will of God and to make that obstinate part of our nature meek and obedient and pliable as the clay in the potter's hands. It means the suppression and possibly the cutting off of appetites, passions, desires, inclinations. It means the hallowing of all aims, the devotion and consecration of all activities. It means the surrender and the stewardship of all possessions to Christ.

I know how hard it is to escape from the tyrannous dominion of self. There is nothing that will wholly dethrone self but the enthroning of Jesus Christ. Self's dominion is too deeply rooted to be abolished by any enthusiasms, however noble they may be, except the one that kindles its undying torch at the flame of Christ's own love. We must let His love and sacrifice come in like a flooding river that cleanses out the filth and floats it all away. The one possibility for complete deliverance from the dominion of self is to be found in the words "for my sake." To find our life in Jesus, to hear these words whispered from His beloved lips, is deliverance indeed.

ALEXANDER MACLAREN

"Whoever finds his life will lose it, and whoever loses his life for my sake will find it."

MATTHEW 10:39

May 17

After Jesus had finished instructing his twelve disciples, he went on from there to teach and preach in the towns of Galilee.

MATTHEW 11:1

Jesus sent out His disciples two by two; then He goes out alone. The groups of two going out was essentially a new school of preparation for them. Even now the Master is signaling a major change to them, forcing them to no longer depend on Him to do the work of ministry as they go out without Him. Yet He does not ask them to go alone, as He does, for they still need each other.

He went forth to preach and to teach and did not sit at home for the purpose of receiving reports from those whom He had sent out. He did not say, "I have delegated the kingdom of heaven to twelve men, and I will rest until they return to tell Me what success it meets in the world." He had been the Master giving commandment and charge, and now He was Himself the slave of slaves. He made Himself of no reputation; He took upon Himself the form of a servant; and He went out to preach the gospel that He had been putting in charge of others. I would rather have heard the Master than the servant; I would rather have had one glance of Him than have spent a lifetime in the sight of the twelve.

But this is not His way: He was with us visibly for a little while, and as a cloud received Him out of our sight, He said, "And surely I am with you always, to the very end of the age" (Matt. 28:20). The Almighty did not allow Himself long incarnation among us: This was His wisdom. It would never have done to have looked upon the physical form longer than men were permitted to do. These revelations are timed: God turns over the pages lovingly, not arbitrarily. He knows precisely when to take His disciples out of one school and send them to another, and he who yields himself lovingly to the guidance of God will remain in that school until he is ready for the revelations and exhortations of some broader and nobler teacher. Yield yourself to divine inspiration: Keep down your impatience as you would keep down a wild beast, and rest peacefully, waitingly, patiently upon God.

JOSEPH PARKER

May 18

John was in prison, in that gloomy fortress of Machaerus that Herod had rebuilt both for a sinful pleasure house and for an impregnable refuge among the severe cliffs of Moab. The halls of luxurious vice and the walls of defense are gone today, but the dungeons are there still, with the holes in the masonry into which the bars were fixed to which the prisoners were chained. No wonder that in the foul atmosphere of a dark dungeon the spirit that had been so undaunted in the free air of the desert began to flag, nor that even he who had seen the fluttering dove descend on Christ's head and had pointed to Him as the Lamb of God experienced his own share of doubts.

We note that John's questions arise when he hears what Christ is doing. We need only recall John's earlier testimony to understand how these works did not seem to line up with his anticipations for the Messiah. Where is the ax that was to be laid at the root of the trees or the fan that was to winnow out the chaff? Where is the fiery spirit that he had foretold? This gentle Healer is not the theocratic judge of his warning prophecies. He is tender and nurturing rather than felling the barren trees. So John began to wonder whether he had been premature in his recognition. Evidently he remained firm in the conviction of Christ's being sent from God and was ready to accept His answer as conclusive, but there is no mistaking his puzzlement by the unfulfilled prophecies.

We may well take to heart the lesson of the fluctuation possible to the firmest faith and pray to be enabled to hold fast what we have. We are wise to do as John did and go straight to Jesus. John was right in believing that Christ must come to judge, but he was wrong in stumbling at the gentleness. Both are needed to make Christ's full character. John did not need to look for someone else, but he did need to realize a second coming of the same Jesus, but then with His ax in His pierced hand.

ALEXANDER MACLAREN

When John heard in prison what Christ was doing, he sent his disciples to ask him, "Are you the one who was to come, or should we expect someone else?"

MATTHEW 11:2–3

Jesus replied, "Go

back and report to

John what you hear

and see: The blind

receive sight, the lame

walk, those who have

leprosy are cured, the

deaf hear, the dead are

raised, and the good

news is preached to

the poor."

MATTHEW 11:4–5

$\mathscr{S}$ee how Jesus Christ treated this inquiry concerning His role as the Messiah. He called attention to the very works that seemed to be a problem. This was Christ's answer, not meta-physical, not doctrinal, not a matter of opinion elaborately stated and eloquently discussed, but facts, provable results, active and noble beneficence. A man's work should praise him; a man's life should be his vindication. You may be ruined by compli-mentary testimonials; you must be your own testimonial if you would vindicate your claim to any degree of authority and sacred influence in society. It is not what others say about you but what you do yourself that must speak for you. Let your own energy, force, wisdom, love, sanctified and inspired from heaven, make such a mark that the doubter himself shall be asked to consider it and decide as to its value.

This is what the Church must do. The Church cannot live in her divinity books. The Church can make no impression upon the age so long as she indulges in merely wordy controversy. What is the Church doing? Are the lepers being cleansed and the blind receiving their sight? Are the deaf hearing and the dead being raised to life? This is the only proof the Church need supply for her divine inspiration and authority, and all this can be done today. These miracles were introductory, and we narrow Jesus' meaning if we see these only as physical occur-rences. Christ said that He was expecting the Church to do greater works than He did. The bad man is a leper, the one who is in intellectual error is the blind man, any sinner is a dead man in desperate need of the good news of the gospel. When the Church works these miracles, she need not defend her credentials and write a great deal about her history and lit-erature. Her true answer is on the public thoroughfares; it is in the homes, lives, and businesses of men and women.

JOSEPH PARKER

May 20

To John the Baptist, locked away in the deep depression of a prison, these words came as comfort to a mind struggling with doubt. The same is true today. I constantly see believers wrestling with doubts who need to receive this word in their hearts.

"Blessed is the man who does not fall away on account of me."

Matthew 11:6

For some it occurs when the novelty of their experience wears off. The special services end, the excitement fades, and they wonder whether anything has changed. Others thought that if they just believed in Jesus, the conflict with sin would be over and they would feel happy forever. They dreamed that if they simply drew their sword all Canaan would be conquered in an hour. Very soon they found it is not so. A sudden victory would suit them, but to carry a cross before winning a crown is not to their liking.

Some have met an opposition they did not expect from their adversaries, while from their friends they have not met with all the respect that they think they ought to have. They did not expect to be laughed at or jeered at. They never counted the cost of following Jesus. Persecution arises, and many are offended. Others are offended because they find that faith involves more self-denial than they had reckoned upon. Over and over, His precepts touch upon their consciences and gall them.

I have known many fine believers who took such a deep offense at what another believer did to them that they allowed that offense to affect their relationship with Christ. An unkind word, a betrayal and an accusation, a wet blanket thrown over us, and we want to give up whatever we are doing. Blessed is he who cannot be offended in this way. Do not be scandalized at Christ on their account.

Look at the life of any saint and you will find one who went through these struggles. Stand firm, press forward, refuse to be disgusted or discouraged. And remember that opposition is very often the sign of coming success.

CHARLES SPURGEON

May 21

"What did you go out into the desert to see? A reed swayed by the wind? If not, what did you go out to see? A man dressed in fine clothes? No, those who wear fine clothes are in kings' palaces. Then what did you go out to see? A prophet? Yes, I tell you, and more than a prophet."

MATTHEW 11:7–9

Jesus proceeds to speak about John as his disciples are leaving. One wonders how so great a Speaker as Jesus will speak about any human creature. He speaks of John in noble terms; His eulogy seems to fill the sky; there is no word too good to be spent upon the character of this modern Elijah.

First, Jesus proceeds to correct the notions of His time concerning John. "What did you go out in the desert to see? A reed swayed by the wind, a man dressed in fine clothes, a prophet?" This is the transition through which every honest man passes when he comes into new social conditions. No minister can arise today who should be enabled by the Lord to do anything who would not pass through precisely these three periods of criticism, unless he died under one of the first two and never came to his due recognition.

Thus, a reed swayed with the wind, a nine-days' wonder, a little fluttering thing in the air, here and gone—that is the first criticism that is passed on any great reformer or noble teacher or self-sacrificing soul. A man clothed in fine clothes, literally, that is the second criticism. Such a man is working for himself; he is doing it all with a purpose; he is trying to make his bed soft, his house rich, his position strong: He has an aim in all this. Time rolls on, and his followers begin reluctantly to say, "He is a prophet." They can turn around as completely as that, and such is our encouragement.

Walk on, persevere, hold the plow handle with all your force; keep at it, John the Baptists, and you pass the period of being a swaying reed, a man clothed in fine clothing—you shall be a prophet, and a greater voice shall say, "Yes, I tell you, and more than a prophet." God give us the strength, patience, and courage to go through the long tunnel that leads to the warm summer sun.

JOSEPH PARKER

May 22

Jesus lays bare the secret of the Baptist's power, and in His praise of John we find the keys to effective service to Christ.

First, Christ praises John's great personal character. He recalls the scenes of popular enthusiasm when all Israel streamed out to the desert preacher. A small man could not have made such an impact. What drew the crowds? It was the qualities required of anyone for spiritual power. The first essential is heroic firm- ness. It was not reeds swaying in the wind by Jordan's banks that drew the crowds. John's whole career was marked by decisiveness, constancy, and courage. Nothing can be done worth doing in the world without a wholesome discipline that keeps a man true to his convictions and tasks, no matter how the wind blows in his face. Such a man must be sure of his message and of himself. The multitudes will not flock to listen to someone devoid of the accent of conviction, nor will truths feebly grasped touch the lips with fire.

Next, John manifested an indifference to material comfort. Silken courtiers do not haunt the desert. If the gaunt ascetic had been a self-indulgent epicure, his voice would never have shaken a nation. The least breath of suspicion that a preacher is such a man ends his power, and ought to end it, for the love of the flesh eats the heart out of goodness and makes the eyes too heavy to see visions.

Third, our Lord speaks of John's great office. He was a prophet. The dim recognitions that God spoke in his fiery words had drawn the crowds, weary of teachers in whose endless jangle and jargon of sophistry was no inspiration. The voice of a man who gets his message first-hand from God has a ring in it that even dull ears detect as something genuine. Alas, for the bewil- dering babble of echoes and the scarcity of voices today!

ALEXANDER MACLAREN

"What did you go out into the desert to see? A reed swayed by the wind? If not, what did you go out to see? A man dressed in fine clothes? No, those who wear fine clothes are in kings' palaces. Then what did you go out to see? A prophet? Yes, I tell you, and more than a prophet."

MATTHEW 11:7–9

"For John came neither

eating nor drinking,

and they say, 'He has

a demon.' The Son of

Man came eating and

drinking, and they say,

'Here is a glutton and

a drunkard, a friend of

tax collectors and

"sinners."' But wis-

dom is proved right by

her actions."

MATTHEW 11:18–19

$\mathcal{E}$very ministry has been rejected, whether ascetic or friendly—each has in turn been despised and rejected of men. You cannot please men who are determined not to be pleased. Men will not look over the fogwall of their prejudices. Here is a minister who will please you; he neither eats nor drinks improperly—what is your judgment? "He has a demon." Here is a friendly man; he comes eating and drinking—what do you say? "A glutton and a drunkard, a friend of tax collectors and 'sinners.'" The truth is, you do not want the minister.

I speak now of those whose hearts are of stone, whose will is marked by invincible obstinance. Will they stick at anything in their road? Not they. "He has a demon"—destroy his character. "He is a drunk and a friend of sinners"—destroy his character. There is nothing too bad for the bad man to do. He would uncrown the monarch and set fire to the throne, he would assault the reputation of angels rather than fail in his malignant purpose.

Blessed Savior, this is Your defense of Your servant. Oh, what shielding! Oh, what gentle protection, what ample security, what a noble eulogy! He is the same yesterday, today, and forever. If we try to serve Him, though our dispensation is brief and small, He will recognize our efforts, and no eulogy shall be so sweet and so full of satisfaction as His will be. Is He your Master? Do you love His name? Do you abide by His cross? Do you live by His Spirit and display His love? Then, though some may say you have a devil and are mad, He will come with the explanation, He will vindicate every servant of His, and your enemies will be clothed with shame, and upon your head shall the crown of His favor flourish.

JOSEPH PARKER

May 24

There is a new tone in the voice of Jesus Christ. All that has yet come out of Him has been an utterance of love and hope and hospitality, great offers of healing and peace and joy. Now comes the tone of reproach which came as a result of labor not misapplied but unworthily received.

To understand in some degree the pathos of this reproach, the bitterness of this cry, we go straight to the reason Jesus gave: because they did not repent. It was not petulance on the part of Christ; there was no tone of merely personal disappointment; it seemed as if He had made the cities worse rather than better; it seemed as if they would have been better if they had never seen Him, for having seen Him, they rejected Him with contempt. No man can hear of Christ, receive an offer of divine mercy, see any display of divine love, without its being a crisis in his personal history. And if he does not accept the offer that was made, it were better for him that the offer had never been presented.

The object that Christ had in view in working miracles was to bring men to repentance. They were wrought not to startle, to please, to amuse, or to gratify curiosity but to bring the heart to contrition. They were assaults upon unbelief, appeals to obstinacy. They were forms and methods of gospel preaching.

Understand, therefore, in reading the miracles, that every one of them has a moral issue in view in the scheme and providence of God. Regarded by themselves, they stun the mind and excite many eager questions, but placed in their right atmosphere and read in the high light of their generous purpose, the miracles are but the emphasis with which divine messages were delivered. The same principle is true in our lives and churches whenever God does a work of power. Let us never fail to heed its message.

JOSEPH PARKER

Then Jesus began to denounce the cities in which most of his miracles had been performed, because they did not repent.

Matthew 11:20

May 25

"Woe to you, Korazin! Woe to you, Bethsaida! If the miracles that were performed in you had been performed in Tyre and Sidon, they would have repented long ago in sackcloth and ashes. But I tell you, it will be more bearable for Tyre and Sidon on the day of judgment than for you."

MATTHEW 11:21–22

*O*ur Lord takes these two little fishing villages, parallels and contrasts them with the two great maritime cities of Tyre and Sidon, and says that these insignificant places have far more light than those had. Then He isolates Capernaum, a place of more importance and His own usual settled residence, and contrasts it with the long-buried Sodom, proclaiming the superiority of the illumination that fell on the more modern three. Why? Because they had Moses, the prophets, the law and temple? By no means. Because they had Him. Jesus sets Himself forth as being the highest and clearest of all the revelations that God has made to the world and asserts that in Him, in His character and deeds, men ought to find motives—motives sweeter, tenderer, stronger than any that the world has ever known—that should bow them in penitence before God. There is no light so bright as to catch a glimpse of the perfect sweetness and perfect beauty of the perfect Jesus Christ.

Might I note that while they stood but in the morning twilight, you and I stand in the noonday blaze. They knew nothing about His cross, death, resurrection, ascension. We stand in the very focus and fountain of the heavenly radiance. A whole Christ, a crucified Christ, a risen Christ, an ascended Christ, a Christ who is the Lord of the Spirit, a Christ who through the centuries is saving and blessing men, a Christ who can point to two thousand years and say, "This is My work, insofar as it is good and noble." This Christ shines with a clearer evidence than the Miracle-worker of Capernaum and Bethsaida. They might be pardoned for doubting whether the light that shone from Him was sunshine or candle, but men today are without excuse.

ALEXANDER MACLAREN

The men of these three little fishing towns were not sinners above other Galileans of their day. Their crime was that they did nothing. No persecution is recorded as having been raised against Christ by them; there were no scornful words said by her. They simply stolidly stood like some black rock in the sunshine and let the sunshine pour down upon them and remained grim and black as ever. That was all.

The thing that brings the severest rebuke from Christ is not angry antagonism but the sleek, passive apathy that is never touched deeper than its ears by the message of God's Word. It is not difficult to do. You have simply to do what some of you are doing and have been doing all your lives as to Christianity, and that is—nothing! You have simply to acquiesce politely and respectfully and say you believe, and there is the end of it. You listen, listen, and listen until your systems have become so habituated to the gospel that it does not produce the least effect. It all runs off you like rain off waterproof. You have water-proofed your consciences and your spiritual susceptibilities by long listening and doing nothing.

Dear friend, we stand in the blaze of the gospel light. Our familiarity with Jesus Christ may be our ruin. Neglect of Christ on your part will bring deeper woes on your head than the people of Capernaum pulled down upon theirs. The brighter the sunshine, the louder the thunder and the fiercer the lightning; the longer the summer day, the longer the winter night; the closer the comet comes to the sun, the farther away it plunges at the other extremity of its orbit into space and darkness. I desire, if I can, to wake some of you to look realities for once in the face, and to be sure of this, that retribution is proportioned to light, and the sin of sins is the rejection of Jesus Christ.

ALEXANDER MACLAREN

"And you, Capernaum, will you be lifted up to the skies? No, you will go down to the depths. If the miracles that were performed in you had been performed in Sodom, it would have remained to this day."

MATTHEW 11:23

May 27

"But I tell you that it will be more bearable for Sodom on the day of judgment than for you."

MATTHEW 11:24

There is a glowing and final proof of the eternal truthfulness of Christ in the fact that He never concealed His own failures. No impostor can afford to make the worst of his case. Impostors magnify their successes; through one success, impostors try to force their way to others. Impostors live in grand reports; they publish their statistics to an admiring world—they never tell their failures. Truth alone loves truth. Jesus Christ never gave us a colored picture of His successes, never hid His disappointments. He did not tell the disciples that Chorazin, Bethsaida, and Capernaum were much better than they looked, and there were wonderful instances of encouragement. No, He was true, He spoke the truth, He confessed the terrific tragedy of His soul's disappointment. "O Jerusalem, Jerusalem, you who kill the prophets and stone those sent to you, how often I have longed to gather your children together, as a hen gathers her chicks under her wings, but you were not willing" (Matt. 23:37).

You will always find Christ consistent with His own truthfulness. He has nothing to color, pervert, distort, tinge with glowing tints, so that He may win further support. He says, "I have toiled but reaped nothing. Though they saw miracles, they did not repent. I came unto my own, and my own received me not." There is a ring of solemn truthfulness in all these declarations. Impostors would have seen the glitter and called it gold. Christ saw the failure and upbraided those who had caused His ministry to return to Him as a bitter disappointment.

It is possible to sin Christ away. I know of no ghastlier sight than the grand external exaltation associated with moral perversity. Jesus sees us as we are; He conceals nothing of the ghastly reality; He makes no false reading of character; He makes no miscalculation of human force and value. Oh, that upbraiding face. Oh, that upbraiding voice—may we never hear it!

JOSEPH PARKER

May 28

*W*ise and learned religious men interpret the great heart of God not by their own hearts but by their intellects. Then, postponing the obedience that alone can give power to the understanding, they press upon men's minds their low interpretations of the will of the Father rather than by their own example impressing the doing of that will upon their hearts. They are the slaves of the letter in all its weakness and imperfection—and will be until the Spirit and the Word, the Spirit of obedience, shall set them free.

Terribly has the gospel of Jesus suffered in the mouths of the wise and the learned! How would it be faring now had its first messages been committed to persons of great repute instead of the simple fishermen? From the first, we would have had a system founded on a human interpretation of the divine gospel rather than the gospel itself. As it is, we have had one miserable system after another usurping its place. But, thank God, the gospel remains!

Had the wise and the learned been the confidants of God, the letter would have usurped the place of the spirit, and a system of religion, with its rickety, rancid plan of salvation, would have been put in the place of the living Christ. The eternal Son, our living Brother, would have been utterly hidden from the tearful eye and aching hearts of the weary and heavy laden.

But the Father revealed His things to babes because the babes were His own little ones, uncorrupted by the wisdom or the cares of the world and therefore able to receive them. The babes are near enough to their Father in heaven and thereby able to interpret the words of the Son. Quickly will the Father seal the old bond when the Son Himself, the first of the babes, comes to lead the children out of the lovely "shadows of eternity" into the land of the "white celestial thought."

GEORGE MACDONALD

At that time Jesus said, "I praise you, Father, Lord of heaven and earth, because you have hidden these things from the wise and learned, and revealed them to little children. Yes, Father, for this was your good pleasure."

MATTHEW 11:25–26

May 29

"Come to me, all you who are weary and burdened, and I will give you rest."

MATTHEW 11:28

To every toiling, heavy laden sinner, Jesus says, "Come to Me...and...rest." But there are many toiling, heavy laden believers, too. For them this same invitation is meant. Note well the word of Jesus if you are heavy laden with your service, and do not mistake it. It is not, "Go, labor on," as perhaps you imagine. On the contrary, it is stop, turn back, "Come to Me and rest." Never, never did Christ send a heavy laden one to work; never, never did He send a hungry one, a weary one, a sick or sorrowing one *away* on any service. For such the Bible only says, "Come, come, come."

The first evangelist of the New Testament records the invitation on which we are writing. The last gives us the similar offer: "If anyone is thirsty, let him come to me and drink" (John 7:37). The New Testament almost closes with the words: "Whoever is thirsty, let him come; and whoever wishes, let him take the free gift of the water of life" (Rev. 22:17).

How many of the Lord's redeemed people have spent hours and days or even months in sorrow and self-reproach from some imagined duty that they did not have the courage or strength to perform, heavy laden all the time! How many can tell of the pressure they have felt to speak to another person about his soul but could not. And how many have done *far worse:* have spoken when they had no message from God and have done harm rather than good. Oh, how different it would have been had they but first come to Jesus and found rest and living water; and then, when the waters were welling up within, the rivers would have flowed naturally and irrepressibly, and the happy countenance would have said more than the heartfelt words were uttering! No one would then have looked at the face of the speaker and *felt,* "What a dreadful religion his must be!" For the "Come" is intended not to exclude the "Go" but to prepare the way for it.

HUDSON TAYLOR

 *May 30*

To be at peace—no longer tossed up and down in the soul—
to be secure, peaceful, joyful, happy, is worth mountains of diamonds. A man's life does not consist of the abundance of the
things that he possesses: Many a poor person is vastly happier
than the possessor of wide estates, for peace comes not with
property but with contentment. The music of peace is not the
jingle of gold and silver. Sweeter bells sound in the pardoned
heart than ever wealth can ring. The herb called heart's–ease
often grows in tiny gardens, and happy is the person who wears
it in his bosom. Rest of soul, for value, outshines all pearls and
rubies, which Jesus promises to give to all who come to Him
for it. Oh, rare peace that comes from the Prince of Peace!

There is no one so fit to run the race of life as the man who has
unloaded his cares and enjoys peace of mind. The man who is
happily restful toward God is the man to fight the battle of life. I
have known a man losing money on the market to step aside
and, breathing a prayer to God, come back calm and composed;
and whereas before, he was ready to plunge into speculation
and lose terribly, he has come back at rest and been in a fit
frame for dealing with his fellowmen. Bring solid rest to the
heart, and you have given the man a fulcrum upon which he
may rest the lever with which he can lift the heaviest weight.

When a man is afraid to die, he may well be afraid to live. He
who cannot look death in the face—and cannot look God in the
face—is a man who has a latent weakness about him that will
rob him of force and courage in the heat of battle. The peace of
God serves as both arms and armor; it is both battle–ax and
breastplate. It will be your heart's comfort and your hand's
strength. It will be good for day and night, for calm and storm.
It has a thousand uses, and all of them are essential to spiritual
well–being.

CHARLES SPURGEON

"Come to me, all you who are weary and burdened, and I will give you rest."

MATTHEW 11:28

May 31

> "Take my yoke upon you and learn from me, for I am gentle and humble in heart, and you will find rest for your souls."
>
> MATTHEW 11:29

It is very remarkable that this is the only passage in the whole New Testament in which the heart of Jesus is distinctly mentioned. "Gentle and humble" remove the fears of any who tremble to approach Him. The words describe His heart as opposed to quickness of anger, haughtiness of spirit, the pretended meekness and mock lowliness that have at times been imposed upon the world. They include a readiness to pardon all past offenses, a willingness to endure yet further offenses, and a welcoming of the lowest, most obscure, and despised of people with all their burdens and needs.

Jesus has in these two words, as with two masterful strokes of the brush, given us a perfect picture of His dear, gentle face, nay, not of His face but of His innermost heart. How I wonder that we are not all in love with Him. "Gentle and humble in heart"—these are two beauties that to sinners' eyes, when sinners know themselves, are the most lovely and fascinating attributes, such as charm their fears and chain their hearts. He who has eyes to see, let him behold the wonder, and looking, let him love.

I beg you to recollect who it is that speaks these words of Himself. As I listened to the verse, at first it spoke to me with a still, small voice and made me very glad. Then, like Moses at the bush, I came closer, but lest I should grow irreverent, it changed its tone, and I heard peal upon peal of thunder issuing from it as I listened to the words "I am." I heard in those words the incommunicable name Jehovah, the Self-existent One! Yet, as I listened awestruck to that thunder's crash, I felt the soft drops of eternal mercy fall upon my brow and heard again the gentle voice of Jesus saying, "Gentle and humble in heart." Jehovah Jesus is gentle, tender, and condescending. What a divine blending of glory and grace! Oh, it is marvelous! Words cannot tell it! Omnipotent, yet humble! Eternal God, yet a patient sufferer!

CHARLES SPURGEON

June 1

His call reaches to the very ends of the earth. This is the Lord's own form of His gospel, intensely personal and direct. "I have rest because I know the Father," He says. "Be meek and lowly of heart toward Him as I am. Let Him lay *my very own yoke* upon you. I do His will, not My own. Take on you the yoke that I wear; be His child like Me; become a babe to whom He can reveal His wonders. Then shall you find rest for your souls. You shall have the same peace I have; you will be weary and heavy laden no more."

Think of it a moment: to walk in the same yoke with Jesus, doing the same labor with Him! Nothing less than this is offered the man who would have rest in his soul, is required of the man who would know the Father, is by the Lord pressed upon him to whom He would give the same peace that pervades and sustains His own eternal heart.

But a yoke is for drawing. And what load is the Lord pulling? Surely it is the will of the eternal, the perfect Father.

How should the Father honor the Son but by giving Him His will to embody in deed, by bringing home His children to the Father's heart! Especially in this work must His yokefellow share. How to draw it, he must learn of Him who draws by his side.

Whoever, in the commonest duties that fall to him, does as the Father would have him do, bears his yoke along with Jesus; and the Father takes His help for the redemption of the world—for the deliverance of men from the slavery of their own rubbish-laden wagons into the liberty of God's children.

Bearing the same yoke with Jesus, the man and woman learn to walk step by step with Him, drawing the cart laden with the will of the Father of both, and rejoicing in the joy of Jesus. He lives for us; we must live for Him. The little ones must take their full share in the great Father's work.

GEORGE MACDONALD

"Take my yoke upon you and learn from me, for I am gentle and humble in heart, and you will find rest for your souls. For my yoke is easy and my burden is light."

MATTHEW 11:29–30

June 2

At that time Jesus went through the grainfields on the Sabbath. His disciples were hungry and began to pick some heads of grain and eat them. When the Pharisees saw this, they said to him, "Look! Your disciples are doing what is unlawful on the Sabbath."

MATTHEW 12:1–2

Jesus Christ treated the Jewish Sabbath in what the Pharisees thought was a rough manner. This was a continual subject of controversy between them. Perhaps no subject of a special kind occupies such difference of opinion between them. The fact was that Jesus was going to establish a Sabbath of His own, and He began to indicate its character by putting the new wine into the old Sabbath bottle and thus breaking it. Always be sure what law it is you are talking about, whether it is incidental and transient. Jesus also notes that by the letter of the law the priests profaned the Sabbath rest in the priestly duties yet they kept it in spirit.

The incidents described here show cases where Jesus believed it was necessary to override the ceremonial law. Hunger, both in His disciples and in David, has no ceremonial law: Where life is in danger, ceremony must go away. The consecrated bread for the priests is not so sacred that David and his followers break the spirit of the law by eating it.

Thus, again, you must distinguish between laws. Always remember that one law belongs to another, and the highest law of life is that man must be preserved. Man's highest interests must be consulted and secured. The law of necessity is above all laws of ceremony. This simplifies the whole Sabbath question if rightly accepted and applied. There are certain necessities that settle everything: What these necessities are must be left to the individual conscience to settle. Do not attempt to draw rules and schedules of observance—all that is mechanical. Life cannot be codified; inspiration is better than regulation. If we have the right spirit, we can easily decide the right action.

JOSEPH PARKER

June 3

The scribes and Pharisees were great readers of the law. They studied the sacred books continually, poring over each word and letter. They have left us a mass of wonderful notes upon the mere words of Holy Scripture that are of very little importance. They might have done the same thing upon another book for that matter, and the information would have been about as important as the facts that they so industriously collected concerning the letter of the Old Testament. They were intense readers of the law and were ready to pick a quarrel at the least inference to a contrary position to their interpretation, ready to use their knowledge as a bird of prey does its talons to tear and rend.

"Haven't you read"—a cutting question to the teachers of the law and Pharisees. Jesus insinuates that the greatest readers of the law then living have not read it at all. "If you had known what these words mean"—meaning, "Your eyes have gone over the words, and you have counted the letters and marked the position of each verse and word, yet you have not read it with any understanding." How tragic was their position to have totally missed the meaning!

Our point is that much apparent Bible reading is not Bible reading at all. The verses pass under the eye, and the sentences glide over the mind, but there is no true reading. One may as well turn the book upside down and spend the same time in looking at the characters in that direction. The soul does not light upon the truth and stay there. Such reading is not reading. Understanding the meaning is the essence of true reading. It is the spirit, the real inner meaning, that is sucked into the soul by which we are blessed and sanctified. We must try to make out, as far as our finite mind can grasp it, what God means in Scripture. Otherwise, we may kiss the book and have no love for its contents; we may reverence the letter and yet really have no devotion toward the Lord who spoke the word to us.

CHARLES SPURGEON

"Haven't you read...Or haven't you read in the Law...If you had known what these words mean..."

MATTHEW 12:3, 5, 7

June 4

"If you had known what these words mean, 'I desire mercy, not sacrifice,' you would not have condemned the innocent."

MATTHEW 12:7

Notice that as our Lord answers the Pharisees He does not question the authority of tradition nor ask where Moses had forbidden what His disciples were doing. Still less does He touch the sanctity of the Jewish Sabbath. He accepts their position for the time and gives them a perfect answer on their own ground. He speaks profound words that touch the deepest truth concerning His own person and His relations to men and that involve the destruction of all temples and rituals. He is all that the temple symbolized. Where He stands is holy ground, and all work done with reference to Him is worship. If, for His sake, His followers had broken a hundred Sabbath regulations, they are guiltless.

So far the Lord has been answering His opponents; now He attacks. The quotation from Hosea is often on His lips. Here He uses it to unmask the real motives of His assailants. Their murmuring came not from more religion but from less love. If they had a little more milk of human kindness in them, it would have died on their lips; if they had grasped the real meaning of the religion they professed, they would have learned that its soul was "mercy"—that is, of course, man's gentleness to man—and that sacrifice and ceremony were but the body, the help, and sometimes the hindrance of that soul. They would have understood the relative importance of disposition and of external worship as end and means and not have visited a mere breath of external order with a heat of condemnation only warranted by a sin against the former. Their judgment would have been more like God's if they had looked at those poor hungry men with merciful eyes and hearts rather than with eager scrutiny that delighted to find them tripping in a triviality of outward observance. What mountains of harsh judgment by Christ's own followers on each other would have been removed into the sea if the spirit of these great words had played upon them!

ALEXANDER MACLAREN

June 5

We used to have a lad here in London at Kennington Gate who would frequently get on the step of a carriage and exhibit his hands, which hung down as if his wrists were broken, and he would cry, "Poor boy! Poor boy!" and appeal to our compassion. I imagine this man to have a similar condition, where through paralysis or some other disease the life had drained from the hand, leaving it shriveled and useless. It had undoubtedly had a devastating effect on this man's life and work.

There sit the haughty, frowning Pharisees. You can easily imagine these fine-looking gentlemen, with fringes on their garments and phylacteries across their foreheads. There, too, are the scribes all wrapped up in their formal array—very grave and knowing men. People were almost afraid to look at them, they were so holy and so contemptuous. See, there they sit, like judges to try the Savior. Now, Christ does, as it were, single out this poor man with the withered hand to be His witness, and by His command He practically asks him which he will do—will he obey the Pharisees or Jesus? It is wrong to heal on the Sabbath day, say the Pharisees. What say you with the shriveled hand? If you agree with the Pharisees, you will decline to stretch out your hand; but if you agree with Jesus, you will be glad to be healed, Sabbath or no Sabbath. The man did as good as vote for Christ when he obeyed and broke ranks with the religious tyrants. When that act of decision is performed, then the healing comes.

What a very beautiful sight to see that limp hand, first hanging down and then stretched out. Do you see the blood begin to flow, the nerves gaining power, and the hand opening like a reviving flower. Oh, the delight of his sparkling eyes as his fingers begin to move! Then the look to the One who healed him!

If the Son shall make you free, you shall be free indeed!

CHARLES SPURGEON

A man with a shriveled hand was there. Looking for a reason to accuse Jesus, they asked him, "Is it lawful to heal on the Sabbath?" Then he said to the man, "Stretch out your hand." So he stretched it out and it was completely restored, just as sound as the other.

MATTHEW 12:10, 13

June 6

He said to them, "If any of you has a sheep and it falls into a pit on the Sabbath, will you not take hold of it and lift it out? How much more valuable is a man than a sheep! Therefore it is lawful to do good on the Sabbath."

MATTHEW 12:11–12

What a curious state of mind the Pharisees had—to believe that Christ could work miracles and to want Him to do one, not for pity's sake but to have evidence for accusing Him! How heartlessly careless of the poor sufferer they are! He for his part stands silent. Desire and faith have no part in evoking this miracle. Deadly hatred and calculating malignity ask for it. Having baited their hook and set the man with his shriveled hand in full view, the Pharisees get into their corners and wait for the event. It is a profound example of the absurdity and cruelty possible when religion is purely about outward observances. Nothing more completely hardens the heart and blinds the senses.

Here Jesus appeals to the natural sense of compassion rather than Scripture. His question takes it for granted that His hearers could answer it in only one way, yet the cold-blooded ingenuity of the rabbis answer it in another. Then Christ binds His first question with another, equally easy to answer. Man's superiority to animals makes His claim for help more impera-tive. Note that He does not say, "It is lawful to heal," but, "It is lawful to do good." Thus, He shows the true justification of healing, namely, that it was a beneficent act, and widening the scope to cover a whole class of cases. The principle is that the charitable assistance of men's needs, of whatever kind, is con-gruous with the true design of that day of rest. Have churches laid that lesson to heart? On the whole, it is to be observed that our Lord distinctly recognizes the obligation of the Sabbath, that He claims power over it, that He permits the pressure of one's own necessities and of others' need of help, to modify the man-ner of its observance, and that He leaves the application of these principles to the spiritual insight of His followers.

ALEXANDER MACLAREN

June 7

When at the word of Jesus of Nazareth the shriveled hand obeyed and became filled with its old human strength, little would the man care that other men—even rulers of synagogues, even teachers of the law and the Pharisees—should question the uprightness of the Healer. The power that restored the gift of God and completed humanity must be of God. Theological arguments may rage, but the man whose hand was restored whole as the other knew it fitting that his hands should match. They might bewilder him with words about commandments and observance, but they could not keep his heart from glad-ness; and being glad, whom should he praise but God? The hand was now as God had meant it to be. Nor could he behold the face of Jesus and doubt that such a man could do only that which was right. God had set him free.

Here, plainly by the record, our Lord gave the man his share, not of mere acquiescence but of active will, in the miracle. If a man is a child of God, he must have a share in the works of the Father. Without such a share in the work as faith gives, the cure will be of little avail. "Stretch out your hand," said the Healer; and the man made the effort. The shriveled hand obeyed and was no more withered. In the act came the cure, without which the act had been confined to the will and had never taken form in the outstretching. The same is true in all spiritual redemption.

In every man, the power by which he does the commonest things is the power of God. The power is not of us. Our power does it, but we do not make the power. This, plain as it is, remains the hardest lesson for a man to learn with convic-tion and thanksgiving. For God has, as it were, put us just so far away from Him that we can exercise the divine thing in us, our own will, in returning toward our source. This is a truth no man can understand, feel, or truly acknowledge, save in proportion as he has become one with his perfect origin, the will of God.

GEORGE MACDONALD

Then he said to the man, "Stretch out your hand." So he stretched it out and it was completely restored, just as sound as the other.

MATTHEW 12:13

June 8

But the Pharisees went out and plotted how they might kill Jesus. Aware of this, Jesus withdrew from that place.

MATTHEW 12:14–15

*B*ecause Jesus had broken the Sabbath, according to the Pharisees, they plotted His death. It is the way of passionate men that they overstep themselves and show by the severity of their penalties some sign of the errors of their supposed piety. This was so extreme that by its own exaggeration, it broke itself and became impiety. But what could you expect from men who actually wrote in plain letters that to eat with unclean hands was more criminal than homicide? It is thus that healing on the Sabbath falls into Pharisaic impiety when it is left without a divine and living center; that is what we come to in the absence of a legitimate and adequate authority. Our morality becomes offensive; we rearrange it: We put it in new lights and place it at new angles, and we make experiments of it, and we run it through all the gamut of our own imagination until it becomes the wildest farce, the most consummate and intolerable nuisance. We want a standard authority, a court of appeal, and a spirit that interprets the law with all the breadth of poetry and yet with all the clearness and narrowness of the highest rectitude. This law and this spirit we find only in Him who is the Son of Man.

When Jesus saw the danger, He withdrew. This was the true courage; it was no use opposing physical force to physical force. The man whose life is founded upon a great plan does not live by mere surprises or allow himself to stoop to another's level. He removes the occasion; he will not even lead his enemies into temptation; he can always get out of the way. This was part of the wisdom of Christ, that He should not bring His enemies into temptation to kill Him. He kept back force by that subtlest and mightiest of all forces, true prudence, for it is not in your fist; that is the lowest of weapons. It is in wisdom, compassion, abstention from violence, in the negativeness that simply withdraws and calmly waits.

JOSEPH PARKER

June 9

*J*esus withdrew from the danger of the Pharisees, but He did not withdraw alone. The multitudinous heart knew Christ; the sectarian heart hated Him.

Realistically, the story might well have read that Jesus was so distressed over His reception by the religious officials that He fell into a great depression, His lips went shut in stubborn silence, and His hand was never put out to bless again, falling in paralysis at his side. Rather, it reads that "he healed all their sick." But there was a council whispering away in a distant city, and the meaning of the whisper was the death of this healing Man. He nevertheless kept on with His healing.

Let that be your policy and mine; if men hate us, let us heal all who come lovingly within our influence. Beware of the evil influences of mere disgust. Never be disgusted. Look at the work and not at the difficulties of the way. Look at the Master and not the provocations given you by others—have the end in view. Jesus Christ endured the cross, despising the shame, looking onward to the glory of what was to come. This is the secret of steady, continuous, and divine work.

Little natures fly off on little excuses. Little natures gather up all the provocations that have been launched against them until they become one great agony that the mind can no longer bear. Jesus Christ kept on healing the multitudes, though councils gathered against Him and officers of the church of His day made it their one business to shed His blood. "Your attitude should be the same as that of Christ Jesus: Who, being in very nature God, did not consider equality with God something to be grasped, but made himself nothing, taking the very nature of a servant, being made in human likeness. And being found in appearance as a man, he humbled himself and became obedient to death— even death on a cross!" (Phil. 2:5–8).

JOSEPH PARKER

Aware of this, Jesus withdrew from that place. Many followed him, and he healed all their sick.

MATTHEW 12:15

June 10

Many followed him,
and he healed all their
sick, warning them not
to tell who he was.

MATTHEW 12:15–16

Jesus Christ did not want His miracles to define Him. It was a poor thing to be known as the chief of magicians, which He might have been mistaken for by those who did not have the true reading of His signs and wonders. He knew that they would take the narrow view, they would read the lines upon the surface, they would not hear the inner music or see the inner light or feel the inner pathos; they would feed their curiosity with signs and wonders and pay no attention to the deeper hunger of the heart.

Jesus never made much of His miracles except in an introductory and illuminative sense. He never wished to be known through His miracles. You cannot point to an instance in which He said, "This miracle is enough to astound the world and bring it to a spiritual conviction regarding my Messiahship." His friends and family were always tempting Him in this direction. They took the low and narrow view, which we are all inclined to make of great souls. They said, "Since you are doing these things, show yourself to the world" (John 7:4). We wonder that they did not do more; we could show them how to come more boldly out and to take the age so as to incite in it a profounder amazement.

That is the vulgar Christianity of our day, not seeing its spiritual aspect, not feeling its tender unction, not knowing the meaning of the compulsion of pure love. Tell me whether the world or the Church has moved one inch beyond this program of the friends and relatives of Jesus Christ. "Make a show of the miracles, publish a list of them, take the greatest place, and repeat these miracles night by night to thronging multitudes." That is a program that makes a splutter at first but dies like a spark in the river. There is no solidity in it. The true program is be true, love the truth, move in God, be silent because of the majesty of your faith. Less faith would mean noise and crying and great demonstration; completeness means quietness.

JOSEPH PARKER

June 11

$\mathcal{O}$ur Savior was God's Servant in the great work of our redemption. He submitted Himself to the Father's will (Heb. 10:7) and set Himself to serve the design of His grace and the interests of His glory. As Servant, He had a great work appointed to Him, and a great trust was placed upon Him. "When the time had fully come, God sent his Son, born of a woman, born under law, to redeem those under law, that we might receive the full rights of sons" (Gal. 4:4–5). Jesus' princely motto was, "I serve."

Jesus Christ was chosen of God as the only person equal to the undertaking of our redemption. None but He was able to do the Redeemer's work or fit to wear the Redeemer's crown. Christ did not thrust Himself upon this work but was duly chosen into it. He is God's Beloved, His beloved Son. Between the Father and the Son there was before all time an eternal and inconceivable fellowship and interchanging of love. In Christ, the Father is well pleased, which denotes the highest complacency imaginable. God declared, by a voice from heaven, that Jesus was His beloved Son in whom He is well pleased; well pleased in Him because He was the ready and cheerful Undertaker of that work of wonder that God's heart was so much upon; and He is well pleased with us in Him, for He has made us accepted in the Beloved (Eph. 1:6).

God put His Spirit upon Christ that Christ should be every way well qualified for His undertaking (Isa. 11:2–3). Those whom God calls to any service, He will be sure to equip and qualify for it. Christ received the Spirit without measure (John 3:34), with power and glory and gladness to proclaim justice to the nations. The way and method of salvation, the justice that is committed to the Son, are not only wrought out by Him as our great High Priest but also shown and published as our great Prophet through the Holy Spirit. Let us make sure that we never let loose of our hope in Him.

MATTHEW HENRY

"Here is my servant whom I have chosen, the one I love, in whom I delight; I will put my Spirit on him, and he will proclaim justice to the nations."

MATTHEW 12:18

June 12

"He will not quarrel or cry out; no one will hear his voice in the streets. A bruised reed he will not break, and a smoldering wick he will not snuff out, till he leads justice to victory."

MATTHEW 12:19–20

We all have our opinion of the meaning of this verse; we rejoice that the Lord Jesus will deal tenderly with the weak in grace and the gentle in heart and are thankful that the text appears to express that consoling truth. I admit that the verse does teach us that, but read the context and judge the meaning for yourself.

The Pharisees endeavored to discover faults in Jesus but could find nothing against Him except in reference of their notions of the Sabbath. Our Lord met their questions boldly and so utterly routed them that one almost pities them while rejoicing over their ignominious defeat. They were beat outright and covered with shame. Our Lord overwhelmed them with His arguments, any one of which completely swept the ground from under their feet. Our Lord's victory was complete and tended to weaken their authority, but He did not push His advantage so as to overturn the sway of these religious teachers. They were before Him as lamps so nearly blown out that nothing but a smoldering smoke remained, but He did not proceed to quench them. In argument He had proved their folly and had crumpled them up till they were like so many bruised reeds, but there He paused. He did not pursue the conflict further but retired into the rural districts of Galilee. Lest a popular controversy and public tumult should arise, every time He wrought a miracle He told the healed one to conceal the fact so that it might be fulfilled, "A bruised reed he will not break, and a smoldering wick he will not snuff out, till he leads justice to victory." Now is the season of His patience, according to Isaiah, but a day of justice and wrath is coming. He forbore to overthrow His antagonists in the days of His flesh, but in the time of His second coming He will break His foes in pieces with a rod of iron.

If Christ would not quench the obnoxious Pharisees, if He does not put down cruel kings and persecutors, how much more will He deal gently with those who are truly seeking Him?

CHARLES SPURGEON

June 13

$\mathcal{M}$ark's gospel tells us that this astonishing explanation of Christ and His work was due to the ingenious malice of an ecclesiastical deputation sent down from Jerusalem to prevent the simple folk in Galilee from being led away by this new Teacher (Mark 3:22). They must have been very hard pressed to explain undeniable but unwelcome facts when they hazarded such a preposterous theory.

Formal religionists never know what to make of a man who is in manifest touch with the unseen. These scribes judged themselves in judging Him and bore witness to the very truths they were eager to deny, for this ridiculous explanation admits the miraculous, recognizes the impossibility of accounting for Christ on any naturalistic hypothesis, and by its outrageous absurdity indicates that the only reasonable explanation of the fact is the admission of His divine message and authority. So we may learn, even from these words, how the glory of Jesus Christ shines, though distorted and blurred, through the fogs of prejudice.

There were never more hostile eyes brought to bear upon any man than the eyes of these ecclesiastical judges. It would have been so easy and triumphant a way of ending the whole business if they could have shown that the miracle was a trick. But the undeniable fact stood before them: a man delivered from a demon whose sight and speech was fully restored. No wonder they must resort to the ridiculous for an explanation.

It is the working of Jesus Christ in the world that has brought all the beneficent, hallowing, elevating, ennobling, refining results that have followed upon the proclamation of His truth in the world ever since. He lifts the whole tone of society, suppresses ancient evils, and bars the doors of old temples of deviltry, lust, cruelty, and vice. But just as on earth He was hindered in the exercise of His supernatural power by men's unbelief, so He is thwarted by His Church and in the world today.

ALEXANDER MACLAREN

But when the Pharisees heard this, they said, "It is only by Beelzebub, the prince of demons, that this fellow drives out demons."

MATTHEW 12:24

June 14

"If Satan drives out Satan, he is divided against himself. How then can his kingdom stand?"

MATTHEW 12:26

It is only by Beelzebub, the prince of demons, that this fellow drives out demons." That is the last resort of Pharisaic prejudice so deep that it will father an absurdity rather than yield to evidence. And Jesus Christ has no difficulty putting it aside, easily noting that Satan would never divide his kingdom.

This explanation witnesses to the insufficiency of all explanations that omit the supernatural. These men knew they were dealing with a man who was in touch with a supernatural world that they could not measure. And so they fell back on "by Beelzebub," admitting that humanity without something more behind it never made such a man as that. It is easy to solve an insoluble problem if you take all the insoluble elements out of it. Some try to do it by taking out all of Christ's miracles and claims, saying nothing about the incarnation, and declaring the resurrection to be unhistorical. But here is the thing to be dealt with—that whole life of the Christ of the Gospels.

Recall our Lord's broad, simple principle: "Make a tree good and its fruit will be good, or make a tree bad and its fruit will be bad" (Matt. 12:33). How do you account for One so radiant, so human and yet so superhuman—where did He come from, and where did the gospel, which has done such things to benefit the world, come from? Serpents' eggs do not hatch out into doves. You cannot account for this by anything short of the belief in His divine mission. This man was no brain-sick enthusiast, and the gospel results rest upon no lie.

Think of the mental condition that could swallow such an explanation. It is more difficult to believe the explanation than the alternative that it is framed to escape. So it is always. The difficulties of faith are small by comparison with those of unbelief, gnats beside camels, and that that is so is plain from the short duration of each unbelieving explanation of Jesus.

ALEXANDER MACLAREN

June 15

*H*ere our Lord throws some light into that dim, unseen world, lifting a corner of the veil that hides it. His words were too solemn to be taken as accommodations to popular prejudice and a great deal too grave to be taken as a mere metaphor.

Jesus tells us that the secret of His power to casting out demons is the Spirit of God. And then He goes on to speak about a conflict that He wages with a strong man, binding the man and carrying off his possessions. He is saying that by His incarnation, life, death, resurrection, ascension, and government at the right hand of God, He has broken the powers of evil in their central hold. He has crushed the serpent's head; and though Satan may still, as Milton puts it, "swing the scaly horror of his folded tail," it is but the flurries of the dying brute. The conquering heel is firmly on his head. Evil is conquered, and Christ is the Conqueror, and by His work in life and death He has delivered those who were held captive of the devil.

That is the only explanation of Jesus Christ—in His person, in His character, in His work, and in the effects of that work in the world—that covers all the facts and will hold water. All others fail, and they mostly fail by boldly eliminating the very facts that need to be accounted for. Let us rather look to Him, thankful that our Brother has conquered, and let us put our trust in Him. For, if His explanation is true, a very solemn personal consideration arises for each of us: "Then the kingdom of God has come upon you." It stands beside us and calls for our obedience. Jesus Christ, and Jesus Christ alone, can cast the evils out of our natures. It is the indwelling Christ who will so fill our hearts that there shall be no aching voids there to invite the return of the expelled tyrants. If any other reformation pass upon us than the thorough one of receiving Him by faith into our hearts, the evil will return. With Jesus inside, it must remain outside.

"But if I drive out demons by the Spirit of God, then the kingdom of God has come upon you."

MATTHEW 12:28

ALEXANDER MACLAREN

June 16

*"And so I tell you,
every sin and
blasphemy will be
forgiven men, but the
blasphemy against the
Spirit will not be
forgiven."*

Matthew 12:31

Having answered His Pharisaic assailants logically, Jesus proceeds to answer them judicially. This severe warning shows that Christianity is more than an argument. An argument it certainly is, having command of all the forces of logic and wit, but Christianity is not a battle of words; it is a judgment upon the spirit, an anathema or a benediction, the fragrance of life unto life or of death unto death. When you touch Christianity, you touch something more than a mere competitor for your intellectual appreciation. Christianity is a stone that, if a man falls upon it, he shall be broken to pieces—happy breaking—or if it falls upon the man, it will grind him to powder, and there are no hands with skill enough to reconstitute the powder into the solid stone.

Men must be warned to beware of this unpardonable sin; it lies within our power to do it. Take care how you lie to the Holy Spirit or deny His ministry or insult His beneficent majesty; take care how you cut yourself off from the currents of life. If a tree could seize itself and drag every fiber of its roots out of the earth, what would become of the tree? All nature would fight against it and kill it, its juices would be sucked out, its veins would be dried up with an everlasting desiccation.

Take care how you uproot yourself and seek isolation; take care how you say you will not have the light and will not have the dew and will not be dependent upon the earth. A man can cut down his imagination, his impulses toward the morning and all its blue and tender light, he can snatch himself away from the altar and never pray another prayer, he can thrust his face into his chest and look downward to the dust to find what he can in the stones beneath his feet, he can rebuke the child who would kiss him and run away from all the influences that would redeem him, and having done so, what has become of him? He is twice dead, for he has offended the Spirit of the universe.

JOSEPH PARKER

June 17

*H*erein we have the connection between character and conduct, how what we do is determined by what we are. It takes a good person to do good things. How shallow is all that talk, "Do, do, do," this, that, and the other thing. All right, but *be;* that is the first thing. Jesus said if you make the tree good, the fruit will take care of itself. The condition of the hidden man of the heart is the all-important thing.

So how do we do that? Whenever a man sets himself, with anything like resolute determination and rigid self-examination, to the task of making himself good, he finds that he is still wrong. Man has power to do much in the direction of self-improvement, but after all that is done, his conscience tells him he is still not good. You may prune, improve the soil, and get bigger fruit, but you will not get better fruit. The plain fact is that the cultivation of self-improvement does little to purify the depths of the heart.

Jesus Christ is the only One who can make us good. He does it by coming to us, to every soul of man on the earth and offering, first, forgiveness for all the past. There is no bondage greater than the consciousness that the past is irrevocable, and this Christ shatters. Then He breathes into us a new life kindred with His own, a new nature that is free from the bonds of past sin. The tree is made good because He makes us into new creations.

Christ makes the tree good in yet another fashion, because He brings to the reinforcement of the new life that He imparts the mightiest motives and sways by love, which leads to imitation of the Beloved, which leads to obedience to the Beloved, which leads to shunning as the worst of evils anything that would break the communion with the Beloved, and which is in itself the decentralizing of the sinful soul from its old center and the making of Christ the Beloved the center around which it moves and from which it draws radiance and light and motion.

ALEXANDER MACLAREN

"Make a tree good and its fruit will be good."

MATTHEW 12:33

June 18

"You brood of vipers, how can you who are evil say anything good? For out of the overflow of the heart the mouth speaks. The good man brings good things out of the good stored up in him, and the evil man brings evil things out of the evil stored up in him."

MATTHEW 12:34–35

The heart is the fountain, the words are the streams. The mouth speaks out of the abundance of the heart as the streams are the overflowings of the spring. Evil words are the natural, genuine product of an evil heart. Nothing but the salt of grace, cast into the spring, will heal the waters, season the speech, and purify the corrupt communication. John the Baptist had called them a "brood of vipers," and they were still the same. The people looked upon the Pharisees as a brood of saints, but Christ calls them the offspring of the serpent, who had an enmity to Him and His gospel. Can the viper be anything but venomous? Christ would have His disciples know what sort of men they were to live among. They are as Ezekiel "among scorpions" (Ezek. 2:6) and must not think it strange if they are stung or bitten.

The heart is the treasury, the words are the things brought out of that treasury, and from them men's characters may be judged. It is the character of an evil man that he has an evil treasure in his heart, and out of it he brings forth evil things. Lusts and corruptions dwelling and reigning in the heart are an evil treasure out of which the sinner brings forth bad words and actions to the dishonor of God and the hurt of others.

Graces, comforts, experiences, good knowledge, good affections, good resolutions, these are a good treasure in the heart: The Word of God is hidden there, the law of God written there, divine truths dwelling and ruling there, are a treasure there, valuable and suitable, kept safe and kept secret, as the stores of the good householder, but ready for use upon all occasions. A good man will bring these forth, will be speaking and doing that which is good, for God's glory and the edification of others. The true believer bears the image of God, both in doing good and in being good.

MATTHEW HENRY

June 19

What was it that they wanted? They sought a merely intellectual gratification, a sign, something to speculate upon, another link in a chain of argumentative evidence. Jesus Christ never came to satisfy the curiosity or mere intellect of man. The gospel has nothing to say to the intellect, stiff and blind in its godless conceit, nothing to utter but a plain disappointing "no." The wisdom of this world is not the wisdom of God. What are called *proofs* to one group do not suffice another. "It is with the heart that a man believes unto righteousness. Blessed are the pure in heart, for they shall see God. To this man will I look, to him who is of a broken and contrite heart." In Isaiah 61 we learn that the meek, the captive, the bound, the tired, the helpless, the mourning, the tearful, the sad—all these are gathered within the enclosure of Christ's purpose, but the merely intellectual and argumentative, where are they? Meanwhile, Christ keeps His great answers and His great promises and benedictions for the meek, the broken-hearted, the sincere, the childlike, and those who have no confidence.

What does Jesus Christ teach in this broad answer? He teaches that there is already enough in human history to satisfy every healthy and sincere mind if it makes the right use of it. Jonah and the Queen of the South stand before them with far less light upon their path, and they will rise up in the judgment to accuse these questioners of their insincerity. All great answers have already been given. They did not lack for more evidence; they needed an understanding heart, a clean heart, a right spirit.

How true is that of the questions we have in our own lives? We do not need a new Bible; we need to read the one we already have in our hands. There is no book of such momentous purpose and significance so little read and so little understood. We need no more proof. What we do need is to make better use of the proof we already have.

JOSEPH PARKER

Then some of the Pharisees and teachers of the law said to him, "Teacher, we want to see a miraculous sign from you."

MATTHEW 12:38

June 20

"The Queen of the South will rise at the judgment with this generation and condemn it; for she came from the ends of the earth to listen to Solomon's wisdom, and now one greater than Solomon is here."

MATTHEW 12:42

To the Jews, Solomon is an ideal figure who appealed so strongly to popular imagination as to become the center of endless legends, whose dominion was the very apex of national glory, in recounting whose splendors the historical books seem to be hardly able to restrain their triumph and pride. His story gives us a richly endowed and many-sided character: He was statesman, merchant, sage, physicist, builder, one of the larger than life men whom the old world produced. Solomon was given a gift of wisdom that was so remarkable that his fame spread to other nations, so much so that the Queen of Sheba traveled far to hear and see him.

Yet we have to take into account the dark moral shadows that fell on Solomon's life and the possible shipwreck of a great character. In Christ we find no falling from a high ideal, no black streak in that flawless white marble. Every type of excellence is in Jesus, a pure white light in which all rays are blended. Solomon wrote and spoke much about wisdom, but he was only wise. Jesus is the "wisdom of God" (1 Cor. 1:24) of which Solomon spoke, the light to which Solomon bore witness and which the Queen of Sheba longed to know. Solomon built the magnificent temple, but it was only a foreshadowing of Jesus, who is Himself the true temple. And while Solomon's temple may be destroyed, Jesus is building up the great Temple of His Church of redeemed people, the eternal temple of which no one stone shall ever be taken down.

Solomon was the ideal king, but a darkness brooded over the later years of his reign in the form of oppression, luxury, and incipient revolt. Contrast that with the deep, inward peace of spirit that Jesus breathes into every person who trusts and obeys Him. Jesus is the true King of righteousness and of peace.

Surely from all these contrasts it is plain that the One who stood before the sign-seeking Pharisees was far greater.

ALEXANDER MACLAREN

June 21

*J*esus gave a broad answer to this inquiry for a sign, and these verses belong with it. I believe that Jesus is saying that the evil spirit is curiosity—idle, vain, self-seeking curiosity—and when once it has been clearly answered by the great replies of history and still wants a further satisfaction and goes out to find it, it will return and become seven times greater than it once was. Beware how you keep your curiosity chained. Strengthen the chain every day. Once a person gets into the spirit of sign seeking and question asking, vital holiness becomes an impossibility. Consider how easy it is to ask for signs, how poor and feeble a condition it is merely to be able to ask questions, to propound difficulties, to suggest problems, and to bewilder and puzzle those who are endeavoring to do great good in the world. You end up so blind that One so great as Jesus can stand in front of you and you don't know who He is.

The same is true morally of all sin. Once you stop a bad habit, you must replace it with something good, or the evil will return stronger than ever. It is not enough to cease to curse; you must learn to pray. It is not enough to break the sin of drunkenness; you must surround yourself with nobler influences and take to yourself a grand moral purpose. No man can remain in the same state from time to time—getting no better, getting no worse—it is not in human nature to be thus stationary. If we are not pursuing the right course, we are getting worse and worse. We do not stand still.

Nor is the corruption of our nature a rapid and visible one; the process is silent, subtle, often invisible, and seldom recognized. It can appear as harmless as asking Jesus for a sign. But the sapping goes on quietly, the strength is sucked out of a person little by little, and the day will come when we sink and perish, and the tremendous reality will be revealed.

JOSEPH PARKER

"When an evil spirit comes out of a man, it goes through arid places seeking rest and does not find it. Then it says, 'I will return to the house I left.'"

MATTHEW 12:43–44

June 22

That same day Jesus went out of the house and sat by the lake. Such large crowds gathered around him that he got into a boat and sat in it, while all the people stood on the shore. Then he told them many things in parables.

MATTHEW 13:1–3

*O*ne can easily imagine our Lord out in the fields, learning life's lessons from the farmer who was plowing, the sower, the reaper, and the harvester who had his fan in his hand with which he was thoroughly purging his flour. As He walked and talked with these various individuals, the Spirit of all truth would descend into His heart and say to Him that all these activities that he had been observing so closely were in all their processes and operations similar to the kingdom of heaven in all its processes, operations, and experiences. As He walked about and meditated, He would draw out to Himself the manifold likenesses between nature and grace, between the labor of the farmer and the labor of the preacher, when He would lay up all His meditations in His mind and heart, till we see and hear it all coming out in the teaching and the preaching found here.

Accordingly, nothing is more likely than that He had led His disciples to the seaside that day along a way that was well-known to Him, a way He had often walked as He went to watch the operations of the farmer to whom that field belonged. And it being the planting time of the year, as the sower that day sowed, some of the seed fell under the feet of the twelve disciples, while flocks of hungry birds swooped down and devoured whole basketfuls of the sower's best sowing. Thus it was that no sooner had our Lord sat down by the seaside than He pointed His disciples back to the field they had just passed through. Not only did He recall to them what they had just seen, but He told them of a lifetime of observations.

Thank God that our Lord always speaks to us in ways that we are familiar with, in words easily understood. May He always make the meaning as equally clear to our hearts.

ALEXANDER WHYTE

June 23

*O*ur Lord begins the parable of the sower with the case in which the seed remains quite outside the soil, in which the Word of God finds absolutely no entrance into the heart or mind. A beaten path runs by the end or perhaps through the middle of the field. It is of exactly the same soil as the rest, but having been packed down, the seed that is sown there has no power to penetrate the hard surface. Hungry birds watch the sower, and as soon as he passes, they swoop down, and away goes the grain. So there is an end to it, and the path is as bare as ever five minutes after it was strewn with seeds.

Here Jesus represents the case of men whose insensibility to the Word is caused by outward things having made a thoroughfare of their natures and has trodden them into incapacity to receive the message of Christ's love. Each footfall along the path has beaten the once loose soil a little firmer. We are made insensitive to the gospel by the effect of innocent and necessary things unless we take care to plow up the path along which they travel and to keep our spirits susceptible by a distinct effort.

The evil one comes for the seed. His agents are these light-winged thoughts that flutter around the hearer as soon as the Word comes. Criticism of the sower, talk about the weather, thoughts of tomorrow, all drive away the Word. Then the whirl of traffic resumes, and the path is soon beaten a little harder. If the seed had got ever so little way into the ground, the sharp beaks of the thieves would not have carried it off. Impressions so slight as Christ's Word makes on busy men are quickly rubbed out. But if the seed soon vanishes, the fault is not in it but in ourselves. Satan may seek to snatch it away, but we can hinder him.

ALEXANDER MACLAREN

"As he was scattering the seed, some fell along the path, and the birds came and ate it up. When anyone hears the message about the kingdom and does not understand it, the evil one comes and snatches away what was sown in his heart."

MATTHEW 13:4, 19

June 24

"Some fell on rocky places, where it did not have much soil. It sprang up quickly, because the soil was shallow. But when the sun came up, the plants were scorched, and they withered because they had no root. ...the man who hears the word and at once receives it with joy. But since he has no root, he lasts only a short time. When trouble and persecution comes because of the word, he quickly falls away."

MATTHEW 13:5–6, 20–21

Many hillsides in Galilee would show a thin surface of soil over rock, like skin stretched tightly on a bone. No roots could get through the rock or find nourishment in it, while the shallow earth and the heat of the underlying stone would accelerate growth. Such premature and feeble shoots perish as quickly as they spring up under the fierce Eastern sun.

The people meant are those of excitable temperament whose feelings lie on the surface and can be raised without first passing through the understanding or the conscience. They are easily played on by the influences of any prevalent emotion or enthusiasm. Their very "joy" in hearing the Word is suspicious, for a true reception of it seldom begins with joy but rather with the sorrow that leads to repentance. The immediate reception of the Word is suspicious, suggesting that there has been no time to consult the understanding; stable resolutions are slowly formed. They see only the sunny side of religion and know nothing of its difficulties and depths. As soon as they face trouble or persecution, all the joyful emotion will ooze out. The same superficial excitability that determined his swift reception of the Word will determine his hasty casting of it aside, and immediately he stumbles. Feeling is in its place down in the engine room, but it makes a poor pilot.

There is another profound truth in this picture. The hard, impenetrable rock lies right under the soil. The nature that is overemotional on its surface is utterly hard at its core. The most heartless people are those whose feelings are always ready to gush; the most unimpressible are those who are most easily brought to a certain degree of emotion.

Let us make sure that faith finds deep roots in us.

ALEXANDER MACLAREN

*I*n this case, the seed fell not only on the ground but also into it, so that it began to grow. The stalk has struggled up through the thorns until you can see its head and are led to expect grain. But go to that apparent grain–ear and feel it: There is nothing in it. You have all the makings of an ear of grain, but it will yield no grain. The grain is so overshadowed with a thicket of thorns and is so choked that it comes to nothing.

Note well that thorns are natural to the soil and were already established there. Any evil that hinders faith is natural to our fallen natures, and the roots of sin run throughout, grasping with marvelous tenacity. They will not give way to the Holy Spirit or to the new life or to the influences of divine grace without a desperate struggle. The roots of the thorns must first be uprooted; the great plow of conviction of sin must tear deep into the soul. Plows that scratch the surface will never do. Let God plow your soul so that His Word can be sown without the thorns.

"The worries of this life" speaks to those who are anxious and mistrustful about temporal things—whether it is to simply have enough to survive or how to get more. It is not a care for God, but it is a care for some vanity or another, such as the ambition to keep up with your fellows, to be respectable, and to keep up appearances. Take heed to anxiety; it will eat the heart out of your faith if you let it.

"The deceitfulness of wealth" speaks to those who have been charmed by the almighty dollar. Riches are evermore deceitful, tricking people who hug them into loving them. I would awake you to the fact that riches worm themselves into a man's heart before he is well aware of it.

Take a good look at your spiritual life. Thorns may not pull the seed up, but they can choke it to death. It may be time to get out the plow and root out the thorns.

CHARLES SPURGEON

"Other seed fell among thorns, which grew up and choked the plants. ...the man who hears the word, but the worries of this life and the deceitfulness of wealth choke it, making it unfruitful."

MATTHEW 13:7, 22

June 26

"Still other seed fell on good soil, where it produced a crop—a hundred, sixty or thirty times what was sown. ...the man who hears the word and understands it."

MATTHEW 13:8, 23

The good soil has none of the faults of the rest of the field. It is loose and thus unlike the path, deep and thus unlike the rocky bit, clean and thus unlike the thorn infestation. Jesus interprets this in one word: *understands*. While others received the Word, and it had some growth in them, the distinction here is surely of a moral nature. Biblical usage of "understanding" regards the action of the whole moral and spiritual nature, not purely the intellectual process. It involves the grasp of the truth with the whole being, the complete reception of the Word of the kingdom not merely into the intellect but into the central self that is the undivided fountain from which flow the issues of life. Only he who has housed the Word deep in his inmost soul "understands it."

The result of that reception into the depths of the spirit is that he "produces a crop." The life of a Christian is the result of the growth in him of a supernatural seed. Fruitfulness is the aim of the sower and the test of the reception of the seed. If there is no crop, manifestly there has been no real understanding of the Word. This is a touchstone that will produce surprising results in detecting spurious Christianity if it is honestly applied. There will be a variety of the degree of fruitfulness according to the thoroughness and depth of the reception of the Word, but the great Sower does not demand uniform fertility. He does, however, look for a crop.

No parable teaches everything. Paths, rocks, and thorns cannot change. But men can plow up the trodden paths and blast away the rock and root out the thorns and, with God's help, open the door of their hearts that the Sower and His seed may enter in. We are always responsible for the nature of the soil.

ALEXANDER MACLAREN

June 27

This saying was frequently on our Lord's lips, and in this instance He is clearly appending it to the parable, which required attention to disentangle the spiritual truth implied. Our Lord used this means to rivet the attention of His hearers, and a striking reappearance of the expression occurs in the book of Revelation. The Christ who speaks to the seven churches from heaven repeats His old Word spoken on earth, that we might listen closely.

We all have ears; therefore, we are all bound to hear. We all have the capacity of hearing in the sense of understanding and obeying the Word that Jesus Christ speaks to us. Herein we have the broadest implication of the universality of Christ's message. Every man has the needs that Christ addresses, and every man has the power of apprehending, of accepting, and of living by the great Incarnate Word and His message to the world.

If we have ears, we are bound to use them. "Let him hear." The power that we possess is the measure of the obligation under which we come. It is criminal for a man having the capacity of grasping the great Revelation of God to turn away from that voice and pay it no heed. For just as truly as light is meant for the eye, so truly are the words of the Incarnate Word meant to be the supreme objects of our attention, of our contemplative regard, and of our practical submission.

We shall not hear without an effort. "Though hearing, they do not hear or understand" (Matt. 13:13) describes countless people. Hearing with the outward ear, there is no hearing in the sense of attending or apprehending or obeying. Many of us are so preoccupied with other things that the trumpets of Sinai might blow in our ears and we would hear them as though we did not hear them. How much easier to miss the Savior's "Come to me."

Beware: If we do not hear, we shall become deaf. If we stop listening to Jesus Christ's voice, we will eventually not hear at all. Let us find ourselves always yielding to God's Word.

ALEXANDER MACLAREN

"He who has ears, let him hear."

MATTHEW 13:9

June 28

> "Whoever has will be given more, and he will have an abundance. Whoever does not have, even what he has will be taken from him."
>
> MATTHEW 13:12

The Lord repeats this saying many times in the Gospels, and in this case it explains why He chose to speak in parables—so that the truth, revealed to the diligent and attentive, might be hidden from the careless. The principles of these words shape all of life. This saying is a paradox, but it is a deep truth. It sounds harsh and unjust, but it contains the very essence of righteous retribution. The paradox is meant to get our attention. The key to it lies here—to use is to have. There is a possession that is no possession. That I have rights of property in a thing, as distinct from your rights, does not make the thing in any deep and real sense mine. What I use I have, and all else is but seeming to have.

Our Lord explains that teaching by parable—a transparent veil over a truth—was adopted so that the veiled truth might be a test as well as a revelation. The revelation that Christ has made comes to us in such a form that by moral affinity we shall be led to recognize and to bow to it or to reject it. He who will be ignorant, let him be ignorant, and he who will come asking for truth, it will flood his eyeballs with a blessed illumination. The veil will but make more attractive to some eyes the outlines of the fair form beneath it, while others will be offended at it.

If you will make that truth your own by loyal faith and honest obedience, if you will grapple it to your heart, then you will learn more and more. Whatever tiny corner of the great whole you have grasped, hold on to that and draw it to yourself, and you will by degrees get the entire, glorious, golden web to wrap around you.

We also have the solemn prospect before us. Hopes unnourished are gone; opportunities unimproved disappear; capacities undeveloped fade; fold after fold, as it were, is peeled off the soul, until there is nothing left but the naked self. He who never responds to the light will surely lose it.

ALEXANDER MACLAREN

June 29

I have no hesitation in saying that this describes the spiritual condition of by far the largest portion of our nation. It is the true enemy of souls. It is not an outright rejection of Christianity but a complacent taking for granted of religious truth, an entire carelessness about God and Christ that plagues us. Disbelief slays its thousands, and dissipation its tens of thousands, but this sleek, well-to-do carelessness its millions. As someone says, it is as if an opium sky had rained down soporifics.

The great cause of this condition is man's evil heart of alienation, the spirit of slumber. There is the indifference springing from the absorbing demands of the present, indifference caused by fear of what the results of attention might be, indifference fed by an indolent acquiescence in the truth, indifference from a familiarity with the truth. And the result is that the gospel river only seems to have worn the soul smooth enough to let it glide past without one stoppage. Like men who live in mountain scenery and no longer know its beauties, the listless eye sees nothing in the gospel but commonplace matter.

Contrast the indolence in spiritual matters that some people have on Sunday with their enthusiasm on Monday. See them slumber at prayer, but see them in a bargain. It is as if a burning mountain with its cataract of fire were suddenly quenched and locked in everlasting frost, and all the flaming glory running down its heaving sides turned into a slow glacier. There comes ice instead of fire, frost instead of flame, snow instead of sparks. It is as if some magician waved a wand and stiffened men into a paralysis. It is an awful thought of how they serve themselves and can be stirred to enthusiasm and how little of all this ever comes to God. The grandest things men can think about, the mightiest realities in the universe, the eternal, the most powerful, these are not seen. Beware of the treacherous indifference that creeps on till, like men in the Arctic regions, the sleepers die.

ALEXANDER MACLAREN

"Though seeing, they do not see."

MATTHEW 13:13

June 30

"But blessed are your eyes because they see, and your ears because they hear. For I tell you the truth, many prophets and righteous men longed to see what you see but did not see it, and to hear what you hear but did not hear it."

MATTHEW 13:16–17

It was a promised blessing that in the days of the Messiah "the eyes of those who see will no longer be closed, and the ears of those who hear will listen" (Isa. 32:3). So the disciples saw the glory of God in Christ's person; they heard the mind of God in Christ's doctrine; they saw much and were desirous to see more and thereby were prepared to receive further instruction. The parables, especially when they were expounded, greatly improved their knowledge, and by them the things of God were made more plain and easy, more intelligible and familiar, and more apt to be remembered.

"Blessed are your eyes." True blessedness, true happiness, is entailed upon the right understanding and due improvement of the mysteries of the kingdom of God. The hearing ear and the seeing eye are God's work in those who are sanctified, and they are the work of God's grace (Prov. 20:12). The eyes of the newest believer who has experienced the grace of Christ are more blessed than those of the greatest scholars, the greatest masters of philosophy, who are strangers to God and who, like the other gods they serve, have eyes but do not see. The knowledge of Christ is a distinguishing favor to those who have it, and upon that account it lays under the greater obligations (John 14:22). The apostles were to teach others and therefore were themselves blessed with the clearest discoveries of divine truth.

This transcendent blessing had been desired by but not granted to many prophets and righteous men. The Old Testament saints, who had some glimpses, some glimmerings of gospel light, coveted earnestly further discoveries. They longed to see what we see, the Substance, that glorious end of those things that they saw but as a shadow, that glorious inside of those things that they could not look into. Such is our privilege and sacred trust.

MATTHEW HENRY

July 1

*I*t was a most diabolical act. Diabolical malice and dastardly cowardice, taken together, could have done no more. That enemy envied with all his wicked heart the farmer's well–plowed, well–weeded, well–sowed field till he said within himself, "Surely the darkness shall cover me." And when the night fell, he filled his seed basket and went out under the night's cover and sowed the whole field over with his diabolical seed. And thus the whole wheat field was destroyed with choking weeds. The best the farmer could do was to have faith and wait patiently for the time of harvest when he could separate the good from the bad.

"But while everyone was sleeping, his enemy came and sowed weeds among the wheat, and went away."

Matthew 13:25

When Jesus interpreted the parable, it was to be the authoritative and the all–comprehending interpretation from that time to the end of the world. At the same time, and in and under that interpretation of His, occasional and provisional and contemporary interpretations and applications of this parable are to be made by each reader according to his or her own circumstances and experiences. Occasions will arise when we must be prepared both by knowledge and by temper to play our part in them like the farmer in his field. We will need the wise–hearted farmer's discretion, patience, and long faith.

How are we to respond when new experiences, new opinions, and new utterances arise in the fields around us? For what purpose, do you think, was this parable spoken to us by our Master but to impose upon us patience, caution, and confidence in the truth and to deliver us from all panic and sudden execution of our fears? Even when what is happening is demonstrably, scandalously, and diabolically the enemy's work, our Lord says to have patience. Let the weeds alone, lest you root up the wheat as well. The day of judgment will come, and it will be clear to all what was real and what was false. Our place is to take the words to heart and humbly apply them to our lives. "Be patient."

ALEXANDER WHYTE

July 2

"When the wheat sprouted and formed heads, then the weeds also appeared. The owner's servants came to him and said, 'Sir, didn't you sow good seed in your field? Where then did the weeds come from?'"

MATTHEW 13:26–27

Side by side with the sower's beneficent work, the counter-working of his enemy goes on. As the one, by depositing holy truth in the heart, makes men children of the kingdom, the other, by putting evil principles there, makes men children of evil. Honest exposition of biblical truth cannot eliminate the teaching of a personal antagonist of Christ nor of his continuous agency in the corruption of mankind. It is a glimpse into a mysterious region, none the less reliable because so momentary. The sulfurous clouds that hide the fire in the crater are blown aside for an instant, and we see. Who would doubt the truth and worth of the unveiling because it is short and partial?

The devil's work is a parody of Christ's. Where the good seed is sown, there the evil is scattered thickest. False Christs and false apostles dog the true like their shadows. Every truth has its counterfeit. Neither institutions nor principles nor movements nor individuals bear unmingled crops of good. Not merely creature imperfections, but hostile adulteration marks them all. The purest metal oxidizes, scum gathers on the most crystal-clear water, every ship's bottom gets foul with weeds. The history of every reformation is the same: radiant hopes darkened, progress retarded, a second generation of dwarfs who are careless and unfaithful guardians of their heritage.

There are, then, two classes of people represented in the parable, and these two are distinguishable without doubt by their conduct. Weeds may look like wheat until the heads show, and then there is a plain difference. Jesus Christ holds the unfashionable "narrow" view that at bottom, a man must be either His friend or His enemy. We are too much inclined to weaken the strong line of demarcation and to think that most men are neither black nor white but gray.

ALEXANDER MACLAREN

July 3

It is always the same. The enemy is as busy as the preacher, suggesting all kinds of doubts, difficulties, and suspicions, prompting all kinds of questions that will break in upon an implicit and loving and loyal obedience to Christ, directing your attention to little points and to transient accidents, the occasion, rather than to its solemn purpose, which is to lift the soul into the light and to clothe it with the very strength of God. The enemy will lure you into considerations of place, manner, and length of service and into a thousand little petty, frivolous discussions and will succeed if he lures the mind away from the sovereign purpose of the occasion—which is to make you pray. And at the end of the day, with bewildered head and heart, neither upward nor downward in its look, but halting, we may have to say, "An enemy did this." So the parable is not ghostly and magical but has its base upon the lines of our common experience.

"An enemy did this."

MATTHEW 13:28

This is precisely the experience of the Church. We are puzzled by the weeds that grow in our own hearts. I see the weeds in your life, and you see them in mine—but there are weeds in all human life, even of the very best kind, and the perplexing inquiry that brings with it a burning agony is, How did the weeds get in here? Didn't these people go to church? Have they never partaken of the Lord's sacrament? Where did the unkind words and actions come from? The two things do not harmonize. Wasn't that man praying in church on Sunday? Then how could he act so unscrupulously in his office on Monday? That woman who sang so lovely in church, how comes she to utter all those discords, those dissonant, harsh-breaking tones of human speech while the cadence of her hymn is trembling and dying in the distant air?

So this parable might have been written yesterday, and we might be reading it for the first time this morning. If Jesus of Nazareth were here today, He could not amend this parable in any of its facts and applications. Surely "an enemy did this."

JOSEPH PARKER

July 4

"The kingdom of heaven is like a mustard seed, which a man took and planted in his field. Though it is the smallest of all your seeds, yet when it grows, it is the largest of garden plants and becomes a tree, so that the birds of the air come and perch in its branches."

MATTHEW 13:31–32

*O*ur Lord discovered the kingdom of heaven everywhere and in everything. As a child He had often sown the least of all seeds in Joseph's garden and had watched that mustard seed springing up till it became a great tree. And with what delight would He see the birds building their nests in the branches of His own mustard tree. It was not the size of the mustard tree that held our Lord's imagination but rather the extraordinary smallness of the mustard seed. Out of that small seed sprang this exquisite little parable, so inexhaustibly rich in its application and fulfillments.

Jesus surely saw countless Old Testament images in His mind. What could be a smaller seed than the lonely call of Abraham into the land of the Canaanites? Or the ark of bulrushes that hid away Moses by the river's bank? Or the shepherd boy who sang to his few sheep on the plains of Bethlehem? Or think of Jesus' own life. Would you see the most wonderful mustard seed that ever was sown? Come and behold the holy thing that lies in the manger of Bethlehem. On and on go the examples.

But it is time to come to ourselves. Every little word that a parent speaks to his child, every action we take toward another person, every glance of our eye and accent of our voice—all are so many mustard seeds down in the garden of someone else's mind and heart. Every little scripture, every little prayer, every little encouragement, every moment spent in sympathy—small seeds dropped that will yet spring up to our everlasting surprise as an everlasting harvest, enriched by the Spirit of God and spreading out into visions of beauty that will sanctify and fortify the soul.

Let us not despise the day of small things. Let us have a great faith in such small things as these.

ALEXANDER WHYTE

July 5

*P*lease note that the kingdom of heaven is available for other uses than those that are sometimes thought to be distinctively spiritual. As with the mustard seed grown into a tree, the birds come and perch in its branches. Did the tree grow for the sake of the birds, or did the birds avail themselves of the hospitality of the tree? It is even so with the kingdom of heaven. Whatever is true has a right to be in the church—all art and science, all business and literature, all recreation and joy. Do not banish these sacred birds from the branches of the church tree, for they are all God's, and if they do not receive hospitality in the church, they will find it elsewhere, and the church will be the loser in the long run.

"...and becomes a tree, so that the birds of the air come and perch in its branches."

MATTHEW 13:32

The church should offer hospitality to all creatures that need lodging, help, defense, education, strength—it should throw itself out in loving and mighty appeal in every direction and offer the hospitality of heaven to all the children of earth. Open your churches for music, open your pulpits for lectures, open your classrooms for amusements, open all your premises that you may spread a meal for the hungry and offer rest to the weary, and eventually those who come will say, "Where are we? This is inspiring music. This is bread truly useful for us in the hunger of life—where are we? What is this building? There is something strange about it. What is so different about these people? What are these books they use?" It may dawn upon them that they are in their Father's house, and they who come to be entertained or fascinated by some transient enjoyment may remain to pray. Do not drive the birds away; do not starve the birds. The church was not distinctively built for any of these outward purposes, but as the birds came and perched in the tree, so may men and women and children, the outcasts, hope-less and heartless ones, come and find it warm in the church and be drawn by its glow of charity still further until at last they enter the sanctuary of truth.

JOSEPH PARKER

July 6

> *"The kingdom of heaven is like yeast that a woman took and mixed into a large amount of flour until it worked all through the dough."*
>
> MATTHEW 13:33

Yeast, or leaven, is generally in Scripture taken as a symbol of evil or corruption, but in this case our Lord lays hold upon the other use of the metaphor. The parable teaches that the effect of the gospel in the society of mankind in whom the will of God is supreme is to change the heavy lump of dough into light, nutritious bread by the power of its fermentation.

Here we glimpse our Lord's attitude as He measures Himself against the world and the forces that were in it. He knows that in Him, the sole representative of the kingdom of heaven upon earth at that moment—because in Him, and in Him alone, the divine will was absolutely and always supreme—lie powers that are adequate to the transformation of humanity from a dead, lumpish mass into an aggregate all-penetrated by a quickening influence. Speaking to the men whom He was charging with a delegated task, He was saying, "You are but twelve men, considered poor and ignorant with no resources at your back, but you have Me, and that is enough, and you may be sure that the tiny morsel of yeast will penetrate the whole mass." Small beginnings characterize the causes that are destined to great endings. The things that are ushered into the world large generally grow very little further and speedily collapse. The force that is destined to be worldwide began with the one man in Nazareth, and although the lump of flour is much larger, He can permeate and transform the mass.

Let us therefore take encouragement from our Lord's parable. If we must stand alone for His kingdom's sake, let us not count heads but measure forces. "What everybody says must be true" is a cowardly proverb. The fact is that what most people say is usually false, and what the few say is most generally true. So if we have to front an embattled mass of antagonism and we are in a miserable minority, never mind! If we have anything of the yeast in us, we are mightier than the lump of dough.

ALEXANDER MACLAREN

There were no banks in ancient times such as we have now, and people who possessed valuable property would often hide it in their fields and in out-of-the-way places. The figure is that of a man who was not looking for treasure but in digging his field came upon it without anticipation, and therefore his joy was the greater.

Without a doubt, the kingdom of heaven is like a treasure hidden in a field: It is a continual surprise. God is able to do exceeding abundantly above all that we ask or think, and He does so all the time. We cannot raise our expectancy to the height of this heaven, but expectation is not forbidden herein in consequence of that solemn and glad fact. We dream of heaven and talk of it and set our poets to work to strike their harps to sweeter and higher strains and tones because, when we have formed our own heaven in the innermost and highest places of our imaginations, it falls short of the reality only by infinity.

Take for your example the testimony of every student of the Bible. Every page is a field in which there is hidden treasure— so say those who have toiled longest in those holy fields. They are the ones who are entitled to testify: Such persons are filled with amazement, new light startles them, unheard music holds their soul in glad enthrallment, presences rise before them, and angels wrestle with them in power that is meant not to destroy but to save and to bless, so that the old man in closing his Bible says, "The last vision is the brightest; the last song was the sweetest. I never knew what this Bible was until now. All the old passages glow with a new meaning; all the sweet and sacred promises come with a deeper significance and more ineffable sweetness." I have always found this to be the case: Every time I conclude my exposition of any portion of holy Scripture, I have not even begun to touch its infinite meaning.

JOSEPH PARKER

"The kingdom of heaven is like treasure hidden in a field. When a man found it, he hid it again, and then in his joy went and sold all he had and bought that field."

MATTHEW 13:44

July 8

"Again, the kingdom of heaven is like a merchant looking for fine pearls. When he found one of great value, he went away and sold everything he had and bought it."

MATTHEW 13:45–46

This is one of those traveling merchants of the East who traversed sea and land in their search for fine pearls. He is never at home. He is always on the lookout for more and more precious pearls, till one day his long search is signally rewarded. Suddenly his eye falls on a pearl the likes of which he had never supposed to exist. Its great size, its perfect form, its exquisite beauty, its dazzling light—he had not expected to see such a gem. Learning what the great price of the pearl was, the merchant sells all that he possesses and immediately buys the pearl.

While the world holds many pearls of great value and worth, our Blessed Lord Himself is the Pearl of all pearls. Knowing that we had sold our own souls away to everlasting loss, Christ entered the soul-market Himself and bought back our souls at a price that has forever put His immense estimate upon us. He who alone knows the exchangeless value of our immortal souls came and redeemed our souls at a price that was worth far more than the whole world, and all our souls to the bargain. For He redeemed our souls at the price of His own perfect blood.

Therefore, our Lord counsels us all to sell all our other pearls, good and bad, great and small, and buy up our own soul unto everlasting life. "What good will it be for a man if he gains the whole world, yet forfeits his soul? Or what can a man give in exchange for his soul?" (Matt. 16:26). He says that any man who holds this whole world in one hand and his immortal soul in the other will be a fool if he holds onto the whole world and lets his soul go. Here before your very eye is the greatest and best pearl in all the world. For Jesus Christ gathers up into Himself all the truth and all the beauty and all the satisfaction that your heart seeks. Yet He comes to us as God's free gift, without money and without price. For the gift of God is eternal life through Jesus Christ our Lord.

ALEXANDER WHYTE

July 9

*I*t was inevitable that the kingdom of heaven should draw within itself every kind. The church has its bad members as well as its good ones. Shall we therefore say there is no kingdom of heaven because of the insincere, the unworthy, and the hypocritical?

Observe, Christ does not hide the fact of a mixture. Christ never hides any ugly facts; He makes more of His own failures than any other man could make of them. He cries over them; He drenches them with tears; He lifts up His voice and fills the whole space of the heavens with His moans. He acknowledges that He would gather Jerusalem to Himself, but they would not. There are miracles that He does not do because of unbelief. And it is no surprise to Him that the children of this world counterfeit the metal of heaven for their own self–interests.

Observe also that the bad do not succeed in hiding themselves. There is no impenetrable secrecy in character. Every bad fish found in the net was cast out. We may be in the visible church and not in the invisible. The Church is a mystical body. Not who was baptized with water but who has been baptized with fire is the deciding question. Not who preached with infinite eloquence but who lived with blameless consistency is the determining question. Not who professed but who carried out will be the rule of judgment.

It requires angels to perform the work of discrimination and separation, and not the fellow members of the church. It is not my business to find out your badness; it is not your business to find out my corruption. I would expel no one from the church unless driven to it by evidence that not only convinced me but also blinded me by its dazzling light. Might the good be larger than the bad in that very soul, and how do I know?

JOSEPH PARKER

"The kingdom of heaven is like a net that was let down into the lake and caught all kinds of fish.... they...collected the good fish in baskets, but threw the bad away. This is how it will be at the end of the age. The angels will come and separate the wicked from the righteous and throw them into the fiery furnace."

MATTHEW 13:47–50

July 10

And he did not do many miracles there because of their lack of faith.

MATTHEW 13:58

One would have thought that no difficulties would have stood in the way of such a preacher as Jesus Christ. The man who could work miracles could surely clear all obstacles out of His path. So it would seem to our ignorance, but it was not so in reality. Jesus Christ complained of difficulties and confessed His inability to remove them. Those difficulties assume a peculiar significance when we remember that Jesus Christ had all the elements that both deserve and command success. His miracles were confessed and admired on every hand. He was the most popular speaker of His day, characterized by marvelous graciousness and wisdom of address, so much so that the most learned wondered and the most illiterate understood, and those who were most ignorant felt the coming upon them of a new and very welcome light.

Still, this man, worker of miracles and speaker of beautiful speeches, failed, in a sense, in His ministry. He did not fail numerically: Great multitudes thronged around Him on the hillside and along the seashore; the popularity of numbers was triumphant—it was never so seen in Israel. Yet every heart was a difficulty, every man was a stumbling block, and in many cases the doctrine was wasted like rain upon the sands. At this place even His miracles were powerless, and He could do but few mighty works—their unbelief was greater, so to speak, than His faith.

I have found it nearly impossible to preach in some towns and places. I may, indeed, utter the intended words, but they come back at me and bring no blessing or answer of human heart along with them. And there are some men to whom we cannot talk. Conversation is stillborn when they are present. I want to say something, but I cannot speak to walking gravestones. We all know the meaning of this lack, some antipathy, some occult and unnamable cause that shuts us up.

But for those who gave Jesus heart-room, their faith works miracles. Let Him be all that He is in fact.

JOSEPH PARKER

July 11

All the historians and biographers of that time, both sacred and secular, agree that Herod Antipas was Herod the Great's son in all that was worst in his father's character. Old Herod, with all his brutalities and deviltries, had at the same time some of the possibilities that go to the making of a great man. But by no possibility could his second son ever have been a great man. Antipas was a weak, cruel, sensual, shallow-hearted creature. He is known to us first as the dupe of a bad woman, then as the murderer of John the Baptist, and then as one of the judges of Jesus Christ. He was that fox who tried to frighten our Lord to flee His work (Luke 13:32), and at last he was that puppet-king and reprobate sinner to whom our Lord would not answer one word (Luke 23:9).

This last point—his reprobation where our Lord would not answer—is the poignant lesson to be drawn from Herod Antipas. Herod's day of grace had lasted long, but it had come to an end. The king had had many opportunities, but all that was long past. Herod had smothered and silenced his conscience long ago, and now he was to be forever let alone. He lived the life of a fox, as our Lord spoke concerning him, and his life ends as a real horror.

It is possible that we can go on exactly like Herod, cheating ourselves and thinking that we are all the time mocking God, till it is too late, for God is not to be mocked by man. David said it impressively: "If I had cherished sin in my heart, the Lord would not have listened" (Ps. 66:18). "Just this once more," we say. "I will reform later." A debt not paid, a grudge kept up, an apology not made, a lie not repented of—all these will do it, and many more. As long as God in your conscience says there is something wrong, you may debate, question, pray, and cry, but the very God of peace will answer you nothing. We need to deal with it before it is too late, before our heart is hardened.

ALEXANDER WHYTE

At that time Herod the tetrarch heard the reports about Jesus, and he said to his attendants, "This is John the Baptist; he has risen from the dead!"

MATTHEW 14:1–2

July 12

Now Herod had

arrested John and

bound him and put him

in prison because of

Herodias, his brother

Philip's wife, for John

had been saying to

him: "It is not lawful

for you to have her."

MATTHEW 14:3–4

If you read Mark's account of the imprisonment of John, you discover that Herod both feared and protected John, was greatly puzzled by his message, yet liked to listen to him (Mark 6:20). Given his opportunity with Herod, John was the more bold with him. The particular sin John reproved Herod for was his marriage to his brother Philip's wife. Herod had enticed Herodias away from Philip and kept her for his own. Here was a complication of wickedness, adultery, and incest along with the wrong done to Philip, who had had a child by this woman. For this sin John reproved Herod, not in oblique allusions but in plain terms: "It is not lawful for you to have her." He did not say it was dishonorable or unsafe, but that it was a transgression of the law. This was Herod's own iniquity, his beloved sin, and therefore John tells him of this specifically. No one, not even princes and the greatest of men, is beyond the law of God. Those who rule over men must not forget that they are as subject to God as other people.

John was imprisoned for his faithfulness to the truth. It was Herod who had John arrested when he continued to preach and baptize and put an end to his work, bound him, and put him in prison. Partly it was to gratify his own revenge and partly to please Herodias, who of the two seemed to be the more incensed against John. Faithful reproofs, if they do not lead to a change in the person, usually provoke; if they do not do good, they are resented as affronts, and those who will not bow to the reproof will fly in the face of the reproved and hate him, as Ahab hated Micaiah (1 Kings 22:8). Perhaps some of John's friends would blame John as indiscreet in his reproof of one so dangerous as Herod, but John's own heart did not reproach him. It is nothing new for God's servants to suffer for doing the right thing. Trouble and hardships, the apostle Paul tells us, accompany those who are the most diligent and faithful in doing their duty (Acts 20:20, 23).

MATTHEW HENRY

July 13

We see in Herod the depths of evil possible to a weak character. The singular double that he, Herodias, and John present to Ahab, Jezebel, and Elijah has been often noticed. In both cases a weak king is drawn in opposite directions by the stronger-willed temptress at his side and by the stern ascetic from the desert. John's undaunted boldness of plain-spoken preaching of morality and repentance shook the king's conscience and appeared at times to sway him toward goodness.

But in the end, Herod's weaker nature yielded to the bitter hatred of Herodias, to the oaths he had spoken, and to the dinner guests who waited to see whether he would keep his word. Herod was a sensual, feeble-willed, easily frightened, superstitious, and cunning despot; and, as is always the case with such, he was driven farther in evil than he meant or wished.

We learn from Herod how far we may go on the road of obedience to God's will and yet leave it at last. What became of his earlier eager listening to John that is recorded in Mark's gospel? All vanished like early dew. Convictions not obeyed harden the heart to stone. Frivolity, lust, and neglect killed the germ of a better life.

Herod also shows us the intimate connection of all sins. The common root of every sin is selfishness, and the shapes that it takes are mutable and interchangeable. Lust dwells hard by hate. Sensual crimes and cruelty are closely akin. The vice that Herod would not surrender dragged behind it a whole tangle of other sins. No sin dwells alone. And the dreadfulness of those sins is that they can so warp a person's conscience that the person would rather murder John than not be polite to visitors by breaking his oath.

ALEXANDER MACLAREN

On Herod's birthday the daughter of Herodias danced for them and pleased Herod so much that he promised with an oath to give her whatever she asked. Prompted by her mother, she said, "Give me here on a platter the head of John the Baptist." The king was distressed, but because of his oaths and his dinner guests, he ordered that her request be granted and had John beheaded in the prison.

MATTHEW 14:6–10

July 14

*John's disciples came
and took his body and
buried it. Then they
went and told Jesus.*

MATTHEW 14:12

The martyrdom having been committed, John's disciples came with heavy feet, with heavy hearts, with tearful eyes, with great groaning, with wonder that might at any moment turn into irreverence and grumbling against heaven's justness. They carried away John's precious body, took it up tenderly, a body that had never known the meaning of luxury, self-care, indulgence, a body held in severest discipline, a gospel in itself of abstention, discipline, and inexorable control. Took up the mutilated body—the lips gone, the eyes gone, who can tell what was being done with the head? Then they buried that precious burden—they had nothing else to do.

Then they went and told Jesus the grim news. He was always hearing calamitous news. To tell our grief is something: To put our distress into words is to get relief. We can tell the Savior everything; we keep back no syllable of the tale. You would be lighter of heart if you would tell the Savior everything that is giving you distress. He is our priest, and to Him we must confess. Tell Him about your difficulty at home, your trouble with your child, your perplexity in business, the distresses for which there are no words—these you can sigh and hint at in your suggestive and eloquent tears. Let there be no lack of confidence between you and your Lord. It is not enough that He knows by His omniscience. He asks us to tell Him as if He knew nothing. Herein is the mystery and the grace and the satisfaction of prayer. Though the Lord knows everything we are going to say, He entreats us to say it, knowing that in the prayer itself is often hidden the contentment of its own answer.

To this Jesus let us cling; to this Jesus let us ever more go. Withhold nothing from the Lamb of God. The bitterer our tale, the sweeter His reply; the more agony there is in our prayer, the greater grace will be in His answer.

JOSEPH PARKER

July 15

$\mathcal{L}$ook at the disciples. A happy thought has occurred to them, and their faces are flushed by its fire. They have been measuring the situation with their calculating eyes, they have seen the sun setting, they have felt the evening chill in the wind, and they think they have thought very kindly of the large crowds who were in this desert place. As if their Master had been absorbed in heavenly contemplations, having in them nothing of care for the present life, they go up and tell Jesus what to do. Their suggestion is at best a copy of the world's benevolence, the same notion of charity that rules nearly all cases where the love of Christ is absent.

How much better to have gone to Jesus and have left the case in His hands. It is always wise to trust omniscience. It is a continual mistake to be making suggestions to divine providence. Remain where you are. Jesus knows when the sun is going down and when your hunger becomes a distress. Do not leave the grounds until He bids you to go. Let us be thankful that we are not left to the devices of the disciples. Let us gladden ourselves with the holy and inspiring thought that the Master still lives.

How did Jesus respond to their suggestion? In contrast to their "send them away," He says, "They do not need to go away. You give them something to eat." How musical His voice sounds after their rough tones. Put the two expressions together and see the infinite discrepancy. The disciples' "Send them away" is exposed for what it is—a rude, vulgar proposition that flows from a selfish mind. Hear the voice that holds in it all heaven's music: "They do not need to go away." That was the revelation, and that is true of human life in all its points, aspects, bearings, and necessities. Wherever Christ is present, He has the power to meet every need and comfort every care. Let us never find ourselves sending away seekers through our own lack of faith.

JOSEPH PARKER

As evening approached, the disciples came to him and said, "This is a remote place, and it's already getting late. Send the crowds away, so they can go to the villages and buy themselves some food."

MATTHEW 14:15

July 16

"We have here only five loaves of bread and two fish."

MATTHEW 14:17

In this miracle we are clearly taught our Christian mission. Behold before you, disciples of Christ, thousands of men, women, and children who are starving for the bread of life. They hunger till they faint. They have spent their money and labors on that which does not satisfy. They collapse in your streets, perishing for lack of knowledge. Open your eyes, let your heart and soul be moved with sympathy. I beseech you, if you cannot help them, weep over them; hear them crying, "Feed us, for we famish."

I think I hear you reason in your heart the same thought as that of the original disciples of Jesus: "Who are we to feed this multitude? Our supplies are so meager we can't feed ourselves. We could never even purchase enough supplies. We are too few, too weak, and too old ourselves. Surely there are others who can feed them." Yet the Master tells you to give them the bread of life. He calls you to practical, personal service, and your Christianity is worth nothing unless it makes you heed His word. Did we say just now we could not? Surely we must recall our words and say, "We must!" The world's only hope, and shall we put it out? The only star that gilds the darkness, and shall we quench it? No! By everything that is tender and gentle in the throbbing of our hearts, we say we must no matter what we feel.

Remember that our duty is to simply bring to Jesus whatever we have. Every talent that we have, whether big or small, is to be brought to Jesus in total consecration. And we ourselves are to come to Him in prayer, as the disciples did at Pentecost, till the Spirit is poured out and we are made strong. Come with faith that Jesus has power to take whatever little means we may have and make it sufficient for mighty ends. A handful of apostles with a score of weaknesses shook the world because they were wholly for God. Put your talents and abilities in the hand of Christ, then go and do good, give to others whatever you can give. This is the way to change the world.

CHARLES SPURGEON

July 17

One can imagine how doubtingly and grudgingly the apostles doled out the bread at first, and how the portion of each was increased as group after group was provided, and no diminishing appeared in Christ's full hands, until all the five thousand were fed and the leftovers lying uncared for proved how sufficient had been the share of each. May we not see in that scene a picture of the full supply for all the needs of the whole world that there is in that Bread of Life that came down from heaven?

The gospel proclaims a full feast, which is enough for all mankind, is intended for all mankind, and shall one day satisfy all mankind.

This universal adaptation of the message of the gospel to the whole world arises from the obvious fact that it addresses itself to universal needs, to the great rudimentary, universally diffused characteristics of human nature, and that it provides for all these, in the grand simplicity of its good tidings, the one sufficing word. It entangles itself with no local or historical peculiarities of the time and place of its earthly origin, which can hinder it in its universal diffusion. It commits itself to no transient human opinions, addresses itself to no sectional characteristics of classes of men. It brushes aside all the surface distinctions that separate us from one another and goes right down to the depths of the central identities in which we are all alike. Christianity sends its shaft down into the deepest depths that are the same in every person—the obstinate willfulness of a nature separated from God and the yet deeper–lying longings of a soul that flames with the consciousness of God and yearns for peace and rest. To the sense of sin and sorrow, to the conscience never wholly stifled, to the desires after good never utterly eradicated and never slaked by anything besides itself, does this mighty word come. For every soul on earth, this living, dying love of the Lord Jesus Christ addresses itself to and satisfies his deepest needs. It is the bread that gives life to the world.

ALEXANDER MACLAREN

They all ate and were satisfied.

MATTHEW 14:20

Immediately Jesus made the disciples get into the boat and go on ahead of him to the other side, while he dismissed the crowd. After he had dismissed them, he went up on a mountainside by himself to pray.

MATTHEW 14:22–23

We wonder how a grand outward ministry can be sustained. The answer is simple in its sublimity. Every outward ministry that is massive, life-taxing in its demands, is sustained by mountain climbing, solitary communion with God, soul fellowship with the Father of all life. The inward man must be renewed day by day: We must deepen the soil if we would enrich the crop. If the Master must have lonely prayer, the servant cannot dispense with secret devotion. It is not enough to pray in others' company in the language of common prayer: We must know the agony, which is joy, of speechless communion and the exquisitely tender gladness of secret fellowship. Oh, for those dewy hours, those opening moments of the day—what conquests may then be won! When our first interview is with God, we cannot fear the face of man.

Jesus Christ could not live within the boundaries that could be touched: He yearned for the infinite and must in His life have an outlet toward the heavens. No traveler accompanied Him. The great wide sky—how wide it can be, let the poet tell me—opened before Him like a door into the central heaven where the throne is and where the Shekinah burned as if glad to see Him back again, poor without Him, owing all its blue and light and tenderness to His presence.

We must have our times of withdrawal from society if we would get a strong hold of life and be master of its vexing details. Do not always be in the crowded streets or in the tumultuous throngs. Five minutes every day alone with God would make us more than conquerors in the day of battle. Fear yourself if you dare not be alone. Solitude, spiritually used, disciplines the soul, fills the heart with heavenly peace, and opens the mind to the daily revelation that God makes to those who love Him. With everything else that we find time for, why not have time for communing with God and reading deeply in His Word?

JOSEPH PARKER

July 19

*J*esus was no stranger who did not.know His way around in the world. The world was His home because it was His Father's house. Even when a boy, He could be no lost child but was with His Father all the time. Think for a moment how Jesus was at home among the things of His Father.

What was His place of prayer? Not the temple, but the mountainside. Where does He find symbols whereby to speak of what goes on in the mind and before the face of His Father in heaven? Not in the temple. Not in its rites, its altars, its Holy of Holies. Rather, He finds them in the world and its lovely, lowly facts—on the roadside, in the field, in the vineyard, in the garden, in the house, in the family, and in the commonest of affairs: the lighting of the lamp, the leavening of the meal, the neighbor's borrowing, the losing of a coin, the straying of a sheep.

All His life Jesus was among His Father's things, either in heaven or in the world. He claimed none of them as His own, would not have had one of them His except through His Father. Only as His Father's could He enjoy them. He had no care for having, as men count having. All His having was in the Father.

To be lord of space, a man must be free of all attachments to place. To be heir of all things, his heart must have no things in it. He must be like him who makes things, not like one who would put everything in his pocket. He must be as the man who makes poems, not the man who gathers books of verse.

I wonder whether Jesus ever put anything in His pocket. I doubt He even had one. Did He ever say, "This is Mine, not yours?" Did He not say, "All things are Mine, therefore they are yours"?

Oh, for His liberty among the things of the Father! Only by knowing them as the things of our Father can we escape enslaving ourselves to them. Through the false, the infernal idea of having, of possessing them, we make them our tyrants, make the relation between them and us an evil thing.

GEORGE MACDONALD

He went up on a mountainside by himself to pray.

MATTHEW 14:23

July 20

During the fourth watch of the night Jesus went out to them, walking on the lake.

MATTHEW 14:25

Not till the final watch of the night does Jesus come, when the disciples have struggled long and hard and the boat is out in the very middle of the lake and the storm is fiercest. We may learn from this the delays of His love. Because He loved Mary and Martha and Lazarus, He stayed still in strange inaction for two days after their message. Because He loved Peter and the praying Church, He let Peter lie in prison till the last hour of the last watch of the last night before his intended execution and then delivered him with a leisureliness that tells of conscious omnipotence. Heaven's clock goes at a different rate from our little timepieces. God's day is a thousand years, and the longest delay is but a little while. When He has come, we find that it is the right time, though before He came He seemed to us to delay.

He comes across the waves. Their restless and yielding crests are smoothed and made solid by the touch of His foot. "He alone stretches out the heavens and treads on the waves of the sea" (Job 9:8). It is a revelation of divine power. It is one of the very few miracles affecting Christ's own person and may perhaps be regarded as being, like the transfiguration, a casual gleam of latent glory breaking through the body of His humiliation and so, in some sense, prophetic. But it is also symbolic. He ever uses tumults and unrest as a means of advancing His purposes. The stormy sea is the recognized Old Testament emblem of antagonism to the divine rule; and just as He walked on the billows, so does He reach His end by the very opposition to it.

In another aspect, we have here the symbol of Christ's using our difficulties and trials as the means of His loving approach to us. He comes, giving a deeper and more blessed sense of His presence by the means of our sorrows than in calm, sunny weather. It is generally over a stormy sea that He comes to us, and golden treasures are thrown on our shores after a tempest.

ALEXANDER MACLAREN

July 21

Faith seems to have a secret instinct revealing her royal character. John is full of love for Jesus and stays within the vessel; but Peter abounds in faith, and he must be doing some high action congruous to the nature of faith. Anybody can walk on land, but faith is a water-walker. Faith says to the mountain to be removed, and it is. Faith loves to deal in great things, in marvelous adventures, in projects beyond human power. We are not to come to God and ask Him to do for us what we can do for ourselves. There is no room for the exercise of faith where reason and human strength will suffice. Faith is a vessel expressly built for the deep seas. She pushes out where she can neither see the shore nor fathom the depth, for she has a compass on board, and she looks up to the stars that God has fixed for her guidance. She has, too, a blessed Pilot, so she feels secure and all at home in the wild waste of waters, with no human eye or hand to help.

If you have faith in God and that faith is an active exercise, I am persuaded you will feel an instinct within you prompting you to dare something more than others have ventured to attempt, eager to honor Jesus Christ more than anyone else could think possible who had little faith or no faith at all. It might be to follow a missionary call or to consecrate more finances to the Lord's work. Blessed it is when faith kindles to furnace-heat and stimulates one to undertake a work for which he would be incompetent! How graciously Christ can make him to walk on the water! It is no novelty for us to put our foot down on what we thought was a wave and find that God had placed a rock there, to rest on the invisible and prove it to be more substantial than the visible. I pray that your faith may grow till you feel compelled to undertake something for Christ that is beyond your own unaided strength, something that He has called you to do but you have never dared try. God will give you the grace to accomplish it.

CHARLES SPURGEON

"Lord, if it's you," Peter replied, "tell me to come to you on the water."

MATTHEW 14:28

July 22

"Come," he said. Then Peter got down out of the boat, walked on the water and came toward Jesus.

MATTHEW 14:29

Faith really does work wonders. I think I see Peter bounding over the bulwarks. How strange to discover that the water was solid marble under his feet! How elated he must have felt—a man with Peter's temperament naturally would so feel—when he began to walk and found the water like a sea of glass beneath his tread! It was a marvelous thing to do. Others have made their way through the sea, but Peter walked over it. The laws of gravitation were suspended for his support. Picture the scene. What Jesus was doing Peter was doing. Faith made Peter to be like his Lord. There were two walking, the one by His own infinite power, the other by the power imparted to him—the power of faith.

It does often seem impossible in certain conditions to act in a Christlike spirit, but faith can make you walk the waves. Your Lord was patient in poverty; faith can make you walk that wave and be patient and contented, too. Christ was gentle under the most dreadful provocations; faith can give you the same gentleness and love to walk those billows, too. Our Lord, in the midst of prosperity, refused worldly honor when they sought to make Him a king. And you in the high places of the earth, tempted by wealth, with flattery poured into your ears, may still walk safely through it all if you have faith in God. Jesus said that if we believed in Him we would do greater works than He did. How remarkable it would be if we believed that! So many of us give up and lie down. How can this be? God dwells in us. When God is thoroughly in a man, and the man knows it, the man is not overwhelmed by difficulties or daunted by sneers. He is not so mindful of his feebleness as to excuse himself from effort or to imagine that he can do nothing. In the confidence of that power that inspires him, he marches boldly on, fully assured that victory awaits him, and he rests not until he realizes that victory. May we always have enough faith to be doing wonders.

CHARLES SPURGEON

July 23

I do not think that Peter's faith became suddenly little; the sight of the boisterous wind simply exposed its weakness. Why did he want to walk on the water? It was because his faith was little. Strong faith is content without signs and marvels. It believes God's bare Word and asks for no confirming miracle; its trust in Christ is such that it asks for no signs at all. Little faith, with its "If it is you," must have signs and wonders, or it yields to doubt. Direct words from God, remarkable dreams, special providences, startling answers to prayer—little faith must be having something out of the ordinary, or it collapses. It is not satisfied with the usual portion of the saints but must have more, do more, and feel more than the rest of the disciples. Why did Peter not stay in the ship like the other brethren? Because he cannot think it really is his Master walking on the sea unless he walks with Him. How dare he ask to do what his divine Lord was doing? Let him be content to share his Lord's humiliation: He ventures far when he asks to partake in a miracle of omnipotence. Am I to doubt unless I can do miracles like those of my Lord? But this is a constant failing of weak faith: It is not content to simply believe.

Weak faith is also too much affected by its surroundings. Are we not as likely as Peter to live by what we feel and see? It is the mark of weak faith that it is all up and then all down. If we live by feelings, we shall live a very wretched life; we shall not live in the Father's house, but we shall be a kind of spiritual gypsy. Strong faith knows where its true standing is, and perceiving this to be unchanging, it concludes that its foundation is as good one day as another, for its standing is in Christ. As the promise upon which it leans is not a variable quantity but is always the same, so its rest is the same. Our God will save all who trust in Him, and that is the top and the bottom of it: Nothing more is required. God help us to rise above our surroundings.

CHARLES SPURGEON

Immediately Jesus reached out his hand and caught him. "You of little faith," he said, "why did you doubt?"

MATTHEW 14:31

July 24

Then some Pharisees and teachers of the law came to Jesus from Jerusalem and asked, "Why do your disciples break the tradition of the elders? They don't wash their hands before they eat!"

MATTHEW 15:1–2

Seldom did Jesus Christ lose His patience, but when that circumstance did occur, it was marked by the utterance of very memorable words. Nor was this loss of patience in the case of Jesus in any sense one of mere irritation or peevishness—it was rather a sense of moral indignation. The answer that He made to the Pharisees and teachers from the metropolis of Jerusalem was an instance of high, noble, moral resentment: It was not anger of a merely personal and selfish kind; it was a grave and solemn judgment. That the leading spiritual men of the day should be putting such trivial questions, should be mocking the spirit of progress by such frivolous inquiries, should be making such mountains out of molehills, roused the divinest anger of an earnest soul.

Consider how this answer of the Savior carries with it some profound suggestion of the supreme purpose of His life. He had not come down to make nice things, to propose violations upon a ceremonial descended from the seniors—He came to save the world. Hence His flashing anger, His burning, scorching retort upon men who wanted to bind down His attention to the smallest frivolities that could engage the intellects of the smallest intellects. From His answers to His opponents, always learn something of Jesus Christ's main object in life.

The difference between the Pharisees and Christ was that they lived in ceremony and He lived in truth. Their religion was a trick in ritual—all religious observances and duties had been reduced to a mechanical standard and arrangement. With the Son of God, religion was life, spirit, a vital principle, a divine inspiration, a continual drawing down from heaven of the energy and the grace needed for the work and suffering of life. Observe, therefore, that the difference between them was not so much measurable in words; it was vital, final, and indestructible.

JOSEPH PARKER

While the Pharisees were finding fault with the disciples on a point of religious tradition, Christ shows them the log in their own eyes for actually violating the law of God when hiding behind the same religious traditions. Although the fifth commandment spoke clearly that children were to honor their parents, the traditions of the elders implied that there was an exception. The tradition said that whenever something was dedicated to the service of the temple, all other obligations, though ever so just and sacred, were thereby superseded, and a man was discharged from them. This was partly a reflection of their devotion to the ceremonial law and partly from their covetousness and love of money, for what was given to the temple they were gainers by. The former was in pretense; the latter was in truth at the bottom of this tradition.

When someone's parents' necessities called for their assistance, they pleaded that all they could spare from themselves and their children had been devoted to the temple. Therefore, their parents must expect nothing from them, and it suggested that the spiritual advantage of what was so devoted would redound to the parents, who must live upon that air. Though the absurdity and impiety of the tradition is evident, under the pretense of spirituality it was made not only passable but also plausible.

Jesus' anger is evident here. "You break the command of God." Call it a tradition of the elders or some other fine spiritual phrase, but illegal trickery will be laid to the charge of those who support and maintain it, as well as of those who first invented it (Mic. 6:16). Christ's disciples must stand upon their guard against any intrusion upon the Word of God, even when it only seems to infringe upon their Christian liberty, as on this issue of hand washing. Whatever leads to disobedience can never make void the command, no matter how spiritual it is made to sound.

MATTHEW HENRY

Jesus replied, "And why do you break the command of God for the sake of your tradition? For God said...But you say...Thus you nullify the word of God for the sake of your tradition."

MATTHEW 15:3–6

July 26

"You hypocrites!
Isaiah was right when
he prophesied about
you: 'These people
honor me with their
lips, but their hearts
are far from me.'"

MATTHEW 15:7–8

It never occurred to the Pharisees and teachers that there could be any answer to their question. Everybody had always yielded to their criticism and judgment and had gone to find out what they ought to do from these great masters of the law. Here is a man who confronts them and challenges the purity of their hearts.

Despite their religious prowess, the Pharisees were locked in a spirit of selfishness, desperately attempting to find in their religious system what can be found only in spiritual reality. Men keep up the framework of appearances to the last: The anxiety of many minds is to save appearances. Jesus Christ never attempted to save appearance at the expense of truth. Are we endeavoring to keep up appearances by our churchgoing, by religious habits and ceremonies for which we have really no heart but which we must appear to respect or else others will begin to imagine the real state of our heart? The Lord's lightning strikes all mere appearances and pretenses. We are killed by our pretensions when they are not supported by an inward reality. What are we in our heart? What is our meaning? What is our purpose? These are the vital questions that men should put to themselves and answer.

This answer was indeed a long thunderstorm. The clouds were, so to speak, gathered from distant skies. Jesus adds in the prophecy of Isaiah. Men are often excited to find out every detail of a prophecy and its fulfillment. Jesus tells us that when we are searching into apocalyptic visions and digging into prophetic mines, wishing to know when times and seasons are accomplished, it may be well to remind our hearts that probably Jesus would fix the great moral accusations of prophecy upon us. While we are seeking to apply some marvelous combinations of dates to some person in history, Jesus might lay His hand upon us and say, "You fool, when the prophet thunders against wrong, all his thunders beat upon your own head."

JOSEPH PARKER

July 27

It was not strange that the Pharisees were offended at this plain truth, for they were men of error and enmity, mistake and malice. Sore eyes cannot bear clear light, and nothing is more provoking to proud impostors than the undeceiving of those whom they have first blindfolded and then enslaved. Christ has shown clearly that it is the Pharisees who defile themselves with what they speak spitefully and censoriously against His disciples. Those who charge guilt upon others for transgressing the commandments of men often bring greater guilt upon them-selves by transgressing the law of God against rash judging.

The disciples thought it strange that their Master should say that which He knew would give so much offense. It was not His normal method. If He had considered how provoking it would be, He would not have said it. But Jesus knew what He said and to whom He said it and what would be the effect of it, and He would teach us that though in indifferent things we must be tender of giving offense, we must not, for fear of that, evade any truth or duty. Truth must be owned and duty done, and if anyone is offended, it is his own fault. It is scandal not given but taken.

Perhaps the disciples themselves stumbled at the Word Christ said, which they thought bold and hardly reconcilable with the law's definitions of clean and unclean meats, and therefore they questioned Christ, that they might themselves be better informed. They seemed to be concerned about the Pharisees, despite their quarrel with them. They would not have the Pharisees go away displeased by what Christ had said. Therefore, though they did not desire Him to retract His com-ments, they hope He will explain it. Weak listeners are often more solicitous than they should be not to have wicked listeners offended. But if we please men with the concealment of the truth and the indulgence of their errors and corruptions, we are not the servants of Christ.

MATTHEW HENRY

Then the disciples come to him and asked, "Do you know that the Pharisees were offended when they heard this?"

MATTHEW 15:12

July 28

"Are you still so dull?" Jesus asked them. "Don't you see that whatever enters the mouth goes into the stomach and then out of the body? But the things that come out of the mouth come from the heart, and these make a man 'unclean.'"

MATTHEW 15:16–18

As many as Christ loves and teaches, He also rebukes. Jesus says in effect, "Have you been so long under my teaching and yet you remain so unskillful in the word of righteousness? No wonder the Pharisees, who know nothing of My kingdom and are unfamiliar with Me, do not understand this doctrine; but you who have heard My teaching and embraced it your-selves and preached it to others, are you also such strangers to the spirit of it?" Had the disciples just arrived in Christ's school, it would have been another matter, but to have been Christ's constant listeners for many months and yet to not understand that moral pollutions are abundantly worse and more dangerous than ceremonial ones was a great reproach to them. Christ expects from us some proportion of knowledge and grace and wisdom according to the time and means we have had, and the disciples' dullness and darkness in this matter is a grief to Christ.

Although Christ did reprove them for their ignorance, He still gives them an explanation. He repeats that the washing of hands may relate to personal cleanliness, but it is not to be rendered a point of conscience. It is not the practice itself but the religious opinion the Pharisees had built upon it that Christ condemns. Rather, the real danger lies within a defiled heart. It is the heart that is "deceitful above all things and beyond cure" (Jer. 17:9), for there is no sin in word or deed that was not first in the heart. "Not a word from their mouth can be trusted; their heart is filled with destruction" (Ps. 5:9).

Never allow the focus of sin to be taken away from the heart. All corrupt thinking, speaking, and acting flow from this foun-tain, and this is where the washing must come. Washed hands count for nothing; a washed heart counts for everything.

MATTHEW HENRY

July 29

The mouth of faith can never be closed, for if ever a person's faith was tried so as to make her cease from prayer, it was that of this Canaanite woman. She had difficulty after difficulty to encounter, and yet she could not be put off from her pleading for her daughter because she believed in Jesus as the great Messiah and she meant to pray to Him until He yielded to her importunity, for she was confident He could chase the demon away.

Here we see that the mouth of faith cannot be closed even on account of the closed ear and the closed mouth of Christ. He answered her not a word. She spoke pitifully, she came and threw herself at His feet, her motherly heart was tender and her cries piercing, and yet He answered her not a word. Yet she was not staggered; she believed in Him, and even He Himself could not make her doubt Him when He remained silent. It is hard when prayer seems to be a failure. Oh, for such a splendid faith that will not doubt even in the face of Christ's apparent refusal.

Nor could her faith be silenced by the conduct of the disciples. Her noise annoyed them, and they wanted her to leave. They even claimed that she was crying out after them, but it was the Master she sought. Sometimes disciples become very important in their own eyes and think that the pushing and crowding to hear the gospel is caused by the people's eagerness to hear them, whereas nobody would care for their poor talk if it weren't for the gospel message that they were to deliver. But despite their rebuff, the woman thought of the horrible miseries of her daughter and pressed straight to the Master's feet. Cold, harsh words and unkind, unsympathetic behavior could not prevent her from pleading with Him in whom she believed, nor should they ever block our path.

CHARLES SPURGEON

A Canaanite woman from that vicinity came to him, crying out, "Lord, Son of David, have mercy on me! My daughter is suffering terribly from demon-possession." Jesus did not answer a word. So his disciples came to him and urged him, "Send her away, for she keeps crying out after us."

MATTHEW 15:22–23

July 30

The woman came and knelt before him. "Lord, help me!"

MATTHEW 15:25

The bitterness of the woman's trial gives the right tone to her prayer. This is her second prayer, and it reflects how Jesus allows us to amend, enlarge, and simplify our prayers. She came and worshiped Him, saying, "Lord, help me!" Sorrow abbreviates our prayers; sorrow teaches true eloquence. When the heart is in the grip of a deadly agony, it knows how to pray. In our ordinary public worship, we must have order and method by which the public can be guided. Beyond all such arrangements there lie the innumerable approaches to heaven, known only to the heart in its keenest pangs. There are times in which no man can teach another how to pray. Bursting out of his throbbing heart will fly the great desire in appropriate speech and tone. Unless we have had experience of this kind, we are not in a proper mood to discuss this type of prayer, and questions regarding this prayer are not to be discussed with cold intellectualism. When your child has been grievously vexed with a devil, when the last hope of your life has been blown out by a sudden and most cruel wind, when you are climbing up steep places and the loose stones are giving way in your hand, you will know whether prayer is a necessity of life or a recreation of the religious fancy.

Our prayers are forced out of us, and being forced out of us by some mighty impulsion that cannot be adequately described in words, they seem to take the kingdom of heaven by force. When men feel the bitterness of sin, they will find right names for Christ. Realize that Jesus Christ is not to be merely approached as an intellectual or historical person. We must feel Christ rather than understand Him, we must wait for His coming rather than surprise Him by our intellectual agility. He is not a subject for our essays and for clever discussions. Christ is the Savior who comes to the heart, the Messenger who finds His way to us along the intricacies and difficulties of our sorrow, the One who visits us in the midnight of our hopeless guilt. May we never miss His approach.

JOSEPH PARKER

When Christ spoke of dogs, he meant that the Gentiles were to Israel as the dogs. Notice that the Canaanite woman did not dispute it but yielded the point by saying, "Yes, Lord." She felt she was worthy only to be compared to a dog. I have no doubt her sense of unworthiness was very deep. She did not expect to win the boon she sought for on account of any merit of her own; she depended upon the goodness of Christ's heart, not of the goodness of her cause, and upon the excellence of His power rather than upon the prevalence of her plea. Yet conscious as she was that she was only a poor Gentile dog, her prayers were not hindered. The mouth of faith could not even be closed by a sense of admitted unworthiness.

No matter what level of unworthiness we find in our hearts, out of the depths, out of the dungeon of self-loathing, still cry out to God, for His salvation rests in no measure or degree upon you or upon anything that you are or have been or can be. It is yours to be empty that Jesus may fill you, yours to confess your uncleanness that He may wash you, yours to be less than nothing that Jesus may be everything to you. Never allow the number, blackness, frequency, or heinousness of your sin to silence your prayers, but though you are not worthy to be set with the dogs of the Lord's flock, open your mouth in believing prayer.

Faith will not allow us to be kept back even in the darkest and most depressing influences. Though cold water was poured upon the flame of this woman's hopes, her faith was not quenched. It was a faith of that immortal kind that nothing can kill, for her mind was made up that whatever Jesus meant or did not mean, she would not cease to trust Him. Though a thousand lions stand in the way when our soul attempts to come to Jesus, let us throw ourselves at His dear feet and never let Him go.

CHARLES SPURGEON

He replied, "It is not right to take the children's bread and toss it to their dogs." "Yes, Lord," she said, "but even the dogs eat the crumbs that fall from their masters' table."

Matthew 15:26–27

August 1

*Then Jesus answered,
"Woman, you have
great faith! Your
request is granted."*

MATTHEW 15:28

$\mathcal{B}$y faith the Canaanite woman's daughter was healed, even though she was an unlikely candidate. By faith the walls of Jericho fell down—yet what more unlikely! We walk by faith. Do we? What record is there on high of things that we have obtained by faith? Is each step each day an act of faith? Do we, as children of God, really believe the Bible? Are we ready to take the place of even a worm, as our Master did: "But I am a worm and not a man" (Ps. 22:6). Or if we realize our power-lessness and our insignificance, do we believe that it is possi-ble—that it is God's will for us—that we should thresh mountains? "Do not be afraid, O worm Jacob," said the Lord by the prophet of old, "I will make you into a threshing sledge, new and sharp, with many teeth. You will thresh the mountains and crush them, and reduce the hills to chaff. You will winnow them, the wind will pick them up, and a gale will blow them away. But you will rejoice in the Lord and glory in the Holy One of Israel" (Isa. 41:14–16).

How then, do we ask, are we to thresh mountains? Let us lis-ten to our Master: "Have faith in God...I tell you the truth, if anyone says to this mountain, 'Go, throw yourself into the sea,' and does not doubt in his heart but believes that what he says will happen, it will be done for him" (Mark 11:22–23). Do you ask when this shall be? The Lord continues in the following verse: "Whatever you ask for in prayer, believe that you have received it, and it will be yours." Let us therefore "not be anx-ious about anything, but in everything, by prayer and petition, with thanksgiving, present your requests to God" (Phil. 4:6).

Now let us stop and ask ourselves: What do we desire? And then let us claim the promise at once. Have we unsaved loved ones? Have we difficulties to conquer? Have we mountains to remove? Then let us take it to the Lord in prayer.

HUDSON TAYLOR

August 2

G reat faith is sometimes found where we least expect it. Our Lord beheld it in a Canaanite woman whose faith was far stronger than His Jewish disciples, who had known the Scriptures since their youth. She was a woman who had great discomfort at home, for the devil was there, tormenting her daughter. It is a dreadful thing to have the devil in your husband or your child when you go home, yet many Christian women have this to bear. Notwithstanding the grave trial, though there was nothing to comfort her at home, she was a woman of great faith. And why shouldn't we be like her? Although your living circumstances may be greatly against your growth in grace, yet why should you not grow to full maturity in Christ? The Lord Jesus can cause you to do so. Though it seems to you that you are stunted by the chill blast and the cruel soil around you, yet Jesus can so nurture you that you become a plant of renown. God can turn disadvantageous circumstances into means of growth. By the holy chemistry of His grace He can bring good out of evil.

Then Jesus answered, "Woman, you have great faith! Your request is granted."

Matthew 15:28

Great faith also sees light in the thickest darkness. Amazingly, she persevered in seeking the Lord when His very words appeared harsh and rejecting. If our Lord spoke to us like that, we would never dare to pray again. But she pleads with Him as readily as if He had given her a promise instead of a rebuff. Great faith can see the sun at midnight. It can reap harvests at midwinter and find rivers in high places. It is not dependent upon sunlight, because it sees that which is invisible by other light. Great faith rests upon the certainty that such a thing is so because God has said it, and it is satisfied with His bare word. If she neither sees nor hears nor feels anything to corroborate the divine testimony, she believes God for His own sake, and Jesus takes great delight in it. Believe Him, then. Believe Him greatly. Believe Him unstaggeringly. Believe His promise without doubt.

CHARLES SPURGEON

August 3

Jesus left there and went along the Sea of Galilee. Then he went up on a mountainside and sat down. Great crowds came to him, bringing the lame, the blind, the crippled, the mute and many others, and laid them at his feet; and he healed them. The people were amazed when they saw the mute speaking, the crippled made well, the lame walking and the blind seeing. And they praised the God of Israel.

MATTHEW 15:29–31

The life of Jesus Christ was one of continual pressure. After healing the Canaanite woman's daughter, He went up on a mountain and sat down to rest. No sooner had He sat down than great multitudes came to Him, bringing a host of physically impaired people and laying them at His feet. We belong to Jesus most when we are in our deepest, most abject helplessness. He does not say, "Take away these burdens and leave the mountain free for My enjoyment"—no, He is a king, and a king must give, a king must identify himself with his subjects, royalty must sympathize. And Jesus healed them, so that those who were borne up the mountain as burdens left it with agility and delight and thankfulness. Then was there great rejoicing among the multitude: They could not deny the wonderful works that had been done. When we see the blind seeing, the crippled made whole, the mute speaking, and the lame walking, it is surely impossible for us to resort to some mere intellectual explanation of these marvelous and astounding disclosures of prayer. The people yielded to the natural instinct, and the mountain throbbed again with the resounding song and shout and jubilance of those who beheld the revelation of the kingdom of gracious power.

Jesus Christ is doing greater works today, and today the world should be filled with the music of worship and thanksgiving to God. Were we not blind and now we see? We were defiled and unclean and corrupt, but we are washed, we are cleansed, we are sanctified. If it is a great thing to see the lame walking and the mute speaking, it is a greater thing to see a bad heart turned to righteousness and to hear blaspheming lips opened in loyal prayer. Such are the continual miracles of Jesus.

JOSEPH PARKER

August 4

$\mathcal{H}$ear this sweet music that rises with the might of gentleness in the desert. It comes upon us suddenly, and yet there
ought not to be any suddenness in such a strain. *Compassion* is
the key word of the Savior's life, the surname of Christ. He
refers to His compassion as if it were a new feature, but what
was the Savior doing all the time but having compassion? The
feeling never ceased: It touched with its own gentleness everything that Christ did. It gave a wondrous expression to His
eyes; it caused the subtlest tones to enter into His gentle yet
all–pervasive and all–penetrating voice; it was the secret and
the very inspiration of His life.

When Christ preached, His words were steeped in feeling;
every sermon therefore came from His heart, belonged to His
heart, expressed His heart's uppermost feeling and purpose.
When Christ denounced, he denounced the Pharisees because
they would not touch the burdens they laid upon others; it was
because He had compassion upon those who were oppressed
and deluded by the tyranny of those who sought to entrap them
in legalism.

"I have compassion." With what richness of tone did He say
that word? It warmed the wilderness when He uttered it; a new
glow of hope pervaded the hearts of all who heard that ineffable
music. The clever man amuses us for a moment, the entertainer
cheers our life on occasion, but we tire of them. But pity, gentle
compassion, noble all–including sympathy is the everlasting
necessity of our lives and the divinest expression of interest.

This is Christ's power over the world—not the splendor of His
intellect, not the fascination of His simple crystal eloquence, but
His care, pity, patience, hopefulness, the heavenly way He has
of stooping down to us and reconstructing our life when it has
been shattered, by whispering into our ear the word of hope
that we dare not whisper to ourselves lest we provoke the
sword of conscience or the sting of outraged memory. By His
love He wins; by His compassion He stands foremost as the
world's Redeemer.

JOSEPH PARKER

*"I have compassion for
these people."*

MATTHEW 15:32

August 5

Then he took the seven loaves and the fish, and when he had given thanks, he broke them and gave them to the disciples, and they in turn to the people. They all ate and were satisfied.

MATTHEW 15:36–37

One point that forever separates Jesus Christ from all other men, even the most tender-hearted and compassionate, stands out in this miracle. It can be said of Christ alone that His resources were equal to His compassion. Our compassion outruns our resources: We are so often utterly helpless we might as well have no senses at all. What we would do, if we could—we would lift up the sick and the weary and make them well in a moment if it was within our power so to do. We would take up the languishing and the death-stricken and make them glad in the summer light and cause them to laugh with new energy and because of new earthly hopes. We would cover up the grave, filling it with flowers, and smooth down the green face of the earth, so that it would be a shame to rip it up again for the purpose of hiding away the life of man. But though this would be the expression of our ignorant compassion, we are left without resource.

Jesus Christ always startled His disciples by the completeness of His proposals. "You give them something to eat," He said, and the disciples immediately answered, "How?" "Go and make disciples of all nations" (Matt. 28:19)—the same completeness and the same compassion, the same determination to meet the necessity of the whole case. Truly, from a human point of view there is as little apparently in the one case as in the other—that is to say, in the case of preaching the gospel to every creature and feeding the multitude with a few loaves and small fishes. What is there in this gospel to preach to every creature? What is there of sufficiency to meet the needs of the human family in all lands in all times? Yet it grows as it is spoken. This message never ends: It halts for a moment to accommodate the weakness of the speaker, but it waits for him; it makes the air throb and burn till he returns to his work, never expressed in final speech. Such is the eternal sufficiency of the gospel to meet every need.

JOSEPH PARKER

August 6

The Pharisees and Sadducees had looked upon the whole demonstration of evidence applied by Jesus Christ in the course of His ministry and were exactly in the same condition of unbelief and disguised and avowed hostility as before. No impression had been made upon them of a vital kind. They had been dazed and stunned by a succession of miracles but had not been convinced. Admitting that great and wonderful cures had been performed, they were piously anxious that now some sign should be shown to them from heaven. You cannot understand the emphasis they pronounced upon that sacred word. A token from heaven would be exactly what their pious and noble minds required. Yes, they had seen wonderful deeds, but these were material and sensational, adapted to the general populous—but they desired a sign from heaven. They considered themselves devout, sweet-souled, godly men, who were alive on the heavenly side of their nature and who would accept any hint or claim that came from the sky in infinite preference to the cures of the leprous, the deaf, the blind, and the maimed.

This is a common corruption. Give them what you may, they always want miracles of another kind. We want sermons of another kind when the devil is twisting his fingers further and further around us. We enjoy the sermons that are delivered but would rather hear a sermon from heaven. We do not deny the truth of what we hear, but we desire something more spiritual. We do not doubt the good that has been done in the past, but we desire to see good of another kind. This is the stock temptation of the old serpent. He says, "What you have is all very good; wonderful doctrine has been propounded, but you should ask for something new, different, better." Old serpent, cunning—and yet his cunning ought now to be so transparent that we should mock it and reject it with bitter scorn. Beware of wrapping a religious cloak around you and seeking a sign from heaven.

JOSEPH PARKER

The Pharisees and Sadducees came to Jesus and tested him by asking him to show them a sign from heaven.

MATTHEW 16:1

August 7

"A wicked and adulterous generation looks for a miraculous sign."

MATTHEW 16:4

Jesus Christ met the pious call for a sign from heaven with a two-edged sword that was driven straight into the guilty hearts. Was not the religious men's pious speech about heaven; was not their question simple and direct; is there any one word in it that could give reasonable offense; did they not belong to the spiritual section of the church, the sighing, crying, and heaven-desiring section of spiritual inquirers? Jesus pulls down their disguise and accosts the devil when he wore an angel's costume.

In the case of Jesus Christ, we must always judge the question by the answer He returns. We do not say everything in words: The big lie is in the heart and not in the speech. Christ answers the question we want to ask and not merely the inquiry we actually put in words. Was not this penetration of character a sign from heaven? Was He ever much grander and nobler than when He faced the religionists and answered a question that flowed from unmixed hypocrisy? Did this man bargain with His age; did He pay a high price for popularity? Was this the way to increase His fame and comfort? Would it not have been better for Him to simply show them some tricks from heaven? Mark the stern and invincible consistency of this man: He will have no compromise with hypocrisy. This is the eternal miracle of truth: It pierces us, being sharper than any two-edged sword. This is the proof of inspiration the Bible always gives. Do not find its inspiration in its literary conscientiousness, in its mechanical consistency, in its artistic finish—find whether it is inspired or not by its moral penetration, moral omniscience, moral authority. In any right reading of the Book, we stand in a holy place, cut off from everything else, made solemn by an unspeakable quietness, so quiet that a whisper is as thunder, so holy that a sight may pollute the awful sanctity. Understand that Jesus has nothing to do with hypocrites but place them under God's judgment.

JOSEPH PARKER

August 8

$\mathcal{V}$iewing the life of Christ, the best that flesh and blood can come up with is a diverse array of conclusions. They saw Jesus as a mysterious person, a holy person, a compassionate person, a wonder-working person; but who He might be they could not make out. Error is multifaceted; truth is one. A thousand lies will live together and tolerate each other. A thousand false gods will stand together in the Pantheon, but if the ark of the true God enters Dagon's temple, Dagon must come down on his face and be dashed to pieces. Jehovah is God alone and will not tolerate a rival. Truth is of necessity intolerant of error. Do not misunderstand me—I believe in the fullest religious liberty and that conscience owes allegiance to none but God. But I speak of principles: Holiness cannot endure sin; righteousness cannot bear injustice; truth cannot consort with error.

Beware of a misty religion! Tighten your grip upon eternal things. Realize the Christ and hold Him fast. Have no second-hand information, no hypothesis, no inference. Let Him reign within your heart as the Son of the living God. Whatever others may say of Jesus, my tongue can never speak a thousandth part of the praises my heart renders to Him, and, alas, my heart does not worship Him a thousandth part as much as He deserves. When I have striven with all my might to extol Him in my preaching, I feel ready to bite my tongue for being so slow and slack. My words are but air, and my tongue but clay, and our Master's glories are too great to be set forth by such poor means. Oh, that we knew how to extol Him! Away with any comparison to Jesus; you are blind as bats! As well might you compare the sun to a glowworm. Come, angels and archangels, and help us with your burning words! Nay, even you must fall. Jesus is infinite, incomparable. The brightness of the Father's glory is not to be set forth by our words.

CHARLES SPURGEON

He asked his disciples, "Who do people say the Son of Man is?" They replied, "Some say John the Baptist; others say Elijah; and still others, Jeremiah or one of the prophets."

MATTHEW 16:13–14

August 9

Simon Peter answered, "You are the Christ, the Son of the living God."

MATTHEW 16:16

There should be no difficulty whatever in distinguishing between the man who has been a long time intimate with Christ and any man who is simply looking upon Christ's history from an outside standpoint. Unction should be in the voice of the one; manifold music should be involved in the one utterance and should pronounce itself in many a happy and suggestive tone. Judgment begins at the house of God, not the judgment of denunciation alone but the judgment of true-hearted criticism. The fire at the center of the earth is hotter than any other fire. So in the church of Christ there should be an all-solving, all-fusing ardor of conviction.

That conviction was sublimely represented in the answer given by Simon Peter. Instantly, with the suddenness of lightning and yet with the graciousness of light, he said, "You are the Christ, the Son of the living God." He was never so great a man before, nor has he ever been a greater man since he returned that infinite reply. Simon Peter was transfigured by his own answer; he was no long a poorly clad fisherman—the fire burned through his clothes: He was the tabernacle of the indwelling God. We know what it is to have a thought in us that transfigures the face and makes the countenance shine with unearthly luster. The great speaker is always surprised by his own utterances, and suddenly there falls upon him an all-transfiguring fire from heaven—the very flesh is a new flesh, and every pore of it an outlet for the inner light. Could we have seen Peter then, we should have seen him at his best—he has never been the same since. Some moments in life can never be repeated. There are some firsts that have no seconds; there are voices that seem to have no echoes. Once for all their ineffable music rolls itself over the welcoming spaces, and it can never be repeated. The day when our voice declares a revelation from heaven is a blessing beyond description.

JOSEPH PARKER

Beloved, if we truly know the Savior, we have not learned it alone by the instruction of other men. Peter had heard others speak, but he did not know Jesus as the Christ till the Father revealed Him. Paul tells us concerning the gospel that he neither received it from men nor was taught it, but he received it by the revelation of Jesus Christ. I grant you that God uses men to instruct us, but all the prophets and apostles could not teach us Christ if the Father did not reveal His Son in us personally. Holy men are the pens, but God Himself must write with them, or they will write nothing on our hearts.

The man who has obtained his religion from other people may have it taken away by other people, but he who has received it from the Father holds it by a tenure that cannot be broken. That which we have learned from the Father will never be unlearned. Nothing can erase what the Holy Spirit has engraved. Beware of a homemade religion created by your own doing. Equally, beware of a religion that is a sort of patchwork made up by the kind contributions of Christian friends, and none of it your own. Beware of the oil that you borrow: You must go to the seller and buy for yourself. No other man can drink from my pitcher; everyone must go the well for himself. There is no safe religion in the world but that which comes through a personal application to Jesus and a reception of Him for yourself. In this matter, God Himself must reveal Jesus to you. The Spirit must take the things of Christ and show them to us, or we shall never receive them. Everyone who has been taught of the Father comes to Jesus and comes to Jesus to remain: Anything short of that is temporary and delusive. Get the better part by sitting at the feet of Jesus, and it will never be taken from you. But religion that does not come by a personal revelation is a mere mirage—there is no reality about it, and it will disappear like a dream of the night.

CHARLES SPURGEON

Jesus replied, "Blessed are you, Simon son of Jonah, for this was not revealed to you by man, but by my Father in heaven."

MATTHEW 16:17

August 11

Jesus replied, "Blessed
are you, Simon son of
Jonah."

MATTHEW 16:17

The four gospels are full of Peter. After the name of our Lord, no name comes up so often in the gospels as Peter's. No disciple speaks so often and so much as Peter. Our Lord speaks oftener to Peter than to any other of His disciples, sometimes in blame and occasionally in praise, as in this instance. No other disciple ever so boldly confessed and outspokenly acknowledged and encouraged our Lord as Peter did repeatedly, and no one ever intruded and interfered and tempted Him as Peter did repeatedly.

Peter's footprints are unmistakable throughout the New Testament. Hasty, headlong, speaking impertinently and unadvisedly, ready to repent, ever wading into waters too deep for him, and ever turning to his Master again like a little child. Peter was sanguine and enthusiastic and extreme both for good and for evil, beyond the other disciples. Peter was naturally and constitutionally of the enthusiastic temperament, and his conversion and call to discipleship did not suppress his true nature. The son of Jonah was, to begin with, a man of the strongest, most willful, and most wayward impulses, impulses that, but for the watchfulness and the prayerfulness of his Master, might easily have become the most headlong and destructive.

All Peter's faults, indeed, lay in the heat of his heart. He was too hot-hearted, too impulsive, too enthusiastic. His hot heart was always in his mouth, and he spoke it all out many a time when he should have held his peace. His Master saw in Simon latent qualities of courage and fidelity and endurance and humility. By degrees, and under the teaching, the example, and the training of his Master, Peter's too-hot heart was gradually brought under control till it became the seat in Peter's bosom of a deep, pure, deathless love and adoration of Jesus Christ. Let us take Peter, come to perfection, for our pattern and our prelate; and, especially, let us watch and work and pray against a cold heart, a chilling temper, a distant, selfish, indifferent mind.

ALEXANDER WHYTE

August 12

The "time" referred to was probably a little more than six months before the crucifixion, when Jesus was just on the point of finally leaving Galilee and traveling toward Jerusalem. It was an epoch in His ministry. The hostility of the priestly party in the capital had become more pronounced, and simultaneously, the fickle enthusiasm of the Galilean crowds, which had cooled by His discouragement, had died down into apathy. Jesus and His followers are about to leave familiar scenes and faces and to plunge into perilous and untrodden paths. Jesus resolves that if they are going to come after Him, it will be with their eyes open. They shall be abundantly certified that their journeying to Jerusalem is not a triumphal procession to a crown but a march to a cross.

Mark the tone of the language, the minuteness of the detail, the absolute certainty of the prevision. This is not the language of a man who simply is calculating that the course that he is pursuing is likely to end in his martyrdom. But the thing lies there before Him, a definite, fixed certainty, every detail known, the scene, the instruments, the nonparticipation of these in the final act of His death, His resurrection, and its date—all manifested and mapped out in His sight, and all absolutely certain. Yet this was by no means the first time the cross was made plain to Christ—its shadow had always darkened the path He traveled.

This "must" was no unwelcome obligation laid upon Him against His will but one to which His whole nature responded and accepted. His willing acceptance of the evil of the cross was owing to His resolve to save the world. He must die because He would redeem, and He would redeem because He could not but love. The "must" was not an iron chain that fastened Him to His cross. The cords of love that fastened Him to the cross was His love for each of us.

ALEXANDER MACLAREN

From that time on Jesus began to explain to his disciples that he must go to Jerusalem and suffer many things at the hands of the elders, chief priests and teachers of the law, and that he must be killed and on the third day be raised to life.

MATTHEW 16:21

August 13

Peter took him aside and began to rebuke him. "Never, Lord!" he said. "This shall never happen to you!" Jesus turned and said to Peter, "Get behind me, Satan! You are a stumbling block to me; you do not have in mind the things of God, but the things of men."

MATTHEW 16:22–23

How vividly the scene of Peter's rash rejection of the Master's teaching is described! The apostle, full of eager love, swift to speak, and driven by unexamined impulse, lays his hand upon Christ and draws Him aside and begins to pour out words that show he has forgotten his confession. "Rebuke" must not be softened down into anything less vehement or more disrespectful. He believes he knows better than Jesus what will happen.

But Peter is not allowed to finish what he began, for the Master, whom he loved unwisely but well, turns His back on him, as in horror, and shows by the terrible severity of His rebuke how deeply moved He is. He repels the hint in almost the same words as He had used to the tempter in the wilderness, of whom that Peter, who had so lately been the recipient and pro-claimer of a divine illumination, has become the mouthpiece. So possible is it to fall from sunny heights to doleful depths! So lit-tle can any divine inspiration be permanent if the man turn away from it to think man's thoughts and set his affections on the things men desire! So certainly does minding these degrade to becoming an instrument of Satan! The words are full of restrained emotion, which reveals how real a temptation Peter had flung in Christ's path. The rock has become a stone of stumbling. The man Jesus shrank from the cross with a natural and innocent shrinking, which never made His will tremulous, but was nonetheless real; and such words from Peter's loving lips did affect Him.

Let us note, on the whole, that the complete truth about Jesus Christ must include these two parts—His divine nature and Messiahship, and His death on the cross—and that neither alone is the gospel, nor is he a disciple, such as Christ desires, who does not cling to both with mind and heart.

ALEXANDER MACLAREN

August 14

The law that ruled the Master's life is here extended to the servants. They recoiled from the thought of His having to suffer. They had to learn that they must suffer too if they would be His. First, the condition of discipleship is set before them as being the fellowship of His suffering. "If" gives them the option of withdrawal. A new epoch is beginning, and they will have to enlist again and do so with open eyes. He will have no unwilling soldiers nor any who have been beguiled into the ranks. No doubt some went away and walked no more with Him.

The terms of service are clear. Discipleship means imitation, and imitation means self-crucifixion. At that time, they could only partially understand what taking up their cross was, but they would apprehend that a martyred master must have followers ready to be martyrs, too. But the requirement goes much deeper than this. There is no discipleship without self-denial, both in the easier form of starving passions and desires and in the harder yielding up the will and letting God's will supplant ours. Only so can we ever come after Him, and of such sacrifice of self, the cross is the eminent example. We cannot think too much of it as the instrument of our reconciliation and forgiveness, but we may, and too often do, think too little of it as the pattern of our lives.

Jesus adds that the desire to save life is the loss of life in the highest sense. If that desire guides us, then farewell to enthusiasm, courage, the martyr spirit, and all that makes man's life nobler than a beast's. He who is ruled mainly by the wish to keep a whole skin loses the best part of what he is so anxious to keep. In a wider application, regard for self as a ruling motive is destruction, and selfishness is suicide. On the other hand, lives hazarded for Christ are therein truly saved, and if they are not only hazarded but actually lost, such loss is gain.

ALEXANDER MACLAREN

Then Jesus said to his disciples, "If anyone would come after me, he must deny himself and take up his cross and follow me. For whoever wants to save his life will lose it, but whoever loses his life for me will find it."

MATTHEW 16:24–25

August 15

"What good will it be for a man if he gains the whole world, yet forfeits his soul? Or what can a man give in exchange for his soul?"

MATTHEW 16:26

What, might I ask, shall it profit a man if he gains the whole world and loses his *sight?* How would you view that proposition? You shall have estates, blocks of houses, mines of gold, luxuries untold, and in exchange you must pay your *sight.* Will you conclude the bargain? What shall it profit a man if he gains the whole world and loses his *hearing?* You shall have diamonds in multitudes that cannot be numbered, servants for every need, and all the delights of the sons of men, but you shall pay your *hearing* in exchange for the bounty; you shall never hear the human voice again, its eloquence, its song, its friendly word, its kind salute—what say you to this offer? Does any man offer the price? Would it be too much to pay? What wonder, then, if Jesus Christ should say, "If you will not pay your sight, if you will not pay your hearing, in exchange for what the world has and can give, what shall it profit you if you gain it all and pay for it with your *soul?* A soul paid for a month's comfort, eternity ruined at the price of a day's release from pain, heaven paid in exchange for hell." These are the ironies of life!

Such things are done every day by men who claim to some measure of intelligence. Within us there is a power against which our best impulses and noblest purposes contend in vain—they go down before its savage strength in utter helplessness and are crushed by its iron heel with all the delight of satisfied malevolence. A wondrous battlefield is the human heart! What is the remedy? Crucifixion we must have. Our opportunity lies in the grand choice between being crucified by others and crucifying ourselves. Jesus laid down His life on His own, and therein was His peace. So we must yield up our will to Christ's own cross.

JOSEPH PARKER

August 16

In the transfiguration we see the radiance of Christ's face and the gleaming whiteness of His clothing that shone like the snow on Mount Hermon when it was smitten by the sunshine. Probably we are to think of the whole body as giving forth the same mysterious light, which made itself visible even through the white robe He wore. This would give beautiful accuracy and appropriateness to the distinctions drawn in the two metaphors—that His face was like the sun, in which the undiluted glory was seen, and His clothes were as white as the light, which is sunshine diffused and weakened. It is clear that the brightness came as a rising from within, not cast from without. Here we find indwelling divine glory, which dwelt in Him as in a shrine, suddenly shining through the veil of His flesh. John explains the event, though his words go far beyond it, when he says, "We have seen his glory, the glory of the One and Only, who came from the Father, full of grace and truth" (John 1:14).

What was the purpose of the transfiguration? Matthew seems to tell us in that "before them." It was for the disciples' sakes, not for Jesus. The new epoch of His life, in which they were to have a share of trial and cross bearing, needed some great encouragement poured into their tremulous hearts. And so, for once, He decided to let them look on His face, shining as the sun, for a remembrance when they saw it covered with shame and spitting and His brow bleeding with thorns. But perhaps we may venture a step further and see here some prophecy of that body as His glory in which He now reigns. How similar does Christ appear here as compared to the Christ that John some years later beholds in the unveiling recorded in the book of Revelation? "His face was like the sun shining in all its brilliance" (Rev. 1:16). The transfiguration of Christ was both a revelation and a prophecy of what was to come.

ALEXANDER MACLAREN

There he was transfigured before them. His face shone like the sun, and his clothes became as white as the light.

MATTHEW 17:2

August 17

*Just then there
appeared before them
Moses and Elijah,
talking with Jesus.*

MATTHEW 17:3

While the three disciples were gazing on Jesus with dazzled eyes, suddenly there stood by Jesus two mighty forms encompassed in the white radiance, walking and talking with the Son of Man. What awe and wonder must have touched the gazers as the conviction of who these men were filled their minds and they recognized the mighty visage of the lawgiver and the prophet! Moses and Elijah were probably sent to bring strengthening words to Jesus, but it was also for the disciples.

Their appearance set forth Christ's death, which was their theme, as the climax of revelation. The Law, with its requirement and its sacrifices, and Prophecy, with its forward-looking gaze, stand there in their representatives and bear witness that their converging lines meet in Jesus. Their presence and their speech were the acknowledgment that this was He whom they had seen from afar; their disappearance proclaims that their work is done.

Their presence also teaches us that Jesus is the life of all the living dead. They are witnesses of an immortal life and proofs that His yet unpierced hands held the keys of life and death. Jesus opened the gate that moves backward to no hand but His and summoned them, and they come with no trailing grave-clothes entangling their feet and own Him as the King of life.

They speak, too, of the eager onward gaze that the Old Testament believers turned to the coming Deliverer. In silent anticipation, through all the centuries, good men had lain down to die, declaring, "I wait for Your salvation." Now these two are brought from their hopeful repose, perchance to learn how near their deliverance was; and behind them we seem to discern a dim crowd of holy men and women who had died in faith, not having received the promises, and who throng the portals of the unseen world, waiting for the near advent of a better Samson to carry away the gates to the city on the hill.

ALEXANDER MACLAREN

August 18

These were the very same words spoken at the baptism of Jesus (Matt. 3:17), and it was the best news that ever came from heaven to earth since man sinned. Christ is the Son, and in Him God is reconciling the world, and in Him God was always well pleased.

This was no vain repetition of the same voice that came from heaven at His baptism, but its doubling was to show the thing was established. It was spoken at His baptism because then He was entering upon His temptation and public ministry. Now it was repeated because He was entering upon His sufferings, which are to be dated from this point, for now, and not before, He began to foretell them, and immediately after His transfiguration it is said (Luke 9:51) that the time had come that He should be received up. These words came to arm Christ against the coming terror and His disciples against the offense of the cross.

The great gospel duty required is that we "Listen to Him!" God is well pleased with none in Christ but those who hear Him. It is not enough to listen, but we must hear Him and believe Him as the great Prophet and Teacher, hear Him and be ruled by Him as the great Prince and Lawgiver, hear Him and heed Him. Whoever would know the mind of God must hearken to Jesus Christ, for by Him God has in these last days spoken to us. This voice from heaven has made all the sayings of Christ as authentic as if they had been thus spoken out of a cloud. God does here, as it were, turn us over to Christ for all the revelations of His mind.

Christ now appeared in glory, and the more we see of Christ's glory, the more cause we have to listen to Him; but the disciples were gazing on the glory. They are therefore told to not look at Him but to hear Him. Their sight of His glory was soon intercepted by the cloud, but their business was to hear Him. We walk by faith, which comes by hearing, not by sight (2 Cor. 5:7).

While he was still speaking, a bright cloud enveloped them, and a voice from the cloud said, "This is my Son, whom I love; with him I am well pleased. Listen to him!"

MATTHEW 17:5

MATTHEW HENRY

August 19

When they looked up,

they saw no one

except Jesus.

MATTHEW 17:8

*W*hen Peter saw our Lord with Moses and Elijah, he exclaimed, "Lord, it is good for us to be here," as if he implied that it was better to be with Jesus and Moses and Elijah than to be with Jesus only. Now it was certainly good that for once in Peter's life he should see Christ transfigured with the representatives of the Law and the Prophets; it might be for that particular occasion the best sight that Peter could see, but ordinarily an ecstasy so sublime would not have been good for the disciples. Peter himself very soon found this out, for when the luminous cloud overshadowed him and the voice was heard from out of the heaven, we find that he with the rest became afraid. The best thing for Peter was not the excessive strain of the transfiguration nor the delectable company of the two great spirits who appeared with Jesus, but the equally glorious, but less exciting, society of Jesus only.

Depend on it, beloved, that ravishing and exciting experiences and transporting enjoyments, though they may be useful as occasional refreshments, would not be so good for every day as that quiet but delightful ordinary fellowship with Jesus only, which should be the distinguishing mark of all Christian life. As the disciples ascended the mountainside with Jesus only, and as they went back again to the multitude with Jesus only, they were in as good company as when they were on the mountain summit, Moses and Elijah being there also. Although Jesus Christ in His common garments might not dazzle their eyes as when they saw His raiment as bright as the light and His face shining as the sun, yet He really was quite as glorious and His company quite as beneficial. Jesus only, as the common Jesus, the Christ of every day, the man walking among men, communing in secret with His disciples, is a better thing for a continuance while we are in this body than the sight even of Jesus Himself in the excellence of His majesty.

CHARLES SPURGEON

August 20

It is obvious that this experience was meant for the disciples alone. We cannot tell all we know: We have secrets that make the heart throb double time, and we would be poor if we parted with them. We have all had experiences of Christ that we could not tell, for no words have been invented for such experiences. Such looks He has given us, such warmth He has communicated to us, such promises He has whispered into the heart— we have laid our head upon His shoulder and cried like little children, and we have been stronger for the sweet sorrow. When we have told all we have to tell, we have not begun the tale: We have secret faiths, secret hopes, secret delights, all in keeping with the central truth but each with an accent unintelligible to the general ear.

This is a hard lesson: "Don't tell anyone what you have seen, until..." Who does not like to speak when he has seen great sights or heard sounds of unusual music? Christ gives the disciples one of their first lessons in the cross. He has just told us, "If anyone would come after me, he must deny himself and take up his cross and follow me" (Matt. 16:24). In this injunction, Jesus causes the disciples to feel the first pressure of what will become a great weight, namely, the cross of crucifixion. Learn the lesson of self-suppression, learn the mystery of silence; the wild-talking man never comes to any rich maturity of life. We must always know more than we have ever told: Every author must be greater than his books, every singer greater than his song, every preacher more than his sermon. Do not babble: Think. Keep all these things and ponder them in your heart— the uses of all will be seen presently. Does Jesus Christ ever tune the instrument for the purpose of hanging it on the wall? He tunes it that He may play eloquent music upon it. So when He grants us white and shining revelations of Himself and His purpose, it is that we may go down the mountain and heal the child possessed by the demon.

JOSEPH PARKER

As they were coming down the mountain, Jesus instructed them, "Don't tell anyone what you have seen, until the Son of Man has been raised from the dead."

MATTHEW 17:9

August 21

"I brought him to your disciples, but they could not heal him."

MATTHEW 17:16

The man whose son was suffering greatly from seizures as well as from a demon had a peculiar speech to make to Jesus: His earnestness made him frank. He did not seek to flatter the disciples or to excuse them but plainly states that they had been of no help. This same charge is brought against the Church today. May I add that it is a charge that is often but too just? The world, like the demon-possessed boy, is at the door of the Church today, and the Church seems to care next to nothing for the sufferer and to have no power over the deadly affliction. The Church has her rituals, her old outworn forms of expression, her decayed machinery, but the miracle-working power, the divine inspiration, the sovereignty over all hindrances and stumbling blocks, alas, where have they fled? What is the Church worth if she cannot cure the lunacy of the world? The Church, like her Master, has nothing to do in the world unless it is to heal and to bless and to save mankind. The Church was instituted not to amuse the world but to save it, not to mock the world by speaking to it a pointless and useless speech but to redeem it through Jesus Christ the Lord.

Discipleship is not enough, for it may be merely nominal. Outward ceremonies and institutional relationships are not enough—these may be only external and momentary and factitious. Discipleship of the heart alone can do any good. The inflamed and inspired heart cannot speak words of weakness; let that heart utter itself, and in its tone there will be the music of a subtle sympathy, and the world will be the better for its illumining and comforting speech. How is it with our hearts? Our hearts are clever enough and clear enough and may be sufficiently stored with a certain kind of information, but what about the heart—its sympathy, its insight, its moral intuition, its redeeming desires, its unity, almost identity, with the Son of God?

JOSEPH PARKER

August 22

*P*rayer and fasting are prescribed by the Lord as the means of joining us to greater power than we possess, and the Church would be far stronger to wrestle with this ungodly age if she used these means. Prayer links us to heaven; fasting separates us from earth. Prayer takes us into the banqueting house of God; fasting delivers the soul from being encumbered with the fullness of bread that perishes. When believers bring themselves up to the uttermost possibilities of spiritual vigor, then they will be able, by God's Spirit working in them, to cast out devils that would otherwise laugh them to scorn. But for all that, there will still remain those mountainous difficulties that must be directly brought to the Master's personal agency for help.

Let me beg you to remember that Jesus Christ is still alive. Simple as that truth is, you need to be reminded of it. We very often estimate the power of the Church by looking at her ministers and members, but the power of the Church does not lie here; it lies in the Holy Spirit and in an ever living Savior. Jesus lives today as He did when that anxious father brought his son to Jesus. We have neither the power to work natural miracles nor the power to work spiritual miracles. Christ has the power to work any kind of wonder, and He is still willing and able to work spiritual miracles. I delight to think of my living Christ, to whom I may bring every difficulty that occurs in my own soul and in the souls of others.

Remember, too, that Jesus lives in the place of authority. All hell confesses the majesty of His power and the splendor of His Godhead. There is no demon, however strong, who will not tremble before Him, and Jesus is the master of hearts and consciences. There cannot be a case too hard for Him. Is Christ unable to save, or are there diseases too many for the Great Physician to heal? Never can it be! Christ outdone by Satan and by sin? Impossible! He breaks the bars of iron and the gates of brass asunder that captives might be brought forth to liberty.

CHARLES SPURGEON

"Bring the boy here to me."

MATTHEW 17:17

August 23

Then the disciples come to Jesus in private and asked, "Why couldn't we drive it out?" He replied, "Because you have so little faith."

MATTHEW 17:19–20

Our faith is ever threatened by subtle unbelief. It appears that the disciples were ignorant of the unbelief that had made them weak. They fancied that they had confidence in their Christ-given power, and they certainly had in some dull kind of fashion expected to succeed in their attempt. But He who sees the heart knew that there was no real living confidence in their souls; and His words are a solemn warning to us all of how possible it is to have our faith all honeycombed by gnawing doubt while we suspect it not, like some piece of wood, apparently sound, the whole substance of which has been eaten away by hidden worms. We may fancy ourselves faithful servants of the gospel, and all the while there may be an utter absence of the one thing that makes our words more than so much wind whistling through an archway. Who among us is not exposed to the assaults of that darkness? Subtly it creeps over us, the stealthy intangible vapor, unfelt till it has quenched the lamp that alone lights the darkness of the mind and clogged to suffocation the laboring lungs.

Let us take heed to ourselves, lest we allow our grasp of our dear Lord's hand to relax. We cannot help seeing the creeping paralysis of hesitancy and doubt that even the power of Christ's name is stealing over portions of the Church and stiffening the arm of its activity. Lips that once spoke with full confidence the words that cast out devils mutter them now languidly with half-belief. Hearts that were once full of sympathy with the great purpose for which Christ died are growing cold to the work of preaching the gospel to the heathen, because they are growing to doubt whether, after all, there is any gospel at all. This icy breath is blowing over our churches and over our hearts. And wherever it reaches, there labor for Jesus and for men languishes, and we recoil baffled with unavailing exorcisms dying in our throats and the rod of our power broken in our hands.

ALEXANDER MACLAREN

August 24

*P*eter's assumption that Jesus will automatically pay the modest temple tax is disputed by Jesus; nevertheless, Jesus waives His entitled exemption "that we may not offend." Few knew, as Peter did, that Jesus was the Son of God; and it would have been a diminution to the honor of that great truth, which was yet a secret, to advance it now to serve such a purpose as the payment of the temple tax. We must sometimes deny ourselves rather than give offense to others (1 Cor. 8:13; Rom. 14:13).

It appears, though, that the poverty of Christ was such that He did not have the two drachmas (about two days' wages) to pay for it. In His ordinary expenses, Jesus lived upon the giving of others (Luke 8:3), and in extraordinary ones, He lived upon miracles. He did not order Judas to pay this out of the common purse that was intended for the benefit of the whole group; that was for subsistence, and He would not ask for that.

We note the power of Christ in getting the money out of a fish's mouth for this purpose. Whether His omnipotence put it there or His omniscience knew it was there, it comes out the same as an evidence of His divinity and that He is Lord of hosts. Even the fish of the sea are under His dominion and command (Ps. 8:5–8).

Observe that Peter must catch the fish by angling. Even in miracles, Christ would use means to encourage our endeavors and to make us ever ready to work for Him. Peter has something to do, and perhaps it came as a lesson to him as well. In this obedience, we find that keeping Christ's command brings its own pay along with it. There is always a great reward in keeping God's commands (Ps. 19:11). In this case, there was just enough money to pay the tax for Christ and Peter. So Christ teaches us to not covet extravagances but, having enough for our present situation, to be content and never distrust God. Let us always make God's providence our storehouse and treasury.

MATTHEW HENRY

"But so that we may not offend them, go to the lake and throw out your line. Take the first fish you catch; open its mouth and you will find a four-drachma coin. Take it and give it to them for my tax and yours."

MATTHEW 17:27

August 25

*H*ow blatantly can we debase the sublimest of subjects! See how they put their words together, and learn from the wild incoherence how possible it is for us to commit the same impious ironies. "Who is the greatest in the kingdom of heaven?"—as if there could be any greatness there of our own making, as if our nature should outshoulder the great dignities, as if we could be *somebody* in the infinite kingdom of light and grace. These men were not struck by the grandeur of the heavenly kingdom; they were plagued with the vexatious question as to which of them should be prominent in it!

Is it not so now to some extent? Are we overwhelmed by the occasion, or do we lift our heads above it and wave our hand over it as if we were bigger after all? In the church, for instance, in holy psalm, in tender prayer, in the reading of the revealed Word, how do we behave ourselves? Do we shrink away into an all but invisible perspective, being nothing when such light shines and such music thrills the air, or do we come forward in bold, plain self-assertiveness? The subject—when the subject is the kingdom of heaven—should always be greater than the men who approach its consideration. In that sense, the altar should be greater than the penitent sinner, for the altar stands for God, and the sinner's only approach should be in a voice that can barely be heard lest his very prayer become an impiety and his intercession aggravate the guilt that he deplores.

One would have thought that men having had given to them the phrase "the kingdom of heaven" would have been dazzled by its glory and so impressed by its tender graciousness that they would never have thought of their position or status within its infinite circumference. I tell you, we all have learned the wicked trick of spoiling everything God gives to us! We have spoiled the earth and would disfigure and mar the very symmetry and music of the stars if we could clutch them.

JOSEPH PARKER

August 26

It was as if Jesus were saying, "You are asking who is the greatest in the kingdom of heaven, forgetting the earlier question—how to get into the kingdom of heaven. Pause before you begin to take your seat in the kingdom; make sure you are in the kingdom itself." The question takes upon itself a thousand accents and smites like a great wind from every corner of heaven. "Before you preach the truth, be sure you feel its power; before you theologize, be sure you can pray; before you debate on things literary and theological, be sure your hearts are broken and all your self-righteousness has been expelled from you like the poison of hell." Let us first consider whether we are in the kingdom, and in proportion as we feel ourselves to be in the kingdom shall we have little concern as to our particular place within the glowing sphere. Words like these of Christ's go right down to the very core and root of things and make us cautious in our questions to Him.

He called a little child and had him stand among them. And he said: "I tell you the truth, unless you change and become like little children, you will never enter the kingdom of heaven."

MATTHEW 18:2–3

It was a great day in the church when that little child stood there and all unconsciously represented the kingdom of heaven. Dear little child!—so little that the Savior took him up into His arms: a hand all dimples, a cheek so fair, made for the kiss of love and trust and blessing, and eyes that had no speculation in them, still a gentle wonder of dreamy love, looking round itself wondering at the scene. And yet that child was made that day to set forth to all the ages the kingdom of God! Where, then, are the great, the noble, the rich, the wise? Where are the ingenious, the learned, the intellectual? Where are they? I have always found that in proportion as a man is truly learned is he truly modest; in proportion as a man is really great is he really childlike. Childlikeness is simplicity, trustfulness, utter unconsciousness in the sense of vain boasting and glory, gentleness, love, sincerity of heart and motive. Here is the practical inquiry for every one of us: Have we the child-heart?

JOSEPH PARKER

August 27

"If your hand or your foot causes you to sin, cut if off and throw it away. It is better for you to enter life maimed or crippled than to have two hands or two feet and be thrown into eternal fire."

MATTHEW 18:8

No person or thing can do our characters as much harm as we ourselves can do. Indeed, none can do them any harm but ourselves. Others may put millstones in the way, but we make them stumbling blocks. The obstacle in the path would do us no harm if it were not for the erring foot, nor the attractive prize if it were not for the hand that itched to lay hold of it, nor the glittering gem if it were not for the eye that kindled at the sight of it. While our Lord has issued a solemn woe of divine judgment on anyone who causes His followers to stumble, let us ourselves be the executioners of the judgment upon the things in ourselves that alone give the millstones their fatal power.

Hand and foot and eye are, of course, regarded as organs of the inward self and symbols of its tastes and capacities. Our Lord takes an extreme case. If members of the body are to be amputated should they cause us to stumble, much more are associations to be abandoned and occupations relinquished and pleasures forsaken if they draw us away. But note the "if." The powers are natural; the operation of them is perfectly innocent, but a man may be ruined by innocent things. It means that anything that draws me away from my relationship with God, however innocent it may be, must come under the knife.

Jesus does not say that we are to abandon all things that are susceptible to abuse, for everything is so. Nor does He mean that we should abandon a duty that causes us to stand in positions full of temptation and danger. But He does mean that we are to suppress capacities, abandon pursuits, and break with associates when we find that they are damaging our spiritual life and hindering our likeness to Jesus. We have to empty our hands of earth's trivialities and weights if we would grasp Christ with them. We have to turn our eyes from earth if we would behold the Master.

ALEXANDER MACLAREN

August 28

The shepherd felt at home with his faithful flock; they had not gone astray, and they gathered about him, and he fed them and took pleasure in them. There is always a great deal to do with sheep: They have many diseases, many weaknesses, many needs. But when you have an attached, affectionate flock about you, you feel at home with them. So the great Shepherd describes Himself as leaving the ninety and nine, His choice flock, the sheep that had fellowship with Him, and He with them. Yes, He leaves those in whom He could take pleasure to seek one that gave Him pain. I will not dwell upon how He left the paradise above and all the joy of His Father's house and came to this bleak world, but I pray you remember that He did so. It was a wonderful descent when He came from beyond the stars to dwell on this obscure globe to redeem the sons of men.

But, remember, He still continually comes by His Spirit. His errands of mercy are perpetual. The Spirit of God moves His ministers, who are Christ's representatives, to forego the feeding of the gathered flock and to seek, in their discourses, the salvation of the wandering ones, in whose character and behavior there is nothing to cheer us. My Master's heart is full of care for all who love Him. He wears their names engraved on the jewels of His breastplate, but yet His heart is always going forth afar after those who have not been brought to Him and after those who once were in His fold but have gone aside and left the flock.

Our Lord leaves the happy and the holy and gives His best thoughts to the lost. He goes out to seek them in a marching forth of power. His divine grace is going forth into the mountains among difficulties and dangers. No dark ravine or high place can daunt His mighty love. What difficulties He conquered, what suffering He endured, what mountains He climbed, that He might seek and save us! Oh, that the Holy Spirit may put such a spirit within us!

CHARLES SPURGEON

"What do you think? If a man owns a hundred sheep, and one of them wanders away, will he not leave the ninety-nine on the hills and go to look for the one that wandered off?"

MATTHEW 18:12

August 29

"And if he finds it, I tell you the truth, he is happier about that one sheep than about the ninety-nine that did not wander off."

MATTHEW 18:13

"If he finds it." That is an awful *if*, when we think of what lies below it. The thing seems an absurdity when it is spoken, and yet it is a grim reality in many lives—that Christ's effort can fail and be thwarted. Not that His search is indifferent or careless, but that we shroud ourselves in darkness through which that love can find no way. It is we, not He, who are at fault when He fails to find that which He seeks. There is nothing more certain than that God and Christ desire the rescue of every man, woman, and child of the human race. Let no teaching blur that sunlit fact. There is nothing more certain than that Jesus Christ has done, and is doing, all that He can do to secure that purpose. If He could make every man love Him and so find every man, be sure that He would do it. But He cannot. There is no person in heaven or earth or hell that has any blame in the matter but the person alone. It is very easy to turn away from the Shepherd's voice. "But since you rejected me when I called and no one gave heed when I stretched out my hand" (Prov. 1:24). That is all! That is what you do, and that is enough.

"If he finds it"—that is a wonderful and merciful phrase. It indicates the infinitude of Christ's patient forgiveness and per-severance. We tire of searching. But Jesus Christ stands at the closed door through the night, with the dew on His hair, unheeded or repelled, like some stranger in a hostile village seeking for a night's shelter. He will not be put away; but after all refusals, still with graciousness He knocks upon the door and speaks into the heart. Christ knows nothing about "incurable cases." If there is the worst man in the world—and perhaps there is—there is nothing but the man's own disinclination to prevent his being brought back and made as pure as an angel. However far you have gone, you have not gone so far but that Jesus' love reaches out through the remoteness to grasp you and draw you to Himself.

ALEXANDER MACLAREN

August 30

How is Christ there? As we, His people, meet, He is there because He is in every one of us. It is a blessed thing to see Christ in His people. I cultivate the practice of endeavoring to see my Lord in all His people, for He is there, and it is irreverent not to honor Him. He is with them and is in them; why should we doubt it? That is something worth remembering. If so many temples of the Holy Spirit gather, why, surely, the Holy Spirit is there, and the place whereon they stand is holy ground. Jesus is in their thoughts, desires, groans, sorrows, spirits, and inmost souls.

"For where two or three come together in my name, there am I with them."

MATTHEW 18:20

Christ is with us in His Word. When the Bible is opened, it is not mere words; it is the living and incorruptible Word of God, and the Christ is in it as the immortal life, the secret life-germ in every seed that we sow. Christ is the way, if we teach men the road to heaven. Christ is the truth, if we preach the doctrines of grace. Christ is the life, if we enjoy and feed upon His precious name. Where His Word is preached, there He is.

Christ is in His ordinances. He has not dissociated Himself from baptism, the blessed symbol in which His death, burial, and resurrection are clearly set forth. He has not separated Himself from His Supper, in which we behold His passion and see the way in which we become partakers of it by feeding upon His body and His blood. He has promised to be with us even to the end of the world in the keeping up of those divine memorials of His incarnation and atonement, His life and death.

And the Lord Jesus is with the assembly by His Spirit. He has sent the Spirit as the Comforter to abide with us forever. You must have felt Him sometimes convincing you of sin, humbling you, then cheering you, comforting you, enlightening you, guiding you, sustaining you, sanctifying you. Oh, what light and life He brings! What love and joy He brings! So He is always among us!

CHARLES SPURGEON

August 31

Then Peter came to Jesus and asked, "Lord, how many times shall I forgive my brother when he sins against me? Up to seven times?"

MATTHEW 18:21

Peter interposes into Jesus' insight in what to do when a brother sins against him and shows that he knows nothing about human nature. We see how grand Christ is by seeing how pitifully little every other person is in comparison. Peter's words are exactly what we would have said. Did it never occur to Peter that he might sin against his brother. Standing there in conscious perfectness of character and disposition, will and thought, godly man, serene and most pious soul, he wonders how often *he* has to play the great man by forgiving somebody else! He starts from the wrong point. The question is not an innocent one; it is steeped in guilt if he did but know it. If one assumes his own sinfulness, he most certain will start the question from the possibility that he may be the offender.

Peter further discloses his littleness by making a suggestion that forgiving a brother seven times perhaps should be the limit. How does this attitude compare with the infinite majesty— "seventy times seven"? The Lord's thoughts are obviously not your thoughts, Peter; neither are His ways your ways. For as the heaven is high above the earth, so are His thoughts higher than your thoughts.

Jesus' answer both awes me and causes me to rejoice. We are called to forgive the repentant brother an uncountable number of times! This is a discipline most severe to my nature. But it also causes me to rejoice, for if God asks so much from me, what will He be prepared to be and to do Himself in reference to my repentance? Laying my finger upon this celestial arithmetic, how might I plead with Him! The Lord is slow to anger, multiplying His pardon. It is not a thin transparent wave He allows to flow over the black stone of my sin, but sea upon sea, He pours upon that blackness, letting it be found no more forever. In that I rejoice!

JOSEPH PARKER

September 1

While scholars differ in the precise amount represented by a talent, the very point of the expression is that millions of dollars—a staggering sum—are owed. A talent was the largest denomination in the currency of the period, signifying that every sin against God is a great sin. He being who He is, and we being who we are, and sin being what it is, every sin is large, although the deed that embodies it may be, when measured by the world's yardstick, very small. The essence of sin is rebellion against God and the enthroning of self as His rival; and all rebellion is rebellion, whether it is blatant opposition or simply sulkily refusing obedience and cherishing thoughts of treason. It may be a small act; it is a great sin. Little rattlesnakes are rattlesnakes with poison fangs as real as the most monstrous of the brood. Do any of us realize, as we all should, the infinite number and the transcendent greatness of our sins against the Father?

A recognized legal right is exercised by the master when he orders that the man, having sinned, be sold as a slave. Our conscience witnesses that this is absolutely just based upon our sin. Yet we cry out for mercy, for we shall repay every penny! Easy to promise. How long will it take the penniless bankrupt to scrape together millions of dollars? But the language of the prayer is all wrong. No! It is impossible that we can repay. No future righteousness has any power to affect the guilt of past sin. There is one thing that does discharge the writing from the page—only the blood of Jesus. We discover a king who, though in former words seemed so harsh with the law, now sounds incredibly merciful, for He not only cancels the debt but also sets us free!

ALEXANDER MACLAREN

"Therefore, the kingdom of heaven is like a king who wanted to settle accounts with his servants. As he began the settlement, a man who owed him ten thousand talents was brought to him. Since he was not able to pay, the master ordered that he and his wife and his children and all that he had be sold to repay the debt. The servant fell on his knees before him. 'Be patient with me,' he begged, 'and I will pay back everything.' The servant's master took pity on him, canceled the debt and let him go."

MATTHEW 18:23–27

September 2

"But when that servant went out, he found one of his fellow servants who owed him a hundred denarii. He grabbed him and began to choke him. 'Pay back what you owe me!' he demanded. His fellow servant fell to his knees and begged him, 'Be patient with me, and I will pay you back.' But he refused. Instead, he went off and had the man thrown in prison until he could pay the debt."

MATTHEW 18:28–30

The conduct described is almost impossibly disgusting and cruel. The debt owed here amounted to a few dollars. Yet the hands that a minute before had been wrung in agony and extended in entreaty now throttled the poor servant; and with the voice that had been plaintively pleading for mercy a minute before, the man gruffly growled, "Pay back what you owe me!" He had just come through an agony of experience that might have made him tender, having received a blessing that might have made his heart glow. But even the repetition of his own petition does not touch him, it avails nothing. And so he flings the poor debtor into prison.

Could a man be like that? The things that would be monstrous in our relations to one another are common in our relations to God. Every day we see and, alas, do the very same thing in our measure and degree. Do you never treasure up somebody's slights? Do you never tuck away the record of some trivial offense against you? It is but a penny against a talent, for the worst that any of us can do to another is nothing as compared with what many of us have been doing all our lives toward God. But we score down our neighbor's act against us with as implacable and unmerciful an unforgiveness as that of this servant in the parable. Do not believe that he was a monster of iniquity. He was just like us. Having been forgiven, he did not forgive.

Our Lord here implies the principle that God's mercy to us is to set the example to which our dealings with others is to be conformed. "Shouldn't you have had mercy...just as I had on you?" (vs. 33) is our Lord's word to us. God's forgiveness is the model and the motive that, brought into our experience, inclines and enables us to forgive. Let us always forgive.

ALEXANDER MACLAREN

September 3

These solemn words close the parable of the unmerciful servant. There can be no doubt whatsoever as to Jesus' position on the theme of retribution and pardon. A child can understand this parable—no secret wizardry prevents us from seeing God's meaning in this great matter of human forgiveness. There is no grammatical puzzle in the interpretation of this parable; do not seek to find any way out of it. It comes to one of two things—either forgive for Christ's sake and be forgiven, or do not forgive and be not forgiven.

Wondrous is the phrase, "from your heart." Forgiveness is sometimes an affair of the lips; pardon is accompanied by a thousand reservations. I know of no men so disinclined to forgiveness than professing Christians. I know ministers of the gospel who have never known the joy of having forgiven a brother. They forgive with parentheses; they forgive with great big *ifs* following the reluctant words. They will forgive but not forget, they will watch, they will wait, they will hope, they will even hope for the best, but it will take a long time to restore confidence! Marvelous Christianity—evangelical doctrine, diabolical temper. Spotless orthodoxy, hideous devilism. Forgiveness should be the *delight* of Christians. Forgiveness must be based upon repentance—there must be confession, or there cannot be pardon. But when that repentance comes, do not take six months to see how the confessor behaves; you, rather, must behave well and forgive immediately. Do not say, "It will be a long time before the old love comes back." Where would you be today if God forgave you with a distinct intimation that He was going to withdraw His old love? Happy is the man who can pray, "Forgive us our debts, as we also have forgiven our debtors." That is the crux of prayer—that is the supreme difficulty of intercession!

JOSEPH PARKER

"This is how my heavenly Father will treat each of you unless you forgive your brother from your heart."

MATTHEW 18:35

September 4

Then little children were brought to Jesus for him to place his hands on them and pray for them. But the disciples rebuked those who brought them. Jesus said, "Let the little children come to me, and do not hinder them, for the kingdom of heaven belongs to such as these."

MATTHEW 19:13–14

The tender scene before us is a lily that cannot be painted. Mothers brought their little children to Jesus. Some of us are carried to God; some of us are brought in loving arms to Christ. We want to bring all men to Jesus. The woman whose husband will not bow to Jesus says, "I will take him to Christ today in some great prayer that is bolder than I have yet ventured to hurl at the very gate and throne of heaven. I will carry him today." O woman, grand heart, she is going to do it by persuasive violence, by gentle force. Your mother says she will carry you to Christ; she says she will believe for you if He will let her. She has so much faith she thinks that she could even include you in the sweep of her trustful belief. How many of us were utterly lost yet our mothers continued to bring us to Jesus? That ought to melt us in tears and break our hearts with infinite contrition. Bring the children to Jesus with your love; don't force them.

Why was Jesus so fond of these little ones? Why did He gather all these little flowers to Himself and bind them to His heart? He tells us, "for the kingdom of heaven belongs to such as these." How He warmed to that kingdom in every aspect of it! When you are in a foreign land and you hear another person speaking in your own language, you say, "How sweet! How homelike! I love the sound of it better than anything." And if He, the Christ of God, saw down here in this rough climate any flower such as He had seen grow upon the heavenly slopes, what wonder if He bent over it and bestowed upon it tenderest and fondest interest. This was Jesus Christ's reason: Whatever represented the kingdom of heaven was precious to Him; wherever He saw any trace or hint of it, there He was in the fullness of His sympathy and in all the tenderness of His music.

JOSEPH PARKER

September 5

*B*y the word *neighbor* we are to understand any person who is near us. The Good Samaritan, when he saw the wounded man on the road to Jericho, felt that the man was his neighbor, and he was bound to love him. That includes all the people nearby—rich or poor, different religion or nationality, competitors in business, enemies, the vulgar and outcasts and lepers. The law of God knows no exception; it claims my love for all. I must love all, and love them as I love myself.

What would our world be like if this law were carried out, even if only within the Church? How many believers really love their neighbors? How many love all the people who go to their church? What about those who differ with you in opinion? Some hardly love their own brothers and sisters. Indeed, some are at daggers drawn with their family members. How can I expect you to love your enemies if you do not love your friends? Perhaps you are angry at your parents or with your spouse for a word spoken earlier in the day. Remember, we are bound to love and honor everyone, not for their goodness or care toward us but simply because the law demands it.

To *love* is a positive command. It is not *the not doing,* it is the doing. It is not enough to not hate your enemy; it is to love him. If the path of love is rough, tread it boldly, and still on, loving your neighbors through thick and thin. Heap coals of fire on their heads, and if they are hard to please, seek not to please them but to please your Master. And remember that if they reject your love, your Master has not rejected it, and your deed is as acceptable to Him as if it had been acceptable to them. Love makes us at all times ready to serve our neighbor, ready to be his footstool if it must be so, that we may be so proved to be the children of Christ. Let love, unconquerable love, dwell in your heart, love that many waters cannot quench, love that the flood cannot drown. Love your neighbors.

CHARLES SPURGEON

"Love your neighbor as yourself."

MATTHEW 19:19

September 6

"All these I have kept," the young man said. "What do I still lack?"

MATTHEW 19:20

We have in the case of the rich young ruler one of the saddest stories in the gospels. It is a true soul's tragedy. He is sincere, but his sincerity lacks the force to lift him over the bar. He wishes to have some great thing asked of him to do but finds the sharp test that Christ imposes too much for him. The truest way to draw sincere souls is not to flatter nor to make entrance easy by dropping the standard or hiding the requirements but to call out all their energy by setting before them the lofty ideal. Easy-going disciples are easily made—and lost. Thorough-going ones are most surely won by calling for entire surrender.

The young man's words indicate astonishment at being deferred to these old, well-worn commandments, and there is a touch of impatience in the reply, "All these I have kept," and more than a touch of self-satisfaction. The law has failed to accomplish one of its chief purposes in the young man in that it has not taught him his sinfulness. He had never gone below the surface of the commandments or below the surface of his acts, or he would not have answered so carelessly. He had yet to learn that the height of "goodness" is reached not by adding some strange new performances to the threadbare precepts of everyday duty but by digging deep in these and bottoming the fabric of our lives on their inmost spirit.

Still he was not at rest, although he had, as he fancied, kept all the commandments. "What do I still lack?" is an honest acknowledgment of the hungry void within which no amount of outward obediences can ever fill. He knows that he has not the inner fountain springing up into eternal life. He is right in believing that the reason for that conscious void is something lacking in his conduct. But Christ will give him no new commandment but a deeper understanding and keeping of the old. When Christ reveals our heart, how close we are to the kingdom!

ALEXANDER MACLAREN

September 7

*W*hen Jesus confronted this young man with the key to eternal life, the man was brought face-to-face, no doubt for the first time, with the true state of his spiritual heart. He was a good man, worthy of the Lord's love. But he was not hungry with the hunger that leads to righteousness.

From what we know of the youth, I do not suppose he was one whom we would call a lover of money or a covetor of his possessions. I imagine he valued his possessions and looked upon them as good, seeing them as something deserved and perhaps meritorious. But our Lord saw that the young man was a slave, for a man is in bondage to whatever he cannot part with that is less than himself. The Lord could have taken his possessions from him, but there would have been little good in that. The Lord wished to accomplish His purpose by the exercise of the young man's will. That would indeed have been a victory for both!

If only he could do as the Lord suggested, the youth would enter into freedom and life, delivered from the bondage by the lovely will of the Lord in him, one with his own. By the putting forth of the divine energy in him, he would escape the corruption that is in the world through lust—that is, the desire or pleasure of *having*.

But the young man would not. The price was too high, and he went away sorrowfully. The Lord had given him the very next lesson in the divine education for which he was ready. It was possible for him to respond, to give birth by obedience, to the redeemed and redeeming will and so be free. It was time the demand should be made upon him, and his refusal allowed him to see what manner of spirit he was of and thus to meet the confusions of soul, the sad searchings of heart that must follow.

A time comes to *every* man and woman when he or she must obey or make such refusal—*and know it.*

GEORGE MACDONALD

Jesus answered, "If you want to be perfect, go, sell your possessions and give to the poor, and you will have treasure in heaven. Then come, follow me."

MATTHEW 19:21

September 8

When the young man
heard this, he went
away sad, because he
had great wealth.

MATTHEW 19:22

*W*hat has become of the eagerness that brought the rich young man running to Jesus, of the willingness to do any hard task to which he was called? It was real eagerness, but shallow. It deceived him. But Christ's words cut down the inner man and laid bare for his own inspection the hard core of selfish worldliness that lay beneath. How many radiant enthusiasms, which cheat their subjects quite as much as their beholders, disappear like tinted mist when the hard facts of self-sacrifice strike against them! How much sheer worldliness disguises itself from itself and from others in glittering garments of noble sentiments that fall at a touch when real surrender is called for! How much "religion" goes about the world and is made "a ruler" of the synagogue in recognition of its excellence, which needs but this Ithuriel's spear to reveal its true shape!

The immediateness of the man's collapse is noticeable. The young man seems to speak no word but stands for a moment as if stunned and then silently turns away. What a moment! His fate hung upon it. Once more we see the awful mystery enacted before our eyes of a soul gathering up its power to put away life. Who will say that the decision of a moment which is the outcome of all the past may not fix the whole future? Christ tore away the veil of surface goodness that hid the man from himself and forced him to a conscious decision.

One sign of grace he does give, in that he went away "sad." He cannot see the fair prospect of the eternal life, which he had in some real fashion desired, fade away without a pain in his heart. If he goes back to the world, he goes back feeling more acutely than ever that it cannot satisfy him. He loves it too well to give it up but not enough to feel that it is enough. Surely, in coming days, that sadness turned to a godly sorrow to work a change of the foolish choice, and we may hope that he found no rest till he cast away all else to make Christ his own.

ALEXANDER MACLAREN

September 9

That it is a very hard thing for a rich man to get to heaven is stated twice by Christ, accented solemnly by His saying, "I tell you the truth." The way to heaven is to all a narrow way, and the gate that leads into it is small but is particularly so to rich people. More duties are expected from them than from others which they can hardly do, and more sins do easily beset them which they can hardly avoid. The rich have great temptations to resist, and many of them are deceitfully affable. It is hard not to be charmed with a smiling world. Rich people have a great account to make up for their estates, their interest, their time, and their opportunities of doing and getting good, above others. It is very rare for a man to be rich and not to set his heart upon his riches, and it is utterly impossible for a man who sets his heart upon his riches to get to heaven. "If anyone loves the world, the love of the Father is not in him" (1 John 2:15). It must be a great measure of divine grace that will enable a man to break through these difficulties.

The disciples were astonished by Jesus' words as the rich young man walked away, and they could not help but wonder out loud, "Who then can be saved?" But when we consider the many difficulties that are in the way of salvation, it is really surprising that anyone is saved. When we think how good God is, it may seem a wonder that so few are His; but when we think how bad man is, it is a wonder that so many are, and Christ will be eternally admired in them. If riches are a hindrance to rich people, are not pride and luxury equally as dangerous to them? But with God, salvation is possible for any man. When men are at a loss, God is not. With men it is impossible that so strong a stream should be turned, so hard a heart softened, so stubborn a will bowed. But with God is power of a new creation for every man.

MATTHEW HENRY

Then Jesus said to his disciples, "I tell you the truth, it is hard for a rich man to enter the kingdom of heaven." When the disciples heard this, they were greatly astonished and asked, "Who then can be saved?" Jesus looked at them and said, "With man this is impossible, but with God all things are possible."

MATTHEW 19:23, 25–26

September 10

Peter answered him,
"We have left every-
thing to follow you!
What then will there
be for us?" Jesus said
to them... "And
everyone who has left
houses or brothers or
sisters or father or
mother or children or
fields for my sake will
receive a hundred
times as much and will
inherit eternal life."

MATTHEW 19:27–29

Christ promised the rich young man that if he would sell all and come and follow Him, he would have treasure in heaven. The disciples had not in fact sold all they had, but they had long since forsaken all to follow Jesus. Peter couldn't help but wonder whether they had sufficiently come up to those terms, yet till now they had never asked, "What then will there be for us?" Though there was no visible prospect of advantage by it, they were so well assured of His goodness that they knew they should not lose by Him at last, and now they asked how Christ would make up their losses to them. It honors Christ to trust Him and serve Him and not to bargain with Him. Now that this young man was gone from Christ to his possessions, it was time for them to think of their future. When we see what others keep by their hypocrisy, it is proper for us to consider what we hope, through grace, to gain not for but by our sincerity and constancy for Christ.

To follow Christ presupposes losses. If we truly forsake these things for Christ's sake, because we cannot keep them and keep a good conscience, Christ undertakes to make it up, for He is able to do it, be it ever so great. No one has ever followed Christ who was not an unspeakable gainer by Him when the account came to be balanced against losses. Christ promises them they shall receive a hundred times as much in the things they have parted with. Whether it be friends or kindnesses, their graces shall increase, their comforts abound, and they shall have tokens of God's love and sweet foretastes of the glory yet to be revealed. And over and above this, Christ promises eternal life! What, then, is one hundred percent profit in this lifetime? If we but mix faith with the promise, surely we should think nothing too much to do, nothing too hard to suffer, nothing too dear to part with, for Him.

MATTHEW HENRY

September 11

Oh, the resplendent glory of God's grace, at whatever age He calls you to Himself. Those called at an early age have delightful reason for admiring sovereign grace, for they are spared the ills and sins of life. Then consider the grace that calls the man at the age of twenty, when the passions are hot, when there is strong temptation to plunge into the vices and the so-called pleasures of life. To be delivered from the charms of sin, this is mighty grace for which God shall have our sweetest song.

To be called of the Lord at forty, in the prime of life. This is a wonderful instance of divine power, for worldliness is hard to overcome and is the sin of middle age. With a family about you, with much business, with the world eating into you as does an ulcer, it is a wonder that God should break through into your life.

At sixty or at eighty, your vessel has begun to rot in the waters of the Black Sea of sin, yet you have a new owner by divine grace! How should you find words with which to express your gratitude! Let us together, called by grace early or late, ascribe it all to the Lord Jesus, and moved by the constraints of His love, let us work with all our hearts for the glory of His name!

I pray you, brethren, allow no idleness to creep over you. If you have sought to extend the Redeemer's kingdom, do it more. Give more, talk more of Christ, pray more, labor more! I often receive the kind advice, "Do less." I cannot do less. Do less! Why, better rot altogether than live the inglorious life of doing less than our utmost for God. Work for the Master! Labor on! We must spend and be spent for Him! Make no reserve for the flesh to fulfill its lusts. And oh, how happy we shall be, if we may be privileged to finish the work and hear Jesus say, "Well done, good and faithful servant! Come and share your Master's happiness!"

CHARLES SPURGEON

"For the kingdom of heaven is like a landowner who went out early in the morning to hire men to work in his vineyard. About the third hour he went out and saw others standing in the marketplace doing nothing....again about the sixth hour and the ninth hour and did the same thing. About the eleventh hour he went out and found still others standing around."

MATTHEW 20:1, 3, 5–6

September 12

"About the third hour he went out and saw others standing in the marketplace doing nothing. He told them, 'You also go and work in my vineyard, and I will pay you whatever is right.'"

MATTHEW 20:3–4

God is infinitely greater than we are, and let us never misunderstand His call to work in His vineyard as though we could do anything meritorious in the eyes of our Maker. He is great and glorious, whatever we may be; and it is for our joy, our safety, our everlasting happiness, that we should become His servants. It is necessary for the right ordering of our lives that our hearts may be in tune to yield the music of joy, that we should be tuned by obedience to His will, and that we should learn to serve Him.

Note that the impulse to serve God always comes from God to us. It never comes from within ourselves first of all. If anyone wills to serve God, there was another will that moved his will, or else his will would never have moved toward God. None of the various men mentioned in this parable went to the vineyard and requested to be employed. The landowner came out into the marketplace and persuaded them to work for him. God the Holy Spirit is able to work upon the judgment, the understanding, the affections, the fears, the hopes, the will of men; and as He works upon them, He makes men willing in the day of God's power so that they turn to Him and enter into His service. The Holy Spirit comes with power by His own effectual calling, and He speaks to us, and we yield to His speaking and give ourselves up to be His servants for the rest of life.

I fear that you may have settled into spiritual idleness. You may have not done anything yet for Christ; you have not even looked to see what you could do. Or you worked for a time but have stopped for a variety of reasons. My fear is that soon you will get settled into this do-nothing style, and you will spend your life achieving nothing for Jesus. Do not stay in that condition a moment longer. The wax is not very soft now; it is beginning to harden. Let the stamp of sovereign grace be pressed upon it that your life may yet bear the impress of Christ.

CHARLES SPURGEON

September 13

Jesus had told them this before and again details the Father's plan to them. Life is a plan—you will have trouble and grievous unrest and dreams that will plague you like enemies at night if you do not seize the all-restful idea that life is not a game of chance but a divine plan. The very hairs of your head are all numbered. Your troubles are all counted, your very tears as well. The valleys before you were all excavated by the divine hand. Every controversy, every crosswind, every cold, steep climb up the barren rocks—all are part of the divine purpose. No temptation comes before you but such as is common to man, and with it God makes a way of escape. Our Father knows the way we take, and when He has tried us, He will bring us forth as gold. The plan for Jesus' life has about it all the beauty and massiveness of an architectural fabric: It is not a heap of loose stones; it is a building with shape and polish and high utility. So is your life.

There are parts of the plan, like this in Christ's life, that you do not like, but you must deal with the plan as an entirety, and do not suppose that the unfinished house is the complete building. Christ saw this as the whole plan, not part of a design, not one little patch plucked out of the pattern—the whole thing is here. Nothing happened to Christ that is not in this paragraph. Equipped with this plan, a man can essentially discount the future; its tragedies come to him in a sense as commonplaces; its crosses are but punctuations of a literature that he himself has written and approved as to its final outcome and significance. We are troubled because we have no outlook: We take in no field of vision; our life comes at us in little pieces, in mocking details; and not knowing what is coming next, we fret ourselves with sore chafing. The one thing we need not know is the details; the great thing we may know is the solemn wholeness.

JOSEPH PARKER

"We are going up to Jerusalem, and the Son of Man will be betrayed to the chief priests and the teachers of the law. They will condemn him to death and will turn him over to the Gentiles to be mocked and flogged and crucified. On the third day he will be raised to life!"

MATTHEW 20:18–19

September 14

"To sit at my right or left is not for me to grant. These places belong to those for whom they have been prepared by my Father."

MATTHEW 20:23

Our Lord does not put aside this request of His apostles as if they were seeking an impossible thing. It is never safe, I know, to argue from the silence of Scripture. There may be many reasons for that silence beyond our knowing, but still it does strike one as noteworthy that when this fond mother and her ambitious sons came with their prayer for preeminence in His kingdom, our Lord did not answer what would have been so obvious to answer if it had been true: "You are asking a thing that cannot be granted to anyone, for they are all upon one level in heaven." He says by implication the very opposite. Not only does His silence confirm their belief that when He comes in His glory, some would be closer to His side than others, but also His plain statement is that in the depth of the eternal counsels and by the preparation of divine grace, there were thrones nearest to His own that some believers should fill "for whom they have been prepared by my Father."

And then, still further, Jesus does not condemn the prayer as indicating a wrong attitude on the part of James and John, though good and bad are strangely mingled in it. We are often told that it is a very selfish request of these men to be excited, encouraged, and strengthened by the prospect of the crown and the rest that remains for the people of God. If so, Christ should have turned to these men and rebuked the passion for reward. But instead of that, He confines Himself to explaining the conditions on which the desire is possible and by implication permits and approves the desire. "You want to sit at My right and My left, do you? You really don't understand what you're asking, but you may do so if you like if you are ready to accept the conditions. It is right that you should want it—not for the sake of being above your brethren but for the sake of being nearest to Me. But there is a cup that you must drink with Me, and it is a place given only to those for whom the Father has prepared."

ALEXANDER MACLAREN

September 15

Christ's disciples must not be like the Gentiles, nor like the princes of the Gentiles. If they are powerful enough, high officials exercise their dominion and authority over their subjects and over one another. These are what they pursue and pride themselves in, and the more they possess, the more they want.

To the disciples of Jesus, the order is simply: "Not so with you." You are to teach the subjects of this kingdom, instruct and beseech them, counsel and comfort them, weep with them and suffer with them, but not exercise dominion or authority over them. This forbids not only tyranny and abuse of power but also the claim or use of any such secular authority as the princes of the Gentiles lawfully exercise. So hard is it for vain men, even good men, to have such authority and not to be puffed up with it and do more harm than good with it that our Lord Jesus Christ saw fit wholly to banish it out of His Church. The apostle Paul himself disowns dominion over the faith of any man (2 Cor. 1:24).

Rather, it is the duty of Christ's disciples to serve one another for mutual edification. This includes both humility and usefulness. The followers of Jesus must be ready to stoop to any position of love for the good of one another; they must submit one to another (1 Pet. 5:5; Eph. 5:21) and edify one another (Rom. 14:19) and please one another for good (Rom. 15:2). The way to be great and first in the kingdom of Christ is to be humble and serviceable. Those who are to be the highest esteemed in the Church are ones who fit this description, not those who hold grand titles and expect a power proportional to their office. The great apostle himself made himself everyone's servant (1 Cor. 9:19), and shall we do less? These honor God most, and those He will honor.

MATTHEW HENRY

"You know that the rulers of the Gentiles lord it over them, and their high officials exercise authority over them. Not so with you. Instead, whoever wants to become great among you must be your servant, and whoever wants to be first must be your slave."

MATTHEW 20:25–27

September 16

"Just as the Son of
Man did not come to
be served, but to
serve, and to give his
life as a ransom for
many."

MATTHEW 20:28

These words declare Christ's preexistence, His voluntary
entrance into the conditions of humanity, and His setting aside
of the glory that He had with the Father before the world was.
We shall never understand the Servant Christ until we understand that He is the Eternal Son of the Father. His service began
long before any of His acts of sympathetic and self-forgetting
lowliness rendered help to us here upon earth. His service
began when He laid aside not the garments of earth but the
raiment of heaven and clothed Himself with the flesh of our
humanity. This was the first, the primary act of His service,
and the sanctity and awesomeness of it run through the list of
all His deeds and make them unspeakably great. It was incredi-
ble that His hands should heal, that His lips should comfort, that
His heart should bleed with sympathy for sorrow. But, oh, it
was more that He *had* hands to touch, lips to speak to human
hearts, and the heart of a man and a brother to feel *with* as well
as *for* us. That He came is the transcendent example of the true
use of greatness; there is the conspicuous instance of the true
basis of authority and rule.

But then, passing beyond this, we may dwell upon the features
of that wonderful life of self-sacrificing service. Think of the
purity of the source from which all these wonders and
blessednesses of service for man flowed. The life of Jesus is
self-forgetting love made visible, presenting in shapes of
loveliness and symmetry the otherwise invisible music of
divine love. He lets us see the rhythm of the Father's heart. No
taint of self was in that service, no sidelong glances at possible
advantages of influence or reputation or the like that so often
damage men's service to others. There was no speck of black in
that lustrous white robe, but all was perfectly unselfish love.
Like the clear sea, weedless and stainless, that laves the marble
steps of the palaces of Venice, the deep ocean of Christ's
service to man was pure to the depths.

ALEXANDER MACLAREN

September 17

It is impossible for us to know the greatness of the price that Jesus paid for us. O Jesus, who shall describe Your agony as the man of sorrows? The sufferings fell on You in one perpetual shower until the last dread hour of darkness. Then not in a shower but in a torrent of grief Your agonies dashed upon You.

See Him yonder! It is a night of cold, but He does not sleep. He is in prayer. Listen to His groans! Did ever man wrestle as He wrestles? Look at His face! Was ever such suffering depicted upon mortal countenance? What is this that stains the ground? It is blood, falling from His body in a sweat of agony! O sufferings that cannot be compassed in language! His words speak of a soul that is exceedingly sorrowful, even unto death. Then He is seized by traitors, hurried through the streets, dragged from one court and then to another, condemned before the Sanhedrin, mocked by Herod, tried by Pilate. His sentence is pronounced: "Let Him be crucified!" Now the tragedy comes to its height. His back is bared; the bloody scourge plows furrows on His back. He is spit upon, plaited with a crown of thorns, and mocked. All silently He sits; He answers not a word. He is driven through the streets with a cross upon His shoulders. Then His arms are stretched out; the four nails are grasped and driven through the tenderest parts of His body. Yet it is not done yet. The cross is lifted and dropped into its hole, putting every bone out of joint. He sighs, He sobs, He sighs, He cries out in agony of being forsaken by His God. No wonder the sun shut its eye from such agony.

But believe me, what our Savior suffered in His body was nothing compared to what He endured in His soul. Suppose a man should pass into hell and suffer the eternal torment for all God's redeemed. He so drank the cup of suffering that there was nothing left of all the pangs and miseries of hell for His people to endure. Now can you dream, can you guess, the great ransom He paid?

CHARLES SPURGEON

"Just as the Son of Man did not come to be served, but to serve, and to give his life as a ransom for many."

MATTHEW 20:28

September 18

Two blind men were sitting by the roadside, and when they heard that Jesus was going by, they shouted, "Lord, Son of David, have mercy on us!" Jesus had compassion on them and touched their eyes. Immediately they received their sight and followed him.

MATTHEW 20:30, 34

No one ever appealed to Jesus Christ for help of this kind in the name of justice. We cannot too strongly keep that fact before the mind. The blind men never said, "We have heard that you cured the leper, therefore in the name of impartiality we charge you to heal us as well." Every petitioner came to Christ along the line of mercy. So it must always be. That God has pardoned one sinner for Christ's sake is no reason why I should go to Him and challenge Him in the name of justice to be as impartial to me as to other men. There are circumstances in life in which we stand alone in the solemnity of perfect individualism, every man carrying his own burden, every man stung by his own sin, every man burned in a hell of his own, and out of the pit of his own particular distress he must vehemently call upon God in the sweet name of mercy.

How did Jesus respond? I read that He had compassion on them. I may pause there, for I know the rest. Once let His compassion be touched, and His omnipotence goes along with it. We may close the book, for we know the rest of the story down to its uttermost line and hue. Immediately the blind men's eyes were touched and restored to sight.

When the soul speaks out with the intensity of conscious need, confronting the great Giver, it speaks in perfect eloquence. Do not attempt to pray until you feel the need, or you will be mocked by your very supplications, and your religion will be turned into skepticism, and your simulating piety will become a sourness in the heart. But when consciously blind, bruised, shattered, wounded, needy, and you hear that the Son of God passes by, then lift up the voice with great shouting and tears and crying, call for Him, and you will touch His compassion as well.

JOSEPH PARKER

September 19

On the day that Jesus Christ made His triumphal entrance into Jerusalem, He was publicly proclaimed as King. Evermore, beyond doubt, we acknowledge Christ to be King in the Church. The children of light are not ashamed but make it their glory to proclaim Him King in the streets. It is a grand day for the kingdom of Christ when the great trumpet is sounded, when His disciples stand in the highways and the voice of wisdom is lifted up in the chief places of the city, at the gates and the marketplaces. We desire the blessings of the gospel to be extended; and we should pray that the gospel may have free course and be glorified, that every street may ring with its charming music, that every alley and court may brighten with salvation, and that no home be left without knowing that Jesus Christ is Lord.

So let us loudly praise the Savior and greatly rejoice in Him as they did in that day. They clapped their hands and called Him "blessed." The whole multitude of His disciples rejoiced with an exceeding loud voice and cried, "Hosanna!" Christ by His Spirit comes with power into our midst; how can we be quiet?

Then our hearts rejoice and leap along in glee like the long frozen brooks when the soft breath of spring has set them free.

There is no joy like the joy of Christ's presence with His people. Oh, that He might send but a revival! Bickerings soon cease, murmurings come to an end, complaints of one another and of God's providence are all hushed. The sense that Jesus Christ is with His people drowns every note of sorrow, and every heart is tuned to loudest notes of thankfulness. O my soul, bless God the Lord, and all that is in me be stirred up. His holy name to magnify and bless, on that auspicious day, when the power of Jesus Christ is revealed. It is a time of singing, of shouting, of exultation, and of intense delight when we go forth to crown Him anew. May our mouth be filled with singing and our tongue with laughter.

CHARLES SPURGEON

"Say to the Daughter of Zion, 'See, your king comes to you, gentle and riding on a donkey, on a colt, the foal of a donkey.'"

MATTHEW 21:5

September 20

The crowds that went
ahead of him and those
that followed shouted,
"Hosanna to the Son
of David!" "Blessed is
he who comes in the
name of the Lord!"
"Hosanna in the
highest!"

MATTHEW 21:9

*W*hen the Jews carried branches about at the feast of tabernacles, they customarily would cry *Hosanna*, and on account of that they called their bundles of branches *hosannas*. *Hosanna* signifies, "O Lord, save us," referring to Psalm 118:25–26, where the Messiah is prophesied of as the Capstone that the builders rejected; and all His loyal subjects are brought in triumphing with Him and attending Him with hearty good wishes to the prosperity of His enterprises.

The hosannas that attended Christ speak of the welcoming of His kingdom. "Blessed is he who comes in the name of the Lord." It was foretold concerning the Son of David that all nations would call Him blessed (Ps. 72:17). Every gospel blessing begins with Christ, and all true believers in all ages concur and call Him blessed; it is the genuine language of faith. First, Jesus Christ comes in the name of the Lord, for He is sent by the Father into the world. Second, the coming of Christ in the name of the Lord is worthy of all praise. Let His coming in the Lord's name be mentioned with strong affections, to our comfort and joyful acclamations, to His glory. Well may we follow Him with our blessings and praise.

The hosannas also intimated their wishing well to His kingdom. "O Lord, grant us success" (Ps. 118:25). They earnestly desired that prosperity and success may attend His kingdom and that it may be a victorious kingdom. It is our duty to earnestly desire and pray for the prosperity and success of Christ's kingdom in the world. "May people ever pray for him and bless him all day long" (Ps. 72:15), that all happiness may attend His interest in the world and that though He ride on a donkey, yet in His majesty He may "ride forth victoriously in behalf of truth, humility and righteousness" (Ps. 45:4). They add, "Hosanna in the highest"—let prosperity in the highest degree attend Him; let Him have a name above every name, a throne above every throne.

MATTHEW HENRY

September 21

Early in His ministry, Jesus visited the temple and cleansed it (John 2:12–16). He now enters it again and finds that the abuses have only grown. Much could be said in defense of the services provided in the temple as convenient and harmless, and they were too profitable to be lightly abandoned. But the altar of Mammon so near the altar of God was sacrilege in His eyes, and though He had passed the traders unmolested many times since that first driving out, now that He solemnly has entered Jerusalem to claim His rights as King, He cannot but repeat it.

It is perhaps significant that His words now have both a more sovereign and a more severe tone than before. Then He had spoken of "My Father's house"; now it is "My house." He is exercising the authority of a son over his own house and bears Himself as Lord of the temple. Before, He charged them with turning the "house into a market"; now, with turning it into a "den of robbers." Evil rebuked and done again is worse than before. Trafficking in things pertaining to the altar is even more likely than other trading to cross the not always very well defined lines that separate business from trickery and commerce from theft.

That lesson needs to be laid to the heart in many quarters now. There is always a fringe of moneyed interests around Christ's Church, seeking gain out of religious institutions, and their stands have a wonderful tendency to creep inward from the court of the Gentiles to holier places. The parasite grows very quickly, and Christ had to deal with it more than once to keep down its growth. If Christ were to come to His house today in bodily form, who doubts that He would begin, as He did then, by driving the traders out of His temple?

ALEXANDER MACLAREN

Jesus entered the temple area and drove out all who were buying and selling there. He overturned the tables of the money changers and the benches of those selling doves. "It is written," he said to them, "'My house will be called a house of prayer,' but you are making it a 'den of robbers.'"

MATTHEW 21:12–13

September 22

The blind and the lame came to him at the temple, and he healed them. But when the chief priests and the teachers of the law saw the wonderful things he did and the children shouting in the temple area, "Hosanna to the Son of David," they were indignant.

MATTHEW 21:14–15

Now that the Lord Jesus has entered and cleansed the temple, along with the purity He brings, we also find Him healing the blind and the lame. Royal state and cleansing severity are wonderfully blended with tender pity and the gentle hand of sovereign virtue to heal. The very manifestation of the former drew the needy to Him; and the blind, though they could not see, and the lame, though they could not walk, managed to grope and hobble their way to Him, not afraid of His severity nor daunted by His royalty. No doubt they haunted the temple precincts as beggars, with perhaps as little sense of its sacredness as the money changers, but their misery kindled a flicker of confidence and desire, to which he who tends the dimmest wick till it breaks into clear flame could not but respond. He who casts out the traders will also heal the needy.

And Jesus encourages and casts the shield of His approval around the children's praise. How natural it is that the children, pleased with the stir and not yet drilled in conventionalism, should have kept up their glad shouts, even inside the temple walls! How their fresh treble voices ring yet through all these centuries! The priests, who though nursing their wrath at all that had been going on were powerless to stop it, could not stand this unseemly noise, though it was praise. Ecclesiastical martinets and men whose religion is mostly ceremony are more indignant about breaches of ceremonial regulations than at holes made in graver laws. Nothing makes men more insensitive to the ring of real worship than being accustomed to the dull decorum of formal worship. Jesus shuts them up by declaring that the ears of God and of the Lord of the temple are more gladly filled with the praises of the "lips of children," who know their weakness and hymn His goodness with simple tongue, than with heartless eloquence of words or pomp of worship.

ALEXANDER MACLAREN

September 23

The chief priests and teachers of the law always come in very conveniently as a sort of shadow to bring out the brightest lights. One feels glad when they put some of their strange questions to the Savior and arouse His spirit to utter precious truths. Their question here is to the effect, "Do You permit these mere children to salute You with hosannas? What do You think of Yourself when Your name is in the mouths of noisy boys and girls who make the temple courts to ring?" I have met with that spirit in these days, for the Pharisees are not all dead. They may be dead literally, but their spiritual successors are still among us. Listen to their criticism: "It is true that there are many converts, but they are mostly young people." A despising of true faith when it is found among the very young is a pernicious evil that springs up again in each generation however diligently we may pull up the weed.

No doubt the Pharisees said, "The children do not even know the meaning of the word *hosanna,* let alone how to apply the term to the man of Nazareth." I have heard the same thing said of certain people. "Oh, it is a congregation of the lower class, the ignorant, uninstructed people. Very sincere and prayerful, but poor and lower class." That judgment tallies with the Pharisees' criticism. The spirit that looks down upon any class of people who sincerely love the Lord is not from heaven; He would never sanction it. We have but one Master, and we are all brethren.

I also think the Pharisees criticized the children's enthusiasm. If the children had chanted in subdued tones, their words might have been acceptable. But how many of us are hindered by our propriety. No doubt, fanaticism is a bad thing, but it is the exaggeration of something that is good. Fire is a bad master, but an exceedingly good servant. Enthusiasm is of God; let us not repress it because we are fearful that it may grow into fanaticism.

CHARLES SPURGEON

But when the chief priests and the teachers of the law saw the wonderful things he did and the children shouting in the temple area, "Hosanna to the Son of David," they were indignant. "Do you hear what these children are saying?" they asked him.

MATTHEW 21:15–16

September 24

And he left them and
went out of the city to
Bethany, where he
spent the night.

MATTHEW 21:17

From the city to the village—it seems to be but a short journey. In point of mileage indeed it was nothing but an easy walk. How far was it? Do not tell me the distance in miles—such journeys are not to be measured by feet. From the city to Bethany was from a battlefield to a home—how far is that? It is the journey from animosity to friendship—who can lay a line upon that immeasurable distance? From the city to Bethany, a journey from tumult and riot and murder to love and rest and tender ministry—who can measure its length in miles? No one.

It was worthwhile making that little change for one night—one quiet look upward, one brief solemn pause in the rush of life, that the head might turn toward the stars and the firmament and the serenities of the upper places. The *house* at Bethany was not grand, but the *home* was lined with the gold of love. We want such a home when the stress is heavy upon us—tears could be shed there without being misunderstood, and the heart could tell its whole tale or remain in total silence, just as the mood determined, and there would be no misconstruction. It was a church in the rocks, it was a sweet sanctuary, just out of the great high road of life's business and sacrifice. Can you retire to such a nest? Happy are you! He who can find a Bethany, a home, a Sabbath in the midst of the week, can bear his burdens with equanimity and grace and hope.

But we must *return,* as did Jesus the following day. The village for rest, the city for toil. Looking ahead, Jesus might easily have said that morning in Bethany, "It is good to be here. Let us stay and let the walls be arms of shelter around us. We should rest till the storms blow away and all God's great sky is shining again in translucent blue above My head." But Jesus returned to His toil, and so must we.

JOSEPH PARKER

September 25

This incident is both a singular miracle and a striking parable. It is an acted parable in which our Lord gives an object lesson. He gets truth before men's eyes that the lesson may make a deeper impression upon the mind and heart. The fruit on the fig trees always preceded the leaves, so the sight of the leaves meant you could expect many baskets of figs. When Christ found none, He simply bade the tree to remain forever fruitless, as it was obviously a blighted tree, and immediately the tree withered.

The tree was a powerful simile of the Jewish state. The nation had promised great things to God. Other nations were like trees without leaves, making no profession of allegiance to the true God, but the Jewish nation was covered with the leafage of supposed spirituality. Pharisees and scribes were sticklers for the letter of the law. Priests made constant cries: "The temple of the Lord." "We have Abraham as our Father" was frequently on their lips. The people were a fig tree in full leaf but fruitless, for they were neither holy nor just nor true nor faithful toward God. It had nothing but a profession of godliness when Christ came, and by His life and words He condemned the Jewish church to remain a fruitless thing. He did not destroy their religious organization, but He left them as they were to wither away from the root.

What a lesson this is to churches! A church may stand prominent in numbers and influence, but if faith and love and holiness have not been maintained, the Holy Spirit has left it to the vain show of a fruitless profession. And what a lesson to individuals! May we tremble, lest, having a profession of godliness, we should wear it conspicuously and yet should lack the fruit bearing. The name of saintship without the sanctity of holiness is a lie, abhorrent to God and man, an offense against truth, and the forerunner of a withering blight.

CHARLES SPURGEON

Early in the morning, as he was on his way back to the city, he was hungry. Seeing a fig tree by the road, he went up to it but found nothing on it except leaves. Then he said to it, "May you never bear fruit again!" Immediately the tree withered.

MATTHEW 21:18–19

September 26

Have we not sometimes been tempted to think that here is a case in which our Lord has not literally and always kept His word? If so, well may He have said to us, "Are you not in error because you do not know the Scriptures or the power of God?" (Mark 12:24). If we had known the Scriptures by searching, we might have known that this is no unconditional promise; this marvelous "whatever" depends on five conditions that we must heed.

1. It must be really, not verbally only, *in the name of Jesus* (John 14:13), asking not in our own name at all, signing our petition, as it were, with His name only, coming to the Father by our Advocate, our Representative. Do we always do this?

2. We must *believe* (Matt. 21:22). The faithful heroes of old received the promises through faith, and there is no new way of obtaining them. Is it any wonder that when we stagger at any promise of God through unbelief we do not receive it?

3. We must *abide in Christ* (John 15:7). Ah! Here is a deeper secret of asking and not having it, because we ask amiss. Not, have we come to Christ, but are we abiding in Him?

4. We must be *keeping His commandments and doing those things that are pleasing in His sight* (1 John 3:22). Only as we are abiding in Him can we bring forth the fruit of obedience, for without Him we can do nothing; only in walking by faith can we do those things that are pleasing in His sight.

5. We must *ask according to His will* (1 John 5:14). When what we ask is founded on a promise or any written evidence of what the will of the Lord is, this is comfortingly clear. But what about petitions that may or may not be according to His will? Surely, then, the condition can be fulfilled only by a complete blending of our own will with His, by His so taking our will, so undertaking it and influencing it for us, that we are led to desire and ask the very thing He is purposing to give.

FRANCES RIDLEY HAVERGAL

September 27

Once again the religious authorities ask Jesus the same question they were always asking. They may craft a thousand varieties of words, but substantially there was one question the enemy asks of Christ—"Who are You, or by what authority do You work, or who gave You this authority, or who is Your Father, or from where do You come?" He was the mystery of His time: He is the mystery of all time. He is there, and yet He seems to have no right to be there. His credentials are not written in official ink or signed by the official hand, and yet there He stands, speaking revelations, working miracles, His smile a heaven, His frown a judgment, and people around Him in great thick files ask who this man is.

Observe how narrow their question is. It is a question about authority. Men who ask narrow questions can never be sincere about great subjects. I venture thus to condense into one sentence what I might speak to you in words of many volumes. Coming to the Bible, coming to Christ with any little, narrow, pedantic question, you never can grapple with the magnificent occasion or extract from the book or the man the vital secret.

Jesus will answer you according to your question. You yourself determine the speech of the Son of God; whenever you are prepared to begin, He will begin with you. How He can tantalize, how He can test the inquirer, how He can spoil the spoiler, how He can hold up to suppressed ridicule the man who would come to Him with taunting question! If you have received no great broad gleaming answer of love and redemption from the Bible, it is because you have come with some little narrow question. Come frankly, with the nakedness of absolute moral destitution, without excuse or plea or self-defense, and knock upon the door of your Father's house, and angels will open it, and all the treasures of the house will be yours, and your very hunger will be turned into the supreme blessing of your life.

JOSEPH PARKER

Jesus entered the temple courts, and, while he was teaching, the chief priests and the elders of the people came to him. "By what authority are you doing these things?" they asked. "And who gave you authority?"

MATTHEW 21:23

September 28

*"Son, go and work
today in the vineyard."*

MATTHEW 21:28

There are certain laws that govern success in the kingdom of grace as well as in the kingdom of nature, and you must study these laws and adapt yourself to them. It would be in vain for the farmer to scatter his seed over the unbroken ground or on preoccupied soil. You must plow and harrow and put your seed in carefully and in proper proportions and at the right time, and then you must water and weed and wait for the harvest.

And just so in divine things. We shall discover that the laws of the spiritual kingdom are quite as certain and unerring in their operation as the laws of the natural kingdom, but through the blindness and obtuseness and unbelief of our hearts, we could not and would not find them out. People get up and fluster about and expect to be able to work for God without any thought or care or trouble. For the learning of worldly professions, they will give years of labor and study, but in their work for God, they would not seem to think it worthwhile to take the trouble to think and ponder, to plan and try to pray and to wrestle with God for wisdom. No, they won't bother with that, but then they fail, grow discouraged, and give up.

This is not the way to begin to work for God. Begin by praying much for Him to show you how and to equip you for the work, and begin in a humble, submissive, teachable spirit. Study the New Testament with special reference to this, and you will be surprised how every page of it will give you increased light. You will see that God holds you responsible for every capacity and influence He has given you, that He expects you to improve every moment of your time, every faculty of your being, every particle of your influence, and every penny of your money for Him. When once you get this light, it will be a marvelous guide in all the other particulars and ramifications of your life. Study your plans. Begin to work for God at once, but begin in the right way!

CATHERINE BOOTH

September 29

The hostility of the tenants in the parable has grown with indulgence. From beating the landowner's servants, they go to killing and stoning. What began with polite hypocrisy and lip obedience changed, under the stimulus of prophetic appeals, to honest refusal, and from that to violence that did not hesitate to slay. The more God pleads with men, the more self-conscious and bitter becomes their hatred; and the more bitter their hatred, the more He pleads and sends other messengers with larger commissions and clearer light. That is always true.

Christ treats the whole long series of violent rejections as the acts of the same set of tenants. The nation was one, as a stream is one; and the Pharisees and the teachers of the law, who stood with frowning hatred before Him as He spoke, were the living embodiment of the spirit that animated all the past. Standing before them, Christ knew Himself to be God's last appeal to that generation, as He is to all men. When it has shot that bolt, the resources even of divine love are exhausted, and no more can be done for the vineyard than He has done for it. We need not wonder at unfulfilled hopes being here ascribed to God. The startling thought only puts into language the great mystery that besets all God's pleading with men which is carried on, though men often fail, and which must, therefore, in view of His fore-knowledge be regarded as carried on with the knowledge that men will fail. That is the long-suffering patience of God.

With what sad calmness does Jesus tell the fate of the son, so certain that it is already as good as done! It was done in their counsels, and yet He does not cease to plead if perchance some hearts may be touched and withdraw themselves from the confederacy of murder.

ALEXANDER MACLAREN

"Last of all, he sent his son to them. 'They will respect my son,' he said. But when the tenants saw the son, they said to each other, 'This is the heir. Come, let's kill him and take his inheritance.' So they took him and threw him out of the vineyard and killed him."

MATTHEW 21:37–39

September 30

"He who falls on this stone will be broken to pieces, but he on whom it falls will be crushed."

MATTHEW 21:44

As Christ's ministry drew to its close, its severity and its gentleness both increased—its severity to the class to whom it was always severe and its gentleness to the class from whom it never turned away. Here there are only words of severity and awful foreboding. Our Lord now throws away even the thin veil of parable and speaks the sternest truth in the nakedest words. He puts His own claim in the plainest fashion, as the capstone on which the true kingdom of God was to be built. He brands the men who stood before Him as incompetent builders who did not know the cornerstone needed for their building when they saw it. He declares, with triumphant confidence, the futility of opposition to Him, even though they will kill Him. Christ is sure that God will build on Him and that His place in the building which shall rise through the ages will be, to even careless eyes, the crown of the manifest wonders of God's hand. Strange words from a man who knew that in three days He would be crucified! Stranger still that they have come true! He is the foundation of the best part of the best man, the basis of thought, the motive for action, the pattern of life, the ground of hope, for countless individuals; and on Him stands firm the society of His Church and is hung all the glory of His Father's house.

All disguise is at an end, and the chief priests and Pharisees are fully aware of Christ's meaning. The tenants' calculation had been that killing the heir would make them lords of the vineyard; the grim fact was that they cast themselves out when they cast him out. He is the heir. If we desire the inheritance, we must get it through him and not kill or reject but trust and obey him. Christ, the rock on which we may pile our eternal hopes and never be confounded, is also the rock that will crush the mightiest opponent as the dust of the summer threshing floor.

ALEXANDER MACLAREN

October 1

$\mathcal{N}$otice the change in the tone of the parables. Compare the parables in the thirteenth chapter of this gospel with the parables that are now before us and see what a wonderful change has taken place in the tone of the speaker. While He was uttering His doctrine, delineating His gospel, and offering it to all mankind, it was like a grain of mustard seed, like a sower going forth to sow seed, or like a net cast into the sea that gathered fish of every kind. Now the parables are judgments: Something has changed since the earlier chapter. The kingdom of heaven assumes another color, speaks in another accent, exhibits itself in another phase. So wonderful is this kingdom—it is to you what you are to it. You determine the attitude of the kingdom of heaven toward yourself. Be needy, be submissive, be expectant of heavenly blessings, and the kingdom of heaven is like a great warm heaven shining upon all your life and offering you all its contents. Be rebellious, frivolous, contemptuous, and the kingdom of heaven is dark with unspeakable tempests, ready to burst upon your life with overpowering destructiveness.

As Jesus Christ came closer to the cross, He saw the kingdom of heaven in a different light. He was the very seer that the times need, the eloquent soul clothed with the prophetic mantle and speaking the thousand tones of apocalyptic language who could see what the kingdom of heaven is like, correctly penetrating the spirit of His age and rightly reading all the meaning of the times passing over Him. It is for us to carry out those parables and multiply them according to the ever-varying color and tone of the times in which we live. If so, the kingdom of heaven will be like a summer day, like a winter night, like an angel of hopefulness, blowing a silver trumpet and calling to a high banquet, or like a spirit, black, grim, fierce, vengeful, going forth to execute divine judgment upon stony hearts and rebellious lives.

JOSEPH PARKER

Jesus spoke to them again in parables, saying: "The kingdom of heaven is like a king who prepared a wedding banquet for his son."

MATTHEW 22:1–2

October 2

"The kingdom of heaven is like a king who prepared a wedding banquet for his son. He sent his servants to those who had been invited to the banquet to tell them to come, but they refused to come."

MATTHEW 22:2–3

This is a most extraordinary marriage and marriage supper and one that goes far beyond anything heard of the marriages of this world. Indeed, this marriage that is in your offer is the only real and true and perfect marriage that has ever been made in this or in any other world. You have been dreaming about marriages all your days, but a marriage like this has never entered your most extravagant imaginations. For this is nothing less than the marriage of the Eternal Son of God with your own immortal soul. You are the bride, and Jesus Christ is the bridegroom, and the Father has sent His servants out to tell you that all things are now ready. And this great marriage has not by any means been made ready in a day. This wedding was actually proposed and planned for and the preparations began to be made for it before the foundations of the world were laid. While I have read many delightful love romances in my day, this great love, and the sometimes smooth and sometimes stormy course it has had to run, quite out of sight eclipses all other romances. The Father, Son, and Holy Spirit are all ready, and it only remains for you to say yes or no.

This very same message and invitation was once sent to a people just like ourselves; and they all, with one consent, began to make excuses. And they were entirely true excuses. All their treasure and consequently all their heart were elsewhere, and they would not have God's Son. Against them, finally, came the anger of Almighty God and the wrath of the Lamb in judgment.

In this parable, it is as if an angel had come straight from heaven to you with an invitation addressed in his hand. There he is, standing before you. Yes, there he is, and it is not the first time he has stood there waiting. Take the Master's invitation, for tomorrow may never arrive.

ALEXANDER WHYTE

October 3

Beloved, the feast is such as you greatly need. Let me tell you what it is. It is pardon for the past, renewal of nature for the present, and glory for the future. Here is God to be our Helper, His Son to be our Shepherd, His Spirit to be our Instructor. Here is the love of the Father to be our delight, the blood of the Son to be our cleansing, the energy of the Holy Spirit to be life from the dead to us. You cannot lack anything that you truly need but what is provided in the gospel, and Jesus Christ will be glorified if you accept it by faith. But here is the hindrance: Men do not accept it.

Nothing so honors a man as for him to accept the gospel invitation. It is no small thing to be a king's son, but those who come to the marriage feast of God's own Son shall become the King's sons themselves—participators in the glory of the great Heir of all things. Just the thought of it makes my heart glow with sacred ardor, and my wonder rises that men do not come to the banquet of love that honors all its guests. When the banquet is so costly to the host, so free to the guest, and so honorable to all concerned, how is it that there should be found anyone so unwise as to refuse the favor. Surely here is an illustration of the folly of the unrenewed heart and a proof of the deep depravity that sin has caused. If men turn their backs on Moses with his stony tablets, I do not marvel, but to despise the loaded table of grace, this is strange. To resist the justice of God is a crime, but to repel the generosity of heaven, what is this? We must invent a term of infamy with which to brand the evil ungratitude. To resist God in majesty of terror is insanity, but to spurn Him in the majesty of His mercy is something more than madness. Sin reaches its climax when it resolves to starve sooner than owe anything to divine goodness. I'm sure the messengers of the king must have been mute with astonishment when they saw the people would not come. Even so, our King calls to His banquet feast again.

CHARLES SPURGEON

"He sent his servants to those who had been invited to the banquet to tell them to come, but they refused to come."

MATTHEW 22:3

October 4

*"The king was
enraged. He sent his
army and destroyed
those murderers and
burned their city."*

MATTHEW 22:7

The king will have a wedding feast, a great banquet, a thousand messengers going forth to call those who were invited to the wedding. He will have trumpets and cymbals and dances and high delight. Such is the conception of God always: He never makes less than a feast. In His original purpose, when His heart speaks out of heaven, before the worlds are made, He says, "I will prepare for all coming ages and coming men an eternal wedding feast, banners, trumpetings, delights, raptures, satisfactions infinite." So He speaks in the background of His own eternity.

When did He ever do less? We can hardly turn over two pages of the inspired Bible story without finding offers of milk and wine and honey and banquets and sacred pleasures and unutterable delights. God's heart will lift its way right up through all the detail of our sin, torment, and pain and will speak hospitable things to the hungry life of human creatures. God calls us to quench our thirst and come to the waters. That is the great cry, crashing, breathing, through the ages, with infinite energy of love. That is God's meaning about us all, to give us satisfaction, to take away the pain of hunger, the fire of thirst, and all that makes life a burden. Give God credit for His purpose.

God has to be forced into judgment: He comes of Himself in love. You have to scourge Him with a judicial attitude, mock Him, taunt Him, break every law He ever made, and spit in the face of His heavens before He will put out His hand for the sword or the rod. But in Himself, in all His heart, there is the one purpose of love, feasting, enjoyment, eternal nourishment, and inward and spiritual delight and growth. When you see His judgment, never miss God's original purpose. God's desire toward the children of men is one of mercy, pity, love, care, supply, answering prayer before the prayer is half spoken, and with a grand amen realizing every petition uttered by the suppliant's pleading lips.

JOSEPH PARKER

October 5

The entrance of the king to see his guests was the crowning point of the entire banquet. Surely this is the case within the Church. What would church fellowship be without the fellowship of God? To sit and rejoice with my brethren is exceedingly delightful, but the best wine is fellowship with the Father and His Son Jesus Christ. Our cry is, "Come, great King, with all Your glorious power, with Your Spirit and Your glorious Son, and manifest Yourself to us."

When the king came into the banqueting chamber, he saw the guests, and they also saw him. It was a mutual revelation. Ever sweet is this to the saints, that their God looks upon them. His look brings no terror to our minds when we are loyal and loving. "My God sees me" is sweet music. We desire to abide forever beneath the divine inspection, for it is an inspection of unbounded love. He sees our faults, it is to remove them; He notes our imperfections, it is to cleanse them away. Behold me, O great King, and lift up Your eyes upon me, accepting me in the Beloved. What joy it is to us who are saved in Christ Jesus that we also can see Him! Though we see through a glass darkly, for as yet we are not fit to behold the full splendor of His Godhead, yet how sweetly does He reveal Himself to our souls and unveil His eternal love.

But the king notices a man who is without a wedding garment and speechless about it. Why is he silent? Surely it was because he was convicted of open, undeniable disloyalty. He portrays someone who makes a profession of faith without care to make it true—willfully despising the Lord's command. Hypocrisy will be found out. The King sees what you lack. Your morality, generosity, high-sounding prayers, and even eloquent discoursing, these cannot conceal from Him the fact that your heart is not with Him. The one thing needful is to accept loyally the Lord as King.

CHARLES SPURGEON

"But when the king came in to see the guests, he noticed a man there who was not wearing wedding clothes. 'Friend,' he asked, 'how did you get in here without wedding clothes?' The man was speechless."

MATTHEW 22:11–12

October 6

Then the Pharisees went out and laid plans to trap him in his words. They sent their disciples to him along with the Herodians.

MATTHEW 22:15–16

You will notice that the attacks made upon the Savior were premeditated, arranged, concerted, so that there might be no weakness on the part of those who were about to approach the great Teacher. No notice was sent of the questions: The preparation was complete on the side of the interrogators without Jesus Christ's having any intimation that an attack was about to be made upon Him. They talked the whole matter over, they proposed and rearranged and amended, and then they settled the terms. Having done so, they went with unanimous purpose to trap the speaker.

It is obvious that the attacks were inspired not by love of truth or by anxiety to know God's mind upon the subjects but by pure hatred of the man. We are told that Jesus clearly understood "their evil intent" (Matt. 22:18). Hence, we see the most unusual combination of parties—Pharisees, Herodians, Sadducees—like a horse and donkey yoked together in one team, like colors that should never have been brought into juxtaposition, stitched together, contrasts that under other circumstances would be accounted anomalies and would evoke destructive criticism. But any union will do where such a man's life is to be taken! Their one combined intent was to strike with a dart the life of Jesus.

This point is the one that brings its severe lesson to us. Herein we find the reality of the inspiration for the attacks made upon Christianity today. Why do men assail the Bible, disputing its integrity and invalidating its claims? It is clearly not about literary discrepancies and incoherences, but it is its moralities that they hate. Loving darkness rather than light, they find fault with any semblance of moral rule that impugns their lifestyle and brings conviction and humiliation. Men would be free to do what they pleased. Be careful, then, how you approach the Savior and His Word. Never put your knife through the Bible's morality to rid yourself of the daily discipline it brings.

JOSEPH PARKER

October 7

$\mathcal{B}$y this clever question, the enemies of Christ hoped to entangle Him and, whichever way He resolved it, to expose Him to the fury either of the jealous Jews or of the jealous Romans. It appeared that His teaching on this could only be concluded as harmful either to the rights of the Jews or to Caesar. Many of the Jews held that because they were descendants of Abraham they should not consent to be in bondage to any man (John 8:33). God had given them a law that they should not set a stranger over them. Did that not imply that they were not to yield any willing subjection to any foreign prince or state? This was an old mistaken belief arising from the pride that brings destruction and a fall and would eventually bring upon them the destruction by the Romans.

But a temptation perceived is half conquered, for our greatest danger lies from snakes under the green grass, and Jesus immediately perceives the trap. Whatever disguise the hypocrite puts on, our Lord Jesus sees through it. He perceives all the wickedness that is in the hearts of pretenders and can easily convict them of it, setting it in order before them. He cannot be imposed upon, as we often are, by flatterings and fair pretenses. He who searches the heart can call hypocrites by their name.

Hypocrites tempt Jesus Christ. They try His knowledge, whether He can discover them through their disguises. They try His holiness and truth, whether He will allow them in His Church. But if they who of old tempted Christ when He was but darkly revealed "were killed by snakes" (1 Cor. 10:9), how much greater will the punishment be when they tempt Him now in the midst of gospel light and love! Those who presume to test Christ will certainly find Him too hard for them and that He is of more piercing eyes than not to see and more pure eyes than not to hate the disguised wickedness of hypocrites, who dig deep to hide their counsel from Him.

MATTHEW HENRY

"Tell us then, what is your opinion? Is it right to pay taxes to Caesar or not?" But Jesus, knowing their evil intent, said, "You hypocrites, why are you trying to trap me?"

MATTHEW 22:17–18

October 8

Then he said to them,
"Give to Caesar what
is Caesar's, and to
God what is God's."

MATTHEW 22:21

Jesus had already gotten them to state that the image on the coins that filled their purses was Caesar's. If Caesar fills the purse, let Caesar command them. It is too late now to dispute paying taxes to Caesar, for taxes are already a province of the empire, and once that relation was admitted, the duty of it must be performed.

Before Pilate, Jesus stated with certainty, "My kingdom is not of this world" (John 18:36), and He shows that He is not about to get entangled in this civil affair. Indeed, He instructs His disciples that the Christian faith is no enemy to civil government but a friend to it. It is the duty of believers to give to government officials that which, according to the laws of their country, is their due. Those officials, being entrusted with the public welfare, the protection of the subject, and the conservation of peace, are entitled to a just proportion of the public wealth and the revenue of the nation. "This is also why you pay taxes, for the authorities are God's servants, who give their full time to governing" (Rom. 13:6). Though it is the constitution that determines what is Caesar's, when that is determined, Christ tells us to pay it.

While we fulfill our civil responsibilities, we must remember to give to God the things that are God's. If our money is Caesar's, our consciences and hearts are God's. God must have the innermost and uppermost place there. We must give to God that which is His due out of our time and our estates, and if Caesar's command interferes with God's, "we must obey God rather than men" (Acts 5:29).

The adversaries of Jesus wanted to make it unlawful to pay taxes to Caesar that they might have a pretense to save their money. Thus many excuse themselves from what they should do. They had also withheld what they owed to God and are reproved for that. While they contended over civil liberties, they had lost the life and power of their religion. Let us never do the same.

MATTHEW HENRY

October 9

*L*ike the angels in heaven, Jesus tells us, we will not marry in heaven. While we are not told all that will change within our glorified natures, it is certain that we shall not marry there.

Like angels in their immortality, so shall we be. No angel was ever carried to his grave, no tomb could encase his free spirit, and the bonds of death could not hold him for a moment. So is it with the freed ones who have passed through the grave and are now with Christ—they cannot die. All the struggles, sicknesses, and tears of earth shall be swept away in the torrent of eternal life that rolls on through endless generations.

The angels bend around the throne in sacred worship. They cast their crowns before the throne upon the glassy sea and worship the Lamb forever and ever. There is never a moment, whether earth is swathed in light or clothed in darkness, in which the Son of God is not adored by ten thousand times ten thousand of these celestial spirits. Cherubim and seraphim perpetually worship the ever-living Son of God. Even so is it with all those whom Christ has redeemed. They too are forever worshiping, paying their perpetual love to Jesus. The elders are represented as standing before the throne with vials full of odors sweet and golden harps, representing the perpetual praises of the glorified Church. How sweet worship often is on earth, but what must it be like in heaven! Such service is to be our portion soon.

Like the angels, we will perfectly do the will of God. No thought of sin ever taints their soul; no syllable of evil ever falls from their holy lips; no thought of transgression defiles their service; no proud thoughts must be cast down. So it is with the saints who dwell in glory with them. They have washed their robes and made them white in the blood of the Lamb. Yonder is the crown of perfect holiness. Only be of good cheer, for through Jesus you shall overcome, and the crown shall be yours.

CHARLES SPURGEON

"At the resurrection people will neither marry nor be given in marriage; they will be like the angels in heaven."

MATTHEW 22:30

October 10

All the law is fulfilled in one word, and that is *love* (Rom. 13:10). All obedience begins in the affections, and nothing in faith is done right that is not done there first. Love is the leading affection which gives law and gives ground to the rest, and therefore that, as the main fort, is to be first secured and garrisoned for God. Man is a being made for love; thus the law is written in the heart, that is, the *law of love*. Love is a sweet word, and if it is the fulfilling of the law, surely the yoke of the command is very easy.

Now God, being good infinitely, originally, and eternally, is to be loved in the first place, and nothing loved beside Him but what is loved for Him. To "have no other gods before me" implies that we must have Him for our God, and that will engage our love for Him. To love God as ours is to love Him because He is ours—our Creator, Owner, and Ruler—and to conduct ourselves to Him as ours, with obedience to Him and dependence upon Him. We must love God as reconciled to us and made ours by covenant.

We are to love God with all our heart, soul, and mind. Some make these to signify one and the same thing, to love Him with all our powers. Others distinguish them; the heart, soul, and mind are the will, affections, and understanding. Our love for God must be sincere love and not in word only, as theirs is who say they love Him but their hearts are not with Him. It must be a strong love; we must love Him in the most intense degree. As we must praise Him, so we must love Him, with all that is within us (Ps. 103:1). It must be a singular and superlative love; we must love Him more than anything else; this way the stream of our affections must entirely run. The heart must be united to love God in opposition to a divided heart. All our love is too little to bestow upon Him, and therefore all the powers of the soul must be engaged for Him. This is the first and great command.

MATTHEW HENRY

# October 11

The second great commandment is like the first, for it is founded upon it and flows from it; and a true love for our brother, whom we have seen, is both an instance and an evidence of our love for God, whom we have not seen (1 John 4:20).

It is implied that we do, and should, love ourselves. There is a self-love that is corrupt and the root of the greatest sins, and it must be put off and put to death. But there is a self-love that is natural and the rule of the greatest duty, and it must be preserved and sanctified. We must love ourselves; that is, we must have a due regard for the dignity of our own natures and due concern for the welfare of our own souls and bodies.

It is prescribed that we love our neighbor as ourselves. We must honor and esteem all men and must wrong and injure none, must have a good will to all and good wishes for all, and, as we have opportunity, must do good to all. We must love our neighbor as truly and sincerely as we love ourselves. In many cases, we must deny ourselves for the good of our neighbor and make ourselves servants to the true welfare of others and be willing to spend our means and expend ourselves for others (2 Cor. 12:15).

The sum and substance of all the precepts of the Law and the Prophets hang upon the law of love for God and neighbor. Take this away, and all falls to the ground and comes to nothing. Rituals and ceremonials must give way to these, as must all spiritual gifts, for love is the more excellent way. This is the spirit of the law, which animates it; the cement of the law, which joins it. It is the root and compendium of the whole Bible, not only of the Law and Prophets but also of the gospel. Into this mold of love let our hearts be poured, and in the defense and evidence of love let us spend our zeal. To the commanding power of these let everything else be made to bow.

MATTHEW HENRY

"And the second is like it: 'Love your neighbor as yourself.' All the Law and the Prophets hang on these two commandments."

MATTHEW 22:39–40

October 12

While the Pharisees were gathered together, Jesus asked them, "What do you think about the Christ? Whose son is he?" "The son of David," they replied. He said to them, "How is it then that David, speaking by the Spirit, calls him 'Lord'?"

MATTHEW 22:41–43

The Pharisees remained gathered together, perhaps preparing another question, but Jesus had been interrogated by them long enough. His questions teach, though. He does not seek to "trap" the Pharisees in their words (Matt. 22:15) nor to make them contradict themselves, but He seeks to bring them full up against a difficulty, that they may open their eyes to the great truth that is its only solution.

His first question, "What do you think about the Christ?" is simply preparatory to the second. The answer that He anticipated was given, for the Davidic descent of the Messiah was universally accepted. One can imagine that the Pharisees smiled complacently at the attempt to puzzle them with such an elementary question, but the smile vanished when the next one came. They interpreted Psalm 110 as Messianic, and David in it called the Messiah "my Lord." How can He be both? Jesus' question is in two forms: "If He is son, how does David call Him Lord?" or, if He is Lord, "how then is He his son?" Take either designation and the other lands you in inextricable difficulties.

Our Lord's purpose in driving the Pharisees into this corner was not to put them to silence (Matt. 22:34) but to bring to light the inadequate conceptions of the Messiah to which exclusive recognition of His Davidic descent necessarily led. David's son would be but a king after the type of the Caesars, and his kingdom as "carnal" as the wildest zealot expected, but David's Lord, sitting at God's right hand and having his foes made his footstool by Jehovah Himself—what sort of Messiah King would that be? The majestic image that shapes itself dimly here was a revelation that took the Pharisees' breath away and made them speechless. Nor are the words without a half-disclosed claim on Christ's part to be that which He was so soon to avow Himself before the high priest as being.

ALEXANDER MACLAREN

October 13

*J*esus Christ had just received a deputation of Pharisees, Herodians, and Sadducees, and that day had utterly humiliated all the men who came to Him with questions that were meant to trap Him. His response had utterly silenced them.

It might be thought, therefore, that He had so cleanly swept out the whole church of His time and dismantled it that He stood before His age as a mere image breaker, a man who smote all existing things of a religious kind. But Jesus was not a mere deconstructionist; knowing that in every crowd there is a preponderance of foolish and unreasonable men, He instantly takes up an affirmative and constructive attitude. It was not His purpose to dishonor the law or to weaken its application in any sense. While there is not one good word that He bestows upon the teachers of the law and the Pharisees, He declares that the law must not suffer because its interpreters are weak or vile men. The law is an eternal quantity, a perpetual dignity that can never be impaired even by the vile behavior of those who interpret it.

Jesus rebukes with no stinted reproach those who had fallen below the dignity and holiness of their sacred vocation. The line He draws is broad and plain, and this was not a speech spoken to a few people now dead and gone. In this exhortation, Christ touches and refutes a fallacy that has found its utterance in all ages of civilized history. That fallacy is that if a man does anything bad, everything good that he touches is to be condemned along with himself. That someone who reads the Bible is a bad person does not mean that the Bible is bad—such is dishonest logic. As strongly as Jesus felt about the religious hypocrisy surrounding Him, He would never allow the Word of God to be damaged by its unworthy teachers. Let us guard it as well.

JOSEPH PARKER

Then Jesus said to the crowds and to his disciples: "The teachers of the law and the Pharisees sit in Moses' seat. So you must obey them and do everything they tell you. But do not do what they do, for they do not practice what they preach."

MATTHEW 23:1–3

October 14

"Woe to you, teachers of the law and Pharisees, you hypocrites! You shut the kingdom of heaven in men's faces. You yourselves do not enter, nor will you let those enter who are trying to."

MATTHEW 23:13

Look at Christ at the center of the great multitude whom He addressed in the eloquent maledictions recorded here. The scribes and the Pharisees, men who have been playing falsely with His name, surround Him: He was not hurling denunciations upon the absent. When did Jesus Christ ever address persons who were not actually before Him? Look over the great throng of hypocrites and blind leaders of the blind all around Him, and then hear this terrible speech. It was a day of great judgment—with lightning and thunder, the earth trembled to the resounding eloquence, and the heavens vibrated as the eloquent tones fell from the lips divine. The men could not run away; He fastened them to earth. They could not lift their fingers to put into their ears, for He held them down, and that day He spoke as He had never spoken before in fullness and breadth and fierceness of moral indignation.

We see in Christ a devotion to truth that clothed Him with sublimest fearlessness. How He lays his great grip upon them and shakes them, and they cannot answer a word. What explanation can there be for this mighty mastery over the leading teachers of His time? Devotion to truth, so complete, so profound, will lift the man above all fear. Men are not continuously strong except in proportion to their devotion to truth: Such men are sublimated by their devotion; they are lifted up into a new and larger self-hood. It is no longer they who speak, but God who speaks in them. The action is not to be measured by their personality; they stand as representatives of the majesty and grandeur of truth. You will be strong only in proportion as the truth is in you.

Jesus Christ could say that He was Himself the Truth. The Truth never blushed, never stammered, never apologized, never compromised. The tone of Truth cannot change; it is royal, commanding; if audacious, simply because complete and infallible.

JOSEPH PARKER

October 15

Christ's all-piercing insight into truth gave Him infinite pre-eminence as a teacher. Here we see somewhat of His intellectual breadth and grandeur coupled with a moral indignation that becomes impatient in the very tones that it utters. How He must have said these words again and again: "You blind fools! How is it that you do not see the right relation and proportion of things? How is it that you mistake the near for the great, the temporal for the eternal? What has become of your common sense or ordinary natural reason? What has fallen upon you, what dementation is this, what sudden insanity, what moral obliqueness? You have lost the first conception of truth, and you have taken upon yourselves metaphysical quibbles and puzzles unworthy of the intellect that God has given you."

This is the inevitable course of wrong thinking in spiritual matters. Men make vain distinctions, they create a series of puzzles, they have so much leisure that it becomes a temptation to them. This is the danger of the Church today. We are so overfed with the gospel, we are so churched and preached to death, that men begin to turn into puzzles the immeasurable, plain, infinite truth of God. We are busy creating sects, schools, denominations, and so-called churches. Perhaps if the fire of persecution should break out among us we would be forced back to great principles, to a proper distinction between the temple and the gold, that we may not be inverting things and putting them into false relations and proportions. If the wolf would come back—the old gray wolf that barked at our heroic fathers, showed its gleaming teeth whenever they came in sight, and sprang upon them in attack—we should get back to right ideas of inspiration, truth, prayer, missions, evangelism, and should cease the small talk about mechanism and fine distinctions that deplete the gospel power.

JOSEPH PARKER

"Woe to you, blind guides! You say, 'If anyone swears by the temple, it means nothing; but if anyone swears by the gold of the temple, he is bound by his oath.' You blind fools! Which is greater: the gold, or the temple that makes the gold sacred?"

MATTHEW 23:16–17

October 16

"Woe to you, teachers of the law and Pharisees, you hypocrites! You give a tenth of your spices... But you have neglected the more important matters of the law— justice, mercy and faithfulness.... You blind guides! You strain out a gnat but swallow a camel."

MATTHEW 23:23–24

*H*ypocrites, who act in religion for themselves and not for God, will do no more in religion than will serve some purpose for themselves. The partiality of the teachers of the law and the Pharisees is seen in their very exact tithing of what would not cost them much but would enhance their reputation before men. Paying tithes was their duty, and Christ is not saying to leave it undone.

But what He condemns them for is that while they tithed their spices they had omitted the more important matters of God's law—justice, mercy, and faithfulness. All the things of God's law are important, but the most important are those that express inward holiness in the heart. Justice and mercy toward men and faith toward God are the important matters of the law—"to act justly and to love mercy and to walk humbly with your God" (Mic. 6:8). This is the obedience that is better than sacrifice or tithe. To be just to the priest in their tithe and yet to cheat and defraud everyone else is to mock God and deceive ourselves. To pay tithe–mint to the priest and to not help the beaten man on the road to Jericho is to come under the judgment without mercy.

"You blind guides!"—for their corrupt living, for their example was as corrupt as their doctrine. In their practice they "strain out a gnat," as if they had a great abhorrence of sin and were afraid of it in the very least instance. But they made no difficulty of those sins that in comparison were as a camel to a gnat. When they devoured widows' houses, they did indeed "swallow a camel." When they gave Judas the price of innocent blood and yet scrupled to put it back into the treasury (Matt. 27:6), when they would not go into the judgment hall for fear of being defiled and yet would stand at the door and cry out against the holy Jesus (John 18:28), they swallowed camels whole. How blind could they possibly be? God keep us from such darkness.

MATTHEW HENRY

October 17

The religious hypocrites were scrupulous about washing cups, pitchers, and kettles (Mark 7:4), and Jesus compares them to cups and dishes washed only on the outside but all the dirt is inside. Theirs was a religion that would only avoid scandalous sins, those that would ruin their reputation with men, but allow themselves in heart-wickedness, which renders them despicable to the pure and holy God.

The practice of the Pharisees was always to make clean the outside. In those things that fell under the observation of their neighbors, they seemed very exact and carried on their wicked intrigues with so much deceit that their wickedness was not suspected. People generally took them for very good men. But within, in the recesses of their hearts and the hidden aspects of their lives, they were full of greed and self-indulgence. While they would seem to be godly, they were anything but that. "Their heart is filled with destruction" (Ps. 5:9), and what we are inwardly is what we are really.

By Christ's accounting, those are blind who are strangers and no enemies to the wickedness of their own hearts, who see not and hate not the secret sins that lodge there. Self-ignorance is the most shameful and harmful ignorance (Rev. 3:17). Christ's rule is, *First clean the inside.* Note, the principal care of each of us should be to wash our hearts from wickedness (Jer. 4:14).

The main business of a Christian lies within, to "purify ourselves from everything that contaminates body and spirit, perfecting holiness out of reverence for God" (2 Cor. 7:1). The secret lusts and inclinations that lurk in the soul, unseen and unobserved, must first be mortified and subdued. Renewing, sanctifying grace can make the inside clean, the heart and spirit can be made new, and there will be a newness of life. This is our first priority.

MATTHEW HENRY

"Woe to you, teachers of the law and Pharisees, you hypocrites! You clean the outside of the cup and dish, but inside they are full of greed and self-indulgence. Blind Pharisee! First clean the inside of the cup and dish, and then the outside also will be clean."

MATTHEW 23:25–26

October 18

"Woe to you, teachers of the law and Pharisees, you hypocrites! You are like whitewashed tombs, which look beautiful on the outside but on the inside are full of dead men's bones and everything unclean. In the same way, on the outside you appear to people as righteous but on the inside you are full of hypocrisy and wickedness."

MATTHEW 23:27–28

The seven woes in this chapter are scathing exposures but full of sorrow as well as severity. The wailing of an infinite compassion rather than the accents of anger sounds in them. The blending of sternness and pity, each perfect, is the characteristic of this wonderful climax of our Lord's appeals to His nation.

If the Talmudic practice is as old as our Lord's time, the annual whitewashing was recently over. Its purpose was not to adorn the tombs but to make them conspicuous so that they might be avoided for fear of defilement. So Jesus would say, with terrible irony, that the apparent holiness of the rulers was really a sign of corruption and a warning to keep away from them. What a blow at their self-complacency! And how profoundly true it is that the more punctiliously white the hypocrite's outside, the more foul is he within, and the wider berth will all discerning people give him! The terrible force of the figure needs no dwelling on. In Christ's estimate, such a soul was the very dwelling place of death, and foul corruption filled its sickening recesses. Terrible words to come from His lips into which grace was poured, and bold words to be flashed at listeners who held the life of the Speaker in their hands!

There are two sorts of hypocrites, the conscious and the unconscious, and there are ten of the latter for one of the former, and each ten times more dangerous. Established religion breeds them, and they are specially found among its defenders. These woes are not like the thunderclaps rolling above our heads while the lightning strikes earth miles away. A religion that is mostly whitewash is as common among us as ever it was in Jerusalem, and its foul corruptions become more rotten every year.

ALEXANDER MACLAREN

October 19

*H*onoring dead prophets was right, but honoring dead ones and killing living ones was conscious or unconscious hypocrisy. The attitude of mind that leads to glorifying the dead witnesses also leads to supposing that all truth was given by them and hence that the living teachers, who carry their message farther, are false prophets. A generation that was ready to kill Jesus in honor of Moses would have killed Moses in honor of Abraham and would not have had the faintest apprehension of the message of either.

It is a good deal easier to build tombs than to accept teachings. Magnifying the past does not imply either the understanding or the acceptance of the principles supposed to be glorified thereby. It may be filled with hollowness of admiration.

Their hypocrisy is unmasked by words that glow with righteous wrath at white heat flashing from Jesus' pained heart. With almost scornful subtlety He lays hold of the words that He puts into the Pharisees' mouths, to convict them of being kindred with those whose deeds they say they disown. For all their protests, Jesus tells them their spiritual kindred goes with bodily descent.

Then come the awful words bidding them to fill up "the measure of the sin of your forefathers." They are like the other command to Judas to do his work quickly. They are more than permission; they are a command, but such a command as, by its laying bare of the true character of the deed in view, is love's last effort at prevention. Mark the conception of a nation's sins as one through successive generations and the other of these as having a definite measure that, being filled, judgment can longer wait. When the last black drop fills the vessel, catastrophe follows.

ALEXANDER MACLAREN

"Woe to you, teachers of the law and Pharisees, you hypocrites! You build tombs for the prophets and decorate the graves of the righteous. And you say, 'If we had lived in the days of our forefathers, we would not have taken part with them in shedding the blood of the prophets.' So you testify against yourselves that you are the descendants of those who murdered the prophets. Fill up, then, the measure of the sin of your forefathers!"

MATTHEW 23:29–32

October 20

"You snakes! You brood of vipers! How will you escape being condemned to hell? Therefore I am sending you prophets and wise men and teachers. Some of them you will kill and crucify... And so upon you will come all the righteous blood that has been shed on earth... I tell you the truth, all this will come upon this generation."

MATTHEW 23:33–36

$\mathscr{I}$t is hard to recognize Christ in these terrible words. We have heard part of them from John the Baptist, and it sounded natural for him to call men snakes and vipers, but it is somewhat of a shock to hear Jesus hurling such names at even the most sinful. But let us remember that He who sees hearts had a right to tell harsh truths and that it is truest kindness to strip off masks that hide from men their real character and that the revelation of the divine love in Jesus would be a partial and impotent revelation if it did not show us the righteous love that is wrath. There is nothing so terrible as the anger of gentle compassion, and the fiercest and most destructive wrath is that of the Lamb.

The woe ends with the double prophecy that that generation would repeat and surpass the fathers' guilt and that on it would fall the accumulated penalties of past bloodshed. God goes on sending His prophets because we reject them; and the more deaf men are, the more does He peal His words into their ears. That is mercy and compassion, that all may be saved; but it is judgment, too, and its foreseen effect must be regarded as part of the divine purpose in it. With great authority, in the face of these scowling Pharisees, Jesus assumes the distinct divine prerogative of sending forth inspired men who, as His messengers, shall stand on a level with the prophets of old.

The punishment of long ages of sin carried on from father to son does in the course of that history of the world fall upon one generation. It takes long for the mass of heaped-up sin to become top-heavy; but when it is so, it buries beneath its down-rushing avalanche one generation of those who have worked at piling it up. Such is the law of the judgment wrought out by God's providence in history.

ALEXANDER MACLAREN

October 21

This is not and could not be the language of a mere man. It would be utterly absurd for any man to say that he would have gathered the inhabitants of a city together as a hen gathers her chicks under her wings. Besides, the language implies that, for many centuries, by the sending of the prophets and by many other warnings, God would often have gathered the children of Jerusalem together as a hen does her chicks. Christ could not have said this if He had been only a man. If His life began at Bethlehem, this would be an absurd statement; but as the Son of God, ever loving the sons of men, ever desirous of the good of Israel, He could say that in sending the prophets, even though they were stoned and killed, He had again and again shown His desire to bless His people. This must be the utterance of the Son of Man, the Son of God, the Christ in His complex person as human and divine.

This verse shows also that the ruin of men lies within themselves. Christ puts this solemn accusation against guilty men very plainly: "I would, but you would not." That is a truth about which I hope we have never had any question. We hold tenaciously that salvation is all of grace, but we also believe with equal firmness that the ruin of man is entirely the result of his own sin. It is the will of God that saves; it is the will of man that damns. The human will is desperately set against God and is the destroyer of thousands of good intentions and emotions, which never come to anything permanent because the will is acting in opposition to that which is right and true. Jerusalem stands and is preserved by the grace and favor of the Most High, but Jerusalem is burned and her stones are cast down through the transgression and iniquity of men, which provoked the justice of God.

CHARLES SPURGEON

"O Jerusalem, Jerusalem, you who kill the prophets and stone those sent to you, how often I have longed to gather your children together, as a hen gathers her chicks under her wings, but you were not willing."

MATTHEW 23:37

October 22

"O Jerusalem,
Jerusalem, you who
kill the prophets and
stone those sent to
you, how often I have
longed to gather your
children together, as a
hen gathers her chicks
under her wings, but
you were not willing."

MATTHEW 23:37

*I*t is a very marvelous thing that God should condescend to be compared to a hen, that the Christ, the Son of the Highest, the Savior of men, should stoop to so quaint a piece of imagery as to liken Himself to a hen.

Those gathered to Christ know that by this wonderful Gatherer, you have been gathered into happy associations. The chicks beneath the wing of the hen look very happy all crowded together. What a sweet little family party they are! How they hid themselves away in great contentment and chirp their little note of joy! Under the wings of the Most High, you find many sweetnesses in this life, many dear and kind friends connected with Christ who love those who are joined to Him.

A hen is to her little chicks a cover of safety. When there is a hawk in the sky, watch the mother bird give her peculiar cluck of warning and quickly gather the little ones under her wings. She loves them; did you ever see a hen fight for her chicks? She may be timid enough at other times, but let her chicks get in danger and she is ferocious to defend them. This is what God is to those who come to Him in Christ Jesus. What a fervency of love we find in the Savior! Oh, to know his love!

The hen is also a constant source of comfort. Whether it is freezing cold or pelting rain, the wings of the hen protect and give the chicks warmth. What a palace it is for the chicks to get there under the mother's wings! Christ also gives us comfort. There is a deep, sweet comfort about hiding yourself away in God, for when troubles come, wave upon wave, blessed is the man who has God to give him mercy upon mercy. Ten thousand things, apart from Him, cannot satisfy you or give you comfort. There, let them all go; but if God is yours and you hide away under His wings, you are as happy in Him as the chicks are beneath the hen.

CHARLES SPURGEON

October 23

*I*magine a river very broad and deep rolling quietly and rhythmically for long miles, not a bubble upon the surface, no noise, no tumult on this noble stream of water, and imagine that stream suddenly coming to a terrific precipice. What a water-fall, what a roar and tumult, what rainbows made by the sun, what snowy veils, what infinite wizardry of shape and sound and suggestion! It does not look like the same water. Nothing is so accommodating as water; one moment it is little drops that sparkle like diamonds in the shining sun; then they gather into great masses and carry navies as if they were straws driven by the wind. There is nothing so genial yet so terrible as water.

It is even so with these speeches of Christ. Up to within a few chapters of these verses, the stream of His talk has rolled for-ward in infinite calmness and nobleness, having no end of sup-pressed power in it. But just recently it has come over a terrific precipice of rocks, and it has been rolling and dashing among us like a fierce waterfall, so that some of us have hardly been able to recognize the grand, eloquent speaker in the recent turmoil and rush of His enthusiasm, passion, and eager, burning conse-cration. Yet the speaker is one and the same, master of all styles. Never did a man speak like this man.

At this moment, the idea of destruction is uppermost in the Savior's mind. The explanation is that His own soul was sor-rowful unto death. When a man's soul is sorrowful, there is nothing being built up outside of it. The universe takes its hue and tone and meaning from the inner experience and con-sciousness of the observer. The cross is already shouldered, the nails are already half in the quivering hands, the blood is already beginning to trickle. So all things are dying around Him: The temple is trembling; the heavens are gathering them-selves into a last agony; the old earth is pained at her heart and will presently give way.

JOSEPH PARKER

"Look, your house is left to you desolate. For I tell you, you will not see me again until you say, 'Blessed is he who comes in the name of the Lord.'"

MATTHEW 23:38–39

October 24

Jesus left the temple and was walking away when his disciples came up to him to call his attention to its buildings. "Do you see all these things?" he asked. "I tell you the truth, not one stone here will be left on another; every one will be thrown down."

MATTHEW 24:1–2

How exquisite was the correspondence between the inner and the outer life of Christ! He saw things with His heart. When He nestled in His Father's bosom and felt all the serenity of that divine warmth, He said, "See how the lilies of the field grow. They do not labor or spin" (Matt. 6:28). That was His view of nature and of life as He laid His hand upon His Father's heart. When He felt His Father's arms strongly around Him He said, "Do not be afraid, little flock, for your Father has been pleased to give you the kingdom" (Luke 12:32). Now that Calvary is in front—Golgatha, the place of skulls and bones, preceded by Gethsemane and all that Gethsemane means—even the temple, marble and gold, the choicest thing of its kind in all the earth, is reeling and trembling and will presently fall flat down, a mass and heap of shapeless stones, as if struck by every wind of heaven. True man, real heart, grand soul, what wonder that He spoke lightning to hypocrites?

Worn and sad of heart, His life a great agony, every look a pain, every pulsation a dying, Jesus walked away from the temple, and His disciples, well-meaning little children, came to Him to show Him the buildings of the temple. They would show Him something that would lure Him from His brooding thought that had so much blood in it. So like children who would show their toys to a boy distressed, they would touch the stones of the beautiful temple with a trembling reverence and seek to charm Him from His grief. Seeing through it all, Jesus replied, "Do not comfort Me with things that perish; do not meet an infinite agony of the heart with things that have the writing of condemnation upon their very stones. Your meaning is good, but you fail to see that soon a great wind will blow through all this temple fabric, and nothing will stand."

JOSEPH PARKER

October 25

The disciples' curiosity was struck concerning the destruction of the temple. The disciples were not struck by what was going to happen immediately in the way of the humiliation and death of Jesus, always seeming to forget the cross, always forgetting the only things they should have remembered, persistently jumping ahead to glories and kingdoms and princedoms and masterships of various degree and name. Jesus could not bind them down to the only thing He came to exemplify and glorify—the principle of self-sacrifice.

Despite their lack of depth, Jesus answers them now with a thunderstorm. Yet amid all that thunderstorm there are streaks of blue sky, outlooks upon silent and beautiful places that may be temple gates or the beginning of infinite sanctuaries. Never was such a speech delivered by mortal lips, its thunder, its silence, its infinite energy, its instruction that might have been whispered in the ear of trouble. It was His own speech in very deed, both in its intellectual capacity, in its moral tone, in its subtle simplicity, in its grand grasp of past, present, and future, in all that was awful in grandeur and all that was luring and tender in heaven's own beauty.

What is the subject? The coming of Christ. How will He come—when shall all these things be—what shall be the sign of His coming? "Tell us," said the eager disciples, "something about it that you have not yet spoken to any human ear." They came to Him privately and clustered about Him. They would have almost crushed Him in their eager love and in the straining of their attention to hear every tone and whisper of that voice. "Tell us."

How could He refuse? Twelve faithful yet fickle men, twelve hearts that had done all they could for Him—it was indeed little, still it was not underestimated by His all-appreciating love. For their sake and ours, He opens to them an amazing panorama of the future that their hearts may be strengthened for the future.

JOSEPH PARKER

As Jesus was sitting on the Mount of Olives, the disciples came to him privately. "Tell us," they said, "when will this happen, and what will be the sign of your coming and of the end of the age?"

MATTHEW 24:3

October 26

The disciples would receive no answer from Christ concerning the time of His return, for it is not for us to know these times (Acts 1:7). But He answers fully the question regarding the signs that would mark the end of the age. It is observable that what Christ says to His disciples tends more to engage their caution than to satisfy their curiosity, more to prepare them for the events that should happen than to give them a distinct idea of the events themselves. Such is the understanding of the times we should all covet.

Christ begins with a caution by foretelling the going forth of deceivers. The disciples expected to be told when these things would happen, to be led into that secret, but this caution is a check to their curiosity: "What is that to you? Mind your duty, follow Me, and do not be seduced from following Me." Those who are most inquisitive concerning the secret things that do not belong to them are most easily imposed upon by seducers (2 Thess. 2:3). Seducers are more dangerous enemies to the Church than persecutors.

There would appear false Christs, coming in Christ's name, assuming to themselves the name peculiar to Him. There was at that time a general expectation of the appearing of the Messiah; they spoke of Him as the One to come. But when He did come, the body of the nation rejected Him, which rejection those who were ambitious of making themselves a name took advantage of and set up their own Christs. History records many such impostors.

The followers of Jesus must be prepared for the deception these false Christs bring. Many, Jesus says, will be deceived. The devil and his instruments may prevail far in deceiving your souls. Many will be imposed upon by their signs and wonders, and many drawn in by the hopes of deliverances from their oppressions. For such the true Church must always be on guard.

MATTHEW HENRY

October 27

_The devil dies hard always. He has made up his mind to not quit us easily; he will have the last pull. Is this your experience? Do not be afraid or cast down by great fear and sorrow as if Christ is not coming to you at all. But you say, "I am only fighting, struggling, praying without an answer, knocking at the door that will not open. Can this be right? I have doubts and worries that I dare not put to words." To me, this reads as if part of the mightier eloquence: "Nation will rise against nation..." Your little cross is cut out of this infinite tree on which is hanging the Son of God. Let no man's heart therefore fail him because he is now only in the tribulation period of this progress. The Son of God is coming, though at present it seems as if He has forsaken the universe.

Nothing happens in all this tumult that was not foreseen. "See, I have told you ahead of time." There are no surprises to omniscience: Nothing happens by accident in all the workings of the universe. There are no accidents in any lawless and incoherent sense of the term. All things work for good to them that love God. Count it all joy when you fall into trials of many kinds, because out of the working of these trials shall come a complete and final peace. What knowledge of human nature is here revealed on the part of the Son of God. He knows the course of truth in the world; He knows precisely what every man will feel, how certain interests will be shocked, and how at the last there will be a fight between evil and good, devil and God, that shall seem to wreck the universe. God knows the whole scene down to Armageddon's bloody field—it is before the divine vision. Not a soul in all the holy army shall be lost, but when the night falls on the ghastly field, only evil shall be wounded and smitten with death. Hope on, live in watchfulness, and loyally follow the Lamb wherever He goes.

JOSEPH PARKER

"Nation will rise against nation, and kingdom against kingdom. There will be famines and earthquakes in various places. See, I have told you ahead of time."

MATTHEW 24:7, 25

October 28

"Then you will be handed over to be persecuted and put to death, and you will be hated by all nations because of me. At that time many will turn away from the faith and will betray and hate each other."

MATTHEW 24:9–10

*O*f all future events, we are as much concerned though commonly as little desirous to know of our own sufferings as of anything else. Christ foretells the coming persecution of His own people and a general falling away of many from the faith.

Believers are told they will be persecuted, perhaps as the apostle Paul was—afflicted with chains and imprisonments, cruel mockings and scourgings (2 Cor. 11:23–25). Jesus adds that they shall be killed. So cruel are the Church's enemies that nothing less will satisfy them than the blood of the saints. And believers shall be hated by all nations because of Jesus. The world was generally filled with enmity and hostility to Christians. What shall we think of this world when the best men have the worst abuse in it? But it is the cause that makes the martyr and comforts him; it is for Christ's sake that believers will be hated. No doubt wherever Christians carry the gospel, the devil will find his kingdom invaded and will rise up in his great wrath.

When the profession of Christianity begins to cost this dearly, Jesus tells us that many will fall away from the faith. The apostle Paul often complained of deserters, who began well, but something hindered them (Gal. 5:7), and John also talks about those who had gone out from them (1 John 2:19). Add to the apostasy the sins of betrayal and hate. Apostates have commonly been the most bitter and violent persecutors. In perilous times, when truth and love are abandoned, treachery and hatred ascend.

Christ has told this ahead of time for our instruction. Suffering times are shaking times, and those fall in the storm who stood in the sunshine. Persecuting times are discovering times. Wolves in sheep's clothing will then throw off their disguise and appear wolves. Many like their religion while they can have it cheap, but if their faith cost them, they fall away quickly.

MATTHEW HENRY

October 29

However many days are bright, and in whatever way all days are good, the reality is that our overall life is a fight. For some of us it is simple endurance; for all of us it has sometimes been agony; for all of us, always, it presents resistance, both inward and outward hindrances, to every noble life, especially to the Christian life.

"But he who stands firm to the end will be saved."

MATTHEW 24:13

Within, weakness, weariness, indolence, bright purposes clouding over, inconsistent wills, and all the works of the flesh continually war against the better self. And without, there is a constant down-dragging that comes from a whole assemblage of external things that solicit and attempt to seduce us. Old legends say that whenever a knight set out upon any lofty quest, his path was beset on either side by voices, some whispering seductions and some shrieking maledictions, but always seeking to distract him from his resolute march toward his goal. Then there are the golden apples rolled upon our path, seeking to draw us away from our standing firm, as well as the burdens of sorrows and cares. Every soldier of the cross of Jesus Christ has met these foes.

To "stand firm" means active persistence as well as patient submission. It is not enough that we should stand and bear the pelting of the storm, unmurmuring and unbowed by it, but we are bound to go on our way, bearing up and steering right onward. Persistent perseverance in the path that is marked out for us is the virtue that our Lord is speaking about. The endurance that wins the soul and leads to salvation is the brave perseverance in the face of all difficulties and in spite of all enemies.

There are many who begin their Christian life full of vigor and with a heat that is too hot to last. But in a few years, the fervency is gone, and they settle into the average, unprogressive Christian, who is a wet blanket to the devotion of the Church. I wonder how many of us would recognize our own former selves if we saw them. To how many of us should the words be rung in our ears: "You were running well; what has hindered you?"

ALEXANDER MACLAREN

October 30

"For as lightning that comes from the east is visible even in the west, so will be the coming of the Son of Man. Wherever there is a carcass, there the vultures will gather."

MATTHEW 24:27–28

This grim parable has a strong Eastern coloring and is best understood by dwellers in those lands who tell us that no sooner is some animal dead than the vultures appear. There may not have been one vulture visible a moment before in the hot blue sky, but taught by scent or by sight that their banquet is prepared, they come flocking in, a hideous crowd around their hideous meal, fighting with flapping wings and tearing it with their strong talons. And so, says Christ, whenever there is a rotting, dead society, a carcass hopelessly corrupt and evil, down upon it, as if drawn by some unerring attractions, will come the angels of the divine judgment.

This principle has operated with unerring certainty through all the course of the world's history (such as the fall of Jerusalem), but it only points to the immensely larger event, the coming of Jesus Christ to judge the world. There is an assured termination of the world's history in that great and solemn day when all men shall be gathered before Christ's throne and He shall judge all nations. Jesus Christ is to return in bodily form to judge all men. The judgment is to be the destruction of opposing forces, the sweeping away of the carcass of moral evil.

At the center of all revelation is the revelation of a God of infinite love, but I cannot forget that there is such a thing as the "terror of the Lord" and that we must strike the solemn note of warning of judgment to come. The gospel is the proclamation of deliverance not only from the power but also from the future retribution of sin. And though the thing that breaks the heart and draws men to God is not terror, but love, the terror must often be evoked in order to lead to love. Judgment is the inevitable issue of the righteousness of the All-ruling God. But no vulture of judgment, wheeling and circling in the sky, will ever touch those whose lives had hidden in Christ their Savior.

ALEXANDER MACLAREN

October 31

There is a day coming when our Lord Jesus will show Himself as the brightness of His Father's glory and the express image of His person. His coming will darken the sun and moon as a candle is darkened in the beams of the noonday sun. "The moon will be abashed, the sun ashamed; for the Lord Almighty will reign on Mount Zion and in Jerusalem" (Isa. 24:23).

The sign that shall appear in heaven is the Son of Man Himself. At His first coming, He was "a sign that will be spoken against" (Luke 2:34), but at His second coming, a sign that should be admired. Yet all the nations will mourn at His coming. "Look, he is coming with the clouds, and every eye will see him, even those who pierced him; and all the peoples of the earth will mourn because of him" (Rev. 1:7). Sooner or later, all sinners will be mourners; penitent sinners look to Christ and mourn in tears, then reap in joy; impenitent sinners shall look on Him whom they pierced and, though they laugh now, shall mourn and weep in endless horror and despair.

The judgment of the great day will be committed to the Son of Man, both in pursuance and in recompense of His great undertaking for us as Mediator (John 5:22, 27). He shall come in the clouds of heaven, as He said at His ascension (Acts 1:9, 11). A cloud will be the Judge's chariot (Ps. 104:3), His robe (Rev. 10:1), His pavilion (Ps. 18:11), and His throne (Rev. 14:14). And His majestic coming on those clouds will be with power and great glory. His first coming was in weakness and lowliness (2 Cor. 13:4), but His second coming will be with power and glory that agree both with the dignity of His person and to the purpose of His coming. "His splendor was like the sunrise; rays flashed from his hand, where his power was hidden. In wrath you strode through the earth and in anger you threshed the nations" (Hab. 3:4, 12).

MATTHEW HENRY

"At that time the sign of the Son of Man will appear in the sky, and all the nations of the earth will mourn. They will see the Son of Man coming on the clouds of the sky, with power and great glory."

MATTHEW 24:30

November 1

*W*hile the Lord tells the disciples much about His second coming, He keeps back the answer to their specific question, When? He is going to tell them, but He will not. He makes a great speech and leaves us in utter ignorance of the one thing we desire to know. Yet He speaks the only word that it is needful for a man to heed to be truly wise: "Watch." The watcher wins; the watcher reads; the watcher sees the coming day. The Son of Man says to us, "You want to see Me coming, to rejoice in My cloudless light, to behold the beauty of My kingdom—Watch." Let us regard this coming of Christ in any light—coming into the individual heart, coming among the nations of the earth, coming in the glory of His power and sovereignty. The dynamics are always the same.

The coming of Christ always makes itself felt through all the space of life. When He moves, He stirs the universe. He cannot come or go as if nothing had happened. He was before all things, and by Him all things consist, and in Him all things are made. The clouds are the trailing of His garments, and on the wings of the wind He flies. What wonder, then, that when He comes there shall be stir, tumult, agitating, shaking, a pulsing through and through the whole life and economy of things? Behold His deity in this very action. The earth would be extinguished in its little cloud, and the nearest star would not know that the spark had gone out—so says the astronomer. But when the sun, at which all lamps are lighted, withdraws, the universe is wrapped in impenetrable and intolerable night. Jesus Christ is the center of all things, His life touches every point and tests every interest. Whenever He moves, creation vibrates to His step. When He came into the world, Herod and all Jerusalem were troubled while others were swept with hope and joy. When He comes into the individual heart, old habits protest, old desires cry out, the whole heaven and earth of the personal life are shaken, and they tremble under His tread.

JOSEPH PARKER

The destruction caused by the deluge was universal. It did not merely sweep away some who were out of the ark, but it swept them all away. Wealthy and poor, brilliant and ignorant, pagan priest and vulgar, young and old—none escaped. A great many had heard of Noah and the ark—some criticized it, others mocked it, some were sympathetic, and a few even helped Noah work on it. Nevertheless, men's universal indifference about their souls remained. They refused to believe and give up their worldliness in the face of judgment and still will do so until the second coming of Christ when the flood of fire comes and sweeps them all away.

Yet all who were in the ark were safe. Nobody fell out of that divinely appointed refuge; nobody died in it; nobody was left to perish. They were all preserved in it, and so will Jesus Christ preserve all in Him. Whoever comes to Him shall be secure. None of them shall perish or be taken out of His hand. Think of the strange collection of creatures they were that were preserved. Snail was as safe as greyhound, squirrel was as secure as elephant—not safe because of what they were but safe because of where they were, namely, in the ark.

When the storm beat upon the ark, it might have destroyed the lion quite as easily as the mouse, but it destroyed neither because the sides of the ark could bear the tempest. When the floods came, the vessel could mount higher and higher and nearer toward heaven, the deeper the waters were. So with us: Let storms and furious tempests come and our sins assail us and our sorrows, too, yet we who are weakest are quite as secure as the strongest because we are in Christ, and Christ shall outlive the storm and bear us upward, nearer and nearer to the heaven of God.

CHARLES SPURGEON

"For in the days before the flood, people were eating and drinking, marrying and giving in marriage, up to the day Noah entered the ark; and they knew nothing about what would happen until the flood came and took them all away. That is how it will be at the coming of the Son of Man."

MATTHEW 24:38–39

November 3

"Therefore keep watch, because you do not know on what day your Lord will come. But understand this: If the owner of the house had known at what time of night the thief was coming, he would have kept watch and would not have let his house be broken into. So you also must be ready, because the Son of Man will come at an hour when you do not expect him."

MATTHEW 24:42–44

The two commands at the beginning and end of the paragraph are not quite the same. To "be ready" is the consequence of watchfulness. The first command is grounded on His coming at a time we do not know, and the second command on His coming at an hour that we do not think; that is to say, it is not only uncertain but also unexpected and surprising.

What is that watchfulness? It is literally wakefulness. We are beset by perpetual temptations to sleep, to spiritual drowsiness and laziness. And without continual effort, our perception of the unseen realities and our alertness for service will be lulled to sleep. The religion of the multitudes is a sleepy religion. It is also a vivid and ever-present conviction of His certain coming and consequently a habitual realizing of the transience of the existing order of things and of the fast-approaching realities of the future. Further, it is the keeping of our minds in an attitude of expectation and desire, our eyes ever traveling to the dim distance to mark the far-off shining of His coming. What a miserable contrast to this is the attitude of professing Christendom as a whole! It is swallowed up in the present, wide awake to interests and hopes belonging to our times but sunk in slumber as to that great future.

It was Christ's purpose that from generation to generation His servants should be kept busy in the attitude of loving expectation—under the absolute certainty that Jesus will return again and with the absolute uncertainty of when it will happen. Christ's coming would be oftener contemplated if it were more welcome. But what sort of a servant is he who has no glow of gladness at the thought of meeting his Lord?

ALEXANDER MACLAREN

*E*verything that our Lord saw on earth seemed to make Him think of the kingdom of heaven. Perhaps our Lord and His disciples were called to that marriage where the original of this parable took place, or perhaps He heard a story like this. While our Lord did not explain the meaning of this parable, its supreme lesson is the richly rewarded wisdom of the five wise virgins. The foolish virgins took no oil with them, but the wise did.

What exactly is the oil in this parable? The answer lies in your own heart. What is it that makes your heart to be so dark and so sad and so unready, sometimes? Why is there so little life and light and joy in your heart? Why is your spiritual experience so flat and stale when it should be as full of gladness as if your whole life were one continual making ready for your marriage? In plain English, it is the absence from your heart of the Holy Spirit.

It is the Holy Spirit who makes God Himself to be so real to us, so full of life and light and blessedness. It is the Spirit who reveals Jesus to us as He is. The fruit of the Holy Spirit in man is love, joy, peace, patience, gentleness, goodness. It is the lack of the Holy Spirit that makes us to be the lump of darkness that we are. If we had God's Holy Spirit shed abroad in our heart, we would make every house in which we live and every company into which we enter like a continual marriage supper. The Holy Spirit is this light-giving and life-giving oil.

You must go to God for the Holy Spirit. God the Father is the real seller of this holy oil. The Holy Spirit proceeds from the Father. Go to the Father before the darkness comes. Have the Holy Spirit already in your heart, and you will never walk in darkness nor be shut out into the darkness, however suddenly the Bridegroom may come.

ALEXANDER WHYTE

"At that time the kingdom of heaven will be like ten virgins who took their lamps and went out to meet the bridegroom. Five of them were foolish and five were wise. The foolish ones took their lamps but did not take any oil with them. The wise, however, took oil in jars along with their lamps"

MATTHEW 25:1–4

November 5

"The foolish ones said to the wise, 'Give us some of your oil; our lamps are going out.'"

MATTHEW 25:8

All spiritual emotions and vitality, like every other kind of emotion and vitality, die unless nourished. There is nothing in our spiritual emotions that has any guarantee of perpetuity in it, except under certain conditions. We may live, and our life may ebb. We may trust, and our trust may tremble into unbelief. We may obey, and our obedience may be broken by the mutinous risings of self-will. There is certainty of the dying out of all communicated life unless the channel of communication with the life from which it was first kindled is kept constantly clear.

Note that these foolish ones did not stray away into forbidden paths. They were simply asleep and had neglected their duty, not having the foresight to look ahead and provide against the contingency of a long time in waiting. If we do not look forward and prepare for possible drains in our powers, we shall be called foolish as well. The thing that makes shipwreck of the faith of many professing believers is not wickedness, nor conduct that would be branded as sin by ordinary people, but simply indolence. If the pipes are not taken care of, they will be clogged, and the rivers of life in Christ Jesus cannot force a way through.

Do you try to keep your lamp lit? There is only one way to do it—that is to go to Christ and get Him to pour His sweetness and power into your heart. The only way to keep our spirit vital and alive is by having recourse, again and again, to the same power that first imparted life to it, and this is done by the first means, the means of simple reliance upon Christ in the consciousness of our own deep need and of believingly waiting upon Him for the repeated communication of the gifts that we have so often neglected. Negligence is enough to slay us. Doing nothing is the sure way to quench the Holy Spirit. You can never have in your heart too much of divine grace. And you will receive all you need if you choose to go and ask it of Him.

ALEXANDER MACLAREN

November 6

I love the expression, "went in with him." I would go nowhere without Him; and if I may go anywhere with Him, wherever He shall lead me, it shall be a happy day to me. You know that our Lord Jesus left it in His will that we are to be with Him in His glory: "Father, I want those you have given me to be with me where I am, and to see my glory" (John 17:24). O beloved, you who know what it is to be one with Jesus, crucified and risen and made to sit together with Him in the heavenly places, you will find something more heavenly about heaven than otherwise had been there when that sweet sentence is true of you: "The virgins who were ready went in with him to the wedding banquet." Jesus Himself shall escort us to our place in glory; He shall conduct us to the sources of highest blessedness, for as was said to John, "The Lamb at the center of the throne will be their shepherd; he will lead them to springs of living water" (Rev. 7:17).

This, it seems to me, is the very center of the bliss of heaven. Heaven is like the Eshcol cluster of grapes, but the essence, the juice, the sweetness of the cluster, consists in that we shall be with Jesus forever. Ah, me! How else could we ever hope to go into the wedding feast if we did not go with Him—hidden behind Him, covered with His righteousness, washed in His blood? John saw the great multitude that no man could number standing before the throne and before the Lamb: "These are they who have come out of the great tribulation; they have washed their robes and made them white in the blood of the Lamb. Therefore, they are before the throne of God and serve him day and night in his temple; and he who sits on the throne will spread his tent over them" (Rev. 7:14–15). All the demands of divine justice will be fully met by the fact that we go in with Jesus. Covered with His righteousness, adorned with His beauties, the beloved of His heart, we shall go with Him to the wedding feast!

CHARLES SPURGEON

"But while they were on their way to buy the oil, the bridegroom arrived. The virgins who were ready went in with him to the wedding banquet. And the door was shut."

MATTHEW 25:10

"It will be like a man going on a journey, who called his servants and entrusted his property to them. To one he gave five talents of money, to another two talents, and to another one talent, each according to his ability. Then he went on his journey."

MATTHEW 25:14–15

In this parable, Jesus teaches us that we are to be in habitual preparation for His return. The Master is Christ, who is the absolute Owner and Proprietor of all persons and things, especially over His Church. The servants are Christians, His own personal servants—born in His house, bought with His money, devoted to His praise, and employed in His work.

When Christ "ascended on high, he led captives in his train and gave gifts to men" (Eph. 4:8). Christ went to heaven as a man going on a journey into a far country. When He went, He took care to furnish His Church with all the things necessary for it during His personal absence. For and in consideration of His departure, He committed to His Church truths, laws, promises, and powers that must be guarded (1 Tim. 6:20). He sent His Spirit to enable His servants to teach and profess those truths, to press and observe those laws, to improve and apply those promises, and to exercise and employ those powers, ordinary or extraordinary.

Christ's gifts to individuals in His Church are rich and valuable, the purchases of His blood inestimable, and none of them inferior. He gave to some more gifts than others, to everyone according to his ability. When divine providence has made a difference in men's ability as to mind, body, estate, relation, and interest, divine grace dispenses spiritual gifts accordingly. All have not alike, for they have not all alike abilities and opportunities. God is a free agent, and "he gives them to each one, just as he determines" (1 Cor. 12:11). Some are cut out for service of one kind, others in another, as the members of the natural body. But every person has at least one gift, and that gift is never to be despised but is to be used faithfully in the Master's service. How important it is that we keep in mind that a day will come when we must give an account for what we have done!

MATTHEW HENRY

*P*raise from Christ's lips is praise indeed, and here He pours it out with warmth and evident delight. His heart glows with pleasure, and His commendation is musical with the utterance of His joy in His servant. When we are tempted to disparage our slender powers as compared with those of His more conspicuous servants and to suppose that all that we do is nothing, let us think of this loving estimate of our poor service.

For such words from such lips, life itself were wisely flung away; but such words from such lips will be spoken in recognition of many a piece of service less high and heroic than a martyr's. Faithfulness is the grace that Jesus praises—manifested in the recognition that the talents were a loan, given to be traded with for Him and to be brought back increased to Him.

The reward of this faithfulness is the appointment to higher office. In Christ's kingdom, the road to advancement is diligence, and the higher a man climbs, the wider is the horizon of his labor. It will be so in heaven. Clearly, this saying implies that in the future life, through a dateless eternity, there will be a continuance in some ministry of love and of the energies that were trained in the small transactions of earth.

The last words of the Lord pass beyond our poor attempts at commenting. No eye can look undazzled at the sun. When Christ was near the cross, He left His disciples a strange gift at such a moment—His joy—and that is their brightest portion here, even though it is shaded with many sorrows. The enthroned Christ welcomes all who have known the fellowship of His sufferings into the fullness of His heavenly joy, unshaded, unbroken, unspeakable, and His followers pass into it as into some broad land of peace and abundance. Sympathy with His purposes leads to such oneness with Him that His joy is ours, both in its occasions and in its rapture. Oh, to drink in His pleasures today!

ALEXANDER MACLAREN

"His master replied, 'Well done, good and faithful servant! You have been faithful with a few things; I will put you in charge of many things. Come and share your master's happiness.'"

MATTHEW 25:21

November 9

> "The man with the two talents also came. 'Master,' he said, 'you entrusted me with two talents; see, I have gained two more.' His master replied, 'Well done, good and faithful servant! You have been faithful with a few things; I will put you in charge of many things. Come and share your master's happiness.'"
>
> MATTHEW 25:22–23

Every good and perfect gift is from above, coming down from the Father of the heavenly lights" (James 1:17). All that men have they must trace to the Great Fountain, the Giver of all good. Do you have talents? Have you time, wealth, influence, and power? Have you powers of speech or of thought? Whatever your position and your gifts may be, remember that they are not yours, but they are lent to you from on high. No man has anything of his own except his sins. All the honor for our ability and the use of it must be unto God, because He is the Giver. The parable teaches us this very pointedly, for it makes every person acknowledge that his talents come from the Lord. Even the man who dug in the earth and hid his Lord's money did not deny that his talent belonged to his master. Although he was exceedingly impertinent, he did not deny this fact, so that even this man was ahead of those who deny their obligations to God, shake their head at the mention of obedience to their Creator, and spend their time and their powers rather in rebellion.

God has made great and decided differences in the talents He has given to individuals, some greater and others less. Remember that in the day of judgment your account must be personal—God will ask you what you did with whatever talents He gave you. We must take our own trial before God's eternal tribunal, and nothing can bias our judge or make Him give an opinion for or against us apart from the evidence. God gives rewards not according to the greatness of the talents with which we have been entrusted but according to our faithfulness in using them. This puts the least gifted believer on an equal basis with the most gifted—each has the opportunity to hear the blessed "Well done, good and faithful servant"! Can you imagine the thrill?

CHARLES SPURGEON

November 10

*W*hat a strangely insolent excuse. To charge an angry master to his face with grasping greed and injustice was certainly not the way to conciliate him. Such language is quite unnatural until we remember the reality that the parable was meant to shadow—the answers for their deeds that men will give at Christ's judgment seat. Then we can understand how, by some irresistible necessity, this man was compelled, even at the risk of increasing the indignation of the master, to turn himself inside out and to put into harsh, ugly words the half-conscious thoughts that had guided his life and caused his unfaithfulness.

Every person will give an account of himself to God. The unabashed impudence of such an excuse is but putting into vivid form this truth—that then a man's actions in their true character, and the ugly motives that underlie them and which he did not always honestly confess to himself, will be clear before him. It will be as much of a surprise to the men themselves, in many cases, as it could be to listeners. Thus, we must examine closely the underside of our lives, the unspoken convictions and motives that work all the more mightily upon us because, for the most part, they work in the dark.

Dear friend, there are two religions in this world: the religion of fear and the religion of love; and if you have not the one, you must have the other. The only way to get perfect love that casts out fear is to be quite sure of the Father–love in heaven that begets it. And the only way to be sure of the infinite love in the heavens that kindles some little spark of love in our hearts here is to go to Christ and learn the lesson that He reveals to us at His cross. Love will annihilate the fear, for the perfect love that casts out fear sublimes it into reverence and changes it into trust. Have you received that love?

ALEXANDER MACLAREN

"Then the man who had received the one talent came. 'Master,' he said, 'I knew that you are a hard man, harvesting where you have not sown and gathering where you have not scattered seed. So I was afraid and went out and hid your talent in the ground. See, here is what belongs to you.'"

MATTHEW 25:24–25

"Take the talent from him and give it to the one who has the ten talents. For everyone who has will be given more, and he will have an abundance. Whoever does not have, even what he has will be taken from him. And throw that worthless servant outside, into the darkness, where there will be weeping and gnashing of teeth."

MATTHEW 25:28–30

The indolent servant is defined by his master as wicked and lazy. The destruction that falls upon him is brought on not by active opposition but by the negative sin of not doing or being what he ought. Unlit lamps and unused talents sink a man like lead. Doing nothing is enough for ruin. The man's fate has a double horror. It is loss and suffering. The talent is taken away and given to the man who had shown he could and would use it.

Gifts not employed for Christ are taken away. How much will go from many a richly endowed spirit that here flashed with unconsecrated genius and force! Even today we see that true possession, which is use, increases powers, and that disuse, which is equivalent to not possessing, robs them. The student's intellect, the craftman's delicate finger, the artist's eye, all illustrate the law on its one side; and the dying out of faculties and tastes, and even of intuitions and conscience, by reason of simple disuse are melancholy instances of it on the other. But Jesus' solemn words seem to point to a far more awful energy in its working in the future when everything that has not been consecrated by employment for Jesus shall be taken away. How much can that be? Enough to see with awe that a spirit may be cut to the bare and still exist.

Once more, like the slow toll of a funeral bell, we hear the dread sentence of ejection to "the darkness" without, where tears are undried and passion unavailing. There is something awful when the most loving lips that ever spoke in love shaped this form of words, so heart-touching in its wailing but decisive proclamation of darkness, weeping, and agony, and cannot but toll them over and over again in our ears, if perchance we may listen and be warned.

ALEXANDER MACLAREN

The teachings of that wonderful last day of Christ's ministry are closed with this tremendous picture of universal judgment. It is a picture to be gazed upon with silent awe rather than to be commented on. There is fear lest, in occupying the mind in the study of the details and trying to pierce the mystery it partly unfolds, we should forget our own individual share in it. Better to burn in on our hearts the thought *I shall be there* than to lose the solemn impression in efforts to unravel the difficulties of the passage. Difficulties there are, as is to be expected in Christ's revelation of so unparalleled a scene. Many questions are raised by it that will never be solved till we stand there. Let us try to grasp the main lessons and not lose the spirit in studying the letter.

The grand teaching is that Christ is the Judge of all the earth. Sitting there, a wearied man on the Mount of Olives, with the valley of Jehoshaphat at His feet, which the Jews regarded as the scene of the final judgment, Jesus declared Himself to be the Judge of the world in language so unlimited in its claims that the speaker must be either a madman or God. Calvary was less than three days off when He spoke this. The contrast between the vision of the future and the reality of the present is overwhelming. The Son of Man has come in weakness and shame; He will come in His glory, that flashing light of the self-revealing God, of which the symbol of the "glory" that shone between the cherubim is said to be Christ's. Then, heaven will be emptied of its angels, who shall gather around the enthroned Judge. Then, He will take His place as Judge and with His glance shall part the infinite multitudes and discern the character of each item in the crowd as easily as the shepherd's eye picks out the goats from the sheep. Men's deeds will compellingly reveal themselves, and Christ will judge.

ALEXANDER MACLAREN

"When the Son of Man comes in his glory, and all the angels with him, he will sit on his throne in heavenly glory. All the nations will be gathered before him, and he will separate the people one from another as a shepherd separates the sheep from the goats. He will put the sheep on his right and the goats on his left."

MATTHEW 25:31–33

November 13

"Then the King will say to those on his right, 'Come, you who are blessed by my Father; take your inheritance, the kingdom prepared for you since the creation of the world.'"

MATTHEW 25:34

This wondrous scene concerns the godly, who are on the right hand of the Son of Man's throne in glory. He who was the Shepherd is here the King, and He speaks with kingdom authority. Christ, who has redeemed the godly from the curse of the law and purchased a blessing for them, commands that blessing on them. Reproached and cursed by the world, they are blessed of the Father, from whom all the blessings in heavenly things flow.

He calls them to "come," in effect saying, "Welcome, ten thousand welcomes, to the blessings of My Father. Come to Me, come to be forever with Me. You who followed Me bearing the cross, now come along with Me wearing the crown. The blessed of My Father are the beloved of My soul who have been too long at a distance from Me. Come, now, come to My bosom, come into My arms, come into My dearest embraces!" With what joy will this fill the hearts of the saints in that day! We now come boldly to the throne of grace, but we shall then come boldly to the throne of glory. This word holds out the golden scepter with an assurance that our sweet communion with God today will one day lead to the perfection of bliss.

Then the saints are provided with a kingdom that the Father has prepared for them. A kingdom is counted as the most valuable possession on earth, and how might one imagine a heavenly kingdom? And what must its happiness be, for it is the product of divine counsel. It is prepared specifically for you, you by name, you personally and particularly, and is adapted in all points to the new nature of your sanctified soul. Amazingly, it was prepared since the creation of the world (Eph. 1:4). The end, which is last in execution, is first in intention with our Father. Infinite Wisdom had an eye to the eternal glorification of the saints. Let us stand in awe that one day we shall inherit a heavenly kingdom via our sonship in Christ. *Come!*

MATTHEW HENRY

November 14

At the final judgment, the righteous did not know they had been doing this; therefore, it had not been done to secure an advantage. The righteous had wholly forgotten the beneficent activities that were attributed to them; therefore, they had not been mere legalists trying to obey the letter of a law and endeavoring to set up, by penance or gift, some claim to the ultimate mercy and clemency of heaven. They had been simply breathing a spirit, embodying an inspiration, setting out in beautiful daily life that which was internal and vital and part of their very nature, and had become such by ministries we call divine and spiritual.

The others had no such spirit; they did not take life other than a daily task, a daily burden, something to be gotten through. If they had been told that by giving a certain portion of food to the poor every day they could have had one heaven, nothing could have been easier for them; but that which appears to be so very easy may sometimes be found to be supremely difficult. Do not imagine that life is a mere question of giving and taking without thought and without purpose: You cannot be mechanically godly with any given issue or with any hope of heaven. Godliness is not a question of mechanics or arrangement, of doing this and partaking of the other. It is a spirit, a life, an invisible but supreme sovereignty of the soul, and he who enjoys the con-sciousness of that sovereignty does good and blushes to find it fame. He has no idea that all of this is coming back to him in certain forms. If he had, he would be a mere investor, a trick-ster in good doing, and that is a contradiction in terms. Our good doing must be our breathing, it must be the habit and spirit of our life, and to be this, it must originate in the cross, take its inspiration from the cross, return for renewal day by day to the cross.

JOSEPH PARKER

"Then the righteous will answer him, 'Lord, when did we see you hungry and feed you, or thirsty and give you some-thing to drink? When did we see you a stranger and invite you in, or needing clothes and clothe you? When did we see you sick or in prison and go to visit you?'"

MATTHEW 25:37–39

November 15

Jesus...said to his disciples, "As you know, the Passover is two days away—and the Son of Man will be handed over to be crucified." Then the chief priests and the elders of the people assembled in the palace of the high priest...and they plotted to arrest Jesus in some sly way and kill him.

MATTHEW 26:1–4

Subtlety—that was their condemnation. Honest men know nothing about sly ways; honest men are fearless; honest men rely upon the instincts of the people; honest men never fear the instincts of a great nation. See how sin debases everything: It turns a grand magisterial function into a machine for the performance of trickery. Sin blights whatever it touches. If it looks at a flower, the flower dies; if it goes through a garden, it leaves a wilderness behind. It is a most damnable thing. See the Sanhedrin, the great council of the nation that should be its pride and crown, that should speak with a voice that would commend itself in every tone to the conscience and inner heart of the people, now conniving, arranging, plotting—and that is the work of the fear that comes of conscious wrong. Fearlessness goes out the front door; honesty speaks aloud in plain language that every man can understand. Honesty can be searched into. Your slyness is your condemnation.

What will Jesus Christ do with the case so vividly and completely before Him? Will Jesus turn away from the great feast of the Jews? No—He will keep the feast, though He must die. He is the Teacher the world wanted; His was the heroism of a moral type that alone could act upon the world like salt to save it from its decay. He will be a true Jew; He will keep the feast, though He will be killed under its sacred banner. But in doing that, He will give the feast its highest meaning. Up till now, the Passover has been but a historical memorial in Israel, getting further and further away from the first incident and losing, by mere lapse of time, much of its first freshness. But Jesus makes all things new. He goes to that last service and lifts it up to its spiritual significance.

JOSEPH PARKER

November 16

In the gospel of John, we learn that it was Judas Iscariot who began the objection and inquired into this matter of waste and by his statement condemned himself. This was not the question of an economist; it was the inquiry of a thief. There is no monetary value that can be given to an act of true worship. Iscariot cannot do anything in the Church but debase and injure it.

A man is not necessarily a Christian because he is a disciple and is seen in the company of believers. A bad disposition misunderstands everything, including Christ. When a Judas looks at a flower, he sends a chill to its little heart; when a Judas kisses your child, he blackens its soul. Do not go to the bad man for high and bright interpretations of life and nature. The bad man cannot give you what you seek. Wherever he is, all the holy spirits vanish and leave him in the vacancy of solitude.

And yet the bad man can use nice words: He talks about the poor. The poor—he would sell his mother's bones to enrich himself! The poor—he would sell the lights from their sockets in the church if he could do it without being caught! Yet he talks about the poor, makes a mouthful of the word, says it with passion as if he cared about the poor. He can care for nothing that is wise, beautiful, tender, and truly necessitous. The disease is vital; the disorder is fundamental. He is bad in the inner fibers, and every look he gives is a blasphemy. He comes into the church and, looking at anything that he may call an ornament, inquires, "Why this waste? Why was it not sold and given to the poor?" He misunderstands all beauty, as if the poor did not benefit from the beautiful thing. Better to learn in Christ's school than in Iscariot's!

JOSEPH PARKER

A woman came to him with an alabaster jar of very expensive perfume, which she poured on his head as he was reclining at the table. When the disciples saw this, they were indignant. "Why this waste?" they asked. "This perfume could have been sold at a high price and the money given to the poor."

MATTHEW 26:7–9

Aware of this, Jesus said to them, "Why are you bothering this woman? She has done a beautiful thing to me. The poor you will always have with you, but you will not always have me. When she poured this perfume on my body, she did it to prepare me for burial."

MATTHEW 26:10–12

*Y*ou cannot have any great life without sentiment. Life is not all cold logic; the flowers are the lovelier for the dews that tremble upon them, and you look so much younger and nobler when the tears of real pity are in your eyes—you are not unmanned; you are more than manned. The bad spirit cannot understand lavish generosity, spiritual suggestiveness, or religious sentiment. Only the beautiful soul can understand the beautiful act. Jesus Christ understood the woman and told her what it meant, though she did not know it. We do not know the meaning of our best acts. I am so afraid that we yield ourselves to those wooden teachers who would always keep us just between two fixed points, who would put down all madness—whereas it is by madness, mistakenly so called, that the world gets on an inch farther on its slow course now and then.

Jesus now becomes the Giver. Making His voice heard above the objections, He tells the disciples what the woman has done. She gave the ointment, He gave the explanation, and in that explanation we have revelation. Our deeds mean more than we sometimes mean them to mean, says Christ. "She did it to prepare Me for burial." That was a new idea; the woman did not intend to suggest death and burial when she came with that perfume. "Ah, but that is exactly what she did," says Christ. "This is like an odor of heaven rising from the grave I shall presently occupy." He gives our actions such great meaning and amplitude of significance! He makes us ashamed of our very prayers because they are to Him so much more than they are to us. He interprets them at the other end and seems to stretch them across the sky, whereas we did but mutter them in helpless and inarticulate necessity. Such is the wonder of Christ!

JOSEPH PARKER

November 18

*W*e are accustomed to think of the betrayer of our Lord as a kind of monster whose crime is so mysterious in its atrocity as to put him beyond the pale of human sympathy. The awful picture that the great Italian poet draws of him as alone in hell, shunned even there, as guilty beyond all others, expresses the general feeling about him. And even the attempts that have been made to diminish the greatness of his guilt by supposing that his motive was only to precipitate Christ's assumption of His conquering Messianic power are prompted by the same thought that such treason as his is all but inconceivable. I cannot but think that these attempts fail and that the narratives of the gospels oblige us to think of his crime as deliberate treachery. But even when so regarded, other emotions than wondering loathing should be raised by the awful story.

There had been nothing in his previous history to suggest such a sin, as is proved by the disciples' later question, "Surely not I, Lord?" (vs. 22), when our Lord announced that one of them would betray Him. No finger pointed to where Judas sat; no suspicion lighted on him. The process of corruption was unseen by all eyes but Christ's. Judas came to his terrible preeminence in crime by slow degrees and by paths that we have all tread. As for his guilt, that is in other hands than ours. As for the growth and development of his sin, let us remember that the possibilities of crime as dark are in us all. And instead of shuddering abhorrence at a sin that can scarcely be understood and can never be repeated, let us be sure that whatever man has done, man may do, and ask with humble consciousness of our own deceitful hearts, "Surely not I, Lord?"

ALEXANDER MACLAREN

Then one of the Twelve—the one called Judas Iscariot—went to the chief priests and asked, "What are you willing to give me if I hand him over to you?" So they counted out for him thirty silver coins.

MATTHEW 26:14–15

And while they were eating, he said, "I tell you the truth, one of you will betray me." They were very sad and began to say to him one after the other, "Surely not I, Lord?"

MATTHEW 26:21–22

None of the disciples could think that he was the traitor, yet none of them could be sure that he was not. Their Master knew better than they did; and so, from a humble knowledge of what lay in them, coiled and slumbering, but there, they would meet His words not with a contradiction but with a question. His answer spares the betrayer and lets the dread work in their consciences for a little longer for their good.

We catch a glimpse here into the possibilities of evil that lie slumbering in all our hearts. Every man is a mystery to himself. In every soul there lie, like hibernating snakes, evils that a very slight rise in the temperature will wake up into poisonous activity. Let no man say in foolish self-confidence that any form of sin is impossible for him.

Remember, all sins are at bottom but varying forms of one root. The essence of every evil is selfishness, and when you have that, you have the source of all wickedness in your heart. Therefore, do not let us be so sure that it cannot be manipulated and flavored into any form of sin. All sin is one at the bottom— living to myself instead of living to God.

Any evil is possible to us, seeing that all sin is but yielding to tendencies common to us all. Cain killed his brother from jealousy; David committed adultery from lust; Judas betrayed Christ because he loved money. Tell me you are never jealous, you never lust, and that the love of money has not got the best of you at times. We all live in the same atmosphere, and the temptations that have overcome those who have committed the worst sins have also appealed to us. One sin opens the door for another, and all sins hunt in packs. So, let us treat our lives with a wholesome self-distrust and say to ourselves, as the good old Puritan divine, looking at a man going to the scaffold, said, "But for the grace of God, there go I!"

ALEXANDER MACLAREN

Here we see the compassion that is the key word of the Savior's life. Except for His pity, most of His miracles never would have been wrought. He wept, He sighed, He pitied, He compassionated with the most tender spirit; and because He had compassion upon those who were needy and in pain or in great distress, He worked miracles for the supply of their necessity.

Jesus has compassion for Judas Iscariot. He does not turn upon Judas and utter these words in a tone of exasperation and resentment. He interprets the great decrees: He stands fast in the tabernacle of God's eternity, and there might have been tears in His eyes when He said, "Woe to that man who betrays the Son of Man." Not, "I threaten you with woe," not, "I will one day repay you for this," not, "This is the day of your triumph, but one day I will punish you." Such a tone would have been out of rhythm with the gospel of His love and also with the thunder of His almightiness; it would have become a quarrel. He regarded it as a fulfillment of prophecy, the final expression of that which had been decreed from eternity. "Woe will be the lot of him who does this. He will suffer for it when he sees one day what he has done. I pity that man that he was ever born."

Jesus pities the man who has fitted himself to carry out this purpose though it be old as the decrees of eternity. There is an aspect of every sinner that touches Him not only with anger but also with pity and real grief. When He sees the man breaking His command right in two, He cries over the poor fool as He sees him doing wrong. That does not excuse the man, but Christ's sorrow when He looks on Judas is real. We are all traitors like Judas. Some have come to public infamy, but all should live in private shame. Jesus never looks with pity upon the sin, yet He never looks without pity on the sinner. His offer of redemption remains.

JOSEPH PARKER

"The Son of Man will go just as it is written about him. But woe to that man who betrays the Son of Man! It would be better for him if he had not been born."

MATTHEW 26:24

November 21

While they were eat-

ing, Jesus took bread,

gave thanks and broke

it, and gave it to his

disciples, saying,

"Take and eat; this is

my body."

MATTHEW 26:26

The Lord's supper is an emblem of the death of Jesus Christ and of the way by which we receive benefit from Him. The bread sets forth His broken body, and the cup His blood. Eating and drinking these elements sets forth the way by which we receive the merit and the virtue of the Lord Jesus Christ, by a faith that is like eating, by a trust that is like drinking, by the reception of Christ spiritually into our hearts. "Take and eat," spiritually understood, are the gospel of the grace of God. Every disciple of Jesus Christ may hear a spiritual voice saying to him concerning Christ, "Take and eat." And to anyone who fears that he is not His disciple, these words are the gift of almighty love.

Jesus holds out the bread and says, "Receive it." No one earns or deserves this bread; it is to be taken. However unworthy I feel, if Jesus says, "Take it," I will take it by grace. Do you need a Savior? There He is; take Him. Do you desire to be delivered from the power of sin; take Him to do it. Do you desire to live a holy, godly life? Here is One who can wash you and enable you to live this way. Take Him; He is as free as the air. You have no more to pay for Christ than you have to pay for your next breath. Take Him in. That is the gospel. Surely the very fact that God would become Immanuel, God with us, and give His entire life for us should convince us to freely receive Him for our every need.

And let us "eat" as well. So receive Christ into your thoughts, your faith, your heart, till at last He gets to be one with you and nourishes your soul, even as food builds up your body. Christ is to become the true nourishment of our soul. Souls have to be nourished by the truth of God; that is their spiritual food; and the Lord Jesus, when we think of Him, meditate upon Him, believe in Him, and receive Him, becomes the food of our heart, the sustenance of our spirit. As we do, we are built up so as to attain the stature of a perfect man in Christ Jesus.

CHARLES SPURGEON

*I*n these words Jesus points out the moment of His whole career that He desires that men should remember. Not His words of tenderness and wisdom; not His miracles, amazing and gracious as they were; not the flawless beauty of His char-acter, though it touches all hearts and wins the most rugged to love and the most degraded to hope, but the moment in which He gave His life is what He would impart forever on the mem-ory of the world. And not only so, but in the rite He distinctly tells us in what aspects He would have that death remembered. Not as the tragic end of a noble career that might be hallowed by tears such as are shed over a martyr's ashes, not as the crowning proof of love, not as the supreme act of patient for-giveness, but as a death for us in which, as by the blood of the sacrifice, is secured the forgiveness of sin.

Within just twenty-four hours of His death, Jesus steps for-ward and says, "I am putting away the ancient covenant, for it is antiquated. I am the true offering and sacrifice, and I am establishing a new covenant sealed in My blood. That blood, when sprinkled on your heart, will thoroughly cleanse you." The power of Christ's sacrifice evokes in our poor souls faith, love, and surrender. It, and it alone, knits us to God; it, and it alone, binds us to the fulfillment of the covenant.

The very heart of Christ's gift to us is the gift of His own very life to be the life of our lives. In deep, mystical reality He Himself passes into our being and becomes one with our spirit. This is the heart of Christianity, the possession within us of the life, the immortal life of Him who died for us. We look forward to that day, after life's weariness and lonesomeness are past, when we will be welcomed to the banqueting hall by the Lord of the feast and sit with Him and His servants who loved Him at that first table and be glad.

ALEXANDER MACLAREN

Then he took the cup, gave thanks and offered it to them, saying, "Drink from it, all of you. This is my blood of the covenant, which is poured out for many for the forgiveness of sins."

MATTHEW 26:27–28

November 23

Then Jesus told them,
"This very night you
will all fall away on
account of me, for it is
written: 'I will strike
the shepherd, and the
sheep of the flock will
be scattered.'"

MATTHEW 26:31

"Struck," but Shepherd still. Strokes do not change character. The Shepherd was not deposed from His tender function; He was scourged, struck, oppressed, and grievously tormented, but He was still a Shepherd. "Scattered," but still the sheep of the flock. Understand that circumstances do not make or unmake you. You are not a Christian because you are comfortable; you are not a sheep of the flock because you are enfolded upon the high mountains and preserved from the ravenous beast. Sometimes the flock is scattered; sometimes the shepherd is struck; but the shepherd is still the shepherd, the flock is still the flock, and the tender relation between the two is undisturbed and indestructible.

If I were a Christian only on my good behavior, woe is me. If I belong to the flock only because of the day's calm or the rich-ness of the pasture and because of the abundance of all I need, my Christianity is no faith at all. It is a thing of circumstances, subject to climatic changes. Any number of accidents may come down upon it and utterly alter its quality and its vital relations. I stand in Christ; I am redeemed with blood; the work is done; when sin abounds, grace does much more abound. The Church was just as much a church when she was in dens and in caves of the earth, destitute, tormented, afflicted, as when she roofed herself with lovely vaulted ceilings and rare lights. Let us more and more understand that our election and standing are of God and are not tossed about, varied and rendered uncertain, by the tumultuous accidents of time or by the sharp variations of a necessary and profitable discipline.

It is the Shepherd who is calm, though He is going to be struck. He has the confidence of the written Word to stand upon. This is not something unexpected or unforeseen: An ancient prophecy is about to be fulfilled, but after that, He points the flock to the broad morning of resurrection and infinite joy.

JOSEPH PARKER

When people boast, such exaggeration is itself a fall. There is a time when even to speak is a vulgarity. There is a time when to contradict is blasphemy. There are times when men should at least think in quietness and nurse their resolutions in the secrecy of unuttered prayer. Some virtues are vices—that is to say, their exaggeration becomes vicious.

Jesus Christ performed what we may call in some sense the last of His miracles. His reply to Peter was a mental miracle, an instance of that foreknowledge of Christ where He read the heart and gave language to the unuttered thought and brought the fire of shame to the cheek of men who supposed that their heart-thoughts were unread and unknown. Christ emphatically defines His disciple's moral lapse within a given period of time. When Peter denied once, he might have recalled almost his breath and denied that he had denied; but this boasting shall be humiliated; there shall be left no doubt or hesitancy on the part of Peter himself that the denial was threefold, complete—in its way, infinite.

For Peter's part, it was honest ignorance, the worst kind of ignorance, the ignorance of one's own heart. Until we know what our heart really is, we can have no conception of what Christ proposes to do. Young, strong, prosperous, with the color of health upon our cheeks and with the energy of health in our step and our appearance, we cannot understand Christ's great speech of the heart. He must reduce us, humble us, grind us to powder, fill us with shame until we weep bitterly, and in that infinite rain of penitence He may say something to us that will lead us to God. Meanwhile He allows the boaster to have the last word, that having his own word ringing in his ear, he may the more accurately and vividly remember it when the stroke falls and his tortuous lips utter the speech of denial.

JOSEPH PARKER

Peter replied, "Even if all fall away on account of you, I never will." "I tell you the truth," Jesus answered, "this very night, before the rooster crows, you will disown me three times."

Matthew 26:33–34

Then Jesus went with his disciples to a place called Gethsemane, and he said to them, "Sit here while I go over there and pray." He took Peter and the two sons of Zebedee along with him, and he began to be sorrowful and troubled. Then he said to them, "My soul is overwhelmed with sorrow to the point of death."

MATTHEW 26:36–38

*O*ne shrinks from touching this incomparable picture of unexampled sorrow for fear lest one's fingerprints should stain it. There is no place here for picturesque description, which tries to mend the gospel stories by dressing them in today's fashions. We must put off our shoes and feel that we stand on holy ground. Though loving eyes saw something of Christ's agony, He did not let them come beside Him but withdrew into the shadow of the gnarled olives, as if even the moonbeams must not look too closely on the mystery of such grief.

Mark how the Man of Sorrows was "overwhelmed with sorrow." Somewhere on the western foot of Olivet lay the garden, named from an oil press in it, which was to be the scene of the holiest and deepest sorrow on which the moon has ever looked. Truly it was "an oil press" in which the "good olive" was crushed by the grip of unparalleled agony and yielded precious oil, which has been poured into many a wound since. The three disciples who witnessed Jesus' transfiguration are allowed to witness this no less wonderful revelation of His glory in His loving submission. A sudden wave of emotion, a storm of agitation, broke over His soul and His calm and forced from His patient lips the unutterably pathetic cry, "My soul is overwhelmed with sorrow to the point of death." No feeble explanation of these words does justice to the abyss of woe into which they let us dimly look.

No word came from the disciples, who were, no doubt, awed into silence by the great grief as the fountains of bitter floods swept over Christ's sinless soul. What lay before Jesus was not merely death but the death that would atone for a world's sin and in which the whole weight of sin's consequences was concentrated. Such is horror and darkness beyond description.

ALEXANDER MACLAREN

The disciples' drowsiness is singularly parallel with the sleep of the same three at the transfiguration—an event that presents the opposite pole of our Lord's experiences and yields so many antithetical parallels to Gethsemane. No doubt the tension of emotion that had lasted for many hours had worn them out; but if weariness had weighed down their eyelids, love should have kept them open. Such sleep of such disciples may have been a riddle, but it resulted in the Savior's gentle surprise and the pain of disappointed love, addressed to Peter especially, as he had promised so much. All that Jesus received in answer to His yearning for sympathy was that those who loved Him most lay curled in deep slumber within earshot of His prayers. If ever a soul tasted the desolation of utter loneliness, that suppliant beneath the olives tasted it.

The gentle reprimand soon passes over into counsel. Watchfulness and prayer are inseparable. The one discerns dangers; the other arms against them. Watchfulness keeps us prayerful, and prayerfulness keeps us watchful. To watch without praying is presumption; to pray without watching is hypocrisy. The eye that sees clearly the facts of life will turn upward from its scanning of the snares and traps and will not look in vain. These two are the indispensable conditions of victorious encountering of temptation. Fortified by them, we shall not fall into temptation, though we encounter it. The outward trial will still be danger or sorrow, but we shall pass through it as a sunbeam through foul air, untainted, and keeping heaven's radiance. To watch and pray will give governing power to the spirit and enable it to impose its will on the reluctant flesh; if we do not, the supremacy of the renewed nature will tend to cease by the unquestioned tyranny of the flesh.

ALEXANDER MACLAREN

Then he returned to his disciples and found them sleeping. "Could you men not keep watch with me for one hour?" he asked Peter. "Watch and pray so that you will not fall into temptation. The spirit is willing, but the body is weak."

MATTHEW 26:40–41

Going at once to Jesus, Judas said, "Greetings, Rabbi!" and kissed him. Jesus replied, "Friend, do what you came for."

MATTHEW 26:49–50

There are some sins against friendship in which the manner is harder to bear than the substance of the evil. It must have been a strangely coarse and cold nature that could think of fixing on the kiss of affection as the concerted sign to point out their victim to the legionaries. Many a man who could have borne to be betrayed by his own friend would have found that heartless insult worse to endure than the treason itself. Yet Christ's words show no agitation in them but carry a grave rebuke as it appeals to former companionship. Christ still recognizes their bond and is true to it. He will still plead with this man who has been beside Him so long, and though Jesus' heart is wounded, He will not cast Judas off.

We are now in the presence of the solemn greatness of divine love. Surely if ever there was a man who might have been excluded from the love of God, it was Judas. Sin is mighty; it can work endless evils on us; it can disturb and embitter all our relations with God. But one thing it cannot do, and that is, make God cease to love us. Love is the very being of God, and He loves us not for reasons in us but in Himself. His love abides with us forever and is granted to every soul of man. Even at the very instant of highest treason, Judas could not escape the lingering tenderness of Jesus and the merciful hand that was extended.

Is there a worse man on earth at this moment? If there is, he, too, has a share in the love of God. Prostitutes and thieves, murderers on death row, souls tormented by unclean spirits, the wrecks of humanity whom respectable Christianity passes by with averted head and uplifted hands, all have a place in His heart. And we, as individuals, have a place in that royal, tender heart. His love is mightier than all our sins and waits not on our merits nor is turned away by our iniquities. He did not begin to love because of anything in us; He will not cease because of anything in us. Let us always yield to His patient pleading.

ALEXANDER MACLAREN

November 28

There can be no limit to the available resources of the Christ of God. Thousands of thousands of angels would fill the air if Jesus willed it. The band that Judas led would be an insignificant squad to be swallowed up at once if the Savior would but summon His allies. Behold the glory of our betrayed and arrested Lord. If He was such then, what is He now, when all power is given Him of His Father! Bear in mind the clear idea that Jesus in His humiliation was nevertheless Lord of all things, and especially of the unseen world and of the armies that people it. The more clearly you perceive this, the more you will admire the all-conquering love that took Jesus to the death of the cross.

Tarry here just a minute to recollect that the angels also are, according to your measure and degree, at your call. You have but to pray to God, and angels shall bear you up in their hands lest you dash your foot against a stone. We do not think enough of these heavenly beings, yet they are all ministering spirits sent forth to minister to those who are the heirs of salvation. Like Elijah's servant, if your eyes were opened, you would see the mountain full of horses of fire and chariots of fire round about the servants of God. Let us learn from our Master to reckon upon forces invisible. Let us not trust in that which is seen of the eye and heard of the ear, but let us have respect to spiritual agencies that evade the senses but are known to faith. Angels play a far greater part in the affairs of providence than we realize. God can raise us up friends on earth, and if He does not do so, He can find us abler friends in heaven. There is no need to pluck out the sword with which to cut off men's ears, for infinitely better agencies will work for us. Have faith in God, and all things shall work for your good. The angels of God think it an honor and a delight to protect the least of His children.

CHARLES SPURGEON

"Put your sword back in its place... Do you think I cannot call on my Father, and he will at once put at my disposal more than twelve legions of angels?"

MATTHEW 26:52–53

November 29

"But how then would the Scriptures be fulfilled that say it must happen in this way?"

MATTHEW 26:54

Peter had been anxious to meet force with force. He, like men of every age, was a victim of the thinking that it was necessary to do something to fight the evil. He failed to see that there is a force of passiveness, an energy of silence, a magnificent retort of nonresistance that is the very mystery of heroism to those who mistake noise for music and tumult for power.

Jesus' instructions that Peter put away the sword said in effect: "Suppose you, Peter, could cut down every man here. What about those who come later? Evil has an indestructible posterity if it is encountered only by force. This disease cannot be cut down with cold steel; it must be met by spiritual and regenerative influences." When force meets force, there are triumphs, there are defeats, there is death: Do not suppose that to strike down an enemy is to overcome the enmity. In these words, Jesus laid down in terms so luminous and definite the philosophy that underlies every beneficent and stable civilization.

Then Christ reminded Peter that all that was happening was in fulfillment of Scripture. Connect yourself with Destiny if you would be calm: Do not live in the dying anecdotes of the passing day. Consider that all things are elect of God and move you in the current of His foreknowledge and forearrangement of things. You will be troubled, tossed about with every wind of doctrine, if you are living only from day to day and upon the breath that is breathed from the human mouth. We must live in the eternity of God if we would be quiet amid all the storm and stress of life. Do not suppose that men come around you accidentally with swords and knives: They know not what they do. If your purpose is right, if your prayer is pure, if your face is set steadfastly toward the Jerusalem in your destiny, you will be an ever-quiet and all-quieting presence in life. Jesus laid His hand upon Destiny as ruled by a personal Will and was unshaken.

JOSEPH PARKER

November 30

*H*ow the Savior was watched, malignly watched, always watched, watched with theological eyes, political eyes, envious eyes, passionate eyes. No wonder! He opposed Himself to the religion of His times—whoever does that dies. He opposed Himself to the orthodoxy, the respectability, and the self-security of His age, and whoever does that dies!

When they urged Jesus to defend Himself, we read these wonderful words: "But Jesus remained silent." That was probably the crowning miracle this side of the cross. The Man of eloquence without a word upon His lips—silence was then truly golden. What made Him so quiet? The struggle in Gethsemane. There was nothing more to be said: The Man who had passed through such experience was bound to be quiet. This was no arrangement or trick. When we return from some funerals we cannot speak. When we spend some places after all-night prayer, we cannot speak for the next three days. We seem to our friends to be distraught but with a singular shining in our face and a new gentleness in the hand. Sorrow conquered must be followed by eloquent silence.

The battle was won in Gethsemane: To have spoken after that would have been to degrade the grandeur of all that made the life of Christ sublime. Yet when He did speak and defined His divinity, He spoke in a fitting tone. What could you do to a man who spoke in this manner? You can strike this man and he does not feel the fist: The soul in that hour is so much greater and grander than the body that the body is but as a dead surface to the hand that abuses it. Live in heaven, live in actual possession of God's blessing, have your tabernacle and your pavilion in eternity, and not a hair on your head shall perish. What could death be to a man who talked as Christ? He had abolished death: They met; they caught each other in their terrific arms; and Death was left where the bloody sweat fell!

JOSEPH PARKER

Then the high priest stood up and said to Jesus, "Are you not going to answer? What is this testimony that these men are bringing against you?" But Jesus remained silent.

MATTHEW 26:62–63

December 1

"Yes, it is as you say,"

Jesus replied. "But I

say to all of you: In the

future you will see the

Son of Man sitting at

the right hand of the

Mighty One and

coming on the clouds

of heaven."

MATTHEW 26:64

*O*ur Lord before His enemies was silent in His own defense, but He faithfully warned and boldly avowed the truth. His was the silence of patience, not of indifference; of courage, not of cowardice. He acknowledged and confessed that He was the Son of God, the promised One, the Messenger from heaven. He did not hold them in suspense but openly declared His Godhead by stating, "It is as you say." He then proceeded to reveal the solemn fact that He would soon sit at the right hand of God, even the Father, and that those who were condemning Him would see Him glorified and in due time would stand at His judgment seat. Our Lord's confession was very full, and happy is he who heartily embraces it.

"In the future you will see." Jesus stood before His enemies, a poor, defenseless man, a spectacle of meek and lowly suffering, led by His captors as a lamb to the slaughter. A lamb in the midst of wolves thirsting for his heart's blood is but a faint picture of Christ standing before the Sanhedrin in patient silence. Yet, this tremendous humiliation did not in the least endanger His after-glory. The lower He stooped, the more sure He was to rise ultimately to His glory. And at this moment He sits at the right hand of power: All power is given to Him in heaven and in earth. He shall come with flaming fire to visit the trembling earth, and kings and princes shall stand before Him, and He shall reign.

Take this spiritual lesson: Never be afraid to stand alone when the truth is to be confessed. Never be overawed by spiritual authorities or daunted by rage or swayed by multitudes. Unpopular truth is eternal. Through flood or flame, in loneliness, in shame, in reproach, follow Jesus! If every step shall cost you scorn and abuse, follow still; yes, to prison and to death, still follow Him. As surely as Jesus will come again, so those who love Him shall sit upon His throne with Him!

CHARLES SPURGEON

December 2

The question that was proposed to Jesus—"Tell us if you are the Christ, the Son of God"—was suggested by the facts of Christ's ministry and not by anything related to this investigation. It was the summing up of the impression made on the ecclesiastical authorities of Judaism by His character and life. While there were outstanding instances in the life of Christ where there was no mistaking Jesus' claim to divinity, they were merely summits that rise above the general level. But the general level is that of one who takes an altogether unique position. No one else professing to lead men in paths of righteousness has so constantly put the stress of his teaching not upon morality nor religion nor obedience to God but upon this, "Believe in me," or ever pushed forward his own personality into the foreground and made the whole nobleness and blessedness and security and devoutness of a life to hinge upon that one thing, its personal relation to him.

People talk about the gentle wisdom that flowed from Christ's lips, about the lofty morality, about the beauty of pity and tenderness, and about all the other commonplaces so familiar to us; we gladly admit them all. But I venture to go a step further and say that the outstanding characteristic that marks Christ's teaching as something new and distinct is not its morality nor its philanthropy nor its meek wisdom nor its sweet reasonableness but its tremendous assertions of His importance.

Jesus' answer to Caiaphas, while plainly claiming to be the Messiah, expanded itself to show the tremendous significance of the Son of God. It involves participation in divine authority and omnipotence. Jesus, at the supreme moment, made the plainest claim to divinity and could have saved His life if He had not done so. Either Caiaphas, in his ostentatious horror of such impiety, was right in calling Christ's words blasphemy, or Jesus is indeed the everlasting Son of the Father, who will come to be our Judge.

ALEXANDER MACLAREN

Then the high priest tore his clothes and said, "He has spoken blasphemy! Why do we need any more witnesses?"

MATTHEW 26:65

December 3

*H*aving heard some of the sublimest words ever spoken by Jesus Christ, the highest representatives of the Jewish nation committed this shameful deed. They spit in the face that is the light of heaven, the joy of angels, the bliss of saints, and the very brightness of the Father's glory. This spitting shows us how far sin will go. If we want proof of the depravity of the heart of man, I will not point you to Sodom and Gomorrah, nor will I take you to places where blood was shed by wretches like Herod and men of that sort. No, the clearest proof that man is utterly fallen and that the natural heart is enmity against God is seen in the fact that they did spit in His face, falsely accuse Him, condemn Him, and hang Him up as a felon that He might die upon the cross. What was there in His whole life that should give them occasion to spit in His face? Even at that moment, did He look with contempt upon them? Not Jesus, for He was all gentleness and tenderness even toward His enemies. He had healed their sick, fed their hungry, and been among them a very fountain of blessing up and down Judea and Samaria. Tell me not of the horrible evils committed by uncivilized men—this is the masterpiece of all iniquity. Humanity stands condemned of the blackest iniquity now that it has gone as far as to spit in Christ's face.

How deep was the humiliation of Christ? That He, the perfect man and perfect God, was made sin for us, was treated with utter shame and contempt. O my Lord, to what terrible degradation were You brought! Into what depths are You dragged through my sin and the sin of all the multitudes whose iniquities were laid upon You! O my brethren, let us hate sin not only because it pierced those blessed hands and feet of our dear Redeemer but also because it dared to spit in His face. Let us bow our heads and blush with shame. Let us think of this marvelous condescension and feel our hearts all on fire with love for Jesus, and let us worship Him forever.

CHARLES SPURGEON

December 4

Peter sat among the servants of the high priest in the court-yard rather than enter the hall and be a comfort to Christ. Bad company is to many an occasion to sin, and those who need-lessly venture upon the devil's ground may expect either to be tempted or to be trapped. Peter certainly was, being ridiculed and abused by their company, exiting with guilt and grief.

Peter was challenged as being a follower of Jesus of Galilee. First one servant girl and then another charged him. The scornful tone of Christ being associated with *Galilee* and *Nazareth* and the disdainful *this fellow* speak of the reproach they felt having Peter in their company. Yet they have nothing to accuse Peter of except that he was with Jesus which, they thought, rendered him a scandalous and suspected person.

Upon the first accusation, Peter gave a shuffling answer. He pretended that he did not understand the charge, that he didn't know whom she meant by Jesus of Galilee or what she meant by being *with* him, even though his heart was bursting with the understanding. It is wrong to misrepresent our thoughts and affections, to pretend we do not understand or remember that which we do apprehend and did think of and remember. This is a convenient form of lying that is not easily disproved, but God knows our hearts (Prov. 24:12). It is yet a greater fault to mask our confession of Christ; it is, in effect, to deny Him.

Upon the next attack, Peter said flat out, "I don't know the man!" Why, Peter? Can you look into the hall at the innocent prisoner and say that you don't know Him? Did you not leave all to follow Him and confess Him to be the Christ, the Son of the Blessed? Have you not known Him better than anyone else? So one sin gives way to the next, and how soon are you fallen.

MATTHEW HENRY

Now Peter was sitting out in the courtyard, and a servant girl came to him. "You also were with Jesus of Galilee," she said. But he denied it before them all. "I don't know what you're talking about," he said. Then...another girl saw him and said...,"This fellow was with Jesus of Nazareth." He denied it again, with an oath: "I don't know the man!"

MATTHEW 26:69–72

Then he began to call down curses on him- self and he swore to them, "I don't know the man!" Immediately a rooster crowed. Then Peter remem- bered the word Jesus had spoken: "Before the rooster crows, you will disown me three times." And he went outside and wept bitterly.

MATTHEW 26:74–75

The hounds of hell have had their turn—spitting in Jesus' face and striking Him with their fists, slapping Him, and mock- ing Him. But something did grieve Christ more than the enemy. Peter cut His heart in two. If it had been an enemy who had done this, Christ could have borne it, but it was Peter, the dis- ciple, the intimate friend, who went to the house of God with Jesus and kept the Passover with Him. That is the sting! Peter said, "I don't know the man!" He even went so far as to curse and swear, saying, "I don't know the man!" That surely is an ancient anecdote. Yes, it is, yet it is not a day old. It was done this morning; we do it in some instances day by day. We are orthodox in conviction; we are heterodox in spirit and action. No enemy can hurt Christ as a friend can hurt Him. The enemy does not get at His heart; the friend does. Something of Peter is living now, living perhaps in the very most of us—not in this rough and violent form but in some mood more subtle yet not less deadly in its expression. O Searcher of hearts, have I denied the Savior—have I made light of His name to avoid the mocking sneer of some enemy? Have I pledged His name to sanctify some bad transaction?

Yet there was one thing about Peter that gives one hope: This was the weakness of violence, and therefore it will have suitable reaction. When he began to curse and swear, I began to have hope for him. If he had said the words coldly, he might never have been restored. The violence of some cases is their hope. The lips now foaming with such madness will presently pray. We say it is never so dark as before the dawn. Have hope for your worst one: He may come back yet. Backsliders return. Do not give up those who have left you as if they would never return. It may be very dark just now, but go to the door and open it. Perhaps there in the darkness we shall find the violent one weeping bitterly.

JOSEPH PARKER

December 6

*W*as ever morning invited to look upon so ghastly a spectacle? Morning and death! There is a grim irony in this conjunction of terms. God sends a fair day upon the earth, and we defile the very dew that glistens upon the heavenly gift. We rise from sleep as men skilled in evil and begin at once, with practiced hands, to rub out the commandments written upon the rocks and to pervert every promise hidden in the sweet flow—ers. Alas, we are proficient scholars in the school of evil; we soon cease to be scholars and become teachers. The morning that once had in it some gladness for us and that came to us as a revelation and a lifting up of the heart now comes with a new chance to serve the devil.

Judas went by night to seek the Lord. It was better. There was a kind of remnant of religion about the traitor when he chose the night for his villainy. He was not quite so bad as he might have been: He waited until darkness. The chief priests and elders seized the morning—thus the whole day has been stained through and through with wickedness; the morning, the night, the shining of the sun and the trembling of the stars, the whole circle of the day has not had one degree of it left without taint and blasphemy and evil.

There are no particular times for sinning. If you want a chance, it will come. Thus a God of pity has to take up every day like a spoiled thing and baptize it and regenerate it and send it upon the earth as a new morning for us. But He never fails to do this. He gives more grace; He will not cast us off forever; He will yet rub out the evil of the day and of the night; He will save us if He can. If lost, we shall be suicides: There shall be no imprint of the fingers of God upon us as having thrust us out when we find ourselves in utter darkness. He lives to save us!

JOSEPH PARKER

Early in the morning, all the chief priests and the elders of the people came to the decision to put Jesus to death.

MATTHEW 27:1

December 7

They bound him, led him away and handed him over to Pilate, the governor.

MATTHEW 27:2

It was Pontius Pilate who crucified our Lord. He was the Roman governor placed at that time over Judah and Jerusalem. What Tiberius Caesar was in Rome, all that Pontius Pilate was in Jerusalem. Pilate's was a much-coveted post among his rivals in Rome, but the insurgent Jews were a difficult people to keep under Caesar's heel. Pilate's position had demanded all his astuteness and statecraft, and it had called forth a good deal of his cruelty.

But of all the problems he faced, nothing had so perplexed him as the widespread and mysterious movement by Jesus of Nazareth. If Pilate had found in Jesus, or in any of His disciples, a single atom of danger to the Roman domination, he would have crushed them. But absolute wolf for Jewish blood as Pilate always was, he was not wicked enough nor wolf enough to murder an innocent man.

Pilate's heart was made of Roman iron, but when Jesus was brought before him that Passover morning, his heart stood absolutely still as he ventured to ask Jesus the staggered question: "Are you the king of the Jews?" What was he to do with Jesus' response and the clamoring of the Jewish authorities before him? Try to get out of it as he did, the chain of his terrible fate was fast closing around his neck, then was cinched by the savage threat: "If you let this man go, you are no friend of Caesar" (John 19:12). That was enough, for at that, Pilate took water, in his defeat and despair, and washed his hands before the multitude.

What would we have done had we been in his place, standing between the deadly anger of Caesar and a just man to be crucified. We would have done just what Pilate did. To protect ourselves and preserve our paying post and life, we too would have washed our hands of it. Who will dare to cast a stone at Pilate? May we learn from his failure and run to that Fount for sin that he had such an awful hand in opening.

ALEXANDER WHYTE

December 8

*J*esus had acted in such a manner as to rouse to very mad-ness the conscience of the man who betrayed Him. Judas was appalled by the issue. No man can betray Christ without first betraying himself. Understand that. No man can give Christ away or sell Him or play foully with any of the great truths of the sanctuary without having first betrayed and sold and damned himself. These are not the actions of the hand, done for a moment, set down and forgotten as accidents of the transient day. You could never have spoken a word against the sanctuary, its Lord, its light, and its revelation, until something had taken place in your own heart amounting to self-betrayal. The vil-lainy is in the heart before it is in the hand. Not only does all history elucidate this, but much of our personal experience and observation goes to confirm it. Who has ever known a man to play falsely with the balances of the sanctuary, with the light and spirit and truth of the holy place, who did not at some time afterward show that before he did so there had been a tremendous collapse in his own heart?

Judas always reveals himself. He never was so revealed to himself as when Christ acted as He did immediately after the betrayal. Christ did not utter any words against Iscariot, but He conducted Himself as to show Iscariot in his true light. This is His method of judgment with us all: He enters into no wordy controversy; He does not requite terms with us or set Himself into weaving elaborate accusations. He so orders His provi-dence, the whole method of His economy, as to bring out of us the reality of our soul. Judas is forced to find an explanation for his actions in his own heart and must confess that he has done something for whose accusation and impeachment there is nothing in human language to touch the tremendous matter. "Innocent blood," says Judas. "The evil is in myself only."

JOSEPH PARKER

When Judas, who had betrayed him, saw that Jesus was condemned, he was seized with remorse and returned the thirty silver coins to the chief priests and elders. "I have sinned," he said, "for I have betrayed innocent blood."

MATTHEW 27:3–4

December 9

"I have sinned," he said, "for I have betrayed innocent blood." "What is that to us?" they replied. "That's your responsibility." "I am innocent of this man's blood," [Pilate] said. "It is your responsibility!"

MATTHEW 27:4, 24

So, what the priests said to Judas, Pilate said to the priests. In Judas' case, the priests contemptuously tell their wretched instrument to bear the burden of his own treachery. Priests though they were, and therefore bound by their office to help any poor creature struggling with a wounded conscience, they had nothing better to say to him than the scornful, "What is that to us?"

Pilate, on the other hand, delivers to the priests the judgment they had given Judas. He tries to shove off his responsibility upon them, and they are quite willing to take it; but the responsibility can be neither shuffled off by him nor accepted by them. His motive in surrendering Jesus to them was nothing more than the cowardly wish to humor his turbulent subjects and so to secure an easy tenure of office. For such an end, what did one poor man's life matter? He knows perfectly well that the Roman power has nothing to fear from this King, whose kingdom rested on His witness to the truth. Knowing that Jesus was innocent, he, as governor, was guilty of prostituting Roman justice and giving up an innocent man to death. No washing of hands will cleanse them.

Here we see a vivid picture that may remind us of what we all know in our own experience—how a man's conscience may be clear-sighted enough to discern and vocal enough to declare that a certain thing is wrong but not strong enough to restrain from doing it. Conscience has a voice and an eye; alas, it has no hands. It shares the weakness of all law; it cannot get itself executed. Men will jump over a fence although the sign says, "No trespassing," and is staring them in the face in capital letters. Your conscience is a king without an army, a judge without officers. Never deceive your conscience with the delusion that your responsibility may be shifted to any other person or thing. Each man has to bear the consequences of his own actions.

ALEXANDER MACLAREN

December 10

We see the governor's wife for only a moment. We hear her for only a moment. But in the space of that short moment, she so impresses her sudden footprint on this page of the gospel that as long as this gospel is read, what she said and did shall be held in remembrance for a most honorable memorial of her.

Both Pilate and his wife were Gentiles, strangers from the covenants of promise. As regards many of the good things of this life—learning, civilization, refinement—they were far advanced. But as regards a knowledge of God, they were not unlike Abram while he still served other gods. They were still at that stage in which God often revealed Himself in a dream to so many individuals before them. Almighty God has complete control and continual command of all the avenues that lead into the soul of man, and He sends His message at the very time and in the way that seems wisest and best in His sight.

We have every reason to believe that Pilate's wife was thoroughly versed in who Christ was. Everything that took place in the province was instantly reported at the Praetorium, including the recent story of Lazarus being raised from the dead. Then comes the remarkable dream. Just what shape did it take? Did she perhaps see Daniel's Ancient of Days on His fiery throne? Whatever its form, the impact was instant and ominous.

Pilate's wife was fearlessly true and faithful to all her light, though it may have as yet been but candlelight. But even candlelight is the same light as the light from the noonday sun. And the lurid light of Pilate's wife's dream came from the Light of the world. And nothing in divine things is more sure than that they who love the light shall have more light sent to them, till they shall have all the light they need. To them their path shall shine more and more to the perfect day. In her response to the light she was given, she becomes our example. Let us heed it as she did.

ALEXANDER WHYTE

While Pilate was sitting on the judge's seat, his wife sent him this message: "Don't have anything to do with that innocent man, for I have suffered a great deal today in a dream because of him."

MATTHEW 27:19

December 11

All the people answered, "Let his blood be on us and on our children."

MATTHEW 27:25

The priests and people gathered were perfectly willing to take from Pilate the burden for killing Jesus upon themselves. They thought that they were doing God a service when they slay His Messenger. They had no perception of the beauty and gentleness of Christ's character. They believed Him to be a blasphemer, and by Jewish law they held it as a solemn religious duty to slay Him. With their awful words, they stand before us as perhaps the crowning instance in biblical history of the possible darkness that may paralyze consciences. Fanatical hatred that thinks itself influenced by religious motives is the blindest and cruelest of all passions, knowing no remorse and utterly unperceptive of the innocence of its victim.

Let us take this thought, dear brethren, as to the awful possibility of a conscience going fast asleep in the middle of the wildest storm of passion, like the unfaithful prophet Jonah in the hold of the heathen ship. You can lull your conscience into dead slumber. You can stifle it so that it shall not speak a word against the worst of your sins. You can do so by simply neglecting it, by habitually refusing to listen to it. If you keep picking all the leaves and buds off the tree before they open, the tree will stop flowering. You can do it by gathering around yourself always and only evil associations and evil deeds. The habit of sinning will lull a conscience faster than almost anything else. Take care of that delicate balance within you, and see that you do not tamper with it or twist it.

Conscience may be misguided as well as lulled. It may call evil good, and good evil. We need a revelation of truth and goodness and beauty outside of ourselves to which we may bring our consciences that they may be enlightened and set right. We need a Bible, and we want a Christ to tell us what is duty as well as to make it possible for us to do it.

ALEXANDER MACLAREN

*W*hat a descent Christ's love for us compelled Him to make! Do not fail to recall that at the very time when they were thus mocking Him He was still Lord of all and could have summoned twelve legions of angels to His rescue. Had He willed it, one glance of those eyes would have withered up the Roman cohorts; one word from those silent lips would have shaken Pilate's palace from roof to foundation; and had He willed it, the vacillating governor and the malicious crowd would together have gone down alive into the pit, as did Korah, Dathan, and Abiram long ago. Lo, God's own Son, heaven's darling and earth's prince, sits there and wears the cruel wreath that wounds both mind and body at once, the mind with insult and the body with piercing pain. His royal face was marred with wounds that could not cease to bleed, trickling faint and slow. Gaze upon Him with enlightened eyes and tender hearts, and you will be able to more fully enter into fellowship with Him in His griefs.

And then twisted together a crown of thorns and set it on his head.

MATTHEW 27:29

I see here a solemn warning against our ever committing the same crime as the soldiers did. "Never!" we respond, but let us not be hasty, for every time we act according to our sinful flesh we crown the Savior's head with thorns. Who has not done this? Dear head, every hair of which is more precious than fine gold, when we gave our hearts to You we thought we should always adore You, that our whole lives would be one long psalm, praising and blessing You. Alas, how far have we fallen short of our own ideal! We have hedged You about with the briers of our sin. We have betrayed You with angry tempers and words spoken that injured; we have been worldly and loved what You abhor; we have yielded to our passions and evil desires. With these we have set upon Your head a coronet of dishonor. We come with the sorrowful and loving penitent and wash Your dear feet with tears of repentance because we have crowned Your head with thorns.

CHARLES SPURGEON

December 13

And sitting down, they kept watch over him there.

MATTHEW 27:36

These soldiers, four in number as we infer from John's gospel, had no doubt joined with their comrades in the coarse mockery that preceded the sad procession to Calvary; and then they had to do the rough work of the executioners, fastening the sufferers to the rude wooden crosses, lifting the crosses, with their burden, fixing them into the ground, then parting the clothing. Then for half a day there they sat, and it was but a dying Jew that they saw, one of three. A touch of pity came into their hearts once or twice, alternating to mockery, but when it was all over, and they had pierced His side and gone back to their barracks, they had not the least notion that they, with their dim, myopic eyes, had been looking at the most stupendous miracle in the whole world's history, had been gazing at the thing that angels desired to behold, and had seen that to which the hearts and the gratitude of millions would turn for all eternity. They shut their eyes that had served them so poorly and went to sleep, unconscious and unmoved that they had seen the pivot on which all of history turned.

Anyone who looks at the cross and sees nothing but a pure and perfect man dying upon it is very nearly as blind as these soldiers. He who sees only an innocent man and patient suffering has seen but an inch into the infinite. If we look on the cross with calm, unmoved hearts, if we look without personal appropriation of that cross and dying love to ourselves, and if we look without our hearts going out in thankfulness and laying themselves at His feet in a calm rapture of lifelong salvation, then we need not wonder that four heathen men sat and looked at Him for four long hours and saw nothing. If we truly see the infinite pathos and tenderness, power, mystery, and miracle of the cross, its image is photographed on our heart; and every day, and all days, we behold our Savior and, beholding Him, we are being changed into His likeness. Let us pray that our eyes may be cleansed, that we may see, and that seeing, we may copy that dying love of Jesus.

ALEXANDER MACLAREN

December 14

It is an old saying that the corruption of the best is the worst. What is more merciful and pitiful than true religion? What is more merciless and malicious than hatred that calls itself religious? These religious leaders, like many persecutors for religion since, came to feast their eyes on the agonies of their victim, and their rank tongues blossomed into foul speech. Yet even a cracked mirror gives a distorted image. Even within their brutal taunts, we find declarations that were absolutely true. The stones flung at the Master turn to roses strewn on His path.

In the cross, Jesus Christ revealed God as God's heart had always yearned to be revealed—infinite in love, forbearance, and pardoning mercy. There was the highest manifestation of the glory of God. Therefore, despite the dying in the darkness, it was the hour when God most delighted in the Savior. In that hour, Jesus carried filial obedience to its utmost perfection; then His trust in God was deepest, even at the hour when His spirit was darkened by the cloud of the world's sin, which He was carrying and which had spread thunderous between Him and the sunshine of the Father's face. For in that mysterious voice, which we can never understand in its depths, there are blended trust and desolation, even in its highest degree: "My God, My God, why have You forsaken Me?"

Let us, led by the errors of these scoffers, grasp the truths that they pervert. Let us see that weak man hanging helpless on the cross, whose "can't save Himself" is the impotence of omnipotence, imposed by His own loving will to save a world by His own sacrifice. Let us crown Him our King, and let our deepest trust and our gladdest obedience be rendered to Him because He did not come down from, but endured, the cross. Let us behold with wonder, awe, and endless love the Father not withholding His only Son but delivering Him up to death for us all.

ALEXANDER MACLAREN

In the same way the chief priests, the teachers of the law and the elders mocked him. "He saved others," they said, "but he can't save himself! He's the King of Israel!"

MATTHEW 27:41–42

December 15

From the sixth hour

until the ninth hour

darkness came over all

the land.

MATTHEW 27:45

There must be a great teaching in this darkness, for every event near the cross is full of meaning. Light will come out of this darkness. I love to feel the solemnity of the three hours of death-shade and to sit down therein and meditate, with no companion but the august Sufferer, around whom that darkness lowered.

Does it not appear as if the death that that darkness shrouded was also a natural part of the great whole? We have grown at last to feel as if the death of Christ were an integral part of human history. Introduce the fall and see paradise lost, and you cannot make the poem complete till you have introduced that greater man who did redeem us and by His death gave us our paradise regained. It is a singular characteristic of all true miracles that though your wonder never ceases, they never appear to be unnatural. The miracles of Christ dovetail into the general run of human history. We cannot see how the Lord could be on earth and Lazarus not be raised from the dead when the grief of Martha and Mary had told its tale. We see the disciples tempest-tossed on the Lake of Galilee and expect Christ to walk on the water to deliver them.

Wonders of power are expected parts of the narrative where Jesus is. Everything fits into its place with surrounding facts. But the miracles of Jesus, this of the darkness among them, are essential to human history. And especially is this so in the case of His death and the darkness that shrouded it. All things in human history converge to the cross, which seems to be not an afterthought or an expedient but the fit and foreordained channel through which love should run to guilty men.

Sit down and let the thick darkness cover you till you cannot see even the cross, and know that out of reach of mortal eye your Lord wrought out the redemption of His people. Jesus wrought a miracle of love by which light has come to those who sit in darkness and in the valley of the shadow of death.

CHARLES SPURGEON

December 16

This cry of Jesus came out of the darkness. Expect not to see through its every word as though it came from on high as a beam from the unclouded Sun of Righteousness. There is light in it, bright, flashing light. But there is a center of impenetrable gloom where the soul is ready to faint because of the terrible darkness.

About the ninth hour Jesus cried out in a loud voice, "Eloi, Eloi, lama sabachthani?"

MATTHEW 27:46

Our Lord was then in the darkest part of His way. He had trodden the winepress now for hours, and the work was almost finished. He had reached the culminating point of His anguish. This is His dolorous lament from the lowest pit of misery— "My God, My God, why have You forsaken Me?" I do not think that the records of time, or even of eternity, contain a sentence more full of anguish. Here the wormwood and the gall, and all the other bitterness, are outdone. Here you may look as into a vast abyss, and though you strain your eyes and gaze till sight fails you, you perceive no bottom. It is measureless, unfathomable, inconceivable. The anguish of the Savior on our behalf is no more to be measured and weighed than the sin that required it or the love that endured it. We will adore where we cannot comprehend.

I hope these words may help the children of God to understand a little of their infinite obligations to their redeeming Lord. You shall measure the height of His love, if it is ever measured, by the depth of His grief, if that can ever be known. See with what a price He has redeemed us from the curse of the law! As you see this, say to yourself: What manner of people should we be? What measure of love should we return to One who bore the utmost penalty that we might be delivered from the wrath to come? I do not profess that I can dive into this deep. I will only venture to the edge of the precipice and bid you look down and pray the Spirit of God to concentrate your mind upon this lamentation of our dying Lord as it rises up through the thick darkness: "My God, My God, why have You forsaken Me?"

CHARLES SPURGEON

December 17

"My God, my God,

why have you

forsaken me?"

MATTHEW 27:46

Without this last trial of all, the temptations of our Master would not have been so full as the human cup could hold. Without this, there would have been one region we must pass—namely, death—wherein we might call aloud upon our Captain, and yet He would not hear us for He would have avoided the fatal spot!

Jesus had emerged from the desert temptations with His path before Him and the presence of His God around Him. Now, after three years of divine action, when His course was run, when His work was finished, when His whole frame was tortured until the controlling brain fell whirling down the blue gulf of fainting and the giving up of the ghost was at hand, when His friends had forsaken Him and fled, then came again the voice of the enemy at His ear: "Despair and die, for God is not with You. Death, not life, is Your refuge. Make haste to Hades, where Your torture will be over. You have deceived Yourself. He never was with You."

"My God, My God, why have You forsaken Me?" the Master cried. For God was His God still, although He had forsaken Him—forsaken *His vision* of Him that His faith might glow out triumphant. But forsaken *Him?* No! Never before had He been unable to see God beside Him. Yet never was God nearer Him than now. The will of Jesus, in the very moment when faith seemed about to yield, was finally triumphant. It had no feeling then to support it, no blissful vision to absorb it. It stood naked in His soul and tortured. Pure and simple and surrounded by fire, His will declared for God. The sacrifice ascended in the cry "My God." His cry of desolation came out of faith. The divine horror of that moment is unfathomable to the human soul, a blackness of darkness. And yet He held fast and believed. In the cry came forth the victory, and all was over soon. Of the peace that followed that cry, the peace of a perfect soul, large as the universe, pure as light, ardent as life, victorious for God and His brethren, He alone can ever know the breadth and length and depth and height.

GEORGE MACDONALD

In actual historical fact, the glorious veil of the temple has been rent. As a matter of spiritual fact, the separating legal ordinance is abolished. For believers, the veil is not rolled up but rent. The veil was not unhooked and carefully folded up and put away so that it might be put in its place at some future time.

Oh, no! The divine hand took it and rent it. It can never be hung up again, for that is impossible. Between those who are in Christ Jesus and the Great God, there will never be another separation. "Who shall separate us from the love of Christ?" (Rom. 8:35). Only one veil was made, and as that is rent, the only separator is destroyed. I delight to think of this. The devil himself can never divide me from God now. He may and will attempt to shut me out from God, but the worst he could do would be to hang up a rent veil. What would that avail but to exhibit his impotence? God has rent the veil, and the devil cannot mend it. There is free access forever between a believer and his God, for the veil is rendered useless.

Some of God's people have not yet realized this gracious fact, for still they worship afar off. Very much of prayer is to be highly commended for its reverence, but it has in it a lack of childlike confidence. I can admire the solemn language of worship that recognizes the greatness of God, but it will not warm my heart or express my soul until it has blended with the joyful nearness of that perfect love that casts out fear and ventures to speak with our Father in heaven as a child speaks with its father on earth. No veil remains. Why do you stand afar off and tremble like a slave? Draw near with full assurance of faith. Jesus has brought you as close to God as even He Himself is. Though we speak of the holiest of all, the secret place of the Most High, yet it is of this place of awe, even of this sanctuary of Jehovah, that the veil is rent. Therefore, let nothing hinder your entrance. Assuredly, infinite love invites you to draw near to God.

CHARLES SPURGEON

At that moment the curtain of the temple was torn in two from top to bottom.

MATTHEW 27:51

December 19

Many women were there, watching from a distance.... Among them were Mary Magdalene... Mary Magdalene and the other Mary were sitting there opposite the tomb. After the Sabbath, at dawn on the first day of the week, Mary Magdalene and the other Mary went to look at the tomb.

MATTHEW 27:55–56, 61; 28:1

Mary (called Magdalene) from whom seven demons had come out" (Luke 8:2). While we know little about Mary and what her seven demons were, the terrible plague of possession is well documented in Scripture. To feel their full power and the whole pain and shame and distress and disgust of their presence, to know their rage and roar and tear and gnash at the heart, is beyond the imagination. To have grappled long, even with one inward demon, and to have him at your throat day and night for years—what a horror, and what a deliverance by Jesus Christ!

Since ever there were women's hearts in this world, were there ever two women's hearts with such emotions in them as when Mary the mother of Jesus and Mary Magdalene stood together beside His cross? Did you ever try to put yourself into their hearts that day? They stood and wept as never another two women have wept since women wept in this world, till John at Jesus' command took His mother away from Calvary and led her to the city. But Mary Magdalene still stood by the cross. She would not be dismissed, and she stood near His crucified feet. All His disciples had fled; thus there were no eyewitnesses to tell us how she stood close to the cross, weeping and ministering to His needs. But on the first day of the new week, we know that she was at the tomb early, and it was to her that both the angel and Jesus appeared (John 20:14–17). She would have been holding His feet there to this day had He not refused her.

It was Mary Magdalene, out of whom He had cast seven demons, to whom Jesus first appeared. It was to her who loved Him best and had the best reason to love Him best of all the people then living in the world. Only love as she loved Him, and Jesus will appear to you also, and call you by your name.

ALEXANDER WHYTE

December 20

$\mathcal{L}$uke tells us that "the women took the spices they had prepared and went to the tomb" (Luke 24:1). Despite being distinctly told by Jesus Christ Himself that He would rise again on the third day, these blessed and affectionate women came with their spices to embalm their Lord! How can you account for this? So treacherous is the memory, or so weak is the heart, that Sight staggers Faith. The women saw Him die; any recollection of a promise of rising again must have died in that death. So forgetting the prediction, or regarding it as a sentiment that had perished rather than as a fact that lay within the possibility of accomplishment, their intention was to embalm the body.

Luke also adds that when the angel said to them, "Remember how he told you...then they remembered his words" (Luke 24:6, 8). But the remembrance of His words would have been of no avail to them two hours before they saw the angel. If the stone had been in place, they would have remembered no such words, but now Sight helped Faith. The grave was empty, celestial visitors were the attendants of that gloomy place, and out of the depths of death they heard the voice of resurrection— "then they remembered." What was it to remember the words when the grave was empty, when angels were filling it with morning light? It was nothing to remember then. True faith sees in the darkness as well as in the light and goes to the grave with only the spices of the immovable certainty of the resurrection and the life.

Cultivate your spiritual memory; live in your remembrances of faith. If you let your yesterdays die, I wonder not that your tomorrows are among the darkest of your fears. Remember the old battles and the old victories and the light that drove them away like shadows that could stand no longer in their presence. Never let Jesus' words be wasted upon you and your experience evaporate and be found no more.

JOSEPH PARKER

After the Sabbath, at dawn on the first day of the week, Mary Magdalene and the other Mary went to look at the tomb.

MATTHEW 28:1

December 21

Death's house was firmly secured by a huge stone; the angel removed the stone, and the living Christ came forth. The massive door was unhinged and rolled away, and henceforth death's ancient prison is without a door. The saints shall pass in, but they shall not be shut in. As Samson arose early in the morning and took upon his shoulders the gates of Gaza—post, and bar, and all—and carried all away and left the Philistine stronghold open and exposed, so has it been to the grave by our Master, who, according to the divine decree, arose in the greatness of His strength and bore away the iron gates of the sepulcher, tearing every bar from its place. The removal of the imprisoning stone was the outward type of our Lord's having plucked up the gates of the grave, thus exposing the old fortress of death and hell and leaving it as a city stormed and taken, forever bereft of power.

Remember that our Lord was committed to the grave as a hostage. "He was delivered over to death for our sins and was raised to life for our justification" (Rom. 4:25). If He had not fully paid the debt for our sin, He would have remained in the grave. But mark Him as He rises, not breaking prison like a felon who escapes from justice, coming forth by his own power with the heavenly officer from the court of heaven to open the door to him, by rolling away the stone. Jesus Christ, completely justified, rises to prove that all His people are, in Him, completely justified and the work of salvation is forever perfect. In the empty tomb we see sin forever put away and death most effectually destroyed. Our sins, which held us captives in death and darkness and despair, have been rolled away, and hence death is no longer a dungeon dark and drear, but only a room we pass through on our way to heaven. Come, let us rejoice in this. Who can bar us in when the door itself is gone. There is nothing to prevent the resurrection of the saints.

CHARLES SPURGEON

The stone rolled away speaks of a foreshadowing ruin. Our Lord came into this world to destroy all the works of the devil. Behold before you the works of the devil pictured as a grim and horrible castle, massive and terrible, overgrown with the moss of ages, colossal, stupendous, cemented with the blood of men, ramparted by mischief and craft, surrounded with deep trenches, and garrisoned with evil spirits. A structure dread enough to cause despair to everyone who goes around it to count its towers and mark its bulwarks.

In the fullness of time, our Champion came into the world to destroy the works of the devil. During His life, Jesus sounded an alarm at the great castle and dislodged here and there a stone, for the sick were healed, the dead were raised, and the poor had the gospel preached to them. But on the resurrection morning, the huge fortress trembled from top to bottom; huge rifts were in its walls; and tottering were all its strongholds. One who was stronger than the master of the citadel had evidently entered it and was beginning to overturn from pinnacle to basement. Jesus tore the one huge cornerstone of death from its position and hurled it to the ground.

It was a prophecy that every stone of Satan's building should come down, and not one should rest upon another of all that the powers of darkness had ever piled up. Evil is still mighty, but evil will come down. Spiritual wickedness reigns in high places, nations still sit in thick darkness, many worship the scarlet woman of Babylon, cruelty and idolatry remain, but Christ has given such a shiver to the whole fabric of evil that the structure will collapse. We have but to work on, use the battering ram of the gospel, and the day must come when righteousness shall triumph. Sing, O heaven, and rejoice, O earth, for there shall not an evil be spared. Truly, there shall not be one stone left upon another in that day.

CHARLES SPURGEON

There was a violent earthquake, for an angel of the Lord came down from heaven and, going to the tomb, rolled back the stone and sat on it.

MATTHEW 28:2

December 23

The angel said to the women, "Do not be afraid, for I know that you are looking for Jesus, who was crucified."

MATTHEW 28:5

*L*et us listen to the angel's sermon. It is a spiritual thing and can be learned only by those whose spirits are awakened to grasp at spiritual truth. "Do not be afraid"—this is the very genius of our risen Savior's gospel. You who would be saved, you who follow Christ, you need not fear. Did the earth quake? Fear not: God can preserve you though the earth is burned with fire. Did the angel descend with terrors? Fear not: There are no terrors in heaven for the child of God who comes to Jesus' cross and trusts his soul to Him who bled thereon. Poor women, is it the dark that alarms you? Fear not: God sees and loves you in the dark, and there is nothing in the dark or in the light beyond His control. Are you afraid to come to the tomb? Does the grave alarm you? Fear not: You cannot die. Since Christ has risen, though you were dead, yet shall you live. Oh, the comfort of the gospel! Permit me to say there is nothing in the Bible to make any man fear who puts his trust in Jesus. Nothing in the Bible, did I say? There is nothing in heaven, nothing on earth, nothing in hell, that need make you fear who trust in Jesus.

"Do not be afraid." The past you need not fear, for it is forgiven. The present you need not fear, for it is provided for. The future is also secured by the living power of Jesus. "Because I live, you also will live" (John 14:19). Fear! How can it remain when Christ has risen from the dead? Do you fear your sins? They are all gone, for Christ had not risen if He had not put them all away. What is it you fear? If an angel bids you to not fear, why will you fear? If every wound of the risen Savior and every act of your reigning Lord consoles you, why will you fear? To be doubting and fearing, now that Jesus has risen, is an inconsistent thing in any believer. Jesus is able to help you in all your temp-tations; seeing He ever lives to make intercession for you, He is able to save you to the uttermost. Therefore, do not fear.

CHARLES SPURGEON

December 24

These good women found that they had lost the presence of Him who had been their greatest delight. "He is not here" must have sounded like another funeral knell to them. They expected to find Him, but He was gone. But then the grief must have been taken out of their hearts when it was added, "He is risen." I gather from this that if God takes away from me any one good thing, He will be sure to justify Himself in having so done, and that very frequently He will magnify His grace by giving me something infinitely better. Did Mary think it would be a good thing to find the body of her Lord? Perhaps it would have given her a melancholy satisfaction. The Lord took that good thing away. But then Christ was risen, and now to hear and see Him, was not that infinitely better?

Have you lost anything around which your heart had inter-twined all its tendrils? You shall find that there is a good cause for the privation. The Lord never takes away a silver blessing without intending to confer on us a golden gain. Depend upon it—for wood He will give iron, and for iron He will give brass, and for brass He will give silver, and for silver He will give gold. All His takings are but preliminaries to larger giving. Though that loss was dear, it will drive you closer to your Savior; His promises shall be more sweet to you, and the blessed Spirit shall reveal His truth more clearly to you. You shall be a gainer by your loss.

"He is not here"—that is sorrowful. But, "He is risen"—what greater joy! Christ, the dead one, you cannot see. You cannot tenderly embalm that blessed body as the women intended. But Christ, the Living One, you shall see; and at His feet you shall be able to worship; and from His lips you shall hear His glad-some voice. This is a lesson well worth remembering. If God apply it to your soul, it may yield you rich comfort. Your heav-enly Father "does not willingly bring affliction or grief to the children of men" (Lam. 3:33). Should the Lord take away one joy from you, He will give you another and a better one.

CHARLES SPURGEON

"He is not here; he has risen, just as he said."

MATTHEW 28:6

December 25

So the women hurried away from the tomb, afraid yet filled with joy, and ran to tell his disciples. Suddenly Jesus met them. "Greetings," he said. They came to him, clasped his feet and worshiped him. Then Jesus said to them, "Do not be afraid. Go and tell my brothers to go to Galilee; there they will see me."

MATTHEW 28:8–10

The women had been at the grave for only a few moments, but they lived more in these than in years of quiet. Time is very elastic, and five minutes or five seconds may change a life. These few moments changed a world. Haste, winged by fear that had no torment and by joys that found relief in swift movement, sent them running, forgetful of conventional proprieties, toward the awakening city. Probably Mary Magdalene had left them as soon as they saw the open grave and had hurried back alone to tell the tidings. And now the crowning joy and wonder comes. How simply it is told! The introductory "Greetings," just hinting at the wonderfulness, and perhaps at the suddenness, of our Lord's appearance, and the rest being in the quietest and fewest words possible. The joy and hope that flow from the resurrection depend on the fact of His humanity. He comes out of the grave, the same brother of our mortal flesh as before. It was no ghost whose feet they clasped, and He is not withdrawn from them by His mysterious experience.

The rush to His feet and the silent clasp of adoration are eloquent of a tumult of feeling most natural which is followed by Jesus' command of practical service that balances what might remain mere emotions. That carries a lesson always in season. We cannot love Christ too much, nor try to get too near Him to touch Him with the hand of our faith, but there is a danger of attempting to bind ourselves to Him with only our emotions. These women were taught that it is better to proclaim Jesus' resurrection than to lie at His feet and that, however sweet the blessedness that we find in Him may be, it is meant to put a message into our lips that others need. Our sight of Him gives us something to say and binds us to say it. Let us make haste to proclaim His message.

ALEXANDER MACLAREN

December 26

*L*ook at the people to whom Jesus sent these words. Remember what they were between the Friday and Sunday morning—utterly cowed and beaten, the women apparently more deeply touched by the personal loss of the Friend and Comforter, and the men apparently, while sharing that sorrow, also touched by despair at the going to the water of all the hopes that they had been building upon Jesus' official character and position. "We had hoped that he was the one who was going to redeem Israel," they said as they walked and were sad (Luke 24:21). They were on the point of parting. The Cornerstone withdrawn, the stones were ready to fall apart. Then came something—let us leave a blank for a moment—then came something; and those who had been cowards, dissolved in sorrow and relaxed by despair, in forty–eight hours became heroes. From that time, when by all reasonable logic and common sense applied to human motives the crucifixion should have crushed their dreams and dissolved their society, a precisely opposite effect ensues, and not only did the Church continue but also the men changed their characters and became, somehow or other, full of the two very things that Christ wished for them—namely, joy and peace.

So what bridges that gulf? How do you get Peter of the Acts of the Apostles out of Peter of the Gospels? Is there any way of explaining the revolution of character that befell him and all of the others, except that the something that came in between was the resurrection of Jesus Christ and the consequent gift of joy and peace in Him, a joy that no troubles or persecution could shake, a peace that no conflicts could for a moment disturb? With their own eyes they saw it was so, and they were forever changed. And when Christ comes to be deep–seated in a person's soul, He is an inward fountain of gladness far better than the greatest of earthly joys. Let Him come in His resurrection power to your heart.

ALEXANDER MACLAREN

Then Jesus said to them, "Do not be afraid. Go and tell my brothers to go to Galilee; there they will see me."

MATTHEW 28:10

December 27

While the women were on their way, some of the guards went into the city and reported to the chief priests everything that had happened. When the chief priests had met with the elders and devised a plan, they gave the soldiers a large sum of money, telling them, "You are to say, 'His disciples came during the night and stole him away while we were asleep.'"

MATTHEW 28:11–13

*N*ote the moral tone of Christ's enemies when confronted with the resurrection. First there was bribery, the money power brought to bear upon those who had some part to play in the transaction. For money you can buy silence; for money you can procure false testimony; for money you can make the next step in your life comparatively easy. Then there were lies. You never find a single sin. Sin does not dwell in solitary places and alone; sin means allies and confederates of every name and color. They were given a short, simple message to deliver and told to stick with it.

The men who can tell lies about themselves can easily tell lies about others, and therefore they engage to say that the disciples came by night and stole Jesus away. The liar takes away the character of other men easily because he was first taken away his own. He who familiarizes himself with suicide of a moral kind falls easily into murder of a moral nature. Expect no justice from the liar. Do not imagine that the liar will become a truthful man on purpose to serve your interests and to promote your good fortune and happy progress. The liar will use you; the false man will tear down all that is sacred in your name, tender in your family, and holy in your household. Falsehood is bad through and through; to it there is nothing sacred. It owns no altar; it respects no oath; it abides by no sacramental bond. It will drink to your health and stab you under the fifth rib; it will smile upon you and plunder not your property but your soul. Do not therefore let us give way to the ever-damaging notion that a man may speak lies in one direction and be quite truthful in another. No such anomalies exist in God's moral creation. He who can deliberately tell one lie will tell a thousand if he has anything to gain by the deluge of falsehoods.

JOSEPH PARKER

December 28

The disciples were sent to the familiar mountain, the grand old hill–church, the familiar place. No dark corner, screened off for dark uses, but a mountain caught by the great light of heaven at every point of its rugged majesty. Not into a cavern, not into a fissure of a rock, not into the depths of some inaccessible forest, but into a mountain. There is health already in these living lines.

Listen to the difference in moral tone surrounding the disciples. The soldiers were told to say, "His disciples came during the night and stole him away." Jesus says to the disciples, "All authority in heaven and on earth has been given to me. Therefore go and make disciples of all nations." Who would not rather take this program as his life guide? In Christianity, when allowed to speak for itself, you always hear a tone of high spiritual robustness. Christianity is a lesson, a message, and has to be taught, and teachers are appointed of God who are qualified by His Spirit and by grace to utter the lesson.

And note how this teaching is bounded. It is only bounded by "all nations." Christianity will not disciple a few; it will not be dwarfed into a sect; it will not be bricked up within given boundaries and held there as the prisoner of any number of partialists. Its wings were meant to flap in the firmament and its voice loud and sweet enough to be heard all over the spaces and to cause its gospel tone to fall like a revelation upon the ear of every listening man.

Compare the breezy, fresh, mountainlike air of the one program with the head–to–head, whispering, collusive program of the enemy. Judge the policies of men by their moral tone. Beware of men who set traps for the catching of the unsuspecting, and have faith in those teachers who have a grand moral tone and who exhibit in every breath and act and word a life worthy of the majesty that they can but imperfectly represent.

JOSEPH PARKER

Then the eleven disciples went to Galilee, to the mountain where Jesus had told them to go.

MATTHEW 28:16

December 29

Then Jesus came to them and said, "All authority in heaven and on earth has been given to me."

MATTHEW 28:18

I have met believers who have tried to read the Bible the wrong way. They have said, "God has a purpose that is certain to be fulfilled; therefore we will not budge an inch. All power is in the hands of Christ; therefore we will sit still." But that is not Christ's way. Based on His power, Christ tells us to go and do something. He puts us on the go because He has all power. I know that many of us have a tendency to say, "Everything is wrong; the world gets darker and darker." We sit and fret together in most delightful misery and try to cheer each other downward into greater depths of despair! Or, if we do stir ourselves a little, we feel that there is not much good in our service and that very little can possibly come of it. This message of our Master is something like the sound of a trumpet. I have given you the strains of a harpsichord, but now there rings out the clarion note of a trumpet. Here is the power to enable you to "go." Therefore, "go" away from your melancholy and ashes and dust. Shake off the negative thoughts. The bugle calls, "Up and away!" The battle has begun, and every good soldier of Jesus Christ must be to the front for his Captain and Lord. Because all power is given to Christ, He passes on that power to His people and sends them forth to battle and to victory.

Believe in this power of Christ and do not seek any other power. There is a craving, often, after great intellectual power; people want "clever" men to preach the gospel. I fear that the gospel has suffered more damage from clever men than from anything else. I question whether the devil himself has ever worked so much mischief in the church of God as clever men have done. We want to have such mental vigor as God pleases to give us, but we remember the word, "Not by might nor by power, but by my Spirit, says the Lord Almighty" (Zech. 4:6). The world is not going to be saved by worldly wisdom or by fine oratory. The power to do this is the power that is in Christ.

CHARLES SPURGEON

December 30

$\mathscr{S}$ome of us fret a good deal about "a sense of His presence," sometimes rejoicing in it, sometimes mourning because
we do not have it, praying for it and not always seeming to
receive it, now on the heights, now in the depths. And all this
April-like gloom instead of steady summer glow, because we
are focusing upon the *sense* of His presence instead of the
changeless *reality* of it.

"And surely I am with you always."

MATTHEW 28:20

All our trouble and disappointment about it are met by His
own simple word and vanish in the simple faith that grasps it.
For if Jesus says simply and absolutely, "And surely I am with
you always," what have we to do with feelings about it? That
overflows all the regrets of the past and all the possibilities of
the future and most certainly includes the present. Therefore, at
this very moment, the Lord Jesus is with you. "I am" is neither
"I was" nor "I will be." It is always abreast of our lives, always
encompassing us with salvation. It is a splendid, perpetual *now*.
We have only to *believe* it and to *recollect* it.

Is it not too bad to turn around upon that gracious presence and
say, "Yes, but I don't realize it!" Then it is, after all, not the
presence but the realization that you are seeking—the shadow,
not the substance! Honestly, it is so! For you have such
absolute assurance of the reality, put into the very plainest
words of promise that divine love could devise, that you dare
not make Him a liar and say, "No! He is not with me!" All you
can say is, "I don't *sense* His presence." Yet He was there with
you while you said it. What must He have thought?

As the first hindrance to realization is not believing His
promise, so the second is not *recollecting* it. If we were always
recollecting, we should be always realizing. But we go forth
from faith to forgetfulness, and there seems no help for it. But
Jesus Himself said that the Holy Spirit should bring all things to
our remembrance. Let us make real use of this promise, and we
shall certainly find it sufficient for the need it meets.

FRANCES RIDLEY HAVERGAL

December 31

"And surely I am with you always, to the very end of the age."

MATTHEW 28:20

The emphatic "I am" not only denotes certainty but also is the speech of Him who is lifted above the lower regions where time rolls and the succession of events occurs. That "I am" covers all the varieties of *was, is, will be.* Notice the long vista of variously tinted days that open here. However many they be, however different their complexion, days of summer and days of winter, days of sunshine and days of storm, days of buoyant youth and days of stagnant, stereotypical old age, days of apparent failure and days of apparent prosperity, He is with us in them all. The days change, but never the Savior. Notice the unlimited extent of the promise—"to the very end of the age." We are always tempted to think that long ago the earth was more full of God than it is today and that way forward in the future it will be fuller again but that this moment is comparatively empty. The heavens touch the earth on the horizon in front and behind, and they are highest and remotest above us just where we stand. But no past day had more of Christ in it than today has, and that He has gone away is the condition of His second coming.

But mark that the promise comes after a command and is contingent, for all its blessedness and power, upon our obedience to the prescribed duty. That duty is primarily to make disciples of all nations, and the discharge of it is so closely connected with the realization of the promise that a nonmissionary church never has much of Christ's presence. But obedience to the King's commands is required if we stand before Him and are to enjoy His smile. If you wish to keep Christ very near you and to feel Him with you, the way to do so is no mere cultivation of spiritual emotion or saturating your mind with spiritual thoughts, though these have their place, but on the dusty road of life doing His will and keeping His commandments.

ALEXANDER MACLAREN